LANGUAGE IN LOUISIANA

Carl A. Brasseaux and Donald W. Davis, series editors

Language in LOUISIANA
Community and Culture

Edited by Nathalie Dajko and Shana Walton

University Press of Mississippi / Jackson

 This contribution has been supported with funding provided by the Louisiana Sea Grant College Program (LSG) under NOAA Award # NA14OAR4170099. Additional support is from the Louisiana Sea Grant Foundation. The funding support of LSG and NOAA is gratefully acknowledged, along with the matching support by LSU. Logo created by Louisiana Sea Grant College Program.

The University Press of Mississippi is the scholarly publishing agency of the Mississippi Institutions of Higher Learning: Alcorn State University, Delta State University, Jackson State University, Mississippi State University, Mississippi University for Women, Mississippi Valley State University, University of Mississippi, and University of Southern Mississippi.

www.upress.state.ms.us

The University Press of Mississippi is a member of the Association of University Presses.

Copyright © 2019 by University Press of Mississippi
All rights reserved

First printing 2019
∞

Library of Congress Cataloging-in-Publication Data

Names: Dajko, Nathalie., editor. | Walton, Shana, 1961– editor.
Title: Language in Louisiana ; community and culture / edited by Nathalie Dajko and Shana Walton.
Other titles: America's third coast.
Description: Jackson : University Press of Mississippi, [2019] | Series: America's third coast series | "First printing 2019." | Includes bibliographical references and index.
Identifiers: LCCN 2019014813 (print) | LCCN 2019022341 (ebook) | ISBN 9781496823854 (hardcover : alk. paper) | ISBN 9781496823878 (pbk. : alk. paper)
Subjects: LCSH: Language and culture—Louisiana. | Language and languages—Variation. | English language—Dialects—Louisiana. | Chitimacha language—Louisiana. | Koasati language—Louisiana. | Tunica language—Louisiana. | Atakapa language—Louisiana. | Cajun French dialect. | Creole dialects—Louisiana. | Creole dialects, French—Louisiana. | Language surveys—Louisiana. | Spanish language—Louisiana. | Vietnamese language—Louisiana.
Classification: LCC P35.5.U6 L365 2019 (print) | LCC P35.5.U6 (ebook) | DDC 409.763—dc23
LC record available at https://lccn.loc.gov/2019014813
LC ebook record available at https://lccn.loc.gov/2019022341

British Library Cataloging-in-Publication Data available

CONTENTS

Preface. VII
    NATHALIE DAJKO AND SHANA WALTON

Acknowledgments XI

Introduction XIII
    CONNIE EBLE

SECTION I: Indigenous Languages 3

1. The Chitimacha Language: A History 9
    DANIEL W. HIEBER

2. Kowassaaton Ilhaalos: Let Us Hear Koasati 28
    LINDA LANGLEY AND BERTNEY LANGLEY

3. The Maintenance of Koasati. 37
    GEOFFREY KIMBALL

4. The Tunica Language. 45
    PATRICIA ANDERSON AND JUDITH M. MAXWELL

5. Ishak Words: Language Renewal Prospects for a Historical
   Gulf Coast Tribe 64
    JEFFERY U. DARENSBOURG AND DAVID KAUFMAN

SECTION II: French in Louisiana 69

6. History and Variation in Louisiana French 75
    NATHALIE DAJKO

7. The Louisiana Creole Language Today..................90
   THOMAS A. KLINGLER

8. The Future of French in Louisiana....................108
   TAMARA LINDNER

9. The Institutionalization of French in Louisiana: History, Successes,
   and Challenges for the Future........................125
   ALBERT CAMP

10. French Education in New Orleans....................140
    ROBIN WHITE

SECTION III: English in Louisiana..................155

11. Cajun English: A Linguistic and Cultural Profile........159
    KATIE CARMICHAEL

12. Do You Know What It Means? New Orleans English......173
    CHRISTINA SCHOUX CASEY

13. The Linguistic Survey of North Louisiana: History and Progress....203
    LISA ABNEY

SECTION IV: New Populations......................227

14. Spanish in Louisiana: A Story of Unplanned Language Revival....229
    RAFAEL OROZCO AND DORIAN DORADO

15. Vietnamese in Louisiana............................246
    ALLISON TRUITT

16. Diverse Linguistic Communities and English "Fluency"
    in New Orleans....................................259
    SHANE LIEF

About the Contributors................................275

Index..279

PREFACE

NATHALIE DAJKO AND SHANA WALTON

In this volume, we bring together researchers and community activists working on different aspects of Louisiana's linguistic heritage. By including in a single volume extensive research on a wide variety of languages by experts on those languages, we want to help dispel the popular image of Louisiana as a primarily francophone state. Beginning with the presence of a multitude of indigenous languages and continuing through waves of immigration, voluntary or not, from both Europe and Africa, Louisiana has never been a monocultural place. That today Louisiana is predominantly monolingual (in New Orleans the rate of monolingual anglicism surpasses 90 percent) is a historical anomaly. In the past, visitors would have expected to find—depending on the era—the hegemony of French and/or English but the actual presence of up to fifty African languages (Hall 1995), large numbers of German and Italian speakers, and smaller numbers of speakers of languages such as Spanish, Greek, Croatian, Hungarian, and Portuguese, to name but a few. Even today, though their speakers may total less than 10 percent of the state's population, dozens of languages are spoken. This volume shows the modern presence and continued importance of many of these languages.

This book also seeks to illustrate the importance of Louisiana as a place in which linguistic research might be done and indeed is needed. The chapters cover a wide range of fields, from language death and revival to variation to language rights. Despite the march toward English monolingualism and the looming disappearance of French (which always somehow manages to survive despite dire predictions that its demise is imminent), Louisiana remains a place rich in scholarly potential.

Finally, this volume presents information that may be of use to both academic and nonacademic readers. We have therefore avoided using technical jargon as much as possible and included explanations where doing so was unavoidable. This book may appeal to linguists seeking an understanding of the state of research on Louisiana languages as well as to members of the general public who wish to better understand Louisiana's linguistic history and current language varieties. Many researchers as well as general readers remain unaware that Native Americans in the state are working to revitalize their languages or that groups like the Koasati have a successful program. Louisiana is, in fact, experiencing a florescence of sleeping languages, as both Chitimacha and Tunica are awakening through tribal linguistic efforts. Many scholars are generally aware of the efforts, but tribal revitalization work has not focused on producing papers for scholarly audiences. This volume provides more information for classroom and research use.

This volume fits within the theory of linguists such as Norma Mendoza-Denton (2008) and Penelope Eckert (2018), at least partially meeting their call to merge sociolinguistic descriptions and ethnographic understandings of variation. Such theorists argue that a full understanding of language variation always involves cultural processes (community). Decoding meaning always requires decoding culture and pulling from community-shared meanings. To truly understand the preservation, maintenance, or revival of a heritage language (like French or Spanish) or a Native language, or to understand the variations within languages (like Cajun English or New Orleans English), we clearly must be able to see the communities of speakers. To this end, each chapter has cultural and historical information about the people who speak the language or variety as well as specific linguistic information. In this way, we recognize both the languages and the communities that maintain, revive, preserve, and teach those languages.

We have attempted to include as many of Louisiana's languages, past and present, as possible. However, some languages unavoidably were omitted. German, for example, is not included in this volume for the simple reason that while Germans comprised an important part of Louisiana history and their presence has had documented long-lasting effects (to take just one example, they are credited with introducing the accordion, an instrument central to both Cajun and Zydeco music), linguistically, the long-term impact of their presence is less clear. George Reinecke (1985) has suggested that the use of *by* to mean *at* (as in *I'm by my mama's house* to mean *I'm at my mama's house*) in New Orleans English could be traced to German *bei*, and it is often suggested, without specific examples, that German is foundational (along with Irish English and Italian) to the working-class white dialect often known as Yat (Mucciaccio 2009:35). But very little if any additional work has documented the linguistic features of the German language in Louisiana, and it seems to have followed the trajectory typical of immigrant languages and passed out of use within a few generations. While reports of German speakers living around Roberts Cove (settled in the late nineteenth century) occasionally surface, we have been unable to verify these claims and suspect that we are dealing with at best a few people who would best be classified as "rememberers." In any case, since German has been the focus of little linguistic inquiry in Louisiana, it was omitted from the volume. The same is true of Irish English (and the possibility that Gaelic was imported to Louisiana with that immigration) and Italian as well as of smaller language communities such as Greek, Croatian, and Hungarian. It is especially true of languages of African origin. Beyond Hall's (1995) excellent treatment of the issue of their presence and continued use into the nineteenth century, at least symbolically, they, too passed out of use and have left no clear and obvious evidence of their passing beyond a few lexical items (most notably *gumbo*). Scholars have yet to examine the issue of these languages' possible continued influence (for example, in nonsegmental areas like intonation) in Louisiana English.

Similarly, the focus on some languages in this volume is slightly stronger than on others simply because of the amount of research that has been conducted on those languages. While our goal is to provide a more balanced view of Louisiana's linguistic heritage than is generally available, we must also acknowledge the state of research. That research has focused primarily on French, with other languages taking a backseat, at least until very recently. The focus on French in both the popular imagination and in the scholarly literature has led to a disproportionate amount of research on that language—ironically, to the particular detriment of English, which has replaced French in importance and is spoken by nearly all residents today. Consequently, our section on French is the largest on a single language (whereas, for example, multiple indigenous languages are grouped together in a single section).

The book is divided into four sections, with the layout reflecting both chronological presence and thematic grouping:

- Indigenous Languages
- Louisiana French Varieties
- Louisiana English Varieties
- New Populations—Major Late-Twentieth-Century and Early Twenty-First-Century Developments

This volume does not cover everything on language in this state. We would love to have more on the variety of north Louisiana Englishes, more on ethnicity and language identity, more on Native languages that are just beginning to revive. We hope that the writings presented here constitute only an initial effort to document for both scholars and the public the range and variety of Louisiana languages. We envision future volumes that include many more languages and language varieties. There is much work to be done in Louisiana, and we look forward to witnessing continued growth in both academic scholarship and community documentation.

A NOTE ON TERMINOLOGY AND TRANSCRIPTION

In this volume, we often use the term *Indian* in reference to the indigenous population. We recognize that the term may be problematic. In Canada, for example, the preferred term for several decades now has been *First Nations*. Our use of *Indian* in this volume is motivated by a desire to reflect the preferences of the communities in question. Sometimes, this preference has been overtly stated: while conducting field research, Nathalie Dajko was party to a conversation in which locals rejected both the terms *First Nations* and *Native American* in favor of *Indian*. Elsewhere, it reflects the usage of the community itself—several chapters are in fact authored or coauthored by community members. In any case, as editors and authors, we have authorized use of the term with caution and out of deference to the communities themselves.

This volume also presents transcription using the International Phonetic Alphabet (IPA). Some authors have chosen to use alternative symbols to those found in the standard IPA—for example, using ž to represent a voiced palatal fricative whereas the standard IPA uses ʒ for this sound. This alternation is the result of differences in usage across fields; those trained in anthropology, especially those working on indigenous languages of the Americas, are more likely to use the former, while scholars of French tend to use the latter. Rather than imposing a single system across chapters, we have allowed authors to use the symbols most commonly used in their fields.

WORKS CITED

Dillard, J. L. 1985. "Language and Linguistic Research in Louisiana." In *Louisiana Folklife: A Guide to the State*, edited by Nicholas R. Spitzer, 35–47. Baton Rouge: Office of Cultural Development. http://www.louisianafolklife.org/LT/Virtual_Books/Guide_to_State/creole_book_guide_to_state.html.

Eckert, Penelope. 2018. *Meaning and Linguistic Variation: The Third Wave in Sociolinguistics*. Cambridge: Cambridge University Press.

Hall, Gwendolyn Midlo. 1995. *Africans in Colonial Louisiana: The Development of Afro-Creole Culture in the Eighteenth Century*. Baton Rouge: Louisiana State University Press.

Mendoza-Denton, Norma. 2008. *Homegirls: Language and Cultural Practice among Latina Youth Gangs*. Malden, MA: Wiley-Blackwell.

Mucciaccio, Francesca. 2009. "'A Gaggle a' Y'ats' and Other Stories: Tracing the Effects of Ideology on Language Change through Indexical Formation in Y'at." Honors thesis, Reed College.

Reinecke, George. 1985. "The National and Cultural Groups of New Orleans." In *Louisiana Folklife: A Guide to the State*, edited by Nicholas R. Spitzer, 55–64. Baton Rouge: Office of Cultural Development. http://www.louisianafolklife.org/LT/Virtual_Books/Guide_to_State/NOGroups.html.

ACKNOWLEDGMENTS

This volume would not have been possible without the support of several people. For help with bibliographic formatting and research, we owe thanks to Travis Fink at Tulane, who checked each chapter to make sure the works cited matched the text and hunted down accidental omissions. We also owe a great debt of gratitude to Michael Picone and an anonymous reviewer for their very careful reading and extensive, insightful comments and helpful suggestions on the text.

We appreciate the contributors' patience as the manuscript underwent several reviews and additional people joined the team after the project was in motion as well as their rapid responses every time we asked them for something. To the press, especially Craig Gill and Emily Bandy, we owe thanks for their frequent assistance, enthusiasm for the book, and good cheer throughout the process.

And of course, we thank our families for their support, moral and otherwise, particularly in the home stretch.

INTRODUCTION

CONNIE EBLE

Louisiana wears an aura of exoticism unmatched by other states. Its citizens revel in their rakish image and like to compare themselves to a piquant local food almost uniquely associated with Louisiana—gumbo. The word *gumbo* came to Louisiana with enslaved Africans and in their Bantu languages meant "okra," a basic ingredient of the traditional dish. Gumbo has no single list of ingredients or combinations thereof. Its base is a spicy soup of indeterminate ingredients to which is added seafood, chicken, turkey, and/or sausage. This hallmark food of Louisiana evolved from the contributions to local cuisine of Native Americans, Africans, and non-Anglo Europeans. The same interplay of cultures that created gumbo can be discerned as an important underpinning of Louisiana's linguistic history. *Language in Louisiana: Culture and Community* shows how linguistic choices in the past and today shape the language life of contemporary Louisiana and reinforce the state's colorful self-image.

When European rulers claimed sovereignty over the area now designated *Louisiana*, it was the homeland of indigenous people speaking several disparate languages as well as a common language for trade. The fate of the people and their languages is familiar. Their communities were diminished drastically by warfare, disease, and displacement, and the disintegration of their communities led to the extinction or near-extinction of their languages.

This volume begins with five essays that sketch the stories of four of Louisiana's indigenous languages: Tunica, Koasati (Coushatta), Chitimacha, and Ishak (Atakapa). All were embedded in parts of rural Louisiana where, until the middle of the twentieth century, French was the ordinary language. When speakers of these languages first learned a European language, it was usually French. Now English is the dominant language of southern Louisiana and likely the first language of tribal members who wish to preserve or revive their ancestral tongue. Tunica, Koasati, Chitimacha, and Ishak exemplify different endangered positions shown by many languages of the world today. Tunica and Ishak are extinct; Koasati still has living speakers; Chitimacha no longer has native speakers but has written texts and even wax cylinder recordings made by scholars in the early twentieth century. For all four languages, varied efforts to preserve and strengthen the language or to bring it back to life are ongoing, with varying degrees of success.

Chitimacha is currently classified an isolate. Linguist Daniel Hieber's essay on Chitimacha not only describes the language and its prospects but also offers an interesting chapter in the history of linguistics. Early in the twentieth century, John Swanton did fieldwork among several indigenous groups in Louisiana, including the Coushatta and Chitimacha, and much of what is known of their languages rests on texts, word lists, and grammars that Swanton created. In the 1930s, linguist Morris Swadesh interviewed the remaining two speakers of Chitimacha, recording them on wax cylinders. Swadesh's extensive unpublished notes and the recordings lay dormant until 1986, when the Library of Congress sent a copy of the cylinders to the tribe. The recovery of these materials has occasioned recent interest by linguists and held out the possibility of reviving their language. Although Chitimacha is not yet demonstrably related to other languages, Hieber's essay points out similarities in verbal structures between Chitimacha and other languages of the Southeast, raising questions of language contact and influence. Not only has Hieber described the language on the basis of documentation recovered decades after the last speakers died, but he has guided the tribe in ambitious and successful efforts to awaken the language from its sleeping state. In 2010, Chitimacha Rosetta Stone was made available without charge to tribal members.

Koasati is a Muskogean language whose speakers came to Elton in Jefferson Davis Parish in southwestern Louisiana in 1884. The story of Koasati and the Coushatta who preserve and honor it is told from different perspectives in two essays.

The first essay shows the day-to-day energy of a planned and intensive program not only to increase the number and fluency of Koasati speakers but also to inspire understanding and respect for their cultural heritage. The essay presents the perspective of well-informed insiders. Linda Langley is an anthropologist at McNeese State University, and Bertney Langley is a member of the Coushatta Tribal Council. Together, they directed the National Science Foundation project that provided the initial resources to document the language of native speakers and to develop an alphabet and twenty-first-century pedagogical tools like apps and computer games. The tribe now publishes a newspaper in Koasati and runs an immersion school with certified teachers.

The second essay on Koasati is representative of the kind of descriptions of indigenous American languages undertaken by linguists and ethnographers beginning in the late nineteenth century. The authors of such descriptions are typically professionally trained, affiliated with universities or learned societies, and outsiders to the communities they observe. For many languages, such published and unpublished descriptions and analyses constitute the sole record.

Anthropologist Geoffrey Kimball has published a grammar and dictionary of Koasati and a collection of Koasati narratives with the University of Nebraska Press. In his essay in this volume, Kimball describes the external factors that have affected the survival and maintenance of Koasati and its prospects for enduring. Unlike the other indigenous languages featured in this volume, Koasati has persisted in unbroken chronology as a living language. Because Koasati was the primary spoken language of the tribal community until the last quarter of the twentieth century, it still has a number of fluent native speakers, though most of them are now over forty. For their first half century in Louisiana, Koasati speakers kept to themselves socially, surrounded by speakers of Louisiana French. They were Protestants, and their English-speaking ministers respected and learned Koasati and had Bible passages and religious services translated into the language. When children began receiving schooling in their community, the English-speaking teachers were respectful of the children's home language. Later Koasati children were assigned to the parish's segregated white public schools. They were bilingual, speaking Koasati at home and English at school and in school activities. More and more Koasati began to graduate from high school and move in social and employment contexts beyond the tribe. The bilingual generation began to be succeeded by young tribal members fluent in English only. In 2007, sensing the dramatic decline in the use of Koasati, the tribe began the Koasati Language Project and obtained a grant from the National Science Foundation to document and archive the language.

Tunica is an isolate: no other documented language appears related to it. Furthermore, it technically fits the definition of a dead or extinct language: the last speaker of Tunica died in 1948 (and his dominant language was French). Linguist Mary Haas documented that last speaker in the 1930s and later published a Tunica dictionary and grammar and texts of stories and songs, but no usable audio recordings of Tunica exist. After many years of effort, in 1981 the Tunica achieved federal recognition as the joint Tunica-Biloxi tribe, which maintains the Tunica-Biloxi Tribal Museum in Marksville in Avoyelles Parish. The museum not only displays artifacts of the tribe's history but also boasts a state-of-the-art artifact conservation and restoration facility. Although the Tunica and Biloxi share much history and culture to justify their association into one tribe for federal recognition, the Biloxi language, now also extinct, is a Siouan language and is not related to Tunica. In the 1990s, tribe member Donna Pierite was inspired to revive the Tunica language and gained the support of the tribal council. She collected all available material on the language and tapped the memories of elders for songs of their childhood. She began teaching others the language and presenting it in performances. In 2010, the tribe approached Tulane University for assistance in revitalizing Tunica, and shortly thereafter the Tunica-Biloxi tribe created its Language and Culture

Revitalization Program. The essay by Judith Maxwell and Patricia Anderson of Tulane University outlines some important features of the Tunica language and explains the challenges in adapting the heritage language to communication needs in the current world.

Ishak, also known inaccurately as Atakapa, is the heritage language of many southern Louisianans, who refer to themselves with names like *French Indians* and *Creole Indians*. Of the four indigenous languages treated in this volume, Ishak faces the greatest challenges. It is an extinct language, and its formal documentation consists almost entirely of word lists and brief texts published by Albert Samuel Gatschet and John Swanton more than a century ago. Further, the tribe has not yet received official federal recognition from the Bureau of Indian Affairs. Nonetheless, members of the Atakapa-Ishak of Southwestern Louisiana and Southeast Texas work to sustain the culture and to revive the sleeping language through their memories of names, phrases, and stories. The tribe has recently joined forces with linguists to produce and publish a new dictionary from the scattered resources.

Tribally affiliated descendants of the indigenous people of Louisiana have experienced an upturn in material prosperity over the past three decades with the ownership of gambling casinos—the Paragon Casino Resort in Marksville for the Tunica, the Coushetta Casino Resort in Kinder for the Koasati, and the Cypress Bayou Casino in Jeanerette for the Chitimacha. Along with relief from poverty, however, has come increased contact with the outside world and access to cultural and educational opportunities that have had important consequences for community identity and ties. The tribes' language revitalization and preservation programs are an effort to retain heritage culture and values in the face of threats from powerful external forces.

At the beginning of the eighteenth century, the lives of the indigenous inhabitants of Louisiana were forever changed by the arrival of Europeans. French speakers were the first Europeans who came as settlers, and the role of the French language in Louisiana to this day dramatically exemplifies the founder principle (or founder effect)—that is, the enduring influence of the initial language of a new community.[1] French is the European language continuously spoken the longest in the state—fully three hundred years. However, French was the official language of Louisiana for only about sixty of those years, because the colony was given to Spain in 1763. However, the people continued to speak French under Spanish rule for the next forty years. Spanish-speaking settlers during that period were few compared with immigrants from France, Canada, and the Caribbean, who continued to seek Louisiana as a francophone destination up to the Civil War. In Louisiana, several varieties of French serving various functions developed. Four essays in this volume describe the important and unique role of French in Louisiana, even as French is now on the brink of extinction in the state and most inhabitants are monolingual speakers of English.

Nathalie Dajko's essay discusses the history, relationship, and salient linguistic features of the three broadly delineated kinds of Louisiana French. Plantation Society French, a variety that developed in tandem with French in France as a consequence of sustained contact, was much like standard continental French. As the language passed through the generations, it fell out of use in the twentieth century. Louisiana Creole originated among enslaved Africans imported into French-speaking Louisiana during the colonial period. Louisiana Regional French developed from several dialects brought to rural southern Louisiana beginning in the colonial period. Among these dialects was the Acadian, brought by French speakers who were expelled from their homeland in Canada by the British in the 1750s and who arrived in Louisiana ten years later. Native speakers of Louisiana Regional French, though now a small and mostly elderly group, included Native Americans, Creoles of color, African Americans, and European Americans of mainly French, Spanish, and German ancestry. Today both Louisiana Creole and Louisiana Regional French are endangered.

Tamara Lindner's essay analyzes perceptions of French among young adults in high school and college enrolled in French language courses in the heartland of Acadiana around Lafayette. She finds that this rising generation believes strongly in the cultural and traditional values of Cajun identity and honors the place of the language in their heritage. However, few feel that knowing Cajun French is now a requirement for claiming Cajun ethnicity. Complementing and paralleling Dajko's essay, Tom Klingler not only describes the development of indigenous Louisiana Creole and its speakers past and present but also gives an overview of the major grammatical features that it shares with other Creoles and that differentiate it from other dialects of Louisiana French. With the prospect of French soon becoming a symbolic relic in Louisiana, Robin White examines in historic perspective recent attention to teaching children French in school. This effort was recognized officially in 1968 with the establishment of a state agency, the Council for the Development of French in Louisiana (CODOFIL). More recently, private schools and public charter schools have attracted enrollment with courses and intensive programs to teach children French, and the state now has more than thirty French immersion schools and programs. These schools, however, teach a standard form of French sometimes called Reference French instead of varieties of Louisiana French.

Despite the romantic status accorded to French, the overwhelming majority of Louisianans—even in southern Louisiana's French triangle—are monolingual anglophones. The displacement of French by English began with the Louisiana Purchase in 1803, especially in northern Louisiana, where early immigration from the United States was heaviest and where French speakers were sparser, except for the area around Natchitoches and the Cane River. Many Americans plus immigrants from Ireland and Germany settled in New Orleans in the second quarter of the nineteenth century. By the end of the Civil War, in which Louisiana aligned itself with other slaveholding southern states in the Cotton Belt, where English had long been the dominant language, English had clearly won out in New Orleans and everywhere else except in the twenty-two parishes of Acadiana.

The essays in the third section of this volume address three perceptibly different kinds of English spoken currently in Louisiana. Katie Carmichael explores Cajun English, a dialect marked by a characteristic rhythm and intonation, consonantal and vowel pronunciations, and words and phrases appropriated from Louisiana Regional French. Most Cajun English speakers do not speak French, but their selective use of Cajun English features marks their identification with the Cajun community. The Englishes of New Orleans sound entirely different from the Cajun English often heard just thirty or forty miles away in Vacherie and other towns upriver or in Thibodaux and elsewhere down the bayou as well as from the northern Louisiana dialects heard in Shreveport and Monroe. The most recognizable and stereotyped variety of New Orleans English is Yat, the dialect of the white working class. In addition to outlining the main linguistic characteristics of Yat, Christina Schoux Casey analyzes the performance and commodification of the dialect and offers a critique of the image it projects—an image that she finds was created by business leaders for the benefit of white tourists. Lisa Abney's study of English in northern Louisiana follows the methodology of *The Linguistic Atlas of the Gulf States* and similar projects that map linguistic variants and posit dialect boundaries based on shared pronunciations and vocabulary. Speakers in north Louisiana sound more like southerners in northern Mississippi, Alabama, and Georgia than they do like inhabitants of the southern part of their own state. This linguistic variation confirms the widespread perception that southern and northern Louisiana are as different as night and day. Abney's research shows, however, that the speech of northern Louisiana is far from uniform and falls into at least three regions whose boundaries run north–south. A theme that runs through these three essays is that the linguistic features of pronunciation, vocabulary, and grammar tell only a part of how English functions in communities in Louisiana. Carmichael shows how Boudreaux and Thibodeaux jokes use Cajun English as a way of eliciting favorable feelings toward a historically unsophisticated community. Schoux Casey notes that in the aftermath of 2005's devastating Hurricane Katrina, New Orleanians have reclaimed local dialects as a sign that the city will prevail and will retain its image as the most interesting and fun-loving city in the United States. Abney uses the narratives elicited by the interview questions of her study to gain insight into the folklore and cultural practices of northern Louisiana.

Although inhabitants of Louisiana and its major city, New Orleans, imagine their state and city as brimming with exotic and foreign flavor, they are not so multicultural or multilingual as other American states and cities of comparable size. The final section of this volume addresses the linguistic challenges that three groups of recent immigrants to the state and city encounter. Following the fall of Saigon in 1975, many Vietnamese refugees came to Louisiana and particularly to the southern part of the state because of its Roman Catholicism and because its subtropical climate and proximity to fishing grounds were similar to their home country. Family and community solidarity are important to the Vietnamese, and while learning English to prosper in their new country, they created centers for worship, day and health care, legal assistance, and socializing that offer the opportunity to maintain the Vietnamese language and its shades of meaning. In her essay, Allison Truitt explains that dialect and lexical differences in Vietnamese often correlate with political allegiance rather than geography. Furthermore, status and politeness relationships are coded into the Vietnamese language, and community members do not wish to lose these important distinctions in the shift to English by younger speakers. To this point, the Vietnamese have insisted on their linguistic rights through constant vigilance. Spanish is a heritage language of Louisiana. Several small communities founded during the Spanish colonial period persist, though they abandoned Spanish in favor of Louisiana Regional French and more recently in favor of English. The newest speakers of Spanish have no link to Louisiana's colonial past. They came in large numbers after Hurricane Katrina for jobs in the construction and service sectors. Rafael Orozco and Dorian Dorado describe the dialect of Spanish that is developing among these speakers as well as their feelings about it. Many wish to learn English for economic reasons while at the same time holding onto Spanish. They confront such issues as which Central American dialect to adopt, whether to create new Spanish words by translating English, and whether to accept code mixing. Smaller and less coherent groups of foreign-language speakers have also made Louisiana their home. Many of them earn their living by driving taxis. Shane Lief details how their imperfectly mastered English suggested unhealthiness, dishonesty, and criminality and led to "English fluency" regulations to protect the public. Lief points out the irony of such xenophobia in a city that prides itself on its laissez-faire attitude and whose major source of revenue is hospitality.

The scholars of language who contributed to *Language in Louisiana: Culture and Community* bring different primary areas of expertise: some are anthropologists, some are experts in English or other languages, some are historians, some are educators, some are traditionally trained in descriptive and historical linguistics, and others are skillful practitioners of the latest techniques of sociolinguistics. But all think of language in the context of the social, cultural, and psychological meanings that it provides to communities. Their essays touch on many issues that interest the greater discipline of linguists today. Among these are language and dialect endangerment, bilingualism, regional versus social dialects, dialect leveling, language as a vehicle of identity, perceptual dialectology, and the commodification of languages and dialects—to name just a few. Taken together, the essays confirm that in Louisiana today, language is a powerful component of everyday life and of the self-image that the state projects to the world.

NOTES

1. Around 1984, Salikoko Mufwene borrowed the term *founder principle* or *founder effect* from the study of population genetics and applied it to linguistic analysis.

LANGUAGE IN LOUISIANA

SECTION I

Indigenous Languages

NATHALIE DAJKO AND SHANA WALTON

Louisiana has been inhabited for somewhere between ten thousand and twelve thousand years. At the time of first human occupation, during the last ice age, Louisiana was a grassy plain populated by megafauna, which were hunted for food. By five thousand years ago, however, the ice age had ended, and the landscape looked more like it does today: dense woodland and swamp. Louisiana—specifically, Watson Brake in Ouachita Parish—is the location of what may be the earliest mound-building site found in North America, and based on archaeological evidence of mound building and earthworks, Poverty Point in northeast Louisiana appears to be the site of the most extensive ceremonial and commerce center in North America during the Archaic period (preagricultural). Over six hundred years, the people of the Poverty Point culture (2200–700 BCE) built structures covering thirty-seven acres, creating some of the first pottery in North America and trading goods with groups across hundreds of miles. Although Poverty Point was abandoned, the population in the region continued to grow, with groups adopting agriculture and becoming sedentary. By 200 BC, the Marksville culture—so named because the first excavation of this cultural group was at Marksville, Louisiana—had domesticated plants (Neuman and Hawkins 1993).

It is in the contact period that we begin to have an idea of the languages spoken in Louisiana; much of our early knowledge comes from accounts by explorers, fur traders, and missionaries such as explorer and naturalist Antoine Simon le Page du Pratz, whose *Histoire de la Louisiane*, published between 1751 and 1753, documents fifteen years living with the Natchez. While we can guess at such things as family affiliation from the writings of early travelers, they do not tend to provide us with dictionaries and grammars. While missionaries have a long history of linguistic documentation, this is not the case for Louisiana (one minor exception is a Choctaw word list compiled by the Jesuit priest

Adrien Rouquette, who died in 1887), so our actual knowledge of indigenous languages during the historic period is minimal.

Much of what is known about the historic period concerns the larger nations such as the Choctaw and Chickasaw, though Kelley (n.d.) and Ellis (2015) note that this is more due to the slanted perspective of historians than to the primary documents, in which the petites nations[1] appear frequently, and which demonstrate their importance on the cultural and political scene. What we know of the languages results almost exclusively from the work of twentieth-century anthropologists, linguists, and tribal researchers. John Swanton, Mary Haas, and Louis Gatschet are among the among the major figures who documented what they could of Louisiana's indigenous languages, most of which were already in steep decline if not nearly extinct by the time they took up the task during the first half of the century.

From twentieth-century sources, then, we have information about a handful of the languages spoken at one time or another in Louisiana. These include Choctaw, Chitimacha, Atakapa, Tunica, Biloxi, and Natchez as well as Mobilian Jargon, the Muskogean-based trade language spoken widely throughout the Lower Mississippi Valley and central Gulf South, with some limited use continuing as late as the mid-twentieth century. We have fragmentary evidence for some languages, including Houma, which Swanton claimed to have documented in the form of a short word list plus a few accompanying phrases following a visit to the lower reaches of Terrebonne Parish in 1906. The nature of that list has been disputed by some sources and buttressed by others. We take no stand on the matter here but present it only as an example of how poorly the languages of the petites nations are represented in the literature. Further complicating the effort to document indigenous languages is the fact that for many people, language is cultural capital, not something to be shared with outsiders. It was common in the South to teach outsiders Mobilian Jargon, the trade language, rather than one's own language (Drechsel 1997:267–70). Consequently, with the violent change that characterized indigenous life in the postcontact era, including war, removal, and decimation from disease that often resulted in the amalgamation of groups that spoke disparate languages, it is likely that several languages and dialects have passed out of existence without ever being known to science. For example, the French slaughtered all but a few of the Washa, meaning that we will almost certainly never know the nature of their language. Others may well still exist, but their existence is only known to a tight-knit community of speakers who choose not to share a precious resource with anyone else.

At the time of contact, several major groups were present in Louisiana. The Muskogean language family probably had the most members, including (among others) Choctaw (though Louisiana's large historical Choctaw population resulted from an influx in the centuries after contact), Bayougoula, Acolapissa, Quinapisa, Tangipahoa, and likely Houma. Caddoan languages dominated in the north and included Natchitoches, Ouachita, and Yatasi. (For a succinct overview of Caddo, see Chafe 2015.) Biloxi, a Siouxan language, was found nearby in roughly what is now coastal Mississippi; Ofo, also Siouxan, was found inland around the modern Louisiana/Arkansas/Mississippi border, near the Tunica and Yazoo settlements. Four linguistic isolates were found in Louisiana or adjacent to it: Natchez, Ishak,[2] Chitimacha, and Tunica. These languages may not have been isolates in the past. For example, the Washa, Chawasha, and Yagenecito were long believed to be speakers of Muskogean languages (given their Muskogean names) but are more recently believed to have been related to the Chitimacha, who occupied the same general area (around Bayou Lafourche, which French explorers first labeled Lafourche des Chetimachas in maps from the 1700s). (For a discussion of possible connections, see Hieber, this volume.)

The forces of colonialization caused major demographic shifts among the indigenous populations (sometimes voluntary, sometimes not). Some languages were lost as a consequence of warfare or disease, and others moved into Louisiana from parts further east. A major westward push by the Koasati resulted in the presence of their language in Louisiana today. The ancestral population lived largely in what is today Alabama. The Tunica moved from the northern reaches of the Louisiana/Mississippi border to find themselves solidly within the modern state of Louisiana. Likewise, the movement of large numbers of Choctaw into the state during the historic period led Choctaw to become a near-generic term for indigenous people in much of the state (Kniffen, Gregory, and Stokes 1987:95).

Even as European settlers displaced and killed the Native people of Louisiana, they often retained Native place-names or derived names from the indigenous people who had been eliminated. For example, Choctaw-speaking guides often led the French through south Louisiana, resulting in waterways with names that include words such as *hacha* (river), *bogue* (creek or stream), *chitto* (big), or *falaya* (long). Hence, waterway names such as the Bogue Chitto River and the Atchafalaya Basin are adopted from the Choctaw names. Town names such as Bogalusa also come from Choctaw. Some place-names mark the region where historic tribal groups lived, such as Ouachita Parish in north Louisiana or Tangipahoa Parish in the region known as the Florida Parishes. As in much of the United States, Louisiana has abundant examples of waterway and place-names derived from Native languages (Kniffen and Hilliard 1988; Leeper 2012).

The upheaval of the historic period is a direct source of the issues, linguistic and otherwise, facing these groups today. In this section, we examine the current state of the language of the Tunica, the Koasati, and the Chitimacha and provide a brief look at beginning work on the Ishak language.

Chapter 1 is an overview of Chitimacha by Daniel Hieber, a linguist who collaborated with the tribe to create language-learning software and is currently working to finalize a new dictionary of the language for use in Chitimacha language classes. He explores several specific features of the language and clues to possible links with languages no longer spoken.

Chapters 2 and 3 explore Koasati, the language of the Coushatta Tribe of Louisiana. The account by Linda Langley, an anthropologist, and Bertney Langley, a researcher and member of the Coushatta Tribe, focuses on the work of the tribe since 2007, when they launched a formal language documentation project. The extensive project resulted in a new alphabet, pedagogical materials, and even a newspaper in Koasati. Geoffrey Kimball, the anthropologist who wrote the first dictionary of Koasati, offers us a look at the language's historical context. He discusses the Koasati's ability to withstand outside pressure to abandon their language, guarding against a shift first to French and then to English until the late twentieth century.

In chapter 4, Patricia Anderson and Judith M. Maxwell present the awakening of the Tunica language after decades of dormancy. Following a brief history of the tribe, they provide a grammatical description of the language based on their analyses of the work of previous anthropologists, especially Haas, who worked with the last speaker of the language, Sesostrie Youchigant, to document it before it passed away. Their chapter concludes with a discussion of the strategies employed by the Tunica-Tulane Working Group to coin new terms for cultural artifacts that did not exist at the time of Haas and Youchigant's work or that were not recorded given the nature of their conversations.

In chapter 5, Jeffery Darensbourg, head of the Alligator Band, Atakapa-Ishak Nation of Southwest Louisiana and Southeast Texas, and linguist David Kaufman offer insight into the beginning process of trying to awaken a sleeping language. They give an overview of the tribal history and the tools they are compiling to begin their work.

NOTES

1. *Petites nations* is the term used by the French to describe smaller polities in native North America (versus larger groups such as the Choctaw and the Chickasaw) that maintained distinct cultural and political identities despite living in close proximity to each other (Ellis 2015:16) and with whom the French had a symbiotic relationship (Usner 1992; Ellis 2015).

2. The Ishak are more commonly known by the name Atakapa (or Attakapa). *Atakapa* is a Muskogean word meaning "people-eaters." Though this name is more commonly used, the Ishak (the people) consider that name derogatory.

WORKS CITED

Chafe, Wallace. 2015. "A Profile of the Caddo Language." In *New Perspectives on Language Variety in the South: Historical and Contemporary Approaches*, edited by Michael D. Picone and Catherine Evans Davies, 43–51. Tuscaloosa: University of Alabama Press.

Drechsel, Emmanuel. 1997. *Mobilian Jargon: Linguistic and Sociohistorical Aspects of a Native American Pidgin*. Oxford: Oxford University Press.

Ellis, Elizabeth. 2015. "The Many Ties of the Petites Nations: Relationships, Power, and Diplomacy in the Lower Mississippi Valley, 1685–1785." PhD diss., University of North Carolina at Chapel Hill.

Kelley, Laura D. N.d. "The Pointe-au-Chien Indian Tribe of Louisiana: Tribal Formation as a Consequence of 18th Century French Geopolitics." Unpublished paper provided by the author.

Kniffen, Fred B., Hiram F. Gregory, and George A. Stokes. 1987. *The Historic Indian Tribes of Louisiana: From 1542 to the Present*. Baton Rouge: Louisiana State University Press.

Kniffen, Fred B., and Sam Hilliard. 1988. *Louisiana: Its Land and People*. Baton Rouge: Louisiana State University Press.

Leeper, Clare. 2012. *Louisiana Place Names: Popular, Unusual, and Forgotten Stories of Towns, Cities, Plantations, Bayous, and Even Some Cemeteries*. Baton Rouge: Louisiana State University Press.

Usner, Daniel H. 1992. *Indians, Settlers, and Slaves in a Frontier Exchange Economy: The Lower Mississippi Valley before 1783*. Chapel Hill: University of North Carolina Press.

CHAPTER 1

The Chitimacha Language: A History

DANIEL W. HIEBER

The history of the Chitimacha language is a remarkable story of cultural survival. This chapter tells a part of that story, discussing the interactions between Chitimacha and other languages in the Southeast prior to colonial contact, the persecution of the Chitimacha people under the French, the language's documentation by early linguists and anthropologists, and finally its modern revitalization.

Chitimacha is a language isolate—that is, unrelated to any other known languages—spoken in the present-day town of Charenton, Louisiana, on the Bayou Teche. Formerly it was spoken over the entire region from the Mississippi River in the east to Vermilion Bay in the west (see figure 1.1). By the time the Chitimacha people first appear in the historic record in 1699 (Margry 1880:155), they had already suffered drastic depopulation, in large part as a consequence of European diseases that had spread outward from Spanish Florida in the early 1500s (Thornton 2004).[1] At the time of contact with the French in 1699, an estimated three thousand Chitimacha people remained (Mooney 1928:9; Swanton 1952:203). Beginning in 1702, Louis Juchereau de St. Denis began a series of unauthorized raids on villages in Grand Terre to obtain captives to sell to French colonists at Mobile. Distrust for the French grew among the Chitimacha, culminating in the murder of Jesuit missionary Jean-François Buisson de Saint-Cosme in 1706. In retaliation, Governor Jean Baptiste Le Moyne de Bienville sent French Canadians and tribal allies in the region to attack the Chitimacha, the first in a series of attacks on the Chitimacha that continued intermittently until a 1718 peace accord (Swanton 1911:337–42). As a result of the many Chitimacha people taken captive during the war, the majority of enslaved people in early colonial Louisiana were Chitimacha (Swanton 1911:338). By 1725, only a few hundred Chitimacha survived, with an estimated one hundred males living at Bayou Plaquemine in present

Figure 1.1. Map of traditional territories of the Chitimacha, Washa, and Chawasha people. The Washa and Chawasha also spoke a variety of Chitimacha. Map from Swanton 1911, plate 1, frontispiece.

Iberville Parish (Rowland and Sanders 1932:528) and a few hundred more people living along the Bayou Teche (see Hoover 1975:44). General population decline continued through the nineteenth century, so that by the early 1900s, only about fifty Chitimacha (among them just a handful of native speakers) remained, situated at the present-day town of Charenton on the Bayou Teche (Gatschet 1883; Swanton 1911).

This state of affairs caused Chief Benjamin Paul (1867–1934), one of the last two fluent speakers of Chitimacha, to despair of the future of his language even as he worked with linguist Morris Swadesh in the early 1930s to record traditional stories: "There were (more) stories about the west, but I have forgotten. I do not know how they begin. There were very many stories about the west. . . . I believe I am doing well. I have not forgotten everything yet. When I die, you will not hear that sort of thing again" (Swadesh 1939d:166).

Chief Paul died in 1934, leaving his niece, Delphine Ducloux (1872–1940) as the last fluent speaker of Chitimacha. Ducloux passed away in 1940, leaving just a handful of elderly basket weavers who continued to use Chitimacha terminology for their weaving.

In 1986, however, the tribe received a delivery from the Library of Congress containing copies of wax cylinder recordings in the language, which Swadesh recorded via Dictaphone with Paul and Ducloux in the 1930s (Swadesh 1931). This was the first time that the language had been heard in decades. According to Chitimacha cultural director Kimberly S. Walden, "The recordings were very hard to understand, especially if you'd never heard the language spoken before. You have to realize that, as long as I was growing up, all we had [of Chitimacha] was a few words on a museum brochure that no one could pronounce" (Rosetta Stone 2007).

Alongside the original wax cylinders stored in the American Philosophical Society Library were Swadesh's field notes and draft grammar, dictionary, and text collection in the language—more than one thousand pages of materials in all (Swadesh 1930, 1939c). The tribe soon initiated the Chitimacha Language Restoration Program. In 1997, under Walden's leadership, the program developed daily language classes at the tribal elementary school as well as a preschool language program and worked with the software company Rosetta Stone to produce language-learning software (Abramson 2010; Bittinger 2010; Hieber 2010). Each of the approximately one thousand registered tribe members today has free access to the software.

In addition, the recent availability of digital copies of archival materials has facilitated a wave of new research on the language. Though Chitimacha featured prominently in the linguistic and anthropological literature in the first half of the twentieth century as a result of Swadesh's fieldwork and that of his predecessor John R. Swanton (Swanton 1917, 1919; Swadesh 1933, 1934a, 1946a), the language received little attention again until the twenty-first century. In the past decade or so, however, Chitimacha has been discussed in several overviews of the languages of the Americas (Mithun 1999; Waldman 2006) and the US Southeast (Brightman 2004; Martin 2004; Goddard 2005) and has been the focus of several theses (Weinberg 2008; Iannucci 2009). A recent proposal (though not widely accepted) also suggested a long-distance genetic relationship with Mesoamerican languages (Brown, Wichmann, and Beck 2014). Numerous studies have examined various aspects of Chitimacha grammar and diachrony, including the development of its class of preverbs (Hieber 2014a, 2018, forthcoming), its system of verbal person marking and agent-patient alignment (Hieber forthcoming), the structure of Chitimacha discourse (Hieber 2016a), and verbal valency and transitivity (Hieber 2016b, 2017).

Since the end of the war with the French in 1718, statements to the effect of "the Chitimacha are now all but extinct" have appeared so many times in the literature—decade after decade well into the twentieth century—as to be absurd (Gatschet 1883; Swanton 1911, 1912; Swadesh 1933). Yet today the language is beginning to thrive again. Far from going extinct, the Chitimacha language has instead awoken from its sleep and entered a modern renaissance. This chapter briefly outlines that story, looking at both the prehistory and history of the Chitimacha language, before turning to some aspects of Chitimacha grammar that appear to be shared with other languages of Louisiana and the Southeast.

CONTACT WITH THE SOUTHEAST

Although the Chitimacha language is an isolate, it shares several grammatical features with other languages of Louisiana and the US Southeast. This section provides just three examples of ways in which the grammar of Chitimacha has been drastically affected by its interactions with other languages in the region: in its use of positional auxiliary verbs, switch-reference, and finally agent-patient marking.

The Muskogean languages to the east, the Tunica language to the north, and the Atakapa language to the west all have a set of verbs called positional auxiliary verbs. These auxiliary verbs indicate the position of the subject—whether sitting, standing, or lying down. This pattern is seen throughout the southeastern United States (Campbell 1997:342). The particular verbs are different for each language, as table 1.1 shows, but the general pattern is the same.

Table 1.1. Comparison of Positional Auxiliary Verbs in Several Southeastern Languages				
Gloss	Chitimacha (isolate)	Atakapa (isolate; Swanton 1929)	Choctaw (Muskogean; Broadwell 2006:209–11)	Tunica (isolate; Haas 1946:349–51)
sit	*hi-*	*kē*	*átta-*	*-na*
stand	*ci-*	*ta*	*hikíya-*	*-hki* (exist)
lie	*pe-*	*tīxt*	*ittóla-*	*-ra*

In Muskogean, these positional auxiliary verbs replaced an earlier set of auxiliary verbs that were incorporated into the main verb, changing their function in the process (Booker 1980:186–87). The same process seems to have occurred in Chitimacha. The future tense marker *-cuy-* (sing.), *-di-* (pl.) clearly derives from the verb *cuw-* (sing.), *dut-* (pl.; go, walk). Likewise, the progressive marker *-qix-* comes from an archaic linking verb *qix-* (be).[2] Originally, *cuw-* and *qix-* were independent auxiliary verbs, and over time they joined with the main verb and became tense markers before being replaced by the new positional auxiliary verbs. These changes directly mirror the ones that took place in Muskogean. So Chitimacha shares not only this grammatical pattern but the history through which the pattern developed.

Another grammatical feature found in Muskogean languages is switch-reference, a method of marking verbs to indicate whether the next clause will have the same subject or a different subject. Chitimacha does not have a specific set of switch-reference markers, as the Muskogean languages do, but it did develop its own means of accomplishing the same function. The participial suffixes -*k* (after consonants), -*g* (after vowels), and -*tk* (after /n/) are either used with auxiliary verbs, as in example (1), or to modify a noun, as in example (2) (Swadesh 1939b:206–7).

(1) Kix qatin   nuhcpa-pa   *giht-k*   hi-qi?[3]
    horse   make.run-NZR   *want*-PTCP   be-NF.SG
    "Do you want your horse to run?" (lit. Are you *wanting* your horse to be made to run?) (Swadesh 1939d:A67f.2)

(2) Kaatspa-nk   qam qoonak   hix   *get-k*   qap   duud-x-naqa.
    stick-INSTR   everything   INSTR   *beat*-PTCP   here   go-IPFV-NF.PL
    (They came *beating* him with sticks and so forth.) (Swadesh 1939d:A9a.2)

However, the participle also developed a third function, allowing clauses to be chained together into long sequences of events or ideas (Hieber 2016a). This typically involves a series of participial clauses each taking the suffix -*k*, followed by a final clause with a fully conjugated main verb. Example (3) illustrates this construction.

(3) Piya   xih   hi   *gaatst-k,*   wetk   we   nux   *gapt-k*   qutp   ki
    cane   belly   there   *cut*-PTCP   then   the   stone   *take*-PTCP leather   in

    qapx   *waatst-k,*   huygi   qapx   *qutii-g,*   wetk   we   piya   gaatsn   ki
    together   *wrap*-PTCP   good   together   *tie*-PTCP   then   the   cane   cut.piece   in

    hi   *xahct-k,*   wetkx   huygi   kas   *hukt-k,*   wetkx   hesigen   qutp
    to   *put.in*-PTCP   then   good   back   *close*-PTCP   then   again   leather

    hi   *gapt-k,*   we   piya   gaatsn   we   qutp   ki   qapx   *waatst-k,*
    there   *take*-PTCP   the   cane   cut.piece   the   leather in   together   *wrap*-PTCP

    huygi   qapx   *qutii-g,*   weyt   hugu   kas   *nucmii-g,*   kas   hamca-ax-naqa.
    good   together   *tie*-PTCP   that   it.is   back   *work*-PTCP   back   keep-IPFV-NF.PL

(They cut a cane joint, take the stones and wrap them in hide, tie them well, put them into the section of cane, cork them well, again take hide and wrap the cane section in the hide, tie it well, and, having prepared it in that way, they save it.) (Swadesh 1939d:A71c.3)

Some expository texts recorded by Swadesh consist almost entirely of such chains of participial clauses, with very few main verbs. Why did this phenomenon become so common in Chitimacha? An examination of how participial clauses are used in the Chitimacha corpus shows that they are used only when the subject of the participial clause is the same as the subject of the following clause (Hieber 2016a). Otherwise, a fully conjugated main verb is used. This is the same pattern of switch-reference as seen in Muskogean, only accomplished indirectly through the participle -*k* rather than with dedicated markers for same and different subjects.

A final example of a grammatical pattern shared with other languages of the Southeast is known as agent-patient marking, where different suffixes are used depending on whether the participant involved in the action has control over it. For example, in Creek (Muskogean), the agent marker -*ay*- is used when the subject acts deliberately, while the patient marker *ca*- is used when the subject lacks control of the action (Martin 2011:168–69). Chitimacha shows a similar pattern but with an important difference: the form of the agent and patient markers is practically the same; instead, the position of the markers differs (Hieber forthcoming). Compare examples (4) and (5).

(4) quc-*ki*-cuy-i
   do-1SG.P-IRR-NF.SG
   (you will do me [well]) (Swadesh 1939d:A49d.16)

(5) quci-cu-*ki*
   do-IRR-1SG.A
   (*I* will do [it]) (Swadesh 1939d:A17e.23)

Example (4) shows that -*ki* appears before the irrealis (future) marker -*cuy*- when the speaker does not have control of the action, whereas example (5) shows that -*ki* appears after -*cuy*- when the speaker does. How did this pattern arise? That the irrealis marker -*cuy*- was originally an auxiliary verb meaning "go," so that the construction in (4) was historically two words, *qucki cuyi*, meaning something like "you will go so that I do" or "you will go and make me do." But when Chitimacha speakers reanalyzed these as a single verb, merging them together, the person suffix -*ki* remained in the middle. Since the -*ki* in the middle referred to the participant having the action done to it, while the -*ki* at the end of the second verb referred to the participant doing the action, these two versions of -*ki* were reanalyzed as the patient and agent suffixes, respectively. These changes were undoubtedly modeled on the similar agent-patient patterns in Muskogean and other languages of the Southeast and would have been facilitated by the simultaneous change in auxiliaries, discussed earlier. This helps explain why in Muskogean the agent and patient suffixes are different forms, while in Chitimacha they are the same form in different positions. Chitimacha co-opted its own native grammatical material for new purposes, mimicking patterns found in other languages of the Southeast.

In all three of these cases, Chitimacha borrowed a grammatical pattern from neighboring languages without borrowing the related vocabulary or grammatical affixes. For instance, Chitimacha borrowed the positional auxiliary pattern yet did not borrow the words for *sit*, *stand*, and *lie*, instead using its own native words. Why did this happen?

The southeastern United States, including Louisiana, is considered a linguistic and cultural area, meaning that the peoples of the region share numerous cultural and linguistic traits that cannot result from a common origin (since Chitimacha is unrelated to any other language in the region): "The defining feature of Native cultures and histories in the region is first, a long history of cultural integration within the region" (Jackson and Fogelson 2004:1). Exogamy (marrying people from outside one's own community) was widespread in the historical Southeast, abetting contact between different cultures in the region (Speck 1907:208). In addition, "the area was integrated by the exchange of goods, people, and ideas such that it comprised one grand diffusion sphere. Communication was facilitated by well marked trail systems and by the use of dugout canoes on the river and coastal courses" (Jackson, Fogelson, and Sturtevant 2004:38). Groups within the Southeast were also highly mobile, often changing the sites of their villages (Swanton 1911:360–64).

What all this means for Chitimacha grammar is that Native Americans in the Southeast were very likely multilingual, knowing the language of their family as their first language, the language of their spouse as their second, and a language of trade and broader communication as a third. Such rampant multilingualism constitutes the perfect environment for grammatical borrowing as occurred in Chitimacha. When speakers adopt another language, they are frequently influenced by ways of speaking from their first language and use structures from the second language in ways that map to structures from their first. Speakers of Chitimacha who also knew a Muskogean language, for example, probably used the auxiliary verb construction to convey the equivalent of the agent-patient distinction. Over time, this construction must have become so frequent as to become routinized and eventually a fixed part of Chitimacha grammar.

So while Chitimacha is an isolate, it was hardly isolated. Instead, the Chitimacha people were part of the diverse cultural exchange of people, goods, and languages of the Southeast that thrived for hundreds of years prior to European contact, a fact that had significant repercussions on the history of the Chitimacha language.

PREHISTORY AND COLONIAL CONTACT

As best we know, the Chitimacha and their ancestors have lived in the Louisiana region for thousands of years. From the archaeology of the region, we know that Chitimacha participated in the Hopewell mound culture, which was distinguished by its large burial mounds, arising around 100 BCE and flourishing with the arrival of farming in the area (ca. 700 ACE) until its decline prior to the fifteenth century (Haywood 2009:3.26). Numerous mound sites have been found along the Bayou Teche (Bernard 2016:25), and the Chitimacha continued to entomb their dead in mounds into the colonial period (Kniffen, Gregory, and Stokes 1987:259) and even the twentieth century, with two mound burials occurring in 1926.

As Jackson, Fogelson, and Sturtevant (2004:39) note, "Ever since the discovery of the elaborated iconography of Mississippian period art, popularizers and scholars have sought to establish connections between the Southeastern Ceremonial complex (formerly called the Southern cult) and the civilizations of Mesoamerica." This holds true for Chitimacha as well. There have been several attempts to show a genetic relationship between Chitimacha and certain languages of Mesoamerica (Brown, Wichmann, and Beck 2014; Swadesh 1960), potentially implying a Mesoamerican homeland for Chitimacha. However, these proposals have not been widely accepted (see Campbell and Kaufman 1983; Campbell 1997 for a critique of older proposals). Moreover, if the suggested relationships are true, they would be at such great time depth that the ancestors of the Chitimacha still could have migrated to Louisiana millennia ago. Indeed, the Chitimacha language shares a sufficient number of grammatical features with other languages of the US Southeast to suggest that the Chitimacha people have lived in their present vicinity for some time.

Like nearly all Native peoples of the Americas, the Chitimacha were subject to European diseases well before making direct contact with the Europeans themselves. Although the documentary and archaeological evidence for mass epidemics is actually rather scant, archaeological evidence and early historical accounts make clear that parts of the Southeast had been greatly depopulated by the time the French settled in Louisiana in 1698 (Thornton 2004). Moreover, exposure to European diseases was continual throughout the colonial period, plaguing Native populations well into the 1800s (Thornton 2004:51). Native American population decline in the Southeast appears to have been more of an ongoing process than a onetime catastrophic event.

In any event, when the Chitimacha first appear in the historical record, their estimated population of about three thousand individuals may have been a mere fraction of their former numbers. They are first mentioned by Iberville on February 17, 1699, when he wrote, "The chief and seven others came to me to sing the calumet ... allying me with four nations to the west of the Mississippi, which are the Mougoulachas, Ouacha [Washa], Toutymascha [Chitimacha], Yagueneschito [Yagnechito]" (Margry 1880:155; translation by author). It is also possible, however, that Europeans encountered Chitimacha-speaking peoples as early as 1543, when Hernando de Soto's expedition reached the mouth of the Mississippi River. When Iberville ascended the Mississippi River some 150 years later, he met several Washa people (Swanton 1911:297), who, along with the Chawasha, were said by Bienville to speak practically the same language as the Chitimacha (Goddard et al. 2004:189). While Swanton (1911:298–300) cautions that the actual settlements of the Washa were most likely further inland on Bayou La Fourche, the Washa were clearly active along the Mississippi. Swanton (1911:342) seems to think that the Chitimacha themselves were also originally situated on the Mississippi, near the northern end of Bayou La Fourche. Indeed, these villages may have been the remnants of the Yagnechito, who lived in the region during the war with the French and were said by Iberville to speak Chitimacha. If the Washa, Chawasha, Yagnechito, or Chitimacha were present along the Mississippi as early as the Soto expedition, they might have met Soto's men. In fact, Swanton (1938) even raises the possibility that one of these groups attacked Soto's men with spears at the mouth of the river, a story that persists in Chitimacha oral history to this day (Laudun 2011). It is also likely that Robert de La Salle, who explored the Mississippi from north to south in 1682, would have met with Chitimacha-speaking peoples, since he also explored the waterways around the Mississippi delta, although there is no evidence of contact with Chitimacha in any of the records from that expedition.

The French did not generally explore either Bayou Teche or Bayou La Fourche (the main areas of Chitimacha settlement) in the early 1700s (Bernard 2016:43; Brightman 2004; Swanton 1911:337), and the war with the French forced the Chitimacha to retreat into the difficult-to-navigate waterways along the sea, so little more is known of the Chitimacha during the colonial era. After peace with the French in 1718, they appear only sporadically in the historical record until the late 1800s. By 1784, the tribe had been reduced to just a few villages—at least two in Iberville Parish around Bayou La Fourche, at least one on Bayou Plaquemine, and two others on Bayou Teche (Charenton and one unknown) (Hutchins 1784:46).

DOCUMENTATION

While the earliest documentation of many languages in the Americas stems from the work of Jesuit missionaries, who were motivated by a desire to preach to Native Americans in their own language, no such work was undertaken for Chitimacha despite an early visit by Jesuit priest Paul du Poisson (1727). However, another common source of documentary materials in the early United States was vocabulary lists recorded as part of a broad research program on Native American languages outlined by Thomas Jefferson. Motivated in part by the philological and historical linguistic research coming out of Europe in the late eighteenth century, Jefferson was fascinated by the questions of whether Native American languages and cultures could be traced to a "common origin" and of their relationships to Indo-European languages. Cognizant of the fact that these languages were rapidly disappearing, Jefferson wrote,

> It is to be lamented then, very much to be lamented, that we have suffered so many of the Indian tribes already to extinguish, without our having previously collected and deposited in the records of literature, the general rudiments at least of the languages they spoke. Were vocabularies formed of all the languages spoken in North and South America, preserving their appellations of the most common objects in nature, of those which must be present to every nation barbarous or civilized, with the inflections of their nouns and verbs, their principles of regimen and concord, and these deposited in all the public libraries, it would furnish opportunities to those skilled in languages of the old world to compare them with these, now, or at any future time, and hence to construct the best evidence of the derivation of this part of the human race. (1801:193–94).

Jefferson also disseminated a standardized 287-item word list comprising what he considered the "most common objects in nature"—*fire*, *water*, and the like. Three members of the American Philosophical Society (of which Jefferson was also a member)—Peter S. Duponceau, Albert S. Gallatin, and John Pickering—pursued Jefferson's program in earnest, collecting numerous vocabularies of Native American languages. Jefferson (1808) compiled these vocabularies into a comparative list, which became the basis for Gallatin's (1836) influential first attempt at a classification of the languages of the Americas.

The first known documentation of the Chitimacha language is a vocabulary recorded in 1802 at Attakapas Post at the request of Martin Duralde, commandant of the Post of Opelousas. A copy the Duralde (1802) vocabulary was sent to Duponceau and today is housed at the American Philosophical Society Library. That vocabulary was later published by Vater (1820), and data from the vocabulary were included in the first major attempt to classify the languages of the Americas by Gallatin (1836) as well as in John Wesley Powell's (1891) revised classification undertaken as part of his work with the Bureau of Ethnography.

The Duralde vocabulary and accompanying anthropological sketch are written in French, and the Chitimacha words likewise use a French orthography (although Duralde says he had transliterated them from a Spanish orthography). Discrepancies in spelling aside, Duralde's list shows no significant differences from later documentation by Albert Samuel Gatschet (1881a), Swanton (1908), and Swadesh (1930) (a fact also noted by Swadesh [1946a:313]). Table 1.2

Table 1.2. Comparison of Chitimacha Vocabulary, 1802, 1881, and 1930

Gloss	Duralde (1802)	Gatschet (1881a)	Swadesh (1930)	Practical*
fire	teppe	tep	tep	tep
water	ko	ku	ku'	kuq
earth	nelle	ne, ne-i	ney'	neyq
air	poko	poko, poku^n	poku	poka
sun	thiaha	tcha, tchia-a	č'a'a	jaqa
moon	pantne	pa^n, pan, pant^n	pan'	panq
star	pacheta	pāshta	pa:šta	paaxta
day, light	uacheta	washta	wašta	waxta
night	timan	tchi'ma	č'ima	jima

* Deviations from the International Phonetic Alphabet are as follows: <aa> = /a:/, <b> = /p'/, <c> = /t͡ʃ/, <d> = /t'/, <dz> = /t͡s'/, <ee> = /e:/, <g> = /k'/, <ii> = /i:/, <j> = /t͡ʃ'/, <oo> = /o:/, <q> = /ʔ/, <ts> = /t͡s/, <uu> = /u:/, <x> = /ʃ/, <y> = /j/.

presents a small selection of vocabulary items comparing the transcriptions of Duralde, Gatschet, and Swadesh and that of the modern practical orthography.

At the end of the nineteenth century, research on Native American languages largely fell under the auspices of the Smithsonian Institution, which founded the Bureau of American Ethnology to research Native American cultures in 1879. Gatschet, a linguist and ethnologist trained in linguistics in Europe who moved to the United States to study Native American languages, joined the bureau when it was formed and did significant work with southeastern languages, including Chitimacha. He visited Charenton for several weeks between December 1881 and January 1882 and worked with Baptiste Angélique at a village on Grand Lake. Angélique was a Creole person of color who grew up in close proximity to the Chitimacha but was not Chitimacha himself. He was approximately seventy-six years old at the time. According to Gatschet (1883:149), roughly sixteen to eighteen Chitimacha people were living on Grand Lake and another thirty-five resided at Charenton, and about half of them still spoke Chitimacha. Gatschet (1881b) recorded enough material for a dictionary consisting of 1,273 file slips (generally with multiple words/phrases per slip) and a long expository text about Chitimacha traditional culture. These materials and his accompanying field notes are now housed in the Smithsonian at the National Anthropological Archives (Gatschet 1881a). Gatschet (1883) published a short anthropological sketch of the Chitimacha but said little about the language other than that it "seems to be extremely polysynthetic" (156). He never published either the texts or vocabulary, but both Swanton and Swadesh obtained copies of Gatschet's materials and incorporated his data into their own.

In the early 1900s, the field of anthropology was undergoing drastic changes as a result of the influence of Franz Boas, the father of modern anthropology. Boas stressed the notion of cultural relativism and the importance of studying cultures on their own terms. Swanton was one of Boas's earliest students at Columbia and in 1900 became the first formally trained anthropologist to join the Bureau of American Ethnology (Jackson, Fogelson, and Sturtevant 2004:35). Swanton became interested in working on Chitimacha after seeing Gatschet's materials in the Smithsonian archives (Swanton 1905) and at Boas's direction traveled to Charenton in 1907, returning again in 1908, 1917, and 1918 (Swanton 1920:2).

Swanton worked with Chief Paul, who is perhaps the person most responsible for the survival of the Chitimacha language today. Paul worked with Swanton during all four of his visits as well as with Swadesh during the 1930s. Approximately 75 percent of all the documentary material on Chitimacha comes from him. According to Swanton (1920:2), "The language has fallen so much into disuse that [Paul] could recall many things only with difficulty and there is reason to believe that it has lost many forms and much of its original richness," but this statement seems to have resulted more from Swanton's inability to puzzle out the grammar of Chitimacha than any linguistic deficiency on the chief's part. Swanton confused an adjective-making suffix, -gi, with a first singular patient suffix, -ki (Swanton 1920; Hieber forthcoming), and calls the first singular gerund -ka a continuative marker (Swanton 1920:31), among other issues. But Chief Paul dictated eighty-eight texts—many quite lengthy—to Swadesh two decades later, with little to no evidence of language obsolescence. Swadesh (1946a:312–13) later observed, "Remarkable in the terminal history of Chitimacha is the purity with which it was preserved. . . . Chitimacha shows no signs of influence by French or English, nor is there anything suggestive of internal disintegration, unless the presence of alternate equivalent forms is such a symptom." Even Swadesh (1939b), whose grammatical analysis is significantly more accurate than Swanton's, attributes certain grammatical alternations to mere free variation, implying a kind of randomness to the language. He says, for example, that "a peculiarity of Chitimacha is the presence of a number of cases of alternate equivalent forms, not different as to meaning. . . . In the adjective there are often three or more forms for the singular, as žiwi, žiwgi, ži·niš, žiwa, žiwg(š) 'bad'" (1946a:315). However, a more detailed look at the Chitimacha corpus shows that these forms are actually the gerund/infinitive "to be bad," the adjective "bad," the patientive adjective "having become/been made bad," the noun "bad thing," and the participle "being bad" (with or without the topic marker -š), respectively.

What Swanton and Swadesh attributed to language obsolescence or lack of grammatical structure was in fact a deft command of the language on the part of Chief Paul. His texts show nuanced control of such semantic subtleties as the agent/patient distinction, use of directional preverbs, and use of various verbal suffixes—constructions that both Swanton and Swadesh had difficulty analyzing. Paul's ability to productively employ grammatical forms in novel constructions becomes more evident when comparing his texts to that of another speaker, Ducloux, who worked with Swadesh in the 1930s. She dictated twenty-two texts, but her discourse shows less productive use of these constructions, some of which seem to have become fossilized expressions. As one example, Ducloux used the word *gapt-* by itself to mean "take away" (Swadesh 1939a:86), whereas Paul used the appropriate preverb to express the sense of "away," depending on context—*hi gapt-* (take there) or *kap gapt-* (take up)—suggesting that Ducloux's ability to use the preverbs productively was not quite as robust as her uncle's. Ducloux also used more French borrowings than did Chief Paul and used the French /v/ where Paul used /w/. For the most part, however, Ducloux's speech was extremely fluent; other differences in the way they used certain constructions are difficult to spot.

The discrepancy between Swanton and Swadesh's descriptions of Chitimacha grammar and Paul and Ducloux's skillful use of the language shows just how easy it was for even cultural relativists in the tradition of Boas to view Native American languages or their speakers as deficient, when in fact the discrepancies were a matter of ignorance on the part of the linguists—a valuable lesson for today's fieldworkers.

Swadesh, a famous student of Edward Sapir, began fieldwork on Chitimacha in 1930, producing the most comprehensive set of documentary materials on the language to date. In 1931, he made a number of wax cylinder recordings, which are still available in digital form (albeit of very poor quality), and by 1934, he had produced sixteen composition notebooks filled with words, sentences, and transcribed texts (Swadesh 1930). By 1939, he had prepared drafts of a dictionary of approximately thirty-five hundred words (Swadesh 1939a); a collection of 120 texts and their translations, with the Chitimacha portion totaling 160 typed pages (Swadesh 1939d); and even a thorough, 238-page descriptive grammar (Swadesh 1939b). These were never published, perhaps partially as a consequence of the political challenges facing Swadesh at the height of the McCarthy era in the late 1940s, when he lost his position at the City College of New York as a result of his leftist political ideologies (Hymes 2006:248–50). Swadesh worked in the Boas Collection at the American Philosophical Society starting in 1949, at which point he seems to have deposited his nearly finished manuscripts and ceased further work on the language.

Though Swadesh's Boasian trifecta of a grammar, dictionary, and text collection was never published, the Chitimacha data he collected and the articles he published using those data came to have a tremendous and enduring impact on the field of linguistics. His work on Chitimacha was influential in his formulation of the phonemic principle (Swadesh 1934b), and indeed, his description of Chitimacha phonology (1934a) was the first sketch of a Native American language to apply phonemic principles. Swadesh (1948) was also one of the first to draw attention to the issue of language endangerment, for which he used Chitimacha as a prominent example. Though Swadesh's controversial theory of glottochronology would later make him well known in linguistics, his first attempt at historical reconstruction was actually an attempt to show a genetic relationship between Chitimacha and Atakapa (Swadesh 1946b, 1947). (This attempt was mostly ignored and receives little credence from modern tribal members or linguists.) The Chitimacha language was therefore a prominent influence on the early development of American linguistics.

REVITALIZATION

After Swadesh's work in the 1930s, very little was done with the Chitimacha language for almost seventy years (though see the comparative work of Haas 1951, 1952). James Crawford (1975:62) recorded fourteen words from Emile Stouff in 1969; one of the few remaining basket weavers still remembers a number of terms relating to weaving; and elderly members of the tribe remembered a few words into the 2000s (Rosetta Stone 2007); however, the language was no longer used in the community. And, as was often the case for Native American communities, tribal members were not made aware that extensive documentary materials existed on their language until the 1980s. Even then, several more years passed before the Chitimacha tribe had the resources to undertake a language revitalization program. The tribe opened a casino in 1992 and used part of the revenue it generated to finance the Cultural Department and hire several tribal members to work on the revitalization project. After enlisting the help of a linguist who had studied under Swadesh decades earlier, the Cultural Department embarked on a broad language revitalization program, beginning work on a comprehensive dictionary aimed at elementary school students, offering both youth and adult language classes, and creating language primers. Today, language instruction starts six weeks after birth at Yaamahana (the Child Development Center, the tribal preschool) and has been incorporated into the K–8 curriculum at the tribal elementary school. Night classes have also been offered for adults, and some of the tribal members who attended that class have gone on to join the revitalization program. For the first time in decades, the Chitimacha language is a prominent feature of public events, with most occasions including an opening prayer and the

Indian Pledge of Allegiance in Chitimacha as well as signs in both English and Chitimacha.

In 2007, the Chitimacha tribe won a worldwide grant competition from the software company Rosetta Stone to create language-learning software. The Rosetta Stone Endangered Language Program, where I served as Editor from 2008 to 2013, worked with various Native American and First Nations educators and nonprofits to produce language-learning software, granting all rights to the sales and distribution of the product to the indigenous organizations. In conjunction with the Endangered Language Program, the Chitimacha Cultural Department worked tirelessly over the course of two years to produce a Chitimacha Rosetta Stone, which was officially released in 2010. The software is now provided free to every tribal member and has been incorporated into the language curriculum in the tribal elementary school. The tribe subsequently invited me to continue working with them in their revitalization efforts, and today, the members of the Cultural Department and I are working to produce various classroom materials and finalize the dictionary for the elementary school.

What Duralde, Gatschet, Swanton, and Swadesh thought was an attempt to capture the last remnant of the Chitimacha language before it faded into history was in fact the beginning of a linguistic revival. Thanks to the inexhaustible work of speakers like Baptiste Angélique, Delphine Ducloux, and especially Chief Benjamin Paul, who spent nearly three decades working with linguists to document his language, as well as the monumental efforts of the Cultural Department of the Chitimacha Tribe, the future of the Chitimacha language is looking bright again.

NOTES

The research in this chapter is based on work supported by the National Science Foundation Graduate Research Fellowship Program, Grant 1144085. Many thanks are due to Chitimacha cultural director Kimberley S. Walden and Dayna Bowker Lee for their detailed feedback and assistance writing this chapter. I also thank Marianne Mithun, Brendon Yoder, and Jared Sharp for taking the time to read an earlier draft and offer comments. All errors or other shortcomings are of course wholly my own.

1. European diseases may have affected the Chitimacha as early as Hernando de Soto's expedition, which reached the mouth of the Mississippi River in 1543 (Swanton 1939).

2. More precisely, *-cuy-/-di-* is an irrealis marker, and *-qix-* is an imperfective.

3. Glossing abbreviations are as follows: A agent, INSTR instrumental, IPFV imperfective, IRR irrealis, NF non-first-person, NZR nominalizer, P patient, PL plural, PTCP participle, SG singular.

WORKS CITED

Abramson, Larry. 2010. "Software Company Helps Revive 'Sleeping' Language." *NPR: All Things Considered*, February 2. http://www.npr.org/templates/story/story.php?storyId=123220585.

Bernard, Shane K. 2016. *Teche: A History of Louisiana's Most Famous Bayou*. Jackson: University Press of Mississippi.

Bittinger, Marion. 2010. "From the Endangered Language Program: Chitimacha Release." *Linguavore*, May 11, 2010. http://blog.rosettastone.com/chitimacha-release/.

Booker, Karen M. 1980. "Comparative Muskogean: Aspects of Proto-Muskogean Verb Morphology." PhD diss., University of Kansas.

Brightman, Robert A. 2004. "Chitimacha." In *Handbook of North American Indians*, vol. 14, *Southeast*, edited by Raymond D. Fogelson, 642–52. Washington, DC: Smithsonian Institution.

Broadwell, George Aaron. 2006. *A Choctaw Reference Grammar*. Lincoln: University of Nebraska Press.

Brown, Cecil H., Søren Wichmann, and David Beck. 2014. "Chitimacha: A Mesoamerican Language in the Lower Mississippi Valley." *International Journal of American Linguistics* 80 (4): 425–74.

Campbell, Lyle. 1997. *American Indian Languages: The Historical Linguistics of Native America*. Oxford: Oxford University Press.

Campbell, Lyle, and Terrence Kaufman. 1983. "Mesoamerican Historical Linguistics and Distant Genetic Relationship: Getting It Straight." *American Anthropologist* 85 (2): 362–72.

Crawford, James M. 1975. "Southeastern Indian Languages." In *Studies in Southeastern Indian Languages*, edited by James Crawford, 1–121. Athens: University of Georgia Press.

Duralde, Martin. 1802. "Vocabulaire de la Langue des Chetimachas et Croyance des Chetimachas." In American Philosophical Society Historical and Literary Committee, American Indian Vocabulary Collection, Mss. 497.V85, American Philosophical Society Library, Philadelphia.

Gallatin, Albert. 1836. "A Synopsis of the Indian Tribes of North America." *Transactions of the American Antiquarian Society* 2:1–422.

Gatschet, Albert S. 1881a. "A. S. Gatschet Vocabularies and Other Linguistic Notes ca. 1881–1886." In Numbered Manuscripts, 1850s–1980s (Some Earlier), MS 1449, Smithsonian Institution National Anthropological Archive, Suitland, MD.

Gatschet, Albert S. 1881b. "Texts of the Shetimasha Language, Spoken in Charenton, St. Mary's Parish, La." In Numbered Manuscripts, 1850s–1980s (Some Earlier), MS 288, Smithsonian Institution National Anthropological Archive, Suitland, MD.

Gatschet, Albert S. 1883. "The Shetimasha Indians of St. Mary's Parish, Southern Louisiana." *Transactions of the Anthropological Society of Washington* 2:148–59.

Goddard, Ives. 2005. "The Indigenous Languages of the Southeast." *Anthropological Linguistics* 47 (1): 1–60.

Goddard, Ives, Patricia Galloway, Marvin D. Jeter, Gregory A. Waselkov, and John E. Worth. 2004. "Small Tribes of the Western Southeast." In *Handbook of North American Indians*, vol. 14, *Southeast*, edited by Raymond D. Fogelson, 174–90. Washington, DC: Smithsonian Institution.

Haas, Mary R. 1946. "A Grammatical Sketch of Tunica." In *Linguistic Structures of Native America*, edited by Charles Osgood, 337–66. New York: Viking Fund.

Haas, Mary R. 1951. "The Proto-Gulf Word for 'Water' (With Notes on Siouan-Yuchi)." *International Journal of American Linguistics* 17 (2): 71–79.

Haas, Mary R. 1952. "The Proto-Gulf Word for 'Land' (With a Note on Proto-Siouan)." *International Journal of American Linguistics* 18 (4): 238–40.
Haywood, John. 2009. *Atlas of World History: From the Ancient World to the Present*. New York: Fall River.
Hieber, Daniel W., ed. 2010. *Rosetta Stone Chitimacha (Sitimaxa)*. Arlington, VA: Rosetta Stone.
Hieber, Daniel W. 2014a. "Category Genesis through Schematicity: On the Origin of Chitimacha Preverbs." Paper presented at the UC Santa Barbara Department of Linguistics 25th Anniversary Reunion, Santa Barbara, CA, October 11.
Hieber, Daniel W. 2014b. "Degrees and Dimensions of Grammaticalization in Chitimacha Preverbs." Paper presented at the Workshop on American Indigenous Languages, Santa Barbara, CA, May 2–3.
Hieber, Daniel W. 2016a. "The Extension of Structure to Discourse: Chitimacha Participles in Discourse and Diachrony." Paper presented at the meeting of the Society for the Study of the Indigenous Languages of the Americas, Washington, DC, January 7–10.
Hieber, Daniel W. 2016b. "Non-Autonomous Valency-Changing Devices in Chitimacha." Paper presented at the workshop on American Indigenous Languages, Santa Barbara, CA, May 6–7.
Hieber, Daniel W. 2017. "Indeterminate Valency and Verbal Ambivalence in Chitimacha." Paper presented at the meeting of the Society for the Study of the Indigenous Languages of the Americas, Austin, TX, January 5–8.
Hieber, Daniel W. 2018. "Category Genesis in Chitimacha: A Constructional Approach." In *Category Change from a Constructional Perspective*, edited by Kristel van Goethem, Muriel Norde, Evie Coussé, and Gudrun Vanderbauwhede, 15–46. Amsterdam: Benjamins.
Hieber, Daniel W. Forthcoming. "Semantic Alignment in Chitimacha." *International Journal of American Linguistics*.
Hoover, Herbert T. 1975. *The Chitimacha People*. Phoenix: Indian Tribal Series.
Hutchins, Thomas. 1784. *An Historical Narrative and Topographical Description of Louisiana, and West-Florida*. Philadelphia: Aitken.
Hymes, Dell H. 2006. "Morris Swadesh: From the First Yale School to World Prehistory." In *The Origin and Diversification of Language*, edited by Joel F. Sherzer, 228–70. New Brunswick, NJ: Transaction.
Iannucci, David J. 2009. "Aspects of Chitimacha Phonology." Master's thesis, University of Utah.
Jackson, Jason Baird, and Raymond D. Fogelson. 2004. Introduction to *Handbook of North American Indians*, vol. 14, *Southeast*, edited by Raymond D. Fogelson, 1–13. Washington, DC: Smithsonian Institution.
Jackson, Jason Baird, Raymond D. Fogelson, and William C. Sturtevant. 2004. "History of Ethnological and Linguistic Research." In *Handbook of North American Indians*, vol. 14, *Southeast*, edited by Raymond D. Fogelson, 31–47. Washington, DC: Smithsonian Institution.
Jefferson, Thomas. 1801. *Notes on the State of Virginia*. Philadelphia: Rawle.
Jefferson, Thomas. 1808. "Comparative Vocabularies of Several Indian Languages, 1802–1808." In American Council of Learned Societies Committee on Native American Languages, Mss. 497.J35, American Philosophical Society Library, Philadelphia.
Kniffen, Fred B., Hiram F. Gregory, and George A. Stokes. 1987. *The Historic Indian Tribes of Louisiana: From 1542 to the Present*. Baton Rouge: Louisiana State University Press.
Laudun, Tika, dir. and prod. 2011. *Native Waters: A Chitimacha Recollection*. Video recording. Louisiana Public Broadcasting.
Margry, Pierre. 1880. *Découvertes et Établissements des Français dans l'Ouest et dans le Sud de l'Amérique Septentrionale (1614–1754): Mémoires et Documents Originaux, Part 4: Découverte*

par Mer des Bouches du Missisipi et Établissements de Lemoyne d'Iberville sur le Golfe du Mexique [Discoveries and Settlements of the French in the West and South of North America (1614–1754): Memoirs and Original Documents, Part 4: Discovery by Sea of the Mouths of the Mississippi and the Settlements of Lemoyne d'Iberville on the Gulf of Mexico]. Paris: Maisonneuve.

Martin, Jack B. 2004. "Languages." In *Handbook of North American Indians*, vol. 14, *Southeast*, edited by Raymond D. Fogelson, 68–86. Washington, DC: Smithsonian Institution.

Martin, Jack B. 2011. *A Grammar of Creek (Muskogee)*. Lincoln: University of Nebraska Press.

Mithun, Marianne. 1999. *The Languages of Native North America*. Cambridge: Cambridge University Press.

Mooney, James. 1928. "The Aboriginal Population of America North of Mexico." *Smithsonian Miscellaneous Collections* 80 (7): 1–40.

Poisson, Paul du. 1727. "Letter from Father du Poisson, Missionary to the Akensas, to Father ***." In *The Jesuit Relations and Allied Documents*, vol. 67, 1610–1791, edited by Reuben Gold Thwaites, 276–325. Abenakis, LA: Burrows.

Powell, John Wesley. 1891. "Indian Linguistic Families of America North of Mexico." In *Seventh Annual Report of the Bureau of Ethnology to the Secretary of the Smithsonian Institution, 1885–86*, edited by John Wesley Powell, 7–148. Washington, DC: Smithsonian Institution.

Rosetta Stone. 2007. "Sleeping Language Gets Help from Rosetta Stone." Press release. http://pr.rosettastone.com/phoenix.zhtml?c=228009&p=irol-newsArticle&ID=1273965.a.

Rowland, Dunbar, and Albert Godfrey Sanders, eds. 1932. *Mississippi Provincial Archives*. Vol. 3, *French Dominion (1704–1743)*. Jackson: Press of the Mississippi Department of Archives and History.

Speck, Frank G. 1907. "Some Outlines of Aboriginal Culture in the Southeastern States." *American Anthropologist* 9 (2): 287–95.

Swadesh, Morris. 1930. "Field Notes on Chitimacha." In American Council of Learned Societies Committee on Native American Languages, Mss. 497.3.B63c G6.3, American Philosophical Society Library, Philadelphia.

Swadesh, Morris, ed. 1931. "Stories in Chitimacha." In American Council of Learned Societies Committee on Native American Languages, Mss. Rec.7, American Philosophical Society Library, Philadelphia.

Swadesh, Morris. 1933. "Chitimacha Verbs of Derogatory or Abusive Connotation with Parallels from European languages." *Language* 9 (2): 192–201.

Swadesh, Morris. 1934a. "The Phonemic Principle." *Language* 10 (2): 117–29.

Swadesh, Morris. 1934b. "The Phonetics of Chitimacha." *Language* 10 (4): 345–62.

Swadesh, Morris. 1939a. "Chitimacha-English Dictionary." In Swadesh 1939c.

Swadesh, Morris. 1939b. "Chitimacha Grammar." In Swadesh 1939c.

Swadesh, Morris. 1939c. "Chitimacha Grammar, Texts, and Vocabulary." In American Council of Learned Societies Committee on Native American Languages, Mss. 497.3.B63c G6.5, American Philosophical Society Library, Philadelphia.

Swadesh, Morris. 1939d. "Chitimacha Texts." In Swadesh 1939c.

Swadesh, Morris. 1946a. "Chitimacha." In *Linguistic Structures of Native America*, edited by Cornelius Osgood, 312–36. New York: Viking Fund.

Swadesh, Morris. 1946b. "Phonologic Formulas for Atakapa-Chitimacha." *International Journal of American Linguistics* 12 (3): 113–32.

Swadesh, Morris. 1947. "Atakapa-Chitimacha *k^w." *International Journal of American Linguistics* 13 (2): 120–21.

Swadesh, Morris. 1948. "Sociologic Notes on Obsolescent Languages." *International Journal of American Linguistics* 14 (4): 226–35.

Swadesh, Morris. 1960. "The Oto-Manguean Hypothesis and Macro Mixtecan." *International Journal of American Linguistics* 26 (2): 79–111.

Swanton, John R. 1905. "Letter to Franz Boas, Oct. 3, 1905." In Franz Boas Papers: Inventory S, American Philosophical Society Library, Philadelphia.

Swanton, John R. 1908. "Chitimacha Vocabulary and Notes, 1908–1931." In Numbered Manuscripts, 1850s–1980s (Some Earlier), MS 4139, Smithsonian Institution National Anthropological Archive, Suitland, MD.

Swanton, John R. 1911. *Indian Tribes of the Lower Mississippi Valley and Adjacent Coast of the Gulf of Mexico.* Washington, DC: Smithsonian Institution.

Swanton, John R. 1912. "Letter to Franz Boas, Nov. 28, 1912." In Franz Boas Papers: Inventory S, American Philosophical Society Library, Philadelphia.

Swanton, John R. 1917. "Some Chitimacha Myths and Beliefs." *Journal of American Folklore* 30 (118): 474–78.

Swanton, John R. 1919. *A Structural and Lexical Comparison of the Tunica, Chitimacha, and Atakapa Languages.* Washington, DC: Smithsonian Institution.

Swanton, John R. 1920. "A Sketch of the Chitimacha Language." In Numbered Manuscripts, 1850s–1980s (Some Earlier), MS 4139, Smithsonian Institution National Anthropological Archive, Suitland, MD.

Swanton, John R. 1929. "A Sketch of the Atakapa Language." *International Journal of American Linguistics* 5 (2–4): 121–49.

Swanton, John R. 1938. "Historic Use of the Spear-Thrower in Southeastern North America." *American Antiquity* 3 (4): 356–58.

Swanton, John R. 1939. *Final Report of the United States de Soto Expedition Commission.* 76th Cong., 1st sess., House Document No. 71. Washington, DC: US Government Printing Office.

Swanton, John R. 1952. *The Indian Tribes of North America.* Washington, DC: Smithsonian Institution.

Thornton, Russell. 2004. "Demographic History." In *Handbook of North American Indians*, vol. 14, *Southeast*, edited by Raymond D. Fogelson, 48–52. Washington, DC: Smithsonian Institution.

Vater, Johann Severin. 1820. *Analekten der Sprachenkunde* [Analects of Linguistics]. Leipzig.

Waldman, Carl. 2006. *Encyclopedia of Native American Tribes.* 3rd ed. New York: Checkmark.

Weinberg, Miranda. 2008. "From Obsolescence to Renaissance: Language Change in Chitimacha." Honors thesis, Swarthmore College.

CHAPTER 2

KOWASSAATON ILHAALOS: LET US HEAR KOASATI

LINDA LANGLEY AND BERTNEY LANGLEY

> Koassaati naathihilkawailiip aatkoaat'hommok iistilkalahǫ.
> *We are told that as long as we can speak Koasati we will remain Indians.*
> —**Koasati Language Committee Exhibit, April 2016**

The Koasati (Coushatta) are Muskogean-speaking peoples who are indigenous to the Southeast, historically inhabiting parts of Tennessee, Alabama, Georgia, Mississippi, Louisiana, Florida, and Texas. The majority of individuals within the Coushatta Tribe of Louisiana have been first speakers of Koasati until the present generation, but English is becoming the dominant language spoken among those tribal members aged twenty years and younger. This chapter presents the tribal community's awareness of and response to its perceived language loss through the development of a comprehensive language documentation and revitalization program.

HISTORY OF THE COUSHATTA TRIBE OF LOUISIANA

The Coushatta Tribe of Louisiana has been located in the piney woods of southwest Louisiana for almost 150 years. After Spanish explorer Hernando de Soto encountered a Coushatta community on an island in the Tennessee River in 1540, the Coushattas relocated several times to avoid European encroachment. By the early 1700s, a large group of the Coushattas had resettled near the present-day town of Coosada, Alabama, and become part of the powerful Muskogean-speaking Creek Confederacy while maintaining their own culture and language.[1] Following the Treaty of San Lorenzo, the influential Coushatta chiefs Stilapihkachatta (Red Shoes) and Pahimikko (Grass Chief) led a group of nearly one thousand Coushattas westward to establish villages in the neutral territory between French, Spanish, American, and Mexican territories. Using existing homestead laws, approximately three hundred Coushattas ultimately settled at Bayou Blue north of Elton, Louisiana, in the 1880s. (For a detailed history of the Coushatta Tribe of Louisiana, see Precht 2007).

The Coushatta people have always been recognized for their strong sense of community and self-determination, qualities gained from years of struggle and numerous relocations. Tribal elders adopted a saying, *The Struggle Has Made Us Stronger*, and eked out a living by farming, working for the local timber companies, and making longleaf pine-needle baskets, which have since become prized collectables. When offered the "opportunity" to join other tribes on reservations in Oklahoma, the Coushatta chiefs politely refused and used existing homestead laws to purchase their own land. When the Bureau of Indian Affairs refused to provide educational assistance for Coushatta children, their families contributed lumber and nails and built a school. After being illegally "terminated" without legislative approval during the Eisenhower administration, tribal members survived for more than twenty years without support from the state or federal governments. During this time, older tribal members report that the elders encouraged patience, stating, "We know who we are. We don't need anyone else to tell us who we are." Tribal leader Ernest Sickey's petitions ultimately succeeded, and the tribe received formal re-recognition from the secretary of the interior in June 1973 (Battise et al. 1983). Even now, researchers find Coushatta historical documents filed under *Creek*, *Choctaw*, and *Cherokee* in such illustrious repositories as the National Archives.[2]

Life in the community changed dramatically when the tribe opened the Coushatta Casino Resort in 1995. The business enterprise grew to be one of Louisiana's largest private employers, significantly impacting the economy in the tribe and surrounding communities. Along with the economic growth and prosperity, the tribe began to see a worrying trend of Native language loss as more families had multiple computers, televisions, and toys that continually streamed the English language into homes. Where Koasati once was spoken everywhere in the community—at the gas station, the convenience store, the Laundromat, community meetings, tribal events, and ball games—it slowly became relegated to gatherings of elders. According to language surveys conducted by the Coushatta Heritage Department in 2010 and 2013, the youngest native Koasati speaker who spoke the language in daily conversation was twenty-five, and less than one-third of the more than nine hundred enrolled members identified themselves as fluent in Koasati. The tribal community began to seek effective ways to promote language and cultural revitalization among tribal youth (B. Langley and Langley 2009; L. Langley, Oubre, and Precht 2009).

THE KOASATI LANGUAGE PROJECT

In the summer of 2006, the authors began working with the Coushatta Tribal Council to develop a comprehensive Koasati language documentation and revitalization plan. They received training in language documentation at the University of Arizona's American Indian Language Development Institute, where they developed a formal language plan.[3] In April 2007, the Tribal Council held a community meeting to present this plan and solicit volunteers to work on the project. More than thirty people signed up, and thus the tribe's first language documentation and revitalization project was born.

From an academic perspective, Koasati had been relatively well documented in the twentieth century compared to many other Native North American languages. Previous Koasati researchers include noted Bureau of American Ethnography researcher John Swanton (n.d.a, b), linguist Mary Haas (1934), Haas's student Lyda Taylor (1940), and linguist Jack Fisher (1963). Linguist Gene Burnham (1979), working with the Summer Institute of Linguistics, also produced Koasati descriptive work and language learning pamphlets in the 1970s, as did fellow institute researcher David Rising (1992). More recently, anthropologist and linguist Geoffrey Kimball produced a Koasati reference grammar (1991), dictionary (1994), and text collection (2010).

Academics and linguists viewing this body of work could readily conclude that Koasati was sufficiently well documented. However, at the inception of the Koasati Language Project, tribal members described a number of difficulties in accessing and utilizing this previous research. The main issue was interpreting the orthography utilized by previous researchers. In addition, tribal members wanted multimedia documentation of everyday conversational language to develop pedagogical materials. Accordingly, the first priority of the newly formed Koasati Language Committee was the development of a tribally approved orthography with which to begin language documentation.

The committee held its first meeting in June 2007; over the course of a weekend workshop, tribal members discussed the relative merits of adopting a spelling system for Koasati (which the community had never previously done), developed a practical orthography, and developed various products in Koasati, including bumper stickers, T-shirts, coloring books, and refrigerator magnets. There was never any discussion of payment or other incentives for committee members; to this day, no one on the committee has asked for compensation for their time. (For an ethnography of the Koasati Language Project, see Hasselbacher 2015a, b).

As Hasselbacher (2015b) has described, the Koasati Language Project generated a lot of excitement about developing a standard way to write the language. Figure 2.1 shows the alphabet developed by the project. According to committee member Claudine Hasting,

Figure 2.1. The Koasati alphabet. Poster by Heather Williams. Reproduced by permission from the Coushatta Heritage Department.

Anap, honaathiikap "Kowassaati naathiihilkạ inchaahilạ" kahhan stachayokpạạhoosit. Inchaalih chabannak statilitik chasankot, kaanon ọntakkotot ommọ, katik, hasaikạạhoosin chikkiililahọ inchaalit. Mootohon, "Inchaahilas" kahhok stiisan stachayokpạạhoosit.

Me, I was really happy when they said they are going to write the Coushatta language. I would try to write it but I never could. I probably didn't do it good, but I have a lot written down. And then, when they said we would write it [as part of the official language project], I was so happy. (Hasselbacher 2015b:135)[4]

In almost nine years of sometimes difficult and tedious language documentation work, meetings of the Koasati Language Committee have remained fun and popular gatherings, well attended, full of laughter, and always accompanied by delicious meals prepared by committee members. Even when differences of opinion arise over such issues as pronunciation or translation, members have agreed to consult others or disagree and move on rather than allow meetings to become bogged down or contentious.[5]

The committee's supportive, altruistic attitude is facilitated by a common understanding at the core of all its activities, which is that the Koasati Language Project has been conceived, initiated, and run by the Coushatta people. They know that it is their project, and they maintain responsibility for all project activities and decisions. When the Language Committee identifies a need for professional expertise outside of the community, they seek linguists[6] and anthropological consultants who work well with the community to provide training in the best practices of language documentation, transcription, archiving, and increasingly language immersion. To date, tribal members have conducted more than one hundred hours of interviews and other speech events, cataloging, transcribing, and translating Koasati texts from numerous speakers.

TRANSITIONING FROM DOCUMENTATION TO REVITALIZATION

By 2012, the National Science Foundation documentation grants had ended and the tribe began to place greater emphasis on language revitalization. The active involvement of the tribal community throughout the project facilitated this transition, because members had consistently requested that documentation be undertaken with the goal of revitalization in mind. For example, tribal members participating in documentation workshops also worked with researchers and students to produce teaching posters, smartphone apps, games, song booklets, children's videos, and other pedagogical materials available through the Language Project website (www.koasatiheritage.org). Printed materials produced in the course of the project—a multimedia dictionary, children's picture dictionary, phrase book, and conversation book—are widely used pedagogical resources within the community (Coushatta Tribe of Louisiana 2011, 2013, 2015; Williams 2010).

Documentation is in many ways easier than revitalization: Linguists have well-developed techniques for making, transcribing, and analyzing recordings, but there are no comparable techniques for reversing language loss and revitalizing an indigenous language. Starting an immersion school involves finding long-term resources, training teachers, and developing a curriculum, all of which are complicated tasks. The community had many discussions regarding revitalization options, including teaching children in an immersion environment. In 2015, Heather Williams became the first tribal member to graduate from college with both a degree in early childhood education and an immersion teaching certificate. She immediately began working to gain Tribal Council approval for partial-immersion teaching of three- to five-year-olds in the tribal Head Start program. Williams is now the school's director and team-teaches immersion classes with an elder speaker who is a longtime language advocate and active member of the Koasati Language Committee. Initial observations indicate that students are actively engaged in the learning process, the immersion classroom is lively and fun, and students are speaking Koasati both at school and in their home environment.

From its inception, the Koasati Language Committee has promoted the use of spoken language in natural settings within the tribal community. Project activities have accordingly incorporated a mixture of informal social activities, such as community gatherings and meetings of basket weavers, with naturally occurring Koasati, and summer camps are held where Koasati is taught to tribal youth. A variety of teaching methods are used, depending on the preferences of the teacher(s) and learner(s). Modified master-apprentice situations are popular, involving small groups of learners and mentors for situations like the Tribal Princess contest (which now requires spoken Koasati from each contestant). In one case, three generations of tribal members worked together to record and teach songs (a semifluent speaker recorded his mother singing an old gospel favorite; another fluent speaker transcribed the song and gave it to her daughter, who used both the recording and the written lyrics to teach the song to a tribal teenager). In June 2016, McNeese State University offered full-immersion Koasati classes for community high school students, the first time that Koasati had been taught anywhere for college credit. Initial assessments indicated that all of the students increased at least one level in spoken and written language proficiency.[7]

In February 2009, the Coushatta Tribe produced its first indigenous-language newsletter, *Kowassaati Aathiihilka* (Koasati News). A stack of newsletters was left on the counter of the Coushatta Café, a popular lunch spot for tribal members and employees. When Loretta Williams, the official transcriber for the Koasati Language Project, went to the café, she read the newsletter out loud to demonstrate that the text did in fact encode Koasati. Asked one man, "Is it really written in Indian?"

A decade later, written Koasati is widely available in the community, though elders still prefer to hear rather than read Koasati. The majority of tribal members are aware of and able to access language learning resources, are comfortable using at least some of these resources, and perceive opportunities to become involved in what is still widely known as the "language project." The initial atmosphere of hesitancy evidenced by the reaction to the first newsletter has shifted dramatically, with tribal members involved in projects such as writing Koasati poems and slogans and the newly opened tribal convenience store including all-Koasati interior signage.[8]

In April 2016, the Coushatta Tribe installed the first-ever public exhibit of tribal history and culture in its casino. The exhibit included both written and spoken Koasati, including committee-approved teaching materials and a poem written by committee members. Summarizing the tribal community's continued enthusiasm for the project, the exhibit declared,

Nashahpak stamaahilkaak komawiichaahoschok.

All things new [that we have started] are helping us.

NOTES

1. When the tribe received federal re-recognition in 1973, it chose the English spelling of its name, which is officially the Coushatta Tribe of Louisiana. Koasati (CKU) is the language of the Coushatta people. For information on the early history of the Coushatta people, see Boyd 1937; Swanton 1922; Hudson 1997. See also numerous period maps.

2. The most humorous example of misidentification occurred at the Smithsonian's Archives, which had filed two seven-inch reel-to-reel tapes of Koasati as "Italian."

3. The first summer at the American Indian Language Development Institute was funded by the National Science Foundation, which has since provided five years of funding for the Koasati Language Project (Grants 0651290 and 1065334). Special thanks to Dr. Susan Penfield, whose work and support at both organizations started and nurtured us along this journey.

4. The authors were surprised to see that the approved orthography was virtually identical to that used by tribal member Douglas John in 1930 and Burnham in the 1970s, with <th> for the lateral fricative, <ch> for the postalveolar affricate, and <aa>, <ii>, and so forth for long vowels (figure 2.1).

5. A major factor in project success is the responsibility that Language Committee members take for every product that emerges. Elders have spent innumerable hours going over every word in the dictionary and rechecking entries to make sure that changes are made. This tendency is so pervasive within the community that Hasselbacher (2015a) uses the term *iterative authorship* to describe it.

6. The Koasati Language Committee is indebted to Dr. Jack Martin of the College of William and Mary, whose contribution of countless hours of his own and his students' work has truly made him *komokla* (our friend). Members of the Koasati Language Committee have worked tirelessly with Martin and other linguists to fill in documentation gaps on Koasati—see, e.g., Gordon, Martin, and Langley 2015.

7. We developed the Koasati evaluation rubric after examining indigenous programs throughout the United States, such as the Salish (http://www.interiorsalish.com/languageassessment.html) and Northwest Tribal (http://pages.uoregon.edu/nwili/language-proficiency-benchmarks)

programs as well as the most commonly used proficiency assessments, including the US, Canadian, and European measures. The Coushatta Tribe thanks Dr. Michelle Haj-Broussard of the University of Louisiana-Lafayette for her assistance in developing this evaluation rubric.

8. The Tribal Council member overseeing the convenience store project worked closely with Language Committee members to make this happen. His decision to use only Koasati signage was unanimously supported by the entire council.

WORKS CITED

Battise, Fulton, Ernest Sickey, Daniel Jacobson, Daniel W. Lay, and Hans W. Baade. 1983. *Congressional Reference to the United States Claims Court No. 3-83, United States Congress.* Washington, DC, filed November 28.

Boyd, Mark. 1937. "Expedition of Marcos Delgado from Apalachee to the Upper Creek Country in 1686." *Florida Historical Quarterly* 16:21–32.

Burnham, Gene. 1979. *Naas Mathaali and Naas Onapa.* Elton: Coushatta Tribe of Louisiana.

Coushatta Tribe of Louisiana. 2011. *Ittooyat Naathiihilkas* (*Koasati Phrase Book*). Elton: Coushatta Tribe of Louisiana.

Coushatta Tribe of Louisiana. 2013. *Koasati Dictionary.* Elton: Coushatta Tribe of Louisiana.

Coushatta Tribe of Louisiana. 2015. *Koasati Conversations.* Elton: Coushatta Tribe of Louisiana.

Gordon, Matthew, Jack B. Martin, and Linda Langley. 2015. "Some Phonetic Structures of Koasati." *International Journal of American Linguistics* 81 (1): 83–118.

Haas, Mary. 1934. "Alibamu-Koasati and Creek Vocabulary and Texts." Field notes. American Philosophical Society, Philadelphia.

Haas, Mary. 1944. "Men's and Women's Speech in Koasati." *Language* 20:142–49.

Hasselbacher, Stephanie. 2015a. "Koasati and 'All the Olden Talk': Ideologies of Linguistic Conservatism and the Mediation of Linguistic Authority." *Native South* 8:31–62.

Hasselbacher, Stephanie. 2015b. "'Written in Indian': Creating Legitimized Literacy and Authorized Speakership in Koasati." PhD diss., College of William and Mary.

Hudson, Charles. 1997. *Knights of Spain, Warriors of the Sun: Hernando de Soto and the South's Ancient Chiefdoms.* Athens: University of Georgia Press.

John, Douglas. 1930. *Dictionary: Coushatta Indian Tribe Language.* Lafayette, LA: Galvez Chapter of the National Society of Daughters of the American Revolution, American Indians Committee.

Kimball, Geoffrey. 1991. *Koasati Grammar.* Lincoln: University of Nebraska Press.

Kimball, Geoffrey. 1994. *Koasati Dictionary.* Lincoln: University of Nebraska Press.

Kimball, Geoffrey. 2010. *Koasati Traditional Narratives: Kowassâa:Ti Incokfa:Lihilkâa.* Lincoln: University of Nebraska Press.

Langley, Bertney, and Linda Langley. 2009. "Kowassaaton Ilhaalos: Let Us Hear Koasati: Developing and Implementing the Koasati Language Project," In *American Indian Language Development Institute: Thirty Year Tradition of Speaking from Our Heart*, edited by Candace K. Galla, Stacey Oberly, G. L. Romero, Maxine Sam, and Ofelia Zepeda, 20–26. Tucson: American Indian Language Development Institute.

Langley, Linda, Claude F. Oubre, and James H. Precht. 2009. "Louisa Williams Robinson, Her Daughters, and Her Granddaughters: Recognizing the Contributions of Three Generations of Coushatta Women in Louisiana." In *Louisiana Women: Their Lives and Times*, edited by Janet Allured and Judith F. Gentry, 155–74. Athens: University of Georgia Press.

Precht, James H. 2007. "'The Lost Tribe Wanders No More': Indian Gaming and the Emergence of Coushatta Self-Determination." PhD diss., Arizona State University.

Rising, David P. 1992. *Switch Reference in Koasati Discourse*. Dallas: Summer Institute of Linguistics; Arlington: University of Texas at Arlington.

Swanton, John R. N.d.a "'First Series' of Koasati Texts, 1912–1920." In Numbered Manuscripts, 1850s–1980s (Some Earlier), MS 4154, Smithsonian Institution National Anthropological Archive, Suitland, MD.

Swanton, John R. N.d.b. "'Second Series" of Koasati Texts, 1912–1920." In Numbered Manuscripts, 1850s–1980s (Some Earlier), MS 1818, Smithsonian Institution National Anthropological Archive, Suitland, MD.

Swanton, John R. 1922. *Early History of the Creek Indians and Their Neighbors*. Washington, DC: Smithsonian Institution.

Taylor, Lyda Averill Paz. 1940. *Plants Used as Curatives by Certain Southeastern Tribes*. Cambridge: Botanical Museum of Harvard University.

Williams, Heather, comp. 2010. *Stahooba Naathiihilka* (*Koasati Picture Dictionary*). Elton: Coushatta Tribe of Louisiana.

CHAPTER 3

THE MAINTENANCE OF KOASATI

GEOFFREY KIMBALL

Koasati, an American Indian language of the Muskogean family, is still spoken in Louisiana, in the second decade of the twenty-first century. It has survived centuries of turbulence, long-distance migration, poverty, and neglect. While under severe pressure from English, especially in recent decades, tribal members are making every effort to preserve the language and ensure that it continues to be spoken by Koasati people of all ages.

Before we discuss how things stand now, we need to know how we arrived here. It is truly marvelous that a group that numbered only a thousand people in the eighteenth century and less than two hundred at the beginning of the twentieth century has preserved its native language and linguistic traditions so well.

At the time of European contact, the Koasati lived in the Upper Tennessee River Valley. Identified with the archaeological culture called the Dallas Focus (Kimball 1994b), they were part of a multiethnic chiefdom called in English Coosa, whose indigenous name, *Kowassa*, is preserved in their self-identification: *Kowassá:ti*; *Kowassa á:ti* (the people of Coosa). At that time, they were part of a dialect chain that extended down the Tennessee River Valley, ending with the Alabama, whose language is today the most similar to Koasati. The introduction of European diseases dramatically decreased the Koasati population, perhaps by as much as 90 percent, and the social upheavals of the early seventeenth century, including the Beaver Wars, eventually caused the remnant Koasati population to migrate to the confluence of the Coosa and Tallapoosa Rivers in Alabama and ally themselves with the Creek Confederacy. In 1795, a large number of Koasati left the Creek Confederacy, settling first in Louisiana and then in three villages in Texas. A further settlement in southwest Louisiana took place in the 1860s near a site known today as Indian Village, and the Koasati gradually migrated there from Texas, although as late as 1910, twenty people continued living in the old village in Texas. In

1884, the Koasati moved from Indian Village to their present location about three miles north of Elton, Louisiana, where they obtained land through the Homestead Act (Kimball 1991:9).

SOCIOLOGICAL SITUATION

At the beginning of the twentieth century, Koasati was one of five Native American languages spoken primarily or uniquely in Louisiana. The others were Atakapa, spoken near Lake Charles in Calcasieu Parish; Biloxi and Tunica, spoken near Marksville in Avoyelles Parish; and Chitimacha, spoken near New Iberia, in St. Mary Parish.[1] By the mid-1970s, Koasati was the only Native American language still serving as the primary speech of a community; all the others were extinct. This linguistic preservation seems to have resulted from of a number of unique factors.

Population

The number of Koasati speakers was relatively large, perhaps three hundred at the beginning of the twentieth century. Immigration from the old Koasati village near San Jacinto, Texas, and from the Alabama Reservation in Texas brought new speakers and their families into the community. In contrast the Chitimacha population at that time numbered fewer than a hundred, while the Tunica population had fallen below fifty.

Social Isolation

While the Koasati had economic contact with their non-Indian neighbors, selling baskets to them and working for local farmers and landowners, they remained aloof, preferring to socialize only with other Indians. For example, one of my consultants, Ed John (1909–86), used to play with the son of one of the local Cajun French farmers. But while John learned to speak French fluently, his father taught the other boy the Mobilian Jargon (the preferred language for use with non-Indians) rather than Koasati (see Drechsel 1997:250–73).

Before 1950, the Koasati opposed marriage of their people with non-Indians. If a suitable spouse were not available in the Koasati community, a person was encouraged to find a spouse among the Alabama, whose language and culture closely resembled that of the Koasati. Failing that, a spouse of Choctaw, Biloxi, or Tunica origin would be acceptable. The great scandal of the 1920s was that of a Koasati woman who left the community and went to New York City to work, returning a few years later with a daughter whose father was Jewish. This focus on Indian-only marriages, especially with the Alabama, who also were continuing to speak their own language, ensured that the children would grow up in a Koasati-speaking environment.[2]

Religion

Along with their self-imposed social isolation, the Koasati became religiously isolated from their neighbors. One factor in the decline in the use of the Chitimacha language and in the Chitimacha switch to French was the fact that they adopted the Roman Catholic religion of their Cajun neighbors (Brightman 2004:651). The Koasati were never evangelized by the Roman Catholic Church, which was the dominant religion of the neighboring non-Indians. Instead, impressed by the Reverend Paul Leeds, a charismatic Protestant missionary, who started preaching in the area in 1893, the Koasati adopted Congregational Protestantism, building St. Peter's Church, still the center of the Koasati community, in 1901 (Leeds 1923). The congregational structure ensured that there was no interference from outside religious bodies in the structure of worship in the church. Furthermore, Leeds was sympathetic to the use of the Koasati language. He learned Mobilian Jargon, and congregant Douglas John presented the minister with a manuscript vocabulary of Koasati to enable him to practice the language (John 1930). The church services were structured in a way that maximized the use of Koasati. While Rev. Leeds preached in English, he had lay ministers translate his sermons into Koasati for the congregation. As a result, biblical stories were cast into traditional Koasati literary forms (see Kimball 2010:179), and Koasati thus became the language of the new religion. Even though the minister of the church was always non-Indian, lay ministers such as Solomon Battise ensured that Koasati continued as the language of church.

Education

At the beginning of the twentieth century, the Koasati did not send their children to school. However, in the second decade of the century, Rev. Leeds decided to establish a school to teach the basics of English and mathematics. L. L. Simmons, who headed the school from 1915 to 1937 was a severe and exacting taskmaster who was nevertheless highly sympathetic to the Koasati language and learned to speak it (Simmons 1920; Kimball 1994a:135), using it both inside and outside the classroom. Bel Abbey (1916–91) remembered

Simmons critiquing one student's handwriting, dismissively saying, "*Koló:si kalásli!* [Chicken scratches!]". The schoolteacher's positive linguistic attitude was another factor that aided in the retention of Koasati as the community language in the twentieth century.

THE BEGINNINGS OF LANGUAGE ATTRITION

By the 1970s, however, changing social and economic factors started to put pressure on the survival of Koasati. Some more observant tribal members, most notably Abbey, recognized this trend early on. Abbey broke with the long-standing tradition of not teaching the language to outsiders, and his efforts were almost entirely responsible for the success of the fieldwork that led to *Koasati Grammar* (Kimball 1991), *Koasati Dictionary* (Kimball 1994), and *Koasati Traditional Narratives* (Kimball 2010).

FACTORS IN KOASATI LANGUAGE ATTRITION

Marriage with Non-Indians

After the 1950s, the Koasati became more open to intermarriage with non-Indians, although they looked at the practice with ambivalence. Martha John (1918–2013), had an otherwise thoroughly traditional outlook but encouraged such intermarriage. The Koasati had suffered a severe drop in population in 1919–20 as a result of the worldwide influenza epidemic, and although the Koasati maintained the tradition of clan exogamy and in fact extended it to surname-group exogamy, by the middle of the twentieth century, all the tribal members had become related to each other, at least to some degree. John, who assisted her mother, a midwife, saw the results of marriage between too-close kin and concluded that the Indians needed outside blood to survive. After John's mother died and left John to raise her two youngest siblings, she encouraged both to marry outside the community, which they did. Intermarriage had consequences for the language, and English became the primary language of mixed homes. While spouses were often interested in the Indian language, there was no mechanism available for teaching them to speak it, and most spouses gained only a rudimentary knowledge of the language and did not speak it to their children. As a result, a group of Koasati children could speak only English.

The Death of the Cajun French Language

For over a century, the Koasati were an island of Indian speech in a sea of rural French. English was a minority language for the first part of the twentieth century, and everyone in the area of Elton spoke their own language rather than English. However, the official prejudice against rural French culminated with the Louisiana Constitution of 1921, which mandated the use of English only in the schools (Picone 1997:123). Children were punished, sometimes cruelly, for speaking French in school, leading parents to stop teaching their children the language. The Koasati gradually became the only people in the area who spoke a language other than English.

Increasing Education

In the 1920s, the Jefferson Davis Parish Board of Education decided that for purposes of schooling, Indians were considered white and thus eligible to attend Elton High School, where the school sports teams were soon named the Elton Indians. Rather than dropping out after a few years, Koasati children increasingly began to graduate from high school. Since English was the only language used at Elton High School, a group of Koasati children soon became fully bilingual in English and Koasati. The increasing socialization with English speakers led to some interesting situations. In the 1990s, I observed the granddaughter of a woman whose primary language was Koasati refuse to speak the language. While she would do whatever her grandmother instructed her to do in Koasati, she spoke to her grandmother only in English. The refusal of an otherwise competent speaker of a language to use it with others would seem to be a mark of language loss. This behavior bears a striking resemblance to what Sesostrie Youchigant, the last speaker of Tunica, reported to Mary R. Haas: whenever his mother spoke to him in Tunica, he responded in French (Haas 1940:10; see also Anderson and Maxwell, this volume).

Change at St. Peter's

Solomon Battise retired from his duties as lay minister at the church and was replaced by his son-in-law, who was non-Indian and did not speak Koasati. English consequently became the language of the church, eliminating the final location in which the language had primary public use. Koasati became restricted entirely to the home.

Economic Change

In 1995, the chronic poverty of the Koasati community was eliminated in one fell swoop with the opening of the Grand Casino Coushatta. Although many older people opposed the casino on moral grounds, the tribal government, chronically underfunded by the US federal government and constantly the victim of the vagaries of national politics, pushed ahead. The casino became popular beyond the wildest expectations of its supporters, providing not only a steady source of income for the tribal government but also a guaranteed income for every registered tribal member. This resulted in an influx of people of part-Koasati heritage whose parents and grandparents had left the community for greater opportunities. Very few of these newcomers spoke Koasati, so English became even more used among tribal members. In addition to providing greater access to health care, building modern houses, and giving homes to landless tribal members, the tribal government also sought to improve the children's relatively poor school performance by establishing a preschool to help prepare children for public school. However, the preschool was English-only, breaking the last link in the chain of language learning, that of grandparent caregivers, and unintentionally ensuring that most young children would not learn Koasati.

THE TWENTY-FIRST CENTURY

In the first years of the century, the Koasati language was no longer in regular use among tribal members younger than thirty, who were switching to English. In the 1980s, the fact that a child spoke Koasati was a given; by 2005, a child who spoke Koasati was considered remarkable. Even among tribal members who did not speak the language, Koasati was still considered valuable in that it was the one thing that made the Koasati different from everyone else. Speaking the language was considered equivalent to being Indian. But what would happen if no one spoke Koasati anymore? What would make someone Koasati besides blood quantum? Bertney Langley, the son of Bel Abbey's sister, keenly felt the growing language. In 2006, with the support of the tribal government, he organized the first Koasati Language Day, at which the questions of how to save the language were first broached. The following year, Langley, with the assistance of his wife, Linda, an anthropologist at McNeese State University in Lake Charles, Louisiana, obtained a grant from the National Science Foundation to create the Koasati Language Project (Langley and Langley 2009), which would document and archive the language. The tribal government subsequently chose an official orthography for Koasati based on recommendations from a committee of Koasati speakers. In the following years, the Koasati Language Project did a tremendous amount of work in recording, transcribing, and archiving linguistic material from many tribal members. A number of these recordings are available through the tribal website (http://koasatiheritage.org); a digital pronouncing dictionary is also available online (http://koasati.wm.edu/). In 2014, the tribe created a Koasati-immersion preschool, and the teachers have done training in how to do immersion. This bodes well for the future of the language, because learning languages is easiest for children, and increasing the number of child speakers is imperative if the language is to survive as a spoken tongue. Trying to encourage older children and young people to learn the language will be difficult; however, the positive attitude of the tribal members toward their language will go a long way toward making this happen. While the long-term future of the Koasati language is still uncertain, it does not appear to be on the verge of disappearing.

NOTES

1. Choctaw was spoken in three small settlements, one in Calcasieu Parish, not far from the Koasati settlement; one near Lacombe, in St. Tammany Parish; and one near Jena, in LaSalle Parish. The Second Choctaw Removal (Roberts 1986:94–111) eliminated all but the Jena community. As for other Native American languages, Ofo was already obsolescent, with only a single semispeaker who had married into the Tunica, and there is no information as to whether Apalachee was still spoken in Rapides Parish at the beginning of the twentieth century. For a reconstruction of Ofo grammar derived in part from John Swanton's documentation of the lone speaker encountered in Marksville and in part from a comparison with cognate morphologies of other Siouan languages, see Rankin 2015.

2. As a rule, the children of a mixed marriage spoke the language of the mother and were considered to be members of her tribe, as they were also of her clan. However, if a child were looked after by one particular set of grandparents, she or he would usually speak the grandparents' language.

WORKS CITED

Brightman, Robert A. 2004. "Chitimacha." In *Handbook of North American Indians*, vol. 14, *Southeast*, edited by Raymond D. Fogelson, 642–52. Washington, DC: Smithsonian Institution.

Drechsel, Emmanuel J. 1997. *Mobilian Jargon: Linguistic and Sociohistorical Aspects of a Native American Pidgin*. Oxford: Clarendon.

Haas, Mary R. 1941. *Tunica*. New York: Augustin.

John, Douglas. [1930]. "How to Talk the Indian Language." Manuscript formerly in the possession of the Reverend and Mrs. Donald Johnson, Kinder, LA.

Kimball, Geoffrey. 1991. *Koasati Grammar*. Lincoln: University of Nebraska Press.

Kimball, Geoffrey. 1994a. *Koasati Dictionary*. Lincoln: University of Nebraska Press.
Kimball, Geoffrey. 1994b. "Making the Connection: Is It Possible to Link the Koasati to an Archaeological Culture?" In *Perspectives on the Southeast: Linguistics, Archaeology, and Ethnohistory*, edited by Patricia B. Kwachka, 71–80. Athens: University of Georgia Press.
Kimball, Geoffrey. 2010. *Koasati Traditional Narratives*. Lincoln: University of Nebraska Press.
Langley, Bertney, and Linda Langley. 2009. "Kowassaaton Ilhaalos: Let Us Hear Koasati: Developing and Implementing the Koasati Language Project." In *American Indian Language Development Institute: Thirty Year Tradition of Speaking from Our Heart*, edited by Candace K. Galla, Stacey Oberly, G. L. Romero, Maxine Sam, and Ofelia Zepeda, 20–26. Tucson: American Indian Language Development Institute.
Leeds, Paul. [1923]. *The End of the Trail*. New York: Congregational Home Mission Society.
Picone, Michael D. 1997. "Enclave Dialect Contraction: An External Overview of Louisiana French." *American Speech* 72:117–53.
Rankin, Robert L. 2015. "The Ofo Language of Louisiana: Recovery of Grammar and Typology." In *New Perspectives on Language Variety in the South: Historical and Contemporary Approaches*, edited by Michael D. Picone and Catherine Evans Davies, 52–71. Tuscaloosa: University of Alabama Press.
Roberts, Charles. 1986. "The Second Choctaw Removal." In *After Removal: The Choctaw in Mississippi*, edited by Samuel Wells and Roseanna Tubby, 94–111. Jackson: University Press of Mississippi.
Simmons, L. Leon. 1920. "Our Indian Parishes in Louisiana." *American Missionary Magazine* 74:670–71.
Williams, Robert S. 1997. "Referential Tracking in Oklahoma Choctaw: Language Obsolescence and Attrition." *Anthropological Linguistics* 41:54–74.

CHAPTER 4

THE TUNICA LANGUAGE

PATRICIA ANDERSON AND JUDITH M. MAXWELL

The Tunica are an indigenous people of the Southeast, historically inhabiting parts of Mississippi, Louisiana, and Missouri. Though surrounded by Muskogean peoples, the Tunica spoke a language unrelated to other known tongues. *Luhchi Yoroni* (the Tunica Language) is currently reawakening. Summer camps, online resources, and activities provide models and venues for renewal.

HISTORY OF THE TUNICA NATION

Archaeological evidence indicates that during the fifteenth and sixteenth centuries, the Tunica lived in large settlements, farming corn, refining and trading salt, and trading horses and dry goods. They situated their towns at the confluences of rivers, including the Sunflower, the Yazoo, the Red River, and the Mississippi, whence they controlled trade. Hoffman (1992:30) characterizes the peoples of these river valleys as having "achieved the highest cultural level in North America north of Mexico." A chiefdom might encompass hundreds of square miles and have thousands of residents. The chief typically resided atop a mound. Other mounds within the township served as ritual spaces. The Tunica practiced a complex religion, especially revering the sun (Hoffman 1992; Morse and Morse 1983). Though tribal members today are Christian, they maintain respect for the natural elements, with special affection for the sun. The last fluent speaker of Tunica, Sesostrie Youchigant, preserved the knowledge of how Sun Woman ascended to the sky:

> Once there was a beautiful Tunica girl. One night, she attended a dance and met a handsome young man. They fell in love. He came courting her in the evenings, and at last they married and he took her to his home. They

climbed up the stairs of his lovely house to his room. But in the morning, when she awakened, she found herself in a nest in a hackberry tree. She also discovered that her husband was a kingfisher who could appear as a man only at night. She knew she could not live with him. She told him that she would sing and dance, blessing him, and when her song finished, she would rise into the sky. So she sang and danced, expressing her love for the kingfisher. As her song ended, she ascended into the heavens, growing brighter and brighter, until she became the sun. Today she shines on all the world, giving light and warmth. The kingfisher remains near the water on the earth below but is beloved by the sun and protected by the Tunica. (adapted from Haas 1950)

The first recorded European contact with the Tunica occurred in 1542, when Hernando de Soto reached the Mississippi River at the town of Quizquiz.[1] The Tunica men were away from the village farming.[2] In their absence, de Soto raided the village, taking many women prisoners and looting provisions. According to the Tunica Museum, the Tunica men rallied to liberate their women. El Inca Garcilaso de la Vega (1951) wrote that the Tunica mustered more than four thousand men within three hours. Brain (1977) observed that the Tunica resistance forced the Spanish to sue for a ceasefire, marking the first Hispanic defeat in de Soto's triumphal march across the Gulf South. However, this brief contact with the Europeans was enough to sow the seeds of contagion. Smallpox and measles decimated the population, and those who survived moved South to smaller riverine communities. In 1699, a French exploratory group found many Tunica villages along the Yazoo and Mississippi Rivers. A Jesuit, Father Antoine Davion, elected to stay among the Tunica to share the Gospel, spending twenty years there before returning to France.[3] His ministry helped solidify Tunica economic and social relations with the French. When more French settlers and explorers came into the region, the Tunica traded with them and soon became their allies against the British and rival indigenous groups such as the Natchez.

Salt had traditionally been a prime trade good of the Tunica. Swanton (1946) noted that the Tunica were still actively engaged in boiling salt water to produce salt for their own use and for trade. He observed that at that time, most of the salt was extracted from northeastern Louisiana. Archaeological evidence suggests that at one time, the Tunica also brought in salt from the Gulf (Brain 1977). The Tunica traded salt with other indigenous groups, with the French, and later with the Spanish.

The Tunica at first prospered through their economic alliance with the French. In 1721, Father Charlevoix wrote of Chief Cahura-Joligo,

The cabin of the chief is very much adorned on the outside.... The inside is dark, and I observed nothing in it but some boxes, which they assured me were full of clothes and money. The chief received us very politely; he was dressed in the French fashion, and seemed to be not at all uneasy in that habit. Of all the savages of Canada there is none so much depended on by our commandants as this chief. He loves our nation, and has no cause to repent of the services he has rendered it. He trades with the French, whom he supplies with horses and fowls, and he understands his trade very well. He has learned of us to hoard up money, and he is reckoned very rich. (Charlevoix 1766:211)

The Tunica moved further south, to the confluence of the Red and Mississippi Rivers, still controlling major trade routes for salt, horses, and dry goods. The Tunica traded with other indigenous groups and heavily with the French. From 1716 to 1729, the Natchez suffered heavy losses in repeated clashes with the French in response to French attempts to displace villages and establish plantations. The Tunica alliance with the French apparently was not lost on the Natchez. In 1729, the Natchez pleaded with Tunica chief Cahura-Joligo to admit them as refugees to his capital. Cahura-Joligo agreed on condition that the Natchez enter unarmed. Promising to lay down their weapons after a manly show of entering in their full regalia, the Natchez feasted and danced with the Tunica late into the night. When the Tunica had retired to their homes, the Natchez, aided by Koroa and Chickasaw warriors waiting in the canebrake outside of town, attacked their hosts in their homes, killing Cahura-Joligo. The Tunica war chief, Brides les Boeufs, rallied his warriors, driving out the invaders after five days of continuous battle (Brain 1977:3).

The seat of Tunica government subsequently moved slightly south on the Mississippi River to a spot about fifteen miles northwest of St. Francisville, Louisiana. From this site, they continued to control trade along the Mississippi and Red Rivers. By this time, they had added horses to their trade inventory, supplying needed livestock, apparently brought up from what is now New Mexico, to French settlers. These active trade networks supplied Tunica families with a wealth of European goods, some of which were interred along with the dead as funeral offerings. In 1968, Leonard Charrier, a guard at nearby Angola prison who was hunting for pots, came across the old Tunica burial ground with its wealth of grave goods. These goods, now known as the Tunica Treasure, were finally recovered by the tribe in the 1980s and are now curated by the tribal museum. Commenting on this array of goods, Brain (1977:3) noted, "The sheer quantity and variety of European items is unparalleled at any other known contemporary native site of the mid-eighteenth century in the Southeast."

In November 1762, via a treaty kept secret for a year, France ceded Louisiana to Spain, seeking to draw Spain into the ongoing French and English conflict (Library of Congress n.d.). In accordance with the treaty, the Spanish aided the American colonists against the English, and Tunica warriors joined forces with the Spanish. In September 1779, they aided Spanish governor Bernardo de Gálvez y Madrid in taking the British outpost at Manchac, on Lake Pontchartrain. That same month, the combined Tunica and Spanish forces drove the British out of Baton Rouge, ending the blockade of the Lower Mississippi River (Caughey 1998). In return for their aid, Gálvez invited the Tunica to settle on the Avoyelles prairie, the area of the current tribal headquarters at Marksville. The Spanish provided the Tunica with land titles, which later US governments consistently failed to recognize. European settlers—ironically, predominantly French, the erstwhile allies of the Tunica—took up Tunica lands, which they registered as previously unoccupied. John Sibley (1806), the first Indian agent of Louisiana, in his report to President Thomas Jefferson, scarcely mentioned the Tunica. Despite being overlooked by early US officialdom, the Tunica maintained their internal coherence. Sesostrie Youchigant, who became the last speaker of the language, was elected chief in 1911. He resigned in 1921 and was succeeded by Ernest Pierite. Pierite, in turn, was succeeded by Eli Barbry, who reached out to other tribes in Louisiana, including the Biloxi, Chitimacha, Coushatta, Avoyelles, and Ofo, seeking to form a group that could demand and receive federal attention and aid. In September 1938, Barbry; his subchief, Horace Pierite Sr.; Sam Barbry; Clarence Jackson; and Joseph Vilmarrette traveled to Washington, DC, to petition for federal recognition. The two Barbrys identified as Tunica, Pierite as Biloxi, Jackson as Choctaw; Vilmarrette was an Avoyelles Parish official. In October, Ruth Underhill of the Education Department of the Bureau of Indian Affairs (BIA) came to assess the conditions of the indigenous communities. She noted that many young people wanted to move to Texas for greater economic opportunities. Underhill reported that there were too few school-age children to merit a separate BIA school and recommended that the group move to Texas. In fact, some members of the tribe did emigrate to Texas; others went north to Chicago. Tunica bands now have subsidiary tribal headquarters in Houston and in Chicago. Successive Tunica chiefs continued to petition the BIA and the federal government for recognition. Under the leadership of Earl J. Barbry Sr., the Tunica-Biloxi tribe finally won recognition from the federal government in 1981.

With recognition and control of tribal lands, the Tunica once again were able to demonstrate their business acumen. In 1994, they opened Louisiana's first land-based casino, the Grand Casino Avoyelles (now the Paragon Casino Resort). They have used funds generated by the casino to pave the roads on the reservation and build a community center and health care and social services centers. In addition, the parish schools, which formerly would not admit Indian children, now send buses onto the reservation to pick up the indigenous students. The community center houses the tribal offices, a tribal museum, and a state-of-the-art artifact conservation and restoration facility, the first of its kind on an Indian reservation. Tunica-Biloxi conservators and students are carefully restoring, examining, and documenting the Tunica Treasure.

In 2010, Brenda Lintinger of the Tribal Council approached Tulane University for aid in revitalizing the Tunica language. Donna Pierite; her daughter, Elizabeth Hixen-Mora; and her son, Jean-Luc Pierite, had been working for years with the documentation left by Mary Haas, Albert Gatschet, and John R. Swanton. Using stories told to Haas by Youchigant and song cycles learned by Donna Pierite from her grandmother and father-in-law, the group developed a repertoire of short (hi)stories and songs, which they perform in the casino atrium as part of the Alligator Show. They have also prepared teaching materials, games, and songs that they present to tribal members at community events, such as elder bingo and the annual powwow. Judith Maxwell and a team of her students from Tulane University have been working with the Pierites to develop further materials. A children's book, *Hichut'una Awachihk'unanahch Fighting Eagles/Tayak Takohkuman Deer and Turtle* has already been published (Tunica-Tulane Working Group 2011), and another volume of three stories, is awaiting publication. The working group has drafted a pedagogical grammar and is compiling on a technical linguistic description. Patricia Anderson (2017) has created an online interactive digital dictionary of the language.

Since 2012, the Pierites, Lintinger, and her sister, Darnée Wambsgans, have run Tunica-language summer camps for tribal children. In 2014, Tulane students joined the effort as camp counselors and language models. The tribe has formed a new governmental division devoted to language and culture renaissance: Development & Programing—Language & Culture Revitalization Program at Tunica-Biloxi Tribe of Louisiana. John D. Barbry serves as the program's director.

The tribe's motto embraces this rich history: *Nis'aha erunasa, sehiti mashuwan* (Cherishing our past, building for our future).

TUNICA-LANGUAGE DOCUMENTS

The Tunica language fell silent on December 6, 1948, with the passing of the last speaker, Sesostrie Youchigant. However, various outside scholars and explorers recorded the Tunica language in writing before Tunica moved into its sleeping state.[4] The Tunica language first entered the written European record in 1700. Davion sent letters outlining missionary work and ethnographic information to the Jesuit seminary in Quebec, where they reside today. Although Davion reportedly spoke the language, his letters contain more information about the Tunica people than about the language.

While the Tunica people can be found across many historical accounts after Davion's departure, the Tunica language was largely ignored and therefore was not fully attested until Albert S. Gatschet (1886a) announced his "discovery" of Tunica to the Bureau of American Ethnology. His letter to the bureau included word lists in both Tunica and Biloxi.[5] Gatschet (1886b) compiled an unpublished, 259-page handwritten manuscript of Tunica grammar, filled with elicited paradigms, collected stories, and ethnographic anecdotes provided by William Ely Johnson. Johnson spoke French, English, Tunica, Choctaw, and Biloxi (Swanton n.d.). In an autobiography given to Gatschet in Tunica, Johnson laments the nonexistence of Tunica elders and claims that he is the last speaker of the language (Gatschet 1886b).

John R. Swanton was the next scholar to spend time with the Tunica language, working intermittently from 1907 to 1910. Swanton had access to Gatschet's materials, which were under Swanton's care at the Bureau of American Ethnology. His primary informant was Tunica chief Volsine Chiki. However, Swanson also used other informants, including Johnson, the "more modern" Eli Barbary (Dorman 1931), and young Sesostrie Youchigant (also known as Sam Young). While Swanton did elicit new Tunica myths and stories, most of his work involved verifying, typing, and reorganizing Gatschet's handwritten information. One such project consisted of typing more than three thousand Tunica-English vocabulary cards for a dictionary. Aside from an article on Tunica grammar (Swanton 1921), Swanton's work remains largely unpublished.

The most comprehensive information about the Tunica language comes from Mary R. Haas and her Tunica-language consultant, Youchigant.[6] Youchigant, the nephew of Volsine Chiki, was born around 1870. As is frequent with last speakers of endangered languages, Youchigant had not had anyone to converse with in Tunica for nearly twenty years when Haas contacted him (Haas 1953). Haas worked with Youchigant from 1933 and 1939. She noted that Youchigant was the only individual who spoke Tunica "with any degree of fluency" and that "although there are a few other Indians of varying degrees of Tunica blood in the vicinity, there is no one sufficiently familiar with the language to converse with Youchigant" (175). Therefore, all of Tunica materials she published were based solely on Youchigant's remembered knowledge.

Sesostrie spoke Louisiana French and English in addition to Tunica, and French was his first language (Haas 1953).[7] Haas (1941:10) "often had the feeling that the Tunica grooves in Youchigant's memory might be compared to the grooves in a phonograph record; for he could repeat what he had heard but was unable to make up new expressions of his own accord." Haas elicited Tunica from Sesostrie in narrative format, drawing data from these stories to compose her dissertation (1935), which was expanded to a full Tunica grammar in 1941. She later published *Tunica Texts* (1950), containing twenty-two myths and stories, followed by the *Tunica Dictionary* (1953).

Although Haas made many wax-cylinder recordings of the Tunica language, including stories and songs, most have deteriorated beyond recognition. Those that have survived are housed at the Survey of California and Other Indian Languages Archive in Berkeley, California, and were optically read in 2015, giving us previously irretrievable glimpses of Tunica as spoken. Nevertheless, while one can hear the intonation of words and phrases, the words themselves are still largely unintelligible and full of static. Careful handwritten transcriptions of the recordings survive in Haas's field notebooks, which reside at the American Philosophical Society's library in Philadelphia. The Tunica Language Project has continued to pursue leads concerning audio copies Haas may have made for other scholars, but no useable Tunica audio has yet been recovered.

FEATURES OF THE TUNICA LANGUAGE

Genetic Relations

Tunica is a language isolate. There have been several attempts to classify in a larger genetic family, including Swanton's "Tunican" (1919), which incorporated Tunica, Chitimacha, and Ishak,[8] and Haas's "Proto-Gulf" (1951), which included Tunica, Natchez, Chitimacha, Muskogean, and Ishak. However, these and other attempts have been proved unreliable at best (Campbell 1997). Nonetheless, Tunica does share areal features with other languages of the southeastern United States. Hopkins (1999) cites four features: (1) presence of labial fricatives and voiceless laterals, (2) classificatory verb roots, (3) an alienable/inalienable distinction for possessed nouns, and (4) verbal distinctions based on the degree of control or volition exhibited by the actor/subject. Heaton (2014) stresses (1) active-stative alignment, (2) positional classifiers of verbs, (3) number suppletion in verb paradigms, and (4) preaspirated voiceless stop phonemes (e.g., /hp/, /ht/, and /hk/). Munro (2015) also lists active-stative alignment but adds four word order traits: (1) subject-object-verb basic word order; (2) possessives before the head noun (a marked feature in languages of the world); (3) adjectives following the nouns they modify; and (4) postpositions rather than prepositions. These features are found in the thirteen language families of the Southeast; they are all attested in Tunica as well. Though no genetic relationships with surrounding languages have been proven for Tunica, the shared areal features show that Tunica speakers participated in the culture sphere of the Gulf South.

Phonology

Tunica has five tense vowels (*i, e, a, o,* and *u*) and two lax vowels (*ɛ* and *ɔ*). The consonant inventory has voiceless stops (*p, t, k,* and *ʔ*),[9] voiceless fricatives (*s, š,*[10] and *h*), the voiceless affricate (*č*),[11] liquids (*r* and *l*), nasals (*m* and *n*), and glides (*w, y*). The category of voiceless stops is further divided into plain and preaspirated stops. The preaspiration is simply a puff of air that precedes the stop closure. This is just the opposite of English voiceless stops, which in word or syllable initial position have a puff of air following the closure. A phonemic distinction between preaspirated and nonaspirated stops exists in Tunica, however: *yapa* (to carry), *yahpa* (to follow).

Singular, Dual, Plural

Tunica recognizes three degrees of number marking. Verbs in the completive and incompletive aspects are marked for number as well as person of the subject. A verbal paradigm then will have separate forms for *I*, *we two*, and *we* (more than two). Table 4.1 shows the forms for the verb *hipu* (dance) in the completive. Nouns are not obligatorily marked for number. Thus, *rushta* may mean either "rabbit" or "rabbits." However, definite nouns, including proper names, are marked for number. Feminine nouns distinguish only singular and plural, while masculine nouns inflect for singular, plural, and dual (table 4.2). Tunica recognizes three degrees of number distinction on verbs and on masculine nouns but only two on feminine nouns.

Table 4.1. *Hipu* (Dance) Sample Conjugation

Person	Singular		Dual		Plural	
1	hipuni	I danced	hip'ina	we two danced	hip'iti	we danced
2 m.	hip'i	you (masc.) danced	hipuwina	you two males danced	hipuwiti	y'all (males) danced
2 f	hipɔ	you (fem.) danced	hipina	you two females danced	hipiti	y'all (females) danced
3 m	hipuwi	he danced	hip'una	two males danced	hiputa	they (males) danced
3 f	hiputi	she danced	hipusina	two females danced	hipusiti	they (females) danced

Table 4.2. Sample Nouns Marked for Number

Singular		Dual		Plural	
Noun	Gloss	Noun	Gloss	Noun	Gloss
tayorum'aha	wild animal	tayorum'ahasinima	wild animal (fem. plural)		
enchayi	my wife	onchayisinima	their wives		
tawakaku	the commander	tawak'unima	the two commanders	tawakasɛma	the commanders
tanisaraku	the young man	tanisar'unima	the two young men	tanisarasɛma	the young men

Gender and Animacy Hierarchy

Tunica has several unique features, including a robust gender system not commonly found in Native North American languages. Masculine and feminine genders are marked in the second and third persons. Further, feminine appears to be the "default" gender in a variety of situations. For example, impersonal phrases such as "it got dark," "it is sunny,"[12] or "that is all" are inflected with the third-person feminine singular subject marker. Passives, though less numerous in Haas's Tunica data, are also inflected with the third-person feminine singular subject marker.

Gender is also closely tied with animacy. Tunica recognizes three distinct animacy groups: inanimate, animate human, and animate nonhuman. In narratives, certain animal protagonists can rise to the level of human animate in their inflection, but they largely follow a separate "nonhuman" pattern.

While marking nouns for number is not required for nonhuman animates and inanimate objects, when it is marked, the pattern is as shown in table 4.3.[13] When referring to humans, however, the noun must be marked for gender, as illustrated in table 4.4. Inanimate and nonhuman animate nouns are marked with a split system; the masculine suffix is used in the singular and dual, while the feminine suffix is used in the plural and collective. This is not the case with human animates, where the default is the masculine suffix if the gender of the person or group of persons is unknown.

Table 4.3. Inanimate Noun Number Inflection

	Singular	Dual	Plural	Collective
Inanimate object or non-human animate of unknown gender	-ku	-unima	-sinima	-hchi

Table 4.4. Human Noun Number Inflection				
	Singular	Dual	Plural	Collective
Referring to a Man	-ku	-unima	-sɛma	-ku
Referring to a Woman	-hchi	-sinima	-sinima	-hchi
Referring to a person of unknown gender or a group of mixed gender	-ku	-unima	-sɛma	-ku

Active-Stative Agreement

Tunica verbs may be divided into several groups according to their inflectional possibilities. There are transitive verbs (those with two arguments, one the subject, the other the object) and intransitive verbs (those with only subjects).[14] The intransitive verbs may be divided into those that attribute an action to the subject and those that describe a state or a mental/physical condition of the subject. Those that report actions are "active" verbs, while those that report conditions or states are "statives."

Active verbs mark their subjects with the same suffixes that mark the subjects of transitive verbs. Stative verbs mark their subjects with prefixes; these prefixes mark objects of transitive verbs. Thus, *I dance* is **hipukani**, while *I am hungry* is **ihkyahpa**.

Table 4.5 compares the forms of transitive and intransitive verbs. The first two rows show the pronominal markers of transitive verbs. The next two rows show active intransitive verbs, with subject markers that match those of the transitive. The final two rows show stative intransitives, with subjects that match the objects of the transitives.

Table 4.5. Transitive Verb Pronominals Contrasted with Intransitives			
Transitive		**Intransitive**	
tihksahchi**kani**	I am bathing her	hara**kani**	I sing
ihkhiru**kati**	She is massaging me	pita**kati**	She is walking
		ihkwana	I am willing
		tihkyari	She is ashamed
Note: Pronouns in **bold**.			

Auxiliary Verbs

Tunica has a set of six intransitive verbs that, in addition to their regular function as main verbs, may serve as helping verbs. As independent verbs, their meanings are *exist, lie, sit, stay, come, go,* and *live.* As helping verbs, they add notions of positionality, movement, and duration. When auxiliary verbs are used, the main verb is inflected for completive aspect and, if transitive, for the object, but the auxiliary carries the subject marking.

The auxiliary 'uta[15] (cause) does not occur as an independent verb but co-occurs with main verbs in the same fashion, following a completive verb and carrying the subject.

(1) uhk'uk'uta < 'uhk (third-person singular masculine object) + 'uk(i) (sit) + 'uta (third-person singular masculine cause; lit. he caused him to sit)

These auxiliary verbs are irregular. Their paradigms are highly suppletive. Table 4.6 shows the conjugation of 'ura (lie) in the completive.[16] The auxiliaries are also used to express the idea of repetitive action. The first consonant and vowel of the auxiliary are copied and prefixed to the stem.[17] This new prefix becomes the stressed syllable (table 4.7). Conditionals are also formed by modifying the auxiliaries. A glottal stop is inserted between the last consonant and vowel (table 4.8). //-k'i// serves as the conditional marker for most verbs. Auxiliaries as well as main verbs may use this form. Only one conditional marker occurs on a given verb. Thus, an auxiliary may either have the infixed //'// or the suffixed //-k'i// but not both (table 4.9). Auxiliaries also interact with the system for indicating positionality or spatial orientation.

Table 4.6. Conjugation of 'Ura (Lay)						
Singular		**Dual**		**Plural/Dual***		
'arani	I lay			'irana		we lay
wira	you (masc.) lay			wirana		y'all (masc.) lay
hɛra	you (fem.) lay			hɛrana		y'all (fem.) lay
'ura	he lay	'urana	two males lay	na'ara		they (masc.) lay
'ara	she lay	sirana	two females lay	na'ara		they (fem.) lay
* A separate dual form exists only in the third person.						

Table 4.7. Auxiliaries Showing Repetitive Action			
Single action		**Repeated action**	
h**ɛ**sa	you (fem.) come	h**ɛ**hɛsa	you (fem.) come constantly
'achi	she sits	'**a**'achi	she sits a lot
'uwa	he went	'**u**'uwa	he went repeatedly
'asani	I came	'**a**'asani	I came often
Note: Stressed syllables in bold.			

Table 4.8. Auxiliaries in the Conditional Mood

Indicative		Conditional	
hɛsa	you (fem.) come	hɛs'a	if you (fem.) come
'achi	she sits	'ach'i	if she sits
'uwa	he went	'uw'a	if he went, were he to go
'asani	I came	'asan'i	if I come, were I to come

Table 4.9. Auxiliaries with the //-k'i// Conditional Ending

Indicative		Conditional	
hɛsa	you (fem.) come	hɛsak'i	if you (fem.) come
'achi	she sits	'achik'i	if she sits
'uwa	he went	'uwak'i	if he went, were he to go
'asani	I came	'asanik'i	if I come, were I to come

Alienability

Tunica nouns can be possessed alienably or inalienably. A small set of objects must be inalienably possessed: body parts, family members, friends, and breechcloth.[18] Any words deriving from root words of the inalienable class are also possessed inalienably, such as bracelet ("arm decorator") or shoes ("that which is worn on the foot"). All other words may appear either in their possessed or unpossessed forms; these take the alienable prefix. The difference between the two forms is marked by an *-hk-* cluster, found only in the alienable set. *Ihk-* means "my, alienable," while *i-* means "my, inalienable."

In Haas's original analysis of the Tunica language, the line between alienable and inalienable was blurred by larger phonological rules. In Tunica, *-hk-* consonant clusters drop when set in front of a sonorant. For example, *tihk + ri* would become *tiri* (her house, alienable) but deceptively looking like *tiri* (*ti + ri*, her house, inalienable). For the purposes of revitalization, the Tunica Language Project has decided to forgo any deletion of *-hk-* consonant clusters in an effort to highlight the distinction between the two types of possession (table 4.10).

Table 4.10. Possession as Constructed by the Tunica Language Project (Tunica Standard)

Haas's Tunica	Tunica Standard	Gloss
wirowinataworu	wihkrowinataworu	your (masc.) book, alienable
sisa	sihksa	their (masc.) dog, alienable
ihkeni		my hand, inalienable
utawakuni		his breechcloth, inalienable

Positionality, Spatial Orientation

The Tunica language is assiduous in indicating the vertical or horizontal orientation of people, things, and actions. Movement and placement of actors and actions provide coherence in Tunica narrative. Stories often begin with the presentation of the protagonists. Rather than simply saying "there is" an alligator, a frog, or a man, Tunica presentationals use auxiliaries that attribute form and position in space. Table 4.11 shows the introductions of story characters. While many animals and things have characteristic positions and forms and thus consistently occur with one auxiliary form (*lie*, *sit*, or *stand*), people may stand, sit, or lie (table 4.12). When the main verb does not indicate a specific position but an auxiliary is used to carry the subject marking, 'una (sit) is used for male subjects but 'ura (lie) is used for female subjects.

Table 4.11. Actors and Their Characteristic Positions as Introduced in a Story

Existential form		Verb in Isolation	
tɔmahkaku 'ura	There is the alligator.	'ura	lie
turunat'ɛku 'una	There is the bullfrog.	'una	sit
toniku kal'ura	There is the man	kal(i) + 'ura > kal'ura	stand

Table 4.12. *The Man* in Various Positions

Sentence		Verb in Isolation	
toniku 'ura	The man is lying down.	'ura	lie
toniku 'una	The man is sitting.	'una	sit
toniku kal'ura	The man is standing.	kal(i) + 'ura > kal'ura	stand

Table 4.13. Positional Prefixes and Sample Uses

Prefix		Compound Form 1		Compound Form 2	
ho-	out	howi	vomit	holu	give out/ exchange
hɔ-	outside	hɔwashi	outdoors	hɔwahta	outside of
ha-	vertical, up, down	hayihta	above	hakaliwi	he went
hi-	here, this	hiyakati	she arrived here	hishtahahki	just this
hɛ-	this proximal	hɛchu'i	Take this!	hɛ'ɛsh	today
ki-	into	kichu	inside of	kipoti	she looked into [it]
lu-	down	luchuhuwi	he spat downward	lucholuti	it dripped down

Positional Prefixes

As table 4.13 shows, a set of prefixes can also be attached to verbs, adverbs, and prepositions to orient the position or movement of a person or object.

Connectives

Hinyatihch, a conflation of **hinahku** (thus, like this) and *yatihch* (when it occurred), is the most common connective used to introduce episodes in narrative. Deixis (pointing—that is, the tracking of the actors and story line in time and space) is central to Tunica storytelling. Within Youchigant's traditional stories, *hinyatich* occurred so often that Haas abbreviated it consistently as *h-hch*.

Neologisms

As with any language that has been dormant for sixty years, the Tunica Language Project requires the use of many words not found in Youchigant's recorded lexicon or in records of Gatschet's interviews with Johnson or Swanton's interviews with Chiki. In some cases, lacunae are present because the object did not exist in the 1930s (e.g., *computer*). Other words are missing because many ordinary conversational interchanges were not elicited or recorded.[19] For modern learners of Tunica (all of whom are native English speakers), the working group used attested Tunica word-building strategies to create expressions that are essential for everyday interactions, including, for example, *sara* (excuse me), *heni* (hello), *tohkuhch* (please), and *tikahch* (thank you).

Other discourse markers such as *oh*, *well*, and *sorry* were not recorded in the strict narrative format of Haas's work but are vital parts of a usable language. Classroom management phrases, such as *May I go to the bathroom?* and *So close!* are also needed for teaching the language.

To tackle these challenges, the Tunica Language Project uses a number of strategies, including compounding, metonymy, back-formation, and calques. Compounding is a very productive process in the Tunica language and constitutes the main strategy for creating neologisms. Words recorded by Haas show that this process was already employed for new terms—for example, *onirɔwahka* (rice) literally means *white man's corn*. Words native to Tunica are also highly descriptive: both *eyutapahka* and *eyutamuri* gloss as "my bracelet," though they literally mean "my arm decorator" and "my arm squeezer," respectively. One example of compounding in new Tunica is the use of *pahi-* (from *pahita*, "lightning") to mean "electric." *Pahitahina* (computer) is literally "electric writer." *Pahitawali* (telephone) means "electric caller," while *pahitawira* (calculator) is "electric counter."

Metonymy is also useful in the creation of neologisms. For example, *kɔra* means "round or disc-shaped" but can also mean "wheel." The Tunica Language Project then extended the meaning to "car." The locative suffix *-shi* makes *kɔrashi* "garage." The word *kosu*, meaning "color," was back-formed from *kosuk'ariya* (rainbow).[20] *Wish'ɛyi* is a direct translation of *firewater*, referring to alcohol. Similarly, *tetimili* (culture) is a calque of the "Red Path."

REAWAKENING

When Haas worked with Youchigant in the summers of 1933–35, he was the last fluent speaker of the language. After his death in 1948, knowledge of the language was fragmented. Some elders recalled songs and practices, such as the Green Corn Ceremony, but public venues for their performance and the passing on of this cultural heritage were lacking. In the 1990s, Donna Pierite had a vision in which it was revealed to her that she would become the tribal language and legend keeper. She conferred with her father-in-law, who took her to the Tribal Council, which confirmed and ratified this spiritual charge. A natural linguist and a language pedagogue (a college and high school teacher of French and Spanish), Pierite collected the available materials on Tunica: Gatschet's papers, Swanton's publication, and Haas's work. After teaching herself the language and learning songs from her father-in-law and from her Choctaw grandmother, Pierite taught Tunica to her children, Elizabeth and

Jean Luc, forming a team of speakers that could lead the way back to a Tunica-language-using community. Jean Luc's gift of graphic design along with the artistry of Donna and Elizabeth was put to use developing basic teaching materials, including word and coloring books, but they were privately produced and had limited circulation.

When the Tunica opened the casino, the Pierites brought the language into the public sphere with their performances of songs and Tunica stories as part of the weekend Alligator Show in the atrium. They also perform at the tribal powwow and at other Louisiana venues, showcasing the language and the Tunica culture.

When Tulane joined in the revitalization efforts at Lintinger's behest, one of the first projects was to compose a set of invocations in Tunica. Both tribal and intertribal meetings and councils begin with a prayer, and in 2010, Lintinger opened the Southeast Regional United Tribes meetings with a Tunica invocation.

In 2011, the tribe published a children's book, *Hichut'una Awachihk'unanahch Fighting Eagles/Tayak Takohkuman Deer and Turtle*, compiled by the Tulane-Tunica Working Group from versions of these stories told by Youchigant in the 1930s. This book and its accompanying CD were distributed to tribal members at the 2011 powwow.

Inspired by the new materials, tribal members sought further instruction in the language and the Tunica-language summer camps were organized. Preparations for the Green Corn Ceremony formed part of the 2014 camp activities, paving the way for the resurgence of this celebration within the wider community. The Pierites also organized language during the school year, and Donna Pierite gave short language lessons at elder bingo events. She and Elizabeth have translated a number of hymns into Tunica and performed them at church and at public holiday celebrations. Further projects for year-round promotion of the language are under way.

In 2013, the Pierites arranged to have signage erected along the Tunica-Biloxi Nature Trail, identifying the local fauna trilingually—in Tunica, French, and English. In 2014, the Tulane-Tunica Working Group developed further signage for the casino and public areas of the reservation. These areas already had English-language signs; the new signage project provided the Tunica equivalents, bringing Tunica language back into the public eye.

Tulane students working closely with the Pierites are developing further teaching materials, including a pedagogical grammar, an introductory language text, an interactive digital dictionary, and a formal descriptive grammar. Jean-Luc Pierite and Elizabeth Hixen-Mora have finished the intensive training program at the Institute of Collaborative Language Research and bring a newly honed set of skills with digital media for language teaching and documentation to the mix. As the language reemerges and meets a new lived reality, new words are being added to the dictionary and to speakers' lexicons. The success of the revitalization program has led Ethnologue to reclassify the language as "reawakening" (Simons and Fennig 2018). Tunica, which slept through the end of the twentieth century, is now facing the challenges of the twenty-first.

Lapuhch! (That would be a good thing!)

NOTES

1. Information from the plaques in the Tunica-Biloxi Museum, Marksville, Louisiana.

2. Brain (1977) notes that the Tunica were unusual among southeastern peoples in that the men did the agricultural work and women worked in the home, making pottery and weaving. La Source, who accompanied a missionary group in 1699, noted that the Tunica were "living entirely on Indian corn, they are employed solely on their fields; they do not hunt like the other Indians" (Shea 1861:81).

3. While history books record him as Antoine Davion, the Séminaire de Québec Archives has his records under the name Albert Davion.

4. Tunica was considered sleeping rather than dead because even though no native speakers remained, some heritage speakers identified with the language. For more on the definition of sleeping languages, see Leonard 2008.

5. Though the Tunica and Biloxi people share a long history, their languages are unrelated; Biloxi is a Siouan language. Like Tunica, there exist no speakers with any knowledge of Biloxi. However the Biloxi language is not currently included in the Tunica-Biloxi's immediate plans for language revitalization.

6. So comprehensive is Haas's work that Swanton himself considered his "material probably made unnecessary by the work of Mary Haas" (Swanton 1930).

7. Haas's term. In section II of this volume, we refer to the variety of French spoken by Youchigant as Louisiana Regional French. For a discussion of Louisiana's French varieties and that spoken by Youchigant in particular, see Dajko, this volume.

8. Ishak is known in historical documents as Atakapa and is the heritage language of the Atakapa Ishak Nation.

9. Glottal stop is written as an apostrophe in the standard script.

10. /š/ is written *sh* in the newly developed orthography.

11. /č/ is orthographic *ch*.

12. References to the actions of the sun and moon as feminine may be correlated with the female persona of these celestial bodies in Tunica mythology. However, this alone does not explain the overall language-wide pattern.

13. Haas (1941) found gender to be lexicalized for inanimate objects, but the Tunica Language Project has assigned these objects a default gender given the high degree of variability and uncertainty Haas notes in the gender of inanimate objects. See Heaton and Anderson 2017.

14. There are also other classes of verbs, including causatives and auxiliaries.

15. Because the auxiliaries are highly variable, I have used the third-person masculine singular as the citation form, following Haas's practice.

16. There is a separate dual form only in the third person.

17. Morphological processes mask this reduplication in two forms, the plurals for ʼura (lie/lay) and ʼuna (sit/sat).

18. Inalienable possession indicates they cannot be separated from that which they are possessed by and must always be referred to with a possessive marker—that is, an arm must always belong to someone.

19. In some cases, Youchigant misremembered or was uncertain, which is understandable given that he had not spoken the language in almost twenty years. However, these cases are rarely encountered in our need for neologisms and are therefore not explored in this essay.

20. *Rainbow*'s meaning includes no reference to color, instead referencing the Crawfish Shaman in the sky, who is believed to have a rainbow painted on his cheek. He appears after storms in which he has sucked crawfish into the air, such as after a whirlwind. In this way, we have extended a word derived from *crawfish* to the word *color*.

WORKS CITED

Anderson, Patricia. 2017. "Yanatame Nisa Luhchi Yoroni: Lexicography, Language Revitalization, and the New Tunica Dictionary." PhD diss., Tulane University.

Barbry, John D. 1994. "Tunica-Biloxi Tribalism and Indian Policy Reform, 1922–1947." Unpublished paper.

Brain, Jeffrey P. 1970. *The Tunica Treasure*. Lower Mississippi Survey Bulletin 2. Cambridge, MA: Peabody Museum of Archaeology and Ethnology.

Brain, Jeffrey P. 1977. *On the Tunica Trail*. Baton Rouge: Louisiana Department of Culture, Recreation, and Tourism, Louisiana Archaeological Survey and Antiquities Commission, 1994.

Campbell, Lyle. 1997. *American Indian Languages: The Historical Linguistics of Native America*. New York: Oxford University Press.

Caughey, John Walton. 1998. *Bernardo de Gálvez in Louisiana, 1776–1783*. Gretna, LA: Pelican.

Charlevoix, Pierre-François-Xavier de. 1766. *A Voyage to North-America*. Vol. 2. Dublin: Exshaw and Potts.

Dorman, Caroline. 1931. "Tunica Stories in English." In Numbered Manuscripts, 1850s–1980s (Some Earlier), MS 4940, Smithsonian Institution National Anthropological Archive, Suitland, MD.

Garcilaso de la Vega, El Inca (Gómez Suárez de Figuero). 1951. *The Florida de la Inca*. Translated and edited by John Grier Varner and Jeannette Johnson Varner. Austin: University of Texas Press.

Gatschet, Albert S. 1886a. Letter to the Director of the Bureau of Ethnology, October 24, 1886. In Numbered Manuscripts, 1850s–1980s (Some Earlier), MS 1347, Smithsonian Institution National Anthropological Archive, Suitland, MD.

Gatschet, Albert S. 1886b. "Vocabulary, Phrases and Sentences, and Texts, October–November 1886." In Numbered Manuscripts, 1850s–1980s (Some Earlier), MS 1301, Smithsonian Institution National Anthropological Archive, Suitland, MD.

Haas, Mary R. 1935. "A Grammar of the Tunica Language." PhD diss., Yale University.

Haas, Mary R. 1941. "Tunica." In *Handbook of American Indian Languages*, edited by Franz Boaz, 4:1–143. New York: Augustin.

Haas, Mary R. 1950. *Tunica Texts*. Berkeley: University of California Press.

Haas, Mary R. 1951. "The Proto-Gulf Word for Water (with Notes on Siouan-Yuchi)." *International Journal of American Linguistics* 17:71–79.

Haas, Mary R. 1953. *Tunica Dictionary*. Vol. 6, no. 2. Berkeley: University of California Press.

Heaton, Raina. 2014. "'Gulf' as an Areal Subgrouping." Paper presented at the Sleeping and Awakened Languages of the Gulf South Conference, New Orleans, March 7–9.

Heaton, Raina, and Patricia Anderson. 2017. "When Animals Become Humans: Grammatical Gender in Tunica." *International Journal of American Linguistics* 83 (2): 341–63.

Hoffman, Michael P. 1992. "Protohistoric Tunican Indians in Arkansas." *Arkansas Historical Quarterly* 51 (1): 30–53.

Hopkins, Nicholas A. 1999. "The Native Languages of the Southeastern United States." http://www.famsi.org/research/hopkins/SouthEastUSLanguages.pdf.

Leonard, Wesley. 2008. "When Is an Extinct Language Not Extinct? Miami, a Formerly Sleeping Language." In *Sustaining Linguistic Diversity: Endangered and Minority Languages and Language Varieties*, edited by Kendall A. King, Natalie Schilling-Estes, Lyn Fogle, Jia Jackie Lou, and Barbara Soukup, 23–34. Washington, DC: Georgetown University Press.

Library of Congress. N.d. "Louisiana as a Spanish Colony."https://www.loc.gov/collections/louisiana-european-explorations-and-the-louisiana-purchase/articles-and-essays/louisiana-as-a-spanish-colony.

Morse, Dan F., and Phyllis A. Morse. 1983. *Archaeology of the Central Mississippi Valley*. New York: Academic Press.

Munro, Pamela. 2015. "American Indian Languages of the Southeast: An Introduction." In *New Perspectives on Language Variety in the South: Historical and Contemporary Approaches*, edited by Michael D. Picone and Catherine Evans Davies, 21–42. Tuscaloosa: University of Alabama Press.

Shea, John D. G., ed. 1861. "Letter of Mr. Thaumur La Source." In *Early Voyages Up and Down the Mississippi River*, 79–86. Albany, NY: Munsell.

Sibley, John. 1806. *Historical Sketches of Several Indian Tribes in Louisiana, South of the Arkansas River and between the Mississippi and River Grand*. Washington, DC: A and G.

Simons, Gary F., and Charles D. Fennig, eds. 2018. "Tunica." In *Ethnologue: Languages of the World*, 21st ed. Dallas: SIL International. https://www.ethnologue.com/language/tun.

Swanton, John R. N.d. "Tunica Texts." In Numbered Manuscripts, 1850s–1980s (Some Earlier), MS 4277, Smithsonian Institution National Anthropological Archive, Suitland, MD.

Swanton, John R. 1919. *A Structural and Lexical Comparison of the Tunica, Chitimacha, and Atakapa Languages*." Washington, DC.: Smithsonian Institution.

Swanton, John R. 1921. "The Tunica Language." *International Journal of American Linguistics* 2:1–39.

Swanton, John R. 1930. "Copy of A. S. Gatschet's Tunica Texts and Swanton's Tunica Texts, Summer, 1930." In Numbered Manuscripts, 1850s–1980s (Some Earlier), MS 4123, Smithsonian Institution National Anthropological Archive, Suitland, MD.

Swanton, John R. 1946. *The Indians of the Southeastern United States*. Washington, DC.: Smithsonian Institution.

Tunica-Tulane Working Group. 2011. *Hichut'una Awachihk'unanahch Fighting Eagles/Tayak Takohkuman Deer and Turtle*. Marksville, LA: Tunica Nation.

CHAPTER 5

ISHAK WORDS: LANGUAGE RENEWAL PROSPECTS FOR A HISTORICAL GULF COAST TRIBE

JEFFERY U. DARENSBOURG AND DAVID KAUFMAN

In this chapter, we provide a brief overview of the Ishak (Atakapan) people. We begin with a discussion of the tribe's history with a focus on ethnonyms and then move on to a discussion of the present status of the language.

ISHAK PEOPLE

The tribe is known by two names: Atakapa, a Muskogean name given by outsiders (generally identified as Choctaw) living on the traditional eastern borders of the tribe's territory, and Ishak, the tribe's traditional name for itself. *Atakapa* (spelled a variety of ways, most notably *Attakapas*, which designated a political region under three separate colonial governing bodies) comes from the Choctaw *hattak apa*, meaning "cannibal" (lit. *hattak* [man, person] + *apa* [to eat]). This name was an epithet (Gatschet and Swanton 1932:1), an attempt to disparage a society with a strongly decentralized governance that lacked the strict hierarchies of the agricultural societies of some of its neighbors. There is little evidence of actual cannibalism among those called Atakapa (Butler 1970), and a sixteenth-century European visitor, Alvar Núñez Cabeza de Vaca (1993), who lived with the tribe following a shipwreck, observed Ishak opposition to cannibalism.[1] The tribe's traditional name for itself, Ishak, means simply "human beings," a common practice among many different tribes (Deloria 1969:103; see also Kniffen, Gregory, and Stokes 1987:44). The tribe should thus be referred to as Ishak or as Atakapa-Ishak if referencing the current tribal organization of the largest group of Ishak people. We refer to the language as Ishak in this essay, though Atakapan is more common in academic publications (*Atakapan* [rather than *Atakapa*] refers to the larger family of languages to which it belonged prior to the population decimation that followed contact with Europeans. Bidai, for example, was also considered Atakapan, as was Akokisa.) Other names tribal members apply to themselves include Les Sauvages, French Indians, Creole Indians, Catholic Indians, and, from the Ishak language itself, Ishak Yukiti (approximately meaning Ishak Natives) (Singleton 2005:15–16). Gatschet and Swanton (1932) cite *Yuk(h)iti* and, of particular note, *Takapo* as additional self-designations.

The Atakapa-Ishak Nation of Southwest Louisiana and Southeast Texas was reorganized in 1996 using both historic names, with much of the work carried out by tribal member Hubert Daniel Singleton (1926–2009) of Lake Charles, Louisiana, who also published several nonscholarly volumes of tribal history and lore. These volumes are quite useful and certainly indispensable to researchers seeking to understand Ishak people from the point of view of the tribe itself. The tribe has played an important role in the culture of the present-day states of Louisiana and Texas, lending cultural influence in music (Singleton [2005] suggests this is true especially of zydeco), food (especially maque choux), and place-names. A US naval vessel, the *Atakapa* ATF-149 (removed from service in 1981) bore the tribe's name. In spite of its historic importance, the tribe is not as well known as many other southern tribes and is often assumed to be extinct.[2] Efforts to increase public awareness of the living contemporary existence of the tribe are ongoing. The tribe does not currently enjoy recognition at the federal level, but it has petitioned for recognition with the Bureau of Indian Affairs, and tribal members regularly participate in cultural events such as powwows, especially within traditional tribal areas in Louisiana and Texas. (For maps of these areas, see Swanton 1911; Newcomb 2004.)

ISHAK WORDS

The Ishak language, as far as can be ascertained by research among tribal members, is currently "asleep."[3] As far as we can tell from informal interviews of Ishak people, the last fluent speaker of Ishak walked on sometime between 1946 and 1970. Alvin "Pem" Broussard, an Ishak-Cajun artist living in Coteau Holmes, Louisiana, can speak a few phrases learned firsthand from speakers of the language decades ago. Some tribal members have memories of long-deceased relatives who "spoke some Indian," but documentation is at best difficult and often impossible to locate. Tribal members who speak a language other than English, especially as a first language, generally speak versions of Louisiana French or Louisiana Creole.

Smithsonian researcher Albert Samuel Gatschet studied speakers of Ishak in Lake Charles, Louisiana, and environs in 1885; his colleague, John R. Swanton, followed up in 1907. Their resulting volume, *A Dictionary of the Atakapa Language Accompanied by Text Material* (1932), is the largest collection of Ishak vocabulary and has a small but significant corpus of Ishak narratives. However, it lacks anything like a phrasebook of the language, which is unfortunate because Gatschet and Swanton had access to fluent speakers who could have assisted in the creation of such a compendium. Most of what is known of the Ishak language comes from this volume. The Bible does not seem to have been translated into Ishak, nor is there a larger-sized nineteenth-century dictionary for Ishak such as exists for Choctaw (Byington 1915). In addition, several shorter works of linguistic analysis either entirely or partially about the Ishak language have been published. Remnants of Ishak endure in some Louisiana place-names, such as Mermentau and Calcasieu, which are named for Ishak chiefs. Few other place-names in Ishak have been preserved, however (see, e.g., Hayward [2016]).

Hubert Singleton added to the Ishak linguistic corpus with *The Indians Who Gave Us Zydeco* (2005), which provided Ishak translations of Roman Catholic texts such as the "Pater Noster" and "Ave Maria" and Christmas carols such as "Silent Night" and "Away in a Manger." Tribal member Tanner Menard, originally from Vermilion Parish, Louisiana, has both composed several songs in the Ishak language and translated some Caddoan songs into Ishak for use in ceremonies of the Native American Church (Lief and Darensbourg 2015).

The most extensive scholarly project on the language in the past century is a new single-volume dictionary currently in process by linguist David Kaufman (forthcoming) that will be published with the support of the Atakapa-Ishak Nation of Southwest Louisiana and Southeast Texas. Kaufman became interested in the project while working on his doctoral dissertation (Kaufman 2014), finding Swanton and Gatschet's dictionary poorly organized and difficult to use, especially because it is organized around word roots and lacks entries for each word separately. The new dictionary will correct this problem and add better cross-references. In addition, Kaufman's revised dissertation has been published as *Clues to Lower Mississippi Valley Histories* (2019), which includes an extensive section on Atakapa-Ishak history and language.

PROSPECTS AND CONCLUSION

While there are presently no fluent or even near-fluent speakers of Ishak, there are language resources, both extant and forthcoming, and living Ishak people who carry on the tribe's culture. Some of these people have expressed interest in basic, practical language materials. The involvement of persons with the desire and expertise to reawaken the Ishak language can preserve, enrich, and embolden the culture of this historic—and living—tribe.

NOTES

A version of this paper was presented at Tulane University's 2014 Conference on Language Revitalization: Sleeping and Awakened Languages of the Gulf South. We are thankful for information, advice, and support from Edward Chretien Jr., principal chief of the Atakapa-Ishak Nation of Southwest Louisiana and Southeast Texas, as well as various other tribal members. We have also benefited from the helpful advice of Shane Lief of Tulane University.

1. Cabeza de Vaca refers to the Ishak as the "Han" people, taking a name for a traditional tribal dwelling as the name of the tribe. For a nonacademic, tribal perspective on the alleged cannibalism and the social impact of the slur on tribal members, see Singleton 2005. There is as yet no contemporary analysis using historiography from the standpoint of critical studies of ethnicity and colonialism.

2. However, tribal members briefly came to the national consciousness after the 2010 BP oil spill in the Gulf of Mexico. NPR reported on the effects of the spill on the Atakapa-Ishak fishing village at Grand Bayou, Louisiana (Burnett 2010).

3. We are particularly grateful to Miami scholar Wesley Leonard for his insight regarding this term.

WORKS CITED

Burnett, John. 2010. "Oil Imperils Native American Town, and Way of Life." *All Things Considered*, June 17. http://www.npr.org/templates/story/story.php?storyId=127902879.

Butler, Joseph T., Jr. 1970. "Atakapa Indians: Cannibals of Southwest Louisiana." *Louisiana History* 11 (2): 167–76.

Byington, Cyprus. 1915. *A Dictionary of the Choctaw Language*. Edited by John R. Swanton and Henry S. Halbert. Washington, DC: Smithsonian Institution.

Deloria, Vine, Jr. 1969. *Custer Died for Your Sins: An Indian Manifesto*. Norman: University of Oklahoma Press, 1988.

Gatschet, Albert S., and John R. Swanton. 1932. *A Dictionary of the Attakapa Language Accompanied by Text Material*. Washington, DC: Smithsonian Institution.

Hayward, Philip. 2016. "Enduring Perceptions: Placenaming and the Perception of Louisiana's Salt Dome Islands." *Island Studies Journal* 11 (2): 417–30.

Kaufman, David. 2014. "The Lower Mississippi Valley as a Language Area." PhD diss., University of Kansas.

Kaufman, David. 2019. *Clues to Lower Mississippi Valley Histories: Language, Archaeology, and Ethnography*. Lincoln: University of Nebraska Press.

Kaufman, David. Forthcoming. *Atakapa Išakkoy Dictionary*. Chicago: Exploration Press.

Kniffen, Fred B., Hiram F. Gregory, and George A. Stokes. 1987. *The Historic Indian Tribes of Louisiana: From 1542 to the Present*. Baton Rouge: Louisiana State University Press.

Lief, Shane, and Jeffrey U. Darensbourg. 2015. "Popular Music and Indigenous Languages of Louisiana." *Proceedings of the Foundation for Endangered Languages* 19:142–46.

Newcomb, William W., Jr. 2004. "Atakapans and Neighboring Groups." In *Handbook of North American Indians*, vol. 14, *Southeast*, edited by Raymond Fogelson and William Sturtevant, 659–63. Washington, DC: Smithsonian Institution.

Núñez Cabeza de Vaca, Alvar. 1993. *Castaways: The Narrative of Alvar Núñez Cabeza de Vaca.* Edited by Enrique Pupo-Walker. Translated by Frances M. López. Berkeley: University of California Press.

Read, William A. 2008. *Louisiana Place Names of Indian Origin: A Collection of Words.* Edited by George M. Riser. Tuscaloosa: University of Alabama Press.

Singleton, Hubert Daniel. 2005. *The Indians Who Gave Us Zydeco: The Atakapa-Ishaks (Uh-TAK-uh-paw-ee-SHAKS) of Southwest Louisiana and Southeast Texas.* 3rd ed. N.p.: Singleton.

Swanton, John R. 1911. *Indian Tribes of the Lower Mississippi Valley and Adjacent Coast of the Gulf of Mexico.* Washington, DC: Smithsonian Institution.

SECTION II

French in Louisiana

NATHALIE DAJKO

It would be impossible to discuss language in Louisiana without addressing the issue of French. The colonial language with the longest continuous presence in Louisiana, French still looms large in the popular imagination. Tourists often arrive in New Orleans looking for French speakers, and the tourism industry uses the language in no small way to promote the state's image. The Council for the Development of French in Louisiana (CODOFIL), established by the Louisiana Legislature in 1968 to promote the use of French, has also recently turned its attention to local varieties as a means of becoming financially viable. Despite the shift to English that has resulted in a nearly monolingual anglophone population, French enjoys a privileged status in Louisiana: it is the language of historic hegemony, and it remains a language with which people identify, even though they may not speak it themselves (Dajko 2018).

French first appeared in the Lower Mississippi Valley with the arrival of explorer Robert René Cavelier, Sieur de La Salle, who descended the Mississippi in 1682 and, standing somewhere near modern Venice, Louisiana, claimed the entire river drainage area for France. However, a real French presence was not established until permanent occupation of the Gulf Coast began in the eighteenth century. The Canadian Le Moyne brothers, Pierre and Jean-Baptiste (known better to history as the Sieur d'Iberville and the Sieur de Bienville, respectively) arrived with a fleet of ships in 1699 to establish a permanent colony. Settlements soon followed: what is now Biloxi, Mississippi, in 1699; present-day Mobile, Alabama, in 1701; Natchitoches, Louisiana, in 1714; Fort Rosalie (Natchez, Mississippi) in 1716; and New Orleans, founded by Bienville, in 1718.

By 1719, the French had started to bring human cargo from Africa to the fledgling colony. Though the importation of enslaved Africans was outlawed by the French in the 1740s, it was reintroduced during the Spanish period (1760–1800). Thus, Louisiana had a strong African presence alongside the French throughout the colonial period. These enslaved people represented dozens of nations and brought at least fifty languages with them, though at least in the early period, Bambara seems to have been predominant (Hall 1995). The meeting of French and African populations resulted in the creation of a new language, based in French but attesting significant grammatical differences that warrant the designation of a separate language, Louisiana Creole.

Significant francophone immigration to Louisiana continued through the Spanish and American (1803–) periods up to the eve of the Civil War, after which it was significantly curtailed, though not extinguished. Two key influxes of francophones included the Acadian resettlement in Louisiana, which started in 1764 and comprised roughly five waves over two decades, and the arrival of people from Saint-Domingue in the wake of the Haitian Revolution in the late eighteenth and early nineteenth centuries.

Louisiana's 1812 statehood ushered in large-scale anglophone immigration, and after the Civil War, English speakers became the hegemonic power in the state. The upper classes abandoned the French language fairly rapidly in favor of the new language of power and industry. Despite the new importance of English, however, French held on for another 170 years, and two varieties, Louisiana Creole and Louisiana Regional French,[1] continue to be spoken primarily in the area of south Louisiana known as the French Triangle or Acadiana (see figures 6.1, 11.1), though they are severely endangered: today, most speakers are over the age of sixty, and while exceptions exist, Louisiana Creole and Louisiana Regional French generally are not being transmitted to children. Louisiana's Native Americans are some of the most conservative in shifting from French to English. French continues to be spoken on a daily basis among people, generally about a generation younger than such speakers elsewhere, who identify as American Indian in Terrebonne and Lafourche Parishes (Picone 1997; Rottet 2001; Dajko 2009; Valdman et al. 2010).

In some historically francophone areas, the language is already gone or effectively so. In the Cane River area, for example, the last known speaker of Creole passed away in 2008, and to the best of our knowledge, the region has only one remaining fluent speaker of Louisiana Regional French, though semi-speakers surely still exist. Likewise, we have been unable to locate a single fluent speaker of heritage French of any kind in New Orleans in more than a decade, though rumors that one or more exist continue to circulate. Louisiana Creole attests significantly fewer speakers than does Louisiana Regional French, and while the Breaux Bridge area has some younger speakers (my students and I interviewed some speakers in their forties in 2011), Louisiana Creole has declined faster than has Louisiana Regional French.

Louisiana's French varieties have attracted a large volume of scholarship and are the best documented of any of Louisiana's languages. (For Creole in particular, see Klingler, this volume.) Academics, most famously Alcée Fortier, began documenting both Creole and Louisiana Regional French in the nineteenth century (e.g., Fortier 1884–85, 1891). By the 1930s, the study of both varieties had become popular subjects for theses and dissertations, with literally dozens produced, many from within Louisiana State University's French studies program. Many if not most of the writers of these studies were native to Louisiana and in some cases were native speakers of the dialects they were describing. Each of the extant varieties has a dictionary compiled by academics; the *Dictionary of Louisiana French as It Is Spoken in Cajun, Creole, and American Indian Communities* (Valdman et al. 2010) is particularly notable for synthesizing the large volume of previous work with current verification to document, as best as possible, variations in pronunciation and the geographic distribution of entries. (For the dictionary's impact on language preservation and reclamation efforts, see Picone 2018:125–27.) Work on an etymological volume to complement the dictionary is currently in progress, led by Albert Valdman with the collaboration of Kevin Rottet and Thomas A. Klingler.

Nonacademics have also joined the push to document (if not actively promote) the language. Perhaps most notably, Father Jules Daigle published *A Dictionary of the Cajun Language* in 1984. Recent years have seen a flurry of publications from laypersons, usually native speakers or semi-speakers eager to document their language before it disappears (see, e.g., Labrie 2009; J. Savoy and Savoy 2009; Voisin 2011; S. Savoy 2014) and hoping to help revive it.

In this section we look at the history, the features, and the future of the two varieties of Louisiana French that are still spoken in the state. In chapter 6, Nathalie Dajko examines Louisiana Regional French, providing an account of its creation and a brief description of the variation it attests, concluding with a discussion of the language's relationship to ethnicity and in particular to American Indian identity.

In chapter 7, Thomas A. Klingler presents a broad overview of Louisiana Creole. He begins with a comprehensive literature review and then provides a brief grammar of the language. He closes with an examination of the current state of the language, with a particular focus on language revival efforts.

In chapter 8, Tamara Lindner considers the issue of decline and revival, examining attitudes toward French among Louisiana's youth. Her surveys of students taking French at the University of Louisiana at Lafayette show that respondents—particularly those who self-identify as Cajun—continue to link language with Cajun identity despite their lack of fluency. Her research suggests that further institutional investments in support of French revival efforts would be well worthwhile.

In chapter 9, Albert Camp, a linguist working at Louisiana State University, has written a broad overview of French education in Louisiana. He offers a focused look at two key programs, CODOFIL, which is working to establish immersion programs, and the Escadrille Louisiane program, which is training Louisiana native French instructors. The latter is a coordinated effort between CODOFIL and the government of France to graduate Louisiana teachers prepared to offer immersion classes. Many of the Escadrille participants do not come from families that historically spoke French.

As a complement to Camp's writing about the state program, chapter 10 offers an in-depth look at French-language schooling in New Orleans. Robin White considers the history of French and bilingual schooling in the city and contrasts both the types of schools and parental motivations for enrolling their children. Modern New Orleanians, living in a nearly exclusively monolingual English city, have very different reasons for wanting their children to pursue an education in a French immersion context than did their counterparts 150 years ago.

NOTES

1. A third variety, Plantation Society French, is still likely used by a number of semi-speakers, and a handful of fluent speakers may still exist. See Dajko, this volume.

WORKS CITED

Daigle, Jules. 1984. *A Dictionary of the Cajun Language*. Ann Arbor: Edwards.
Dajko, Nathalie. 2009. "Ethnic and Geographic Variation in the Lafourche Basin, Louisiana." PhD diss., Tulane University.
Dajko, Nathalie. 2018. "The Continuing Symbolic Importance of French in Louisiana." In *Language Variation in the New South: Contemporary Perspectives on Change and Variation*, edited by Jeffrey Reaser, Eric Wilbanks, Karissa Wojcik, and Walt Wolfram, 153–74. Chapel Hill: University of North Carolina Press.
Fortier, Alcée. 1884–85. "The French Language in Louisiana and the Negro-French Dialect." *Transactions of the Modern Language Association of America* 1:96–111.
Fortier, Alcée. 1891. "The Acadians of Louisiana and Their Dialect." *Publications of the Modern Language Association of America* 6 (1): 64–94.
Hall, Gwendolyn Midlo. 1995. *Africans in Colonial Louisiana: The Development of Afro-Creole Culture in the Eighteenth-Century*. Baton Rouge: Louisiana State University Press.
Labrie, Denise. 2009. *Parle Creole French: Southern Louisiana Dialect*. Lexington, KY: CreateSpace.
Picone, Michael D. 1997. "Enclave Dialect Contraction: An External Overview of Louisiana French." *American Speech* 72 (2): 117–53.
Picone, Michael D. 2018. "Language Variety in Louisiana: Trends and Implications." In *Language Variety in the New South: Contemporary Perspectives on Change and Variation*, edited by

Jeffrey Reaser, Eric Wilbanks, Karissa Wojcik, and Walt Wolfram, 113–34. Chapel Hill: University of North Carolina Press.

Rottet, Kevin. 2001. *Language Shift in the Coastal Marshes of Louisiana*. New York: Lang.

Savoy, Joseph, and Scott Savoy. 2009. *The Cajun Home Companion*. Lexington, KY: CreateSpace.

Savoy, Scott. 2014. *The Cajun Home Companion*. Vol. 2. Lexington, KY: CreateSpace.

Valdman, Albert, Kevin J. Rottet, Barry Jean Ancelet, Richard Guidry, Thomas A. Klingler, Amanda LaFleur, Tamara Lindner, Michael D. Picone, and Dominique Ryon. 2010. *Dictionary of Louisiana French: As Spoken in Cajun, Creole, and Native American Communities*. Jackson: University Press of Mississippi.

Voisin, Gordon. 2011. *Cajun Vocabulation*. Bloomington: iUniverse.

CHAPTER 6

HISTORY AND VARIATION IN LOUISIANA FRENCH

NATHALIE DAJKO

Popular understandings of Louisiana French present a story of immigration, subsequent isolation, and the survival of a single regional variety of French. The recorded history is far more complex, however, involving the meeting of many regional French dialects, the creation of a new language based in French, and the survival of a variety that bears influence from multiple sources. And while popular culture often focuses on the myth of one variety of French (often called Cajun French), linguists have traditionally recognized three types of French in Louisiana: Colonial French, Louisiana Creole, and Cajun French. But this three-way distinction and the terms used may also lead to misunderstanding.

The term *Colonial French* is most accurately used to reference the French spoken by the earliest (eighteenth-century) colonists, most of whom were drawn from the lower classes and spoke various French dialects. We have no record of this variety, though we may glean clues from extant varieties that descend from it. Confusingly, however, the term has also been used anachronistically in the literature to refer to a variety that developed in tandem with the nineteenth-century French of France as a consequence of continued ties to the metropole via immigration (of wealthier people) and education (of the planter class), though people from many walks of life ultimately spoke this variety. Ample documentation exists for this variety: it was nearly indistinguishable from modern Standard French and differs primarily by only a few lexical items: *banquette* for "sidewalk" (cf. *trottoir*), for example. Given its linguistic distinctness from the French spoken by the earliest colonists and given that it developed in the postcolonial (i.e., post–Louisiana Purchase) period, the term *Plantation Society French* (Picone 1998, 2015) was coined to alleviate the confusion. Today, Plantation Society French is nearly dead; only a handful of speakers, if any, likely survive.

The remaining two varieties are also endangered, but a solid community of speakers still exist for both, with most speakers living in south Louisiana's French Triangle (also known as Acadiana) (figure 6.1). Louisiana Creole, a French-based language likely created in Louisiana in the eighteenth century by African-born slaves (Neumann 1985; Marshall 1989; Klingler 2003a; Klingler and Dajko 2006), bears resemblances to other French-based Creoles worldwide. (For a more detailed discussion of Louisiana Creole, see Klingler, this volume.)

Though often presented as the result of an ethnic group practicing isolated language maintenance, the subject of this chapter, Louisiana Regional French—more commonly called Cajun French[1]—is more properly understood to be the complex product of extensive dialect mixing across centuries of contact. In this chapter, I outline a brief history of the language and then discuss the variation found within it, demonstrating that while the language varies along both geographic and ethnic lines, ascribing provenance to any given feature is difficult and that the reasons why features are retained or lost as languages change over time may be obscure. While Louisiana Creole is regionally variable as well—for example, while most speakers around the state use an apical flapped *r* sound (the sound that in American English is conceived of as a variant of /t/ or /d/, as in *waiter* or *wader*), speakers in St. Tammany Parish around Lacombe use a uvular *r* (the *r* used in Standard French),[2] and in Natchitoches the verb *gen* (to have) may be used in a long form, *ganyen*—I limit my comments here to Louisiana Regional French.[3]

DEVELOPMENT AND NATURE OF LOUISIANA REGIONAL FRENCH

The commonly used label *Cajun French* bolsters the most common misunderstanding surrounding the nature of Louisiana Regional French: that it is simply the descendant of Acadian French, isolated for generations in Louisiana. While the term *Cajun* does in fact derive from *Acadian*, and Acadian French is a part of the linguistic makeup of Louisiana Regional French, it is in fact descended from multiple French dialects brought in by successive waves of francophone immigrants. For this reason, among others,[4] while most speakers call their dialect Cajun French,[5] when discussing it in an academic setting I prefer to follow Klingler (2003b) and use the term *Louisiana Regional French*.

The earliest settlers to Louisiana included people from the metropole and from existing colonies, including Canada. They were primarily soldiers and lower-class citizens (Usner 1992:32–33; Brasseaux 2005), many of whom came from the Paris region (Brasseaux 2005:16). Given their origins, they likely spoke *le français populaire* (popular French)—the nonstandard language of the Parisian working class that derived from multiple nonstandard regional dialects (Lodge

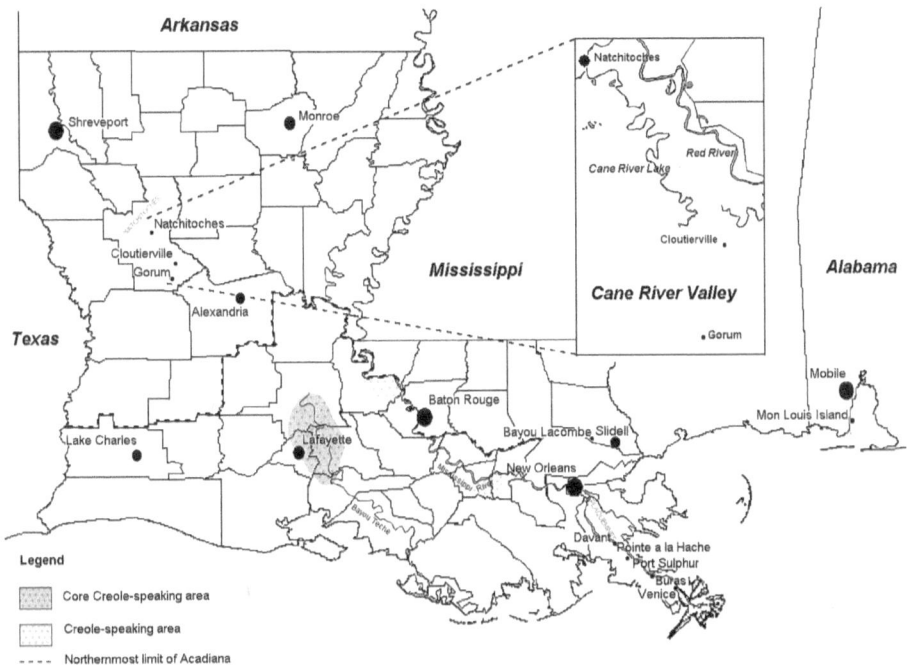

Figure 6.1: French-speaking regions of Louisiana. Map by the author.

2004)—and other nonstandard *oïl*[6] dialects (Klingler 2003a:xxix; Brasseaux 2005; Klingler 2009).[7] Though related and therefore sharing many features, these dialects were nonetheless distinct from each other. The 1764–85 Acadian immigration brought between twenty-six hundred and three thousand speakers of Acadian French (Brasseaux 1987, 1992:4, 2005:17), a dialect descended largely from that spoken in the Poitou-Saintonge region in western coastal France and, like most of the earlier-arriving varieties, classified as a northern *oïl* dialect. Roughly half of these immigrants had been displaced for thirty years prior to coming to Louisiana, spending much of that time in cities on the French Atlantic seaboard (Brasseaux 1987). They were followed by a large influx of refugees from Saint-Domingue (modern Haiti), who presumably spoke either Haitian Creole, the precursor of modern Standard French, or both, depending on whether they were free or enslaved, among other factors. Until the eve of the Civil War, immigration from France continued alongside large-scale immigration from Germany, Ireland, and the American states (Brasseaux 2005). Many of these settlers remained in the New Orleans area, though a number also spread out into the Louisiana countryside. The nineteenth-century French immigrants tended to be wealthier and better educated than the earliest settlers and, alongside the local gentry, they continued sustained contact with the metropole, especially by sending their children to school there (Klingler 2003a:xxviii). As a result, Louisiana's elites came to speak a dialect very close to modern Standard French that linguists call Plantation Society French (Picone 1998, 2015). Until the Civil War and the economic collapse that followed, tension between the francophone groups of different social classes and origins kept the groups fairly separate from each other (Brasseaux 1992:104–5). During the Reconstruction era, however, this state of affairs changed drastically. Acadians married non-Acadians at rates sometimes surpassing 50 percent (Brasseaux 1992:106–7), resulting in a synthetic culture that incorporated Acadian and non-Acadian customs and language even in areas in which Acadian settlers predominated (Brasseaux 1992:109).

The most parsimonious explanation for the general uniformity of Louisiana Regional French is that merging of cultures and languages in a region that supported multiple French dialects caused a good deal of dialect leveling (Brasseaux 1992:109; Rottet 2004; Picone 2006; Valdman et al. 2010:ii). Speakers across the state use *asteur*, for example, for "now" (cf. standard *maintenant*), and the construction *être après faire quelque chose* (lit. to be after doing something) to indicate progressive action is universal. Across Acadiana, speakers use nasal pronunciations of vowels before *n*, *m*, and *ng*. Moreover, the palatal nasal found in words like *cogner* (to strike/bump/knock) or *campagne* (countryside) (in Spanish, this sound is represented by *ñ*, as in *año* [year]) is absent in Louisiana and typically is replaced by a nasalized vowel followed by a palatal semiconsonant (the initial sound in *yellow*, known as a *yod*): *cogner* [kɔ̃je] or [kɔ̃jɛ̃], *campagne* [kãpãj]. However, a good deal of variation still exists, at times throwing into question the extent of any leveling that may have taken place (Rottet 2004; Picone 2006).

Of course, Louisiana Regional French speakers, like speakers of any language, may also make stylistic choices. So, much as an English speaker might choose to describe a particularly large house as "very big," "really big," or "big big," depending on audience, setting, and/or intended effect, a Louisiana Regional French speaker may select from among a range of synonymous intensifiers (e.g., *bien* or *joliment*) or may elect to reduplicate an adjective or adverb: *il y avait une grande grande maison* (lit. there was a big, big house). This chapter focuses on variation related to factors such as region and ethnicity rather than on stylistic choices.

Louisiana French's differences from Standard French do not mean that the dialect is incomprehensible to the majority of francophones (as is often claimed, particularly by nonspeakers). Indeed, because of shared origins, Louisiana French bears much resemblance to spoken regional varieties in France. When a member of a Facebook group for Cajun French speakers and those wishing to learn to speak the dialect posted a series of twenty recordings (VielleLouisiane 2016) and asked group members to identify whether the speakers were from France or Louisiana, no one got more than seventeen correct. The recordings were short and in some cases not ideal for the purpose (for example, one clip was of a woman singing, which can often present problems for dialectal identification), but the exercise nonetheless highlighted the similarities between the varieties. All of the recordings from France presented speakers of nonstandard varieties, generally from Normandy or Poitou, that shared many features with Louisiana Regional French (such as apical *r*).

Despite a legacy of intermarriage with speakers of other languages, including Spanish, German, English, and indigenous languages, the only language to have left a significant trace of its passing is English. That said, early on, French speakers frequently cohabited with American Indian women in particular, and a number of salient vocabulary items are borrowed from indigenous languages, including *bayou* and *chaoui* (raccoon), both from Choctaw. The presence of Canadians among the founding population led to the introduction of a few indigenous words of nonlocal origin, such as *maringouin* (mosquito), in some areas (see Picone 1996; Klingler, Picone, and Valdman 1997). These outside influences are not sufficient to prevent intercomprehension.

LEXICAL, SEMANTIC, AND MORPHOLOGICAL DIFFERENCES

Perhaps the most obvious regional differences in any language tend to be lexical. People immediately notice when someone uses the term *pop* rather than *soda* to refer to a sugary carbonated drink, and such utterances often prompt people to ask for (or attempt to guess) the origin of the person who uses the "incorrect" term. In Louisiana, lexical differences abound. For example, in Lafourche Parish, a mosquito is a *moustique*, while in Terrebonne it is a *maringouin*.[8] A wall is an *entourage* in Terrebonne and Lafourche Parishes but a *muraille* in Grand Isle. In some areas, to run is *galoper*; in others, *courir*. One may be *fatigué(e)* or *lasse* (tired) after a long day of work. A small street may be a *manche* or simply a *rue* or a *chemin*); a tree is either an *arbre* or a *bois*. In the Lafourche Basin, both *bombe* and *chaudière* are used for "cooking pot."

What might be the most impressive example of variation can be found in the third-person-plural pronouns: Louisiana French boasts five different ways to say *they*: *ils*, *eux-autres*, *eux*, *eusse*, and *ça*. In very restricted contexts (those in which the subject has previously been clearly established), the pronoun may be dropped entirely.[9] In many regions, a single variant is preferred over the others (though it may not be used exclusively). In the Lower Lafourche Basin, speakers overwhelmingly use *eusse*. In Thibodaux, however, all five variants are used fairly interchangeably (Dajko 2009).

Finally, a few words may have different meanings in different parts of the state. For example, while I was doing my fieldwork in Terrebonne and Lafourche Parishes, there was some argument about whether *chaudière* and *bombe* really represented the same thing. While I elicited the terms using a sentence I provided for translation, a few interviewees declared that a *bombe* was a kettle— that is, a pot used for a specific purpose. The most striking example, however, is in interrogative pronouns. The French spoken in most areas differentiates the inanimate pronoun *quoi* (what) from the animate *qui* (who). However, in some areas (most notably Terrebonne and Lafourche and variably but predominantly in Avoyelles and Evangeline Parishes), speakers use only a single pronoun, *qui*, to cover both meanings. This can lead to occasional confusion, as many people seem unaware of this variation.

Louisianans may also sometimes employ different morphological strategies. For example, when conjugating a verb in the present tense with the third-person-plural pronoun *ils*, they may use the null suffix (i.e., they simply pronounce the stem), as in *ils dansent* [idãs], pronounced identically to the singular *il danse*,[10] or they may use the *-ont* [-ɔ̃] suffix (pronounced like *non* or *mon*) and produce *ils dansont* [idãsɔ̃]. An example of variation not in kind but in degree is the use of distinct (including irregular) subjunctive verb forms by Cajuns and American Indians in Terrebonne and Lafourche Parishes. In French, a few verbs use distinct forms when conjugated for subjunctive mood: *je finis* [ʒəfini] (I finish) versus *je finisse* [ʒəfinis], for example (cf. present indicative *je marche* versus subjunctive *je marche*). Marking subjunctive mood is disappearing in both France (Battye and Hintze 1992:346) and Louisiana; the rate at which subjunctive forms appear in Louisiana may vary by community. In Terrebonne Parish, Cajuns are three times more likely (26.8 percent vs. 8.3 percent) to use distinct subjunctive forms than are Indians. Furthermore, variation exists in the form the subjunctive may take. In my work in that area, I encountered two forms for the verb *avoir* (to have):

(1) faut que t'**aies** une licence pour *drive* (shared with Standard French)
(2) faut que t'**avoye** une licence pour aller *drive*

Such variation is a little more uncommon than is difference in word choice or pronunciation and is complicated by language attrition as a consequence of the shift to English. For example, in Louisiana, the first-person subjunctive form of the irregular verb *pouvoir* (to be able) is often *je peuve*, following the regular pattern, which bases the subjunctive form on the third-person-plural form of the present indicative (*ils peuvent*; the final *-ent* is silent in French).

In Standard French, the subjunctive form uses a separate stem to produce *je puisse*. Regularizations like this may just as easily be attributed to leveling as to attrition, as both processes may produce them.

PRONUNCIATION

As is true with the lexicon, pronunciation of Louisiana French is characterized by a general uniformity. In all regions, for example, the /h/ that has disappeared from Standard French, known as the *h aspiré*, is pronounced in words of Germanic origin such as *honte* (shame). Vowels that precede nasal consonants (e.g., /n/ and /m/) are generally nasalized themselves; this is the same phenomenon that exists in English, where the vowel in *ran* is different than that in *rat* (this is easily verified by pinching one's nose shut and pronouncing both words in sequence; a vibration can be felt when pronouncing the vowel in *ran*). And as previously noted, Louisiana French generally lacks the palatal nasal /ɲ/, the sound found in words like *campagne* or the Spanish *año*. As noted earlier, Louisiana Regional French overwhelmingly attests the apical tap/flapped *r* (/ɾ/), though a few areas that were either home to speakers of Plantation Society French or closely connected to them (notably, Grand Isle and Plaquemines Parish) instead use the uvular *r* found in Standard French (Picone 1998, 2015). There is evidence that the uvular *r* may previously have been more widespread (Dajko and Klingler 2013), suggesting that the general uniformity observed is relatively recent. Nevertheless, many features are variable, even within a single region. For example, a frequently heard alternation in Louisiana French is that of [z] pronounced [ʒ] (and likewise the voiceless counterpart [s] alternates with [ʃ]), so that *chose* becomes *choge* or *chez* becomes homophonous with *c'est*. In Terrebonne-Lafourche, this phenomenon particularly affects the words *chose* (and its composite *quelque chose*) and *chez*, though my data also include attestations of *zuste* (*juste*), *soisir* (*choisir*), *ch'était* (*c'était*), *chigner* (*signer*), and *Etage-Units* (*Etats-Unis*), among others. In other areas, including Evangeline Parish, I have encountered such examples as *chaige* (*chaise*) and *chemige* (*chemise*). The feature seems to be stable at least for some lexical items for some speakers and variable for others. *Chez* was nearly always *sez* in Terrebonne-Lafourche, but I did encounter a few instances of *chez*. Likewise, a speaker I interviewed in Evangeline Parish systematically pronounced *chemige* rather than *chemise*. Conversely, *choge* varied considerably in my data from Terrebonne Parish, with speakers using the [ʒ] variant (i.e., *choge*) 27 percent of the time during a translation exercise, when they were (presumably) paying careful attention to their speech and using their most standard register, and 14 percent in spontaneous speech. These numbers are hard to compare, given the large number of people who did not use the word at all in either context. Still, enough speakers used both forms, even in the same context, to show that the feature is variable and to suggest that it may be affected by style, at least for some speakers.

Another variant that may or may not be related to style is the alternation of the pronunciation of orthographic *oi* between [wɑ] and [wɛ] or [ɛ] in words such as *boîte* (box) and *droite* (right). The [wɛ] pronunciation was historically prestigious in France until it was overtaken by /wɑ/; it survives in a number of regional Frenches, such as that spoken in Quebec, and in Haitian Creole. In those places, it is applied in most contexts; for example, in Quebec, *moi* may be pronounced *mweh*. In Louisiana, however, the [wɛ] pronunciation is restricted to a very small number of words. In my data from Terrebonne/Lafourche, it affects only *boîte* and *droite* (*bwette* and *drette*) and the subjunctive forms of *avoir* (to have), *être* (to be), and *voir* (to see), which are *avoye*, *soye*, and *voye* (effectively [avwɛj] *avway*, [swɛj] *sway*, and [vwɛj] *vway*), respectively. Elsewhere in the state, this pronunciation occurs in a few more words, including *froid*, pronounced *frette*. At least in Terrebonne/Lafourche, both forms are attested, sometimes in the speech of a single speaker (except in the subjunctive forms, which are always pronounced [wɛ]). It is unclear whether the variation results from style (i.e., the standard pronunciation presumably would prevail in careful contexts, as is true for other style-based variation in the area) given the near absence of the words in recordings of casual speech and the difficulty in steering conversation to elicit them more than once.

CORRELATES TO VARIATION AND ATTEMPTS TO EXPLAIN DISTRIBUTION

Some variation in Louisiana patterns fairly neatly in terms of geography. For example, the use of *arbre* or *bois* (tree) roughly follows the path of the Atchafalaya River, with *bois* used almost exclusively to the east and *arbre* to the west. More often, however, the variation does not follow any neat geographic line, and scholars have often been stymied in their attempts to explain the distribution. For example, as noted above, while much of Louisiana uses *quoi* (what) and *qui* (who), in some areas (such as Terrebonne and Lafourche Parishes and nearly always in Evangeline and Avoyelles Parishes), only *qui* is used to express both concepts. Rottet (2004) further notes that the use of the *-ont* ending on verbs when conjugated in the third person plural using the pronouns *ils* (e.g., *ils dansont* [they dance]) patterned alongside *quoi* in areas of heavy Acadian settlement. However, research by Picone (2006) and Dajko (2007) shows that *quoi* and *-ont* are also found together in areas where nearly no Acadians have settled, such as Natchitoches Parish, significantly mitigating the explanatory value of Rottet's analysis. In fact, Louisiana presents a number of conundrums when historic demographics are considered. Acadians settled heavily in the area around Lafayette and later around modern Thibodaux. However, in Lafayette, the alternation of /ʒ/ with /h/ (rendering *jamais* as *hamais* or *manger* as *manher*), a feature common to Acadian French (Hewson 2000), is unknown; that feature is heavily documented in lower Lafourche Parish between Golden Meadow and Larose,[11] which had fewer Acadian settlers, and its incidence rapidly declines outside of the core area. It is still well attested, though at a lower rate, in lower Terrebonne Parish; however, it is almost entirely limited to the lower reaches of those two parishes. Only sporadic attestations occur in the otherwise very standard-like French on Grand Isle (only thirty minutes away), and it is rare even in the upper reaches of Lafourche Parish, where the second wave of Acadian immigrants settled in the 1780s. Of course, the feature is not exclusive to Acadian French (Hewson 2000), so its presence in lower Lafourche might be explained as the result of the presence of people from some other region that attests the feature. Moreover, the group of Acadians who settled in upper Lafourche had spent a generation in western France, some of them in cities (La Rochelle, Bordeaux) essentially adjacent to the region of France in which the feature has been documented (Brasseaux 1987; Horiot and Gauthier 1995:219) and in which some of the Acadians acquired spouses before arriving in Louisiana. It is possible that these later Acadians took the feature down the bayou with them and it was subsequently lost in the upper reaches of the parish, as it had been elsewhere for earlier Acadian arrivals. It remains odd, however, that a feature well documented in Acadia should appear in Louisiana in an area where fewer Acadians settled and be absent or nearly absent from areas of heavy Acadian settlement, and this distribution highlights the difficulties of tracking the dialectal origins of a feature. Other Acadian features are also present only in limited form in Louisiana. For example, the palatalization of [k] and [g] to [tʃ] and [dʒ] before front vowels in casual contexts, so that *qui* becomes *tchi* and *coeur* becomes *tchoeur*, is systematic in Acadian French (Hewson 2000) but lexicalized in Louisiana, where it occurs in very few words and in some regions, at least, is not variable. In Terrebonne-Lafourche, for example, I encountered it only in *geuele* (mouth),[12] *queue* (tail), and *cul* (ass), which were nearly always *djeule*, *tcheu*, and *tchul*, respectively (three interviewees used the standard *queue*, and one also used *gueule*). I was repeatedly assured that some people would pronounce *guèpe* (wasp) as *djèpe*, but in hundreds of interviews, I encountered it only rarely, suggesting it is limited to only a handful of speakers. In other regions, I have also encountered sporadic attestations such as *tchuisse* (*cuisse* [thigh]) or *tchuisine* (*cuisine* [kitchen]). Given the retention of a nonstandard feature such as the ʒ/h alternation in the Lower Lafourche

Basin, however, we might also expect to see more [k] replaced with [tʃ], but we do not. Moreover, a host of Acadian features, such as the pronunciation of /ɔ̃/ as [ɛ̃y] so that *non* sounds to the English ear much like a very nasal *néo* simply do not appear anywhere in Louisiana.

Conversely, linguistic variation sometimes clearly follows geographical provenance. Baronian (2010) has shown that such features as the assibilation of /t/ and /d/ before front high vowels (*du* becomes *dzu*, for example, and *petit* is *petsit*), though weaker in Louisiana than in Quebec, can be traced to the heavily Quebecois ancestry in Evangeline Parish, where it is found. The conundrums, however, highlight the fact that the dialects that found their way to Louisiana were often very similar and that what appears to be leveling may simply result from the presence of a now nonstandard feature in multiple dialects.

Variation also exists along ethnic lines. Dajko (2009) has shown that systematic differences exist between white and American Indian speakers of Louisiana Regional French in the Lower Lafourche Basin. The most important of these differences include the use of a single pronoun for both male and female subjects in the third person singular (*il*, the masculine pronoun, is used to refer to both men and women), increased progressive nasalization among Indian speakers (so that *mais* is pronounced identically to *main*), and the replacement of /ʒ/ with /z/ in careful speech, resulting in a three-way divide wherein /ʒ/ may be /h/ in casual contexts and /z/ in very formal ones. Only the use of feminine *il* is exclusive to the Indian community, though not all speakers use it. Most features that vary are not exclusive to a given community and are only more common in the speech of one region or group than another.

FRENCH VARIATION, LABELS, AND IDENTITY

Though Louisiana Regional French may vary along ethnic lines, this correlation is not perfect. Moreover, the labels speakers give their language often ignore linguistic features altogether. While all speakers generically use *French* to refer to any form of the language, speakers may also use ethnically based terms when they wish to differentiate their language from that spoken elsewhere in the world or when they wish to signal its importance to their ethnic identity. Klingler (2003b) has shown that while Louisiana Creole tends to be spoken by people who identify as black and Louisiana Regional French tends to be spoken by those who identify as white, there are many white speakers of Louisiana Creole, just as there are black speakers of Louisiana Regional French. However, white speakers tend to call their language *Cajun French*, in accordance with the way they identify ethnically, even if they speak something that linguists would label *Creole*, and black speakers tend to label both themselves and their language *Creole*, even if they speak something that linguists would call *Louisiana Regional French*. When questioned, speakers demonstrate that they are well aware of this discrepancy, and many will happily explain that while everyone in their area speaks the same way, they give their language different names. Conversely, people are also very capable of identifying Creole speakers, even if those speakers call themselves and their language *Cajun French*, and vice versa. This is particularly true in Bayou Boeuf and in nearby Des Allemands, where speakers have frequently asked me to explain how people who grew up as neighbors can speak so differently from each other.

Louisiana francophones are also sensitive to differences within a single variety. In my research, I found that prairie residents were very good at identifying speakers from the bayou based on a twenty-second sound recording, and speakers from upper Lafourche immediately recognized lower-bayou residents but were hard-pressed to explain just what had tipped them off. This ability to easily identify differences does not translate to giving the language a different name, however. If anything, Louisiana francophones tend to dismiss the differences as lacking in meaning. In short, linguistic variation is recognized as interesting (often even amusing) but not generally indicative of anything important.[13] After I completed a 2008 presentation detailing the variation found in Lafourche Parish that showed a neat up-the-bayou versus down-the-bayou separation for several features, a resident who had participated in the study told me that my students and I had "made too much of" the variations we found.

One exception to both of these tendencies (at least until very recently) is the French spoken by American Indians. Though the language as it is spoken in the Lafourche Basin does attest some clear differences from that spoken by Cajuns in the area, and residents are conscious of at least the use of feminine *il* and may be subconsciously aware of other variation,[14] the Indians I interviewed in 2007 almost always called their language *Cajun French* if they gave it a more specific label than *French*. In recent years, however, I have seen more frequent mentions of *Indian French* or *Houma French* from residents of the lower bayous, sometimes with insistence that the differences result from influence from (an) indigenous language(s).

The fact that ethnic groups may rebrand French under an ethnically based name indicates the strong role that French (in any form) plays in the creation of ethnic identity for several different groups, including the indigenous population. In Terrebonne-Lafourche, for example, French is strongly associated with Indianness despite the application of the *Cajun* label and despite the language's association with Cajun identity among both insiders and outsiders. As one interviewee noted, "I used to work as a school substitute teacher. A lot of the younger generation didn't want to learn French, because automatically when you talk French, you was known as Indian. And a lot of them didn't want to be recognized as Indian." Another interviewee noted that Indian identity was eroded when children were sent to school, where they were forbidden from speaking French, a sentiment echoed in the Pointe au Chien Indian Tribe's petition for federal acknowledgment (PACIT 2005:9). I have also encountered this association of Indian identity with the French language (though not exclusively) at a Tunica-Biloxi powwow in Marksville in 2011, where a mother-son-daughter trio of singer-storytellers provided entertainment in both Tunica and French. After finishing a song in French, they explained that it was also a Tunica heritage language, as important to them as any other. This sentiment was echoed by participants at Tulane's 2014 Conference on Language Revitalization, who thanked a speaker who was a member of the Pointe au Chien Indian Tribe for including French in her discussion.

French has been spoken in Louisiana for more than three hundred years. Although it has undergone many modifications during this time, it remains recognizable as French, regardless of where and by whom it is spoken. Generations of people—some of French extraction, some not; some indigenous, some not—grew up speaking it and in doing so made it their own. Indeed, even nonspeakers having no known ancestral connection to French and having virtually no command of French are aware that the language occupies a special place in the collective identity of Louisiana, setting the state apart from the rest of the nation. In Louisiana, French belongs to everyone.

NOTES

The research presented in this chapter was supported in part by grants from the National Science Foundation (Doctoral Dissertation Improvement Grant 0745971), the Louisiana Board of Regents (Special Incentives for Doctoral Students at Severely Impacted Campuses Program), and the Jacobs Research Fund Kinkade Grant, Whatcom Museum, Bellingham, Washington.

1. However, a number of residents, predominantly young activists, strongly prefer the term *Louisiana French* as a neutral, more inclusive term than *Cajun French*.

2. It is also found in Louisiana Regional French in some areas.

3. The varieties often overlap considerably and may be hard to distinguish from each other (Klingler 1994).

4. These reasons include that many speakers of Louisiana Regional French are not of Acadian descent and that many claim African ancestry and often label their language *Creole*, though linguistically it would not be classified as such. Others identify as American Indian.

5. The term *Louisiana French* is problematic in this context because speakers of each of the three varieties of French call their language simply *French* (as well as by other names), and Louisiana French could easily be misunderstood to be any one of the three. Consequently, here I use *Louisiana Regional French*, though this term is never used in conversation with Louisiana residents.

6. The descendants of Latin in what is now France are roughly classified as either *oïl* or *oc* dialects, based on the regional variation in the pronunciation of the ancestral Vulgar Latin word for "yes." The northern *oïl* eventually became the modern *oui*.

7. For a variety of issues related to appraising the French of the founding population along the Gulf Coast and Lower Mississippi, see Picone 2015.

8. Though these terms are not limited to these parishes. The *Dictionary of Louisiana French* (Valdman et al. 2010) is not an exhaustive resource but nevertheless provides examples of regional attestation for each term it documents.

9. This is true of all the pronouns; it is not exclusive to the third-person plural.

10. Also the Standard French pronunciation for both; the spellings are retained from a time long past when the final *-e* and *-ent* were pronounced.

11. And in that area, unlike in Acadia, other sibilants may also be replaced with /h/, though at a much lower rate. Most frequently, though not at the rate that it occurs with /ʒ/, /z/ is affected. *Nous-autres* thus becomes *nouh-autres*, and *maison* becomes *maihon*. The voiceless counterparts /ʃ/ and /s/ are also affected, though relatively rarely.

12. In Standard French, *geuele* refers to an animal's mouth. In my research in Terrebonne-Lafourche, however, asking people to translate "The dog had a bone in his mouth" elicited only *bouche*, which in France is used to refer solely to people's mouths. I finally got *djeule* by asking people to translate "That woman has a big mouth"—that is, she talks too much. The term clearly is used derisively.

13. There are certainly a few exceptions to this rule. Michael D. Picone (personal communication, May 27, 2018) notes that in Terrebonne and Lafourche Parishes in the 1990s, speakers who identified as Houma claimed significant differences between their French and that of their Cajun neighbors, though they did not give it a different label. They further identified indigenous lexical items (e.g., *chaoui* ['raccoon'])—all of which are also found in the speech of Cajuns across the state—as diagnostic items. But in the roughly 150 interviews I conducted, I only occasionally encountered anyone (Indian or Cajun) who claimed a difference in the way Indians and Cajuns spoke, and those who did make such claims noted that any differences were minor. No one who made the claim pointed to indigenous words of any sort as examples. Instead, they noted the use of feminine *il*. Picone may have encountered a few militants who were deeply concerned with distinguishing their group from others. Their claims are ultimately borne out (though not in the way they asserted), but the feeling that differences lack significance generally predominates.

14. A perception exercise I conducted suggests that residents may be able to tell apart Cajun and Indian speakers; however, the features used to identify speakers can only be guessed at pending further research on the topic.

WORKS CITED

Baronian, Luc V. 2010. "L'Apport Linguistique Québécois en Louisiane." In *Actes du XXVe Congrès International de Linguistique et de Philologie Romanes*, edited by Maria Iliescu, Heidi Siller-Runggaldier, and Paul Danler, 7:231–40. Berlin: Mouton de Gruyter.

Battye, Adrian, Marie-Anne Hintze, and Paul Rowlett. 1992. *The French Language Today*. New York: Routledge.

Brasseaux, Carl A. 1987. *The Founding of New Acadia*. Baton Rouge: Louisiana State University Press.

Brasseaux, Carl A. 1992. *Acadian to Cajun: Transformation of a People, 1803–1877*. Jackson: University Press of Mississippi.

Brasseaux, Carl A. 2005. *French, Cajun, Creole, Houma: A Primer on Francophone Louisiana*. Baton Rouge: Louisiana State University Press.

Dajko, Nathalie. 2007. "French in the Cane River Region: Implications for Louisiana French Dialectology." Paper presented at the Southeastern Conference on Linguistics, Natchitoches, LA, April 13.

Dajko, Nathalie. 2009. "Ethnic and Geographic Variation in the Lafourche Basin." PhD diss., Tulane University.

Dajko, Nathalie, and Thomas A. Klingler. 2013. "La Consonne Rhotique Apicale et Dorsale en Louisiane Francophone." Paper presented at the Journées Phonologie du Français Contemporain, Paris, December 7.

Hewson, John. 2000. *The French Language in Canada*. Munich: Lincom Europa.

Horiot, Brigitte, and Pierre Gauthier. 1995. "Les Parlers du Sud-Ouest." In *Français de France et Français du Canada: Les Parlers de l'Ouest de la France, du Québec et de l'Acadie*, edited by Pierre Gauthier and Thomas Lavois, 187–249. Lyon: Université Lyon III Jean Moulin, Centre d'Études Linguistiques Jacques Goudet.

Klingler, Thomas A. 1994. "L'Insécurité Linguistique dans les Communautés Francophones Périphériques." *Cahiers de l'Institut de Linguistique de Louvain* 20 (2): 123–29.

Klingler, Thomas A. 1998. "Français Cadien, Créole des Blancs, et Créole des Noirs en Louisiane." In *Français d'Amérique: Variation, Créolisation, Normalisation*, edited by Patrice Brasseur, 206–16. Avignon: Centre d'Études Canadiennes, Université d'Avignon.

Klingler, Thomas A. 2003a. *If I Could Turn My Tongue Like That: The Creole of Pointe Coupée Parish*. Baton Rouge: Louisiana State University Press.

Klingler, Thomas A. 2003b. *Language Labels and Language Use among Cajuns and Creoles in Louisiana*. https://repository.upenn.edu/pwpl/vol9/iss2/8/.

Klingler, Thomas A. 2009. "How Much Acadian Is There in Cajun?" In *Acadians and Cajuns: The Politics and Culture of French Minorities in North America*, edited by Ursula Mathis-Mosen and Günter Beschof, 91–103. Innsbruck: Innsbruck University Press.

Klingler, Thomas A., and Nathalie Dajko. 2006. "Louisiana Creole at the Periphery." In *History, Society, and Variation*, edited by Clancy J. Clements, Thomas A. Klingler, Deborah Piston-Hatlen, and Kevin J. Rottet, 11–28. Amsterdam: Benjamins.

Klingler, Thomas A., Michael D. Picone, and Albert Valdman. 1997. "The Lexicon of Louisiana French." In *French and Creole in Louisiana*, edited by Albert Valdman, 145–81. New York: Plenum.

Lodge, Anthony. 2004. *A Sociolinguistic History of Parisian French*. Cambridge: Cambridge University Press.

Marshall, Margaret. 1989. "The Origins of Creole French in Louisiana." *Regional Dimensions* 8:23–40.

Neumann, Ingrid. 1985. "Bemerkungen zur Genese des Kreolischen von Louisiana und seiner historischen Relation zum Kreolischen von Haiti." In *Akten des 1. Essener Kolloquiums über "Kreolsprachen und Sprachkontakte,"* edited by Norbert Boretzky, Werner Enninger, and Thomas Stolz, 87–113. Bochum: Brockmeyer.

PACIT (Pointe au Chien Indian Tribe). 2005. Petition for Federal Recognition, Part II. Copy provided by Patty Ferguson-Bohnee.

Picone, Michael D. 1996. "Stratégies Lexicogéniques Franco-Louisianaises." *Plurilinguismes* 11:63–99.
Picone, Michael D. 1998. "Historic French Diglossia in Louisiana." Paper presented at the Annual Meeting of the Southeastern Conference on Linguistics, University of Southwestern Louisiana, Lafayette, March 26–28.
Picone, Michael D. 2006. "Le Français Louisianais hors de l'Acadiana." *Revue de l'Université de Moncton* 37 (2): 221–31.
Picone, Michael D. 2015. "French Dialects of Louisiana: A Revised Typology." In *New Perspectives on Language Variety in the South: Historical and Contemporary Approaches*, edited by Michael D. Picone and Catherine Evans Davies, 267–87. Tuscaloosa: University of Alabama Press.
Rottet, Kevin J. 2004. "Inanimate Interrogatives and Settlement Patterns in Francophone Louisiana." *French Language Studies* 14:169–88.
Usner, Daniel H., Jr. 1992. *Indians, Settlers, and Slaves in a Frontier Exchange Economy: The Lower Mississippi Valley before 1783*. Chapel Hill: University of North Carolina Press.
Valdman, Albert, Kevin J. Rottet, Barry Jean Ancelet, Richard Guidry, Amanda LaFleur, Thomas A. Klingler, Tamara Lindner, Michael D. Picone, and Dominique Ryon. 2010. *Dictionary of Louisiana French: As Spoken in Cajun, Creole, and Native American Communities*. Jackson: University Press of Mississippi.
VielleLouisiane. 2016. *Louisiana French or French?* Audio recording. https://www.youtube.com/watch?v=HvcRWHIo-rU.

CHAPTER 7

THE LOUISIANA CREOLE LANGUAGE TODAY

THOMAS A. KLINGLER

Louisiana Creole is a French-based language that bears many resemblances to the other French Creoles of the world and to Haitian Creole in particular. It is spoken today by rapidly dwindling numbers of people in several noncontiguous regions of Louisiana that constitute linguistic islands. These include the area around False River in Pointe Coupee Parish and the German and Acadian coasts of the Mississippi River in St. James and St. John-the-Baptist Parishes. The largest concentrations of speakers today, however, are found along and near Bayou Teche in southwest Louisiana, in towns such as Cecilia, Henderson, Parks, St. Martinville, and Catahoula (see figure 6.1). The language formerly was much more widely spoken across south Louisiana and beyond, including in New Orleans and on the north shore of Lake Pontchartrain as well as along the Cane River in Natchitoches Parish, in coastal Mississippi, and in the Mobile, Alabama, area (see, e.g., Marshall 1989; Klingler and Dajko 2006).

There are no reliable figures for the current number of speakers of Louisiana Creole; the 2013 US Census Bureau estimate of 6,706 speakers is probably not far off, though it likely overstates the number (US Census Bureau 2009–13). The labels that speakers use to identify their language variety do not always correspond to those that linguists use. (For a discussion of the problem of language labels and ethnic labels in Louisiana, see Klingler 2003b, 2009.) For example, speakers have a strong tendency to refer to their language using the same label that they use to identify themselves ethnically, meaning that many self-identified Creoles—who are typically black or of mixed racial background—also refer to the type of French they speak as *Creole*. In some cases, that language is what I refer to here as *Louisiana Creole*, but it is often much closer to the so-called Cajun French of the speakers' white neighbors. It is likely, therefore, that some of the 6,706 self-declared speakers of "Creole French" or "French Creole" were in fact speakers of Louisiana French.

Just as there are black (as well as American Indian) speakers of Louisiana French, there are white speakers of Louisiana Creole.[1] This is the case in most Creole-speaking areas and especially in Pointe Coupee Parish and in Cecilia, Henderson, and Catahoula. In areas where both Creole and Louisiana French are spoken, many people speak both varieties. That Louisiana French, though stigmatized in relation to Standard French and English, was traditionally considered more prestigious than Creole is evident in the tendency of bidialectal speakers to prefer Louisiana French in formal interview settings even when they have been asked to speak Creole and even when it is their native language (see, e.g., Klingler 2013).

The resemblances between the creole languages of Louisiana and Haiti, along with the fact that more than ten thousand former residents of the French colony of Saint-Domingue—which became Haiti after its independence in 1804—made their way to Louisiana in the early nineteenth century, have led some to assume that the Creole language was imported to Louisiana from Haiti (see, e.g., Maguire 1979:2; Trépanier 1988, 134; Brasseaux and Conrad 1992:xi). Neumann (1985a) and I (Klingler 2003a) argue, however, that the features shared by the two creoles are not sufficient to prove that Louisiana Creole represents an imported version of Haitian Creole. Evidence shows that a creole language existed in Louisiana well before the influx of former residents of Saint-Domingue (Klingler 2003a). The Spanish transcript of a 1795 slave trial, for example, refers to *Criollo* (Creole) as spoken by both enslaved people and whites in the Pointe Coupee post, and the first (albeit cursory) grammatical description of the language appeared in 1807 (Robin 1807) based on the author's visit to Louisiana several years earlier (Klingler 2003a:44–46; Ricard 1992). This linguistic and historical evidence supports the idea that Creole is indigenous to Louisiana and was not imported from elsewhere.

RESEARCH ON LOUISIANA CREOLE

The mid- to late nineteenth century saw the publication of a number of poems and songs in Creole that were either written or collected by white Louisianans familiar with the language (see Neumann-Holzschuh 1987). But scholars and other writers did not begin to take a scientific interest in Louisiana Creole until the 1880s, when three articles describing the language were published (Mercier 1880; Harrison 1882; Fortier 1884–85). While Mercier and Fortier, both of whom were native speakers of the language, treated it with a certain objectivity and even respect, Harrison's article betrays racist and classist attitudes toward both the language and its speakers—black and white—that were typical of the time.[2] In the early twentieth century, seven master's students at

Louisiana State University produced theses that either described some aspect of the language or recorded elements of folklore in it (Trappey 1916; Bourgeois 1927; Durand 1930; Lavergne 1930; Jarreau 1931; Bienvenue 1933; Perret 1933), and in 1935 Lane published an article on Louisiana Creole in the premier linguistics journal, *Language.*

The first book-length study of the language appeared in 1942, including a good if short description of the Creole of St. Martin Parish and a collection of proverbs, superstitions, poetry, and folktales as well as a series of La Fontaine's fables translated into Creole by the author, James Broussard. Broussard (1942:x) was a professor of Romance languages at Louisiana State University who by his own account learned the language from his nurse and spoke it "exclusively up to the age of seven" and then "bilingually with French" for the remainder of his life. While Broussard writes fondly of the language of his childhood, he also paternalistically ascribes childlike features not just to the language but also to its African American speakers, to whom he credits its creation: "Because of its naïve simplicity, its inherent melody, its soothing rhythm, this dialect has expressed the sweetest memories of my childhood. It is particularly dear to me. It should prove of interest to scholars who like to see what a simple, emotional, and highly imaginative race can fabricate out of a cultured language to serve as a medium for their thoughts" (x).

The first and to my knowledge only African American scholar to publish studies of Louisiana Creole was Raleigh Morgan (1959, 1960, 1970), who produced a series of articles on the subject. Although not a native speaker, Morgan was a trained linguist who based his studies on fieldwork conducted in St. Martin Parish.

As the field of creole studies within linguistics developed with increasing rapidity after the 1960s, more linguists turned their attention to Louisiana. In 1979, Albert Valdman, a specialist in French outside of France and in Haitian Creole, published an important article that analyzed Creole-French diglossia in nineteenth-century Louisiana plantation society as represented in Alfred Mercier's novel, *L'Habitation Saint-Ybars* (1881). German scholar Ingrid Neumann (1985b) published a landmark study of the Creole of Breaux Bridge. In addition to a thorough grammatical description of the language, Neumann's work included an examination of its history and development, an assessment of its sociolinguistic situation at the time, a collection of transcribed conversations and folktales, and a lexicon. Neumann also published an edited collection of nineteenth-century texts in Louisiana Creole (Neumann-Holzschuh 1987) and several articles exploring various aspects of the language (Neumann 1984, 1985a); more recently, she edited a collection of the Louisiana State University master's theses on Creole (Neumann-Holzschuh 2011).

Also in the 1980s, linguist Margaret M. Marshall published several articles on Louisiana Creole, including an analysis of the linguistics situation in St. James Parish in terms of a post-Creole continuum (Marshall 1987) and a description of the now-extinct Creole of Mon Louis Island, Alabama, the existence of which had previously been unknown to linguists (Marshall 1991).

Publications on the language grew more numerous in the following decade. Kevin J. Rottet (1992) produced a generative analysis of verb movement in Creole, and I published several articles and book chapters on various aspects of the language, including its origins and development, the relationship between its use and ethnic identity, and the question of how to best represent it orthographically (Klingler 1994a, b, 1996, 1997, 1998). Valdman (1992, 1993, 1996a, b) also published a series of articles on Creole as well an edited volume devoted to both the French and Creole languages in Louisiana (Valdman 1997). In her master's thesis and a book chapter, Karin Speedy (1994, 1995) explores the possibility that Louisiana Creole underwent two separate geneses, one along the Mississippi River and a later one in the Bayou Teche region, a hypothesis against which I have argued (Klingler 2000, 2003a). The most significant work to emerge in this period is undoubtedly the *Dictionary of Louisiana Creole* (Valdman et al. 1998), created by Valdman, Marshall, Rottet, and me. Based primarily on fieldwork conducted by the editors, it provides an extensive inventory of the lexicon of the language, though it is no longer in print; however, a PDF version is available on CD-ROM from the Creole Institute at Indiana University.

Research on Louisiana Creole has continued steadily into the twenty-first century. In *If I Could Turn My Tongue Like That: The Creole of Pointe Coupee Parish, Louisiana* (Klingler 2003), I sought to do for the Creole of Pointe Coupee Parish what Neumann (1985) had done for the Breaux Bridge region. Like Neumann's work, my volume includes a grammatical description as well as an examination of the origin and development of the language, an assessment of its sociolinguistic situation, and transcribed excerpts of interviews with speakers. I have also published articles on topics such as the sometimes-uncertain linguistic boundary between Louisiana French and Creole and the ambiguity of language labels such as *Cajun* and *Creole* (Klingler 2003b, 2005), while Dajko and I (Klingler and Dajko 2006) used data from geographically marginal Creole-speaking isolates such as Natchitoches, St. Tammany, and Plaquemines Parishes as a window onto the history of the language's development and spread. The new century also saw the emergence of a new generation of scholars working on the language, including Élsie Angélique Bergeron Gardner, who wrote a 2011 doctoral dissertation on nonverbal communication among Creoles in Pointe Coupee Parish, and Oliver Mayeux, a doctoral candidate at the University of Cambridge whose 2015 master's thesis examines the morphosyntax of "new" speakers of Creole—those who are learning as adults today. In 2017, he presented part of his doctoral research on number and gender agreement in the determiner phrase. N. A. Wendte at Tulane University is also completing a doctoral dissertation on Creole and French, with a focus on language and identity among self-described Creoles in southeast Texas and southwest Louisiana. In 2017, Wendte, Mayeux, and Herbert Wiltz (n.d.), a native speaker of Creole who published a series of language lessons in *Creole Magazine* in the early 1990s (see, e.g., Wiltz 1991), created a short pedagogical text on the language.

The work done on Louisiana Creole in the past 150 years represents a substantial body of research. Perhaps paradoxically, however, it is today both one of the most seriously endangered creole languages and among the most thoroughly described.

LINGUISTIC FEATURES

A few salient features most clearly distinguish Louisiana Creole from Standard French and especially Louisiana French, with which it shares many structural elements and most of its lexicon. (For more in-depth treatments of Louisiana Creole, see Broussard 1942; Neumann-Holzschuh 1985a; Valdman and Klingler 1997; Klingler 2003a.) Like all languages, Louisiana Creole is characterized by a great deal of variation linked to geography, style, ethnicity, and other factors. Here I distinguish between a type of Creole whose features are furthest removed from French, typically referred to as a *basilectal* variety in creole studies, and a *mesolectal* variety that shares a greater number of features with French. On the whole, the Creole of nineteenth-century texts such as those found in Neumann-Holzschuh (1987) is more basilectal in nature than the Creole spoken today, a circumstance that is likely the result of Creole speakers' prolonged contact with speakers of Louisiana French. This variation also correlates to some degree with race and ethnicity, as the Creole of whites tends to show more mesolectal features than the Creole of blacks. However, no one today speaks a purely basilectal Creole: all speakers use some mesolectal features but differ in how many and how often. (For further discussion of basilectal and mesolectal Creole, see Klingler 2003a, 2014; Neumann 1984, 1985b.)

The Sound System

The vowels of Louisiana Creole are the same as those of Louisiana French. However, in basilectal Creole, the vowels /y/ (as in *jus* [juice] and *sucre* [sugar]), /ø/ (as in *feu* [fire] and *creux* [hollow, deep]), and /œ/ (as in *sœur* [sister] and *cœur* [heart]), which are pronounced with the tongue positioned toward the front of the mouth while the lips are simultaneously rounded, are unrounded to /i/, /e/, and /ɛ/ (as in *frère* [brother]), respectively. Thus, for example, *jus* and *feu* are pronounced like *ji* and *fé*. Both Louisiana Creole and Louisiana French differ from Standard French in showing widespread nasalization of vowels that occur before a nasal consonant such as *n* or *m* (a phenomenon known as regressive nasalization), so that the bolded vowels in *je**u**ne* (young) and *p**o**mme* (apple) are pronounced with a strong nasal quality. Unlike Louisiana French, however, Louisiana Creole also shows widespread progressive nasalization, in which vowels that follow a nasal consonant are nasalized (e.g., the bold vowel in *conn**a**ît* [know]).

Louisiana Creole also shares its consonants with Louisiana French. In both languages, the *r* is most commonly pronounced with the tip of the tongue in contact with the alveolar ridge, similar to the *r* of Spanish. In the moribund Creole of New Orleans and St. Tammany Parish, however, the *r* is similar to the uvular, as in Standard French. In basilectal Creole, *r* is dropped before another consonant or word finally: *frère* (brother) > *frè*; *parler* (to speak) > *paler*.

GRAMMAR

Nouns, Determiners, and Adjectives

Nouns: One feature that most clearly distinguishes Louisiana Creole from Louisiana French is the tendency to add (agglutinate) to the beginning of some nouns a full syllable that derives from a definite or partitive determiner in French. In Creole, however, this element has lost its original function and merely become an integral part of the noun without changing its meaning. This is demonstrated by the fact that the agglutinated noun can be preceded by another determiner or adjective, as in *mo la-maison* (my house), in which *la-maison* derives from French *la* (the) + *maison* (house) but in Creole is treated as an unanalyzable unit in which *la* has no discernable function. The French plural definite determiner *les* and partitive determiners *du* and *des* can also be agglutinated in this way: *to les-tripes* (your intestines), *un gros di-bois* (a big tree) (in which the rounded vowel /y/ of *du* has been unrounded to /i/), *six des-œufs* (six eggs). Agglutination of these elements is highly variable and occurs much more rarely in mesolectal speech.

Gender on Nouns: As in Standard French, Louisiana French nouns have grammatical gender: each one is arbitrarily classified as either masculine or feminine, and determiners and adjectives that qualify them vary accordingly (e.g., *la maison* [the house, fem.] versus *le café* [the coffee, masc.]). In the Creole of nineteenth-century texts, nouns do not have grammatical gender, meaning that the same determiner and adjective forms are used for all nouns regardless of whether they are treated as masculine or feminine in French (e.g., French *ma farine* (my flour, fem.), *mon sac* (my bag, masc.) versus Creole *mo farine, mo sac*. Most speakers today, however, use gender marking in at least some contexts.

Determiners

In basilectal Creole, the singular indefinite determiner (or indefinite article) is *un* (pronounced [ɛ̃]), and plural indefiniteness is expressed by the absence of an article. Today most speakers also use a feminine form *une* [ɛ̃n] and often use the form *des*, as in French, to express plural indefiniteness.

The definite determiners (or definite articles) of basilectal Creole are singular *-la* and plural *-yé* placed after the noun, which differs significantly from the prenominal determiners *le* (masc.), *la* (fem.), and *les* (pl.) of French: Creole *chat-la* (the cat), *chat-yé* (the cats) versus French *le chat, les chats*. In function, the Creole definite determiner occupies an intermediate space between the definite and demonstrative determiners of French or English. Here again, however, many of today's speakers tend to replace these postnominal forms with their prenominal French equivalents.

Table 7.1 shows the possessive determiners (or possessive adjectives) of basilectal Louisiana Creole. The plural is formed by adding *-yé* after the noun: *to dents-yé* (your teeth). In mesolectal Creole, however, the pluralizer *-yé* tends to be discarded in favor of the French-like prenominal forms *mes, tes, ses* for the singular persons. Mesolectal Creole also frequently shows gender markings on the possessive determiners, although, as in French, this applies only to the singular persons: *ma, ta, sa*. In addition to these determiners, Creole has a series of emphatic possessive determiners that are identical in form to the possessive pronouns.

The forms of the demonstrative determiners (or demonstrative adjectives) vary by region. In Pointe Coupee Parish, the most common forms are *-ça-là* and *-ca-yé* placed after the noun (*n-homme-ça-là* [this/that man], *monde-ça-yé* [these/those people]), whereas in Breaux Bridge, the most common form of the plural is *les* + noun + *-ça-là/-là-la* (Klingler 2003a:181–83; Neumann 1985b:136).

Adjectives

Unlike French, in which most adjectives have distinct masculine and feminine forms, Creole adjectives typically do not show gender distinctions: French *un nouveau livre* (a new book, masc.), *une nouvelle maison* (a new house, fem.) versus Creole *un nouveau livre, un nouveau la-maison*. Feminine forms such as *nouvelle* are not uncommon among some speakers today, however.

Table 7.1. Possessive Determiners

Person	Singular	Plural
1	mo	no, nous
2	to	vous-autres
3	so	yé

Source: Klingler 2003a:186

Table 7.2. Personal Subject Pronouns

Person	Singular	Plural
1	mo	nous, nous-autres
2	to (informal)	vous-autres, 'ous-autres, 's-autres, vous, ou (formal)
3	li	yé

Source: Klingler 2003a:206

Table 7.3. Personal Emphatic and Nonsubject Pronouns

Person	Singular	Plural
1	mo, mon, moi, moin	nous-autres, 'ous-autres
2	toi	vous-autres, 'ous-autres
3	li	yé, ça

Source: Klingler 2003a:206

Pronouns

As can be seen by comparing tables 7.1, 7.2, and 7.3, considerable overlap occurs between the possessive determiners and the personal pronouns of Creole. The vowel of the subject forms *mo, to, li, vous, nous,* and *yé* is often dropped, especially before a following vowel, as these examples illustrate:[6]

> *To gain to la-montre encore?* (Do you still have your watch?)
> *Mo dis, "Vous est garder pou' vous madame?"* (I said, "Are you looking for your wife?")
> *Nous té connaît voler whiskey nous popa.* (We used to steal our father's whiskey.)
> *M'olé couri la chasse 'cureuil.* (I want to go squirrel hunting.)
> *T'as jamais connaît!* (You'll never know!)
> *Mon m' pas connait arien pou' li.* (I don't know anything about him.)
> *C'est ça l' dit nous-autres.* (That's what he told us.) (modified from Klingler 2003a:206–7)

Table 7.4 shows the possessive pronouns of Louisiana Creole. In a common mesolectal pronunciation of these pronouns, the sound [k] (represented by -qu-) is realized as [tʃ], represented by -tch-: *motchenne, totchenne*. This pronunciation makes it easier to see the origin of these forms in *mo, to, vo,* + *tienne*, which is the feminine of the second-person-singular possessive pronoun in French.

Table 7.4. Possessive Pronouns		
Person	Singular	Plural
1	moquenne	noquenne
2	toquenne (informal)	voquenne (formal)
3	soquenne	yéquenne
Source: Klingler 2003a:212		

The demonstrative pronouns in Pointe Coupee Parish are identical to the demonstrative determiners: *ça-la* (sing.), *ça-yé* (pl.):

*Mo gain en zyé. Mo pas gain passé un. . . . Mo gain juste **ça-là**.* (I have one eye. I only have one. I just have this one.)
***Ça-yé** ca READ et yé ca écrit.* (Those [people] can read and write.) (Klingler 2003a:317)

In Breaux Bridge, the most common forms of the demonstrative are *ci-là(-là)* in the singular and *cez-là(-là), lez-là(-la)* in the plural (Neumann 1985b:174).

Verbs

In the basilectal Creole of nineteenth-century texts, verbs typically have a single form in all contexts and are thus not conjugated at all. Today, all speakers use more than one form for some verbs. More specifically, Creole verbs today may be divided into two broad classes, those that have only a single form and those that have a long form in some contexts and a short form in others. Single-form verbs include *boit* (to drink), *connaît* (to know), *couri* (to go), *fait* (to do, make), *gain* (to have), and *olé* (to want), while verbs with two forms include *laime/laimé* (to like, love), *mange/mangé* (to eat), *ouv'/ouvert* (to open), and *vend/vende* (to sell).

The distribution of the long and short forms of two-form verbs is clear cut in the Creole of Breaux Bridge (Neumann 1985b:187–99): the short form is used in the imperative and to express a habitual or universal present (e.g., "We eat out every Friday" or "Vegetarians don't eat meat"), while the long form is used in all other contexts, including to express past tense, after another verb, and after the series of preverbal tense and aspect markers. The following examples illustrate the use of the long and short forms of the verb *to eat*:

> *To **manges** ça 'ec des gratons* (You eat that with cracklins)
> *Lapin **mangé** tout l'affaire* (Rabbit ate the whole thing) (modified from Neumann 1985b:195–96)

In the Creole of Pointe Coupee Parish, the use of long and short verb forms follows a similar pattern, but there is much greater variation. For example, whereas only the long verb form is used after the marker *té* in Breaux Bridge, in Pointe Coupee either verb form may be used after this marker. (For a detailed presentation of the distribution of long and short forms in Pointe Coupee, see Klingler 2003a:237–42.)

Preverbal Markers of Tense, Mood, and Aspect

Like other Creole languages of the world, Louisiana Creole expresses notions of tense, mood, and aspect primarily through the use of a series of markers placed before the verb rather than through a set of complex verb endings as in French (with the long verb forms constituting an exception to the absence of verb endings in Creole). The markers of Louisiana Creole are:

- *té*, the marker of "anteriority," which indicates a past state in the case of adjectives and stative verbs and a pluperfect or an habitual past before verbs expressing an action
- *apé/ap/est*, which expresses the progressive nature of an action; *est* is used only in Pointe Coupee
- *a/va/aller*, which expresses a future action, and *sa*, which expresses a future state; *aller* does not occur in Pointe Coupee in this function
- *sé*, which expresses the conditional (although *té* can also serve in this function)
- *bin* (been) is a borrowing from English that has a similar use in Creole, marking "an action or state that began before, and continued up to, a subsequent point in time" (Klingler 2003a:162–263)

It is possible to combine markers: for example, *té* + *apé* > *t'apé*, which expresses a past progressive. The following examples illustrate the use of these markers:

*Yé **té** si faim* (They were so hungry; = past state)

*C'est trist' éna des places nous passé ao yé . . . pas fini ôté dibri-là, ao STORM-là **té** passé* (It's sad, there were places we passed where they hadn't finished removing the debris, where the storm had passed; = pluperfect)

*Quand to **té** coupe des-cannes à la main* ([In the days] when you cut sugar-cane by hand; = habitual past)

*M'**apé** réponde* (I'm answering; = progressive)

*Doleau-là **est** galoper* (The water is running; = progressive)

*Mo **té est** danser* (I was dancing' = past progressive)

*Vous pas crois l'**a** chiner?* (Don't you think he'll win?; = future)

*Si mo **té** connait li té là, mo **sé** pas vini* (If I'd known he was there, I wouldn't have come; = conditional)

*Nous **té bin est** voler* (We had been stealing; = pluperfect progressive) (Klingler 2003a:256–63)

The Copula

An important way in which Louisiana Creole differs from Louisiana French but is similar to other creole languages is its use of the copula, which is typically absent in the present tense before adjectival, adverbial, and prepositional complements:

Li si __ doucement (He's so slow)
Mo sœur [sɛ] *__ malade* (My sister is sick)
To manman et to popa, yé __ ici? (Your mother and father, are they here?)
Mo frère [frɛ] *__ dans la court* (My brother is in the yard) (Klingler 2003a:289)

Whereas in nineteenth-century texts, the copula was also absent before noun predicates, today *c'est*, which Neumann (1985b:247) analyzes "as a form that is intermediate between a copula and a presentative," is nearly always used in this context.

*Mo **c'est** un docteur* (I'm a doctor)
*To **c'est** un Yankee?* (Are you a Yankee?) (Klingler 2003a:290)

Insofar as this feature makes Louisiana Creole closer to French, it is another example of the generally more mesolectal character of modern-day Creole as compared to that of the nineteenth century.

Creole also has a copula *yé* that occurs in clause-final position, such as in certain interrogative structures and cleft structures used for highlighting:

Qui l'heure [lɛ] *li yé?* (What time is it?)
C'est comme ça mo piti-yé yé (That's how my children are) (Klingler 2003a:295)

LEXICON

Louisiana Creole shares the vast majority of its lexicon with Louisiana French (see Klingler, Picone, and Valdman 1997), although the forms of some words are altered in basilectal Creole—for example, through the unrounding of rounded vowels and through agglutination on nouns. However, a small number of lexical items have very different forms in the two varieties and thus constitute one of the clearest ways of distinguishing them, as table 7.5 illustrates. While the Creole forms are almost never heard in these meanings in Louisiana French, for some items, many Creole speakers also use forms that are closer to those of Louisiana French, such as *pé/peut* for "can, to be able to," *aller* for "to go," and *vé/veut* for "to want."

Table 7.5. Key Lexical Differences between Louisiana Creole and Louisiana French		
Louisiana Creole	**Louisiana French**	**English**
capab	pouvoir	can, to be able to
couri	aller	to go
gain	avoir	to have
olé	vouloir	to want

The primary source of the lexicon of Louisiana Creole and Louisiana French is the regional and popular varieties of French spoken in Louisiana during the colonial period. For example, *grouiller* (to move), *espérer* (to wait), and *rester* (to live, inhabit) are widely attested in these meanings in various French dialects but do not correspond to Standard French usage, which prefers *bouger*, *attendre*, and *habiter*, respectively. In addition to words inherited from regional and popular French, Louisiana French and Creole have borrowed a great number of items from various other languages. (For more on the origins of the Louisiana French lexicon, see Read 1931.)

These include Native American languages (*bayou*, *caouenne* [snapping turtle], *chaoui* [raccoon], *maringouin* [mosquito], *pacane* [pecan]), African languages (*cala* [rice fritter], *gombo* [gumbo, okra]), Spanish (*tchaurisse* [chorizo], *pobon* [jar]), and English (*char* [car], *drive, game, gone, padna* [friend < partner], *stove, truck*). Not surprisingly, a great number of borrowings from Native American languages are in the domain of nature, referring to flora, fauna, and other natural phenomena unknown to Europeans when they arrived in the New World, while modern technology is heavily represented in the borrowings from English.

THE TWENTY-FIRST CENTURY

Given Louisiana Creole's demographic picture, its future prospects are not bright. Most remaining speakers are elderly, and with very rare exceptions, the language is not being transmitted to younger generations in the home. Of the fifty people I interviewed for my 2003 study of Pointe Coupee Creole (Klingler 2003a), only a handful were still living in 2018, and finding Creole speakers in the area has become difficult. The situation is less dire in the Bayou Teche region, where more speakers reside, but even there, the language is rarely being passed on to children, placing its future in doubt. Nevertheless, previous predictions of the death of Louisiana Creole have proven premature (Klingler 2003:xxxiii), and the language may live on well into the future.[3]

Efforts to revalorize and revitalize the Louisiana Creole language have, at least until recently, not benefited from some of the advantages enjoyed by similar efforts on behalf of Louisiana (Cajun) French. The most obvious reason is the much greater demographic weight of those who consider themselves Cajuns and those who speak "Cajun" French. This demographic importance, along with the fact that self-identified Cajuns are usually white and have thus not suffered from the same racial discrimination that for so long marginalized the blacks and Creoles of color who make up a significant portion of the Creole-speaking population, has translated into greater visibility and political influence. Although the Council for the Development of French in Louisiana (CODOFIL), a state agency founded in 1968 to preserve and promote French, was long criticized for focusing on Standard French rather than Louisiana French, it became associated with the Cajun community and the promotion of its culture and heritage (see Henry 1997; Bernard 2003). CODOFIL's embrace of things Cajun is part of a broader trend that began around the 1960s and has witnessed the transformation of Cajun people, culture, and language from targets of ridicule and stigmatization to sources of pride.[4] The results of this transformation are visible in the commodification of the Cajun label on food, music, and all manner of other products.

While similar efforts have sought to promote Creole culture and language, they have generally come later and been less visible than those benefiting the

Cajun community. One obstacle confronting such efforts is the complex history and use of the word *Creole* itself. Although it historically referred to people born in the Louisiana colony but whose origins lay elsewhere—typically in France or, in the case of the enslaved population, Africa—its meaning was highly contested in the post–Civil War period, when whites who had always considered themselves Creole insisted that the term applied solely to them and could not be and never had been applied to blacks or people of mixed race despite ample historical evidence to the contrary (see Dominguez 1986). Today, the term is most commonly understood to refer to African Americans or persons of mixed race (often referred to as Creoles of color) who are of Catholic and francophone background, even if they may have changed religious affiliation and now speak only English. Because of the multiple meanings of the term, Creole organizations that have formed over the last twenty-five years or so have often faced the question of just who they consider Creoles to be, and their history has not been devoid of racial tensions, whether between white and nonwhite members or between black and lighter-skinned Creole of color members.

The Creole organizations that have formed over the past two to three decades are CREOLE Inc., based in the Lafayette area; the Creole Heritage Center, based at Northwestern State University in Natchitoches and serving the long-standing Creole community of the Cane River area; Les Créoles de Pointe Coupée, in New Roads; and the Louisiana Creole Research Association (LA Creole), in New Orleans. While Les Créoles de Pointe Coupée formed largely so that younger members of the Pointe Coupee Creole community could learn the Creole language from their elders (Gardner 2016), the other organizations have broader agendas and have focused only tangentially on issues of language. In the early 1990s, CREOLE Inc. member Herbert Wiltz wrote a Creole lesson in the short-lived monthly *Creole Magazine*, but the column ended when the magazine ceased publication. The Creole Heritage Center announced a Creole-language documentation project on its website (https://creole.nsula.edu/creole-language/), but the only product of that project available so far is a video showing Creole people speaking what, from a linguistic point of view, is Louisiana French, not Louisiana Creole (Creole Heritage Center 2010).[5]

Yet the demand for opportunities to learn the Creole language remains strong, especially among younger Creoles who want to reclaim this part of their cultural heritage. To the extent that the demand is being met, it is primarily on the Internet, thanks above all to materials created by Christophe Landry, a Louisiana Creole from New Iberia who recently completed a doctorate in the United Kingdom. These materials include an electronic version of the *Dictionary of Louisiana Creole* (http://www.louisianacreoledictionary.com/) and a "Louisiana Creole/Kouri-Vini Practice Group" on Facebook (https://www.facebook.com/groups/LouisianaCreolePraticeGroup/), which at the time of this writing had

564 members. Landry's once-popular "Louisiana Creole Virtual Tutorials" site no longer exists, but a group of linguists and language activists have created a Memrise site featuring online Creole lessons (https://www.memrise.com/course/1046984/kouri-vini-louisiana-creole-language/).

Since the Creole language is not being passed on to younger generations in the home and few, if any, native speakers remain who are young enough to have children, the language's survival clearly depends on the increased availability of such language learning resources and the "new speakers" they create. As Mayeux (2015) shows, this Creole is bound to differ from that spoken natively by their ancestors. But these speakers' determination to reclaim the language testifies to it its continuing importance as a symbol of the Creole community's identity. Only time will tell whether the language will survive as a viable means of communication or eventually be reduced to playing a purely symbolic role.

NOTES

1. No American Indian community of Louisiana Creole speakers appears to currently exist, though it is very likely that some Indians spoke Creole at one time. For a study of French-speaking American Indians in Lafourche and Terrebonne parishes, see Dajko 2009.

2. According to Harrison (1882:289), "Illiterate white folk and Africans of the purest blood, catching by ear the more or less indistinct utterances of the landed and commercial aristocracy around them, have reproduced in their own way, otographically, so to speak the message delivered to their far from fastidious sensorium, producing a dialect resembling French in a fashion that suggest the relation between the *Æthiopica* of Uncle Remus and current English."

3. Nearly ninety years ago, Lafayette Jarreau (1931:vi) of Pointe Coupee Parish wrote that the Creole language, "theoretically speaking, will no longer exist anywhere in Louisiana in about fifty years from now."

4. CODOFIL has more recently embraced the Creole community and the Creole language, even if the agency's resources for helping to preserve either Louisiana French or Louisiana Creole are limited. Indeed, CODOFIL's mission has recently been redefined by Act 651: the agency's purpose is "to preserve, promote, and develop Louisiana's French **and Creole** culture, heritage, and language" (emphasis added), and the structure of the CODOFIL board has recently been changed to include members from the Creole community, one of whom is to be nominated by CREOLE Inc.

5. I do not mean to imply that the Center is mistaken in calling the language *Creole*, since this is the label often given to it by self-identified Creoles who speak it. However, based on this video, the project does not appear to be devoted—or at least not exclusively devoted—to the documentation of Louisiana Creole as I define it here.

WORKS CITED

Bienvenu, Charles Joseph. 1933. "The Negro-French Dialect of Saint Martin Parish." Master's thesis, Louisiana State University.

Bourgeois, Eugène Oliver. 1927. "Creole Dialect." Master's thesis, Louisiana State University.
Brasseaux, Carl A., and Glenn R. Conrad. 1992. Introduction to *The Road to Louisiana: The Saint-Domingue Refugees, 1792-1809*, edited by Carl A. Brasseaux and Glenn R. Conrad, vii-xviii. Lafayette: Center for Louisiana Studies, University of Southwestern Louisiana.
Broussard, James Francis. 1942. *Louisiana Creole Dialect*. Baton Rouge: Louisiana State University Press.
Creole Heritage Center. 2010. *Time to Learn French Creole*. Video recording. https://www.youtube.com/watch?v=9E9iHs6S47w.Dajko, Nathalie. 2009. "Ethnic and Geographic Variation in the French of the Lafourche Basin." PhD diss., Tulane University.
Durand, Sidney Joseph. 1930. "A Phonetic Study of the Creole Dialect." Master's thesis, Louisiana State University.
Fortier, Alcée. 1884-85. "The French Language in Louisiana and the Negro-French Dialect." *Transactions of the Modern Language Association of America* 1:96-111.
Gardner, Angélique Élsie Bergeron. 2011. "Nonverbal Communication among Pointe Coupee Creoles." PhD diss., Louisiana State University.
Gardner, Angélique Élsie Bergeron. 2016. Personal communication, January 7.
Harrison, J. A. 1882. "The Creole Patois of Louisiana." *American Journal of Philology* 3 (2): 285-96.
Jarreau, Lafayette. 1931. "Creole Folklore of Pointe Coupee Parish." Master's thesis, Louisiana State University.
Klingler, Thomas A. 1994a. "Langues Moribondes et Identité Ethnique: Le Cas du Créole Louisianais." *Etudes Créoles* 17 (1): 39-49.
Klingler, Thomas A. 1994b. "Norme, Tourisme, et Étiolement Linguistique Chez les Créolophones en Louisiane." *Cahiers de l'Institut de Linguistique de Louvain* 20 (2): 123-29.
Klingler, Thomas A. 1996. "Comment Écrire le Créole Louisianais?" *Plurilinguismes* 11:179-203.
Klingler, Thomas A. 1997. "Colonial Society and the Development of Louisiana Creole." In *Language Variety in the South Revisited*, edited by Cynthia Bernstein, Thomas Nunnally, and Robin Sabino, 140-51. Tuscaloosa: University of Alabama Press.
Klingler, Thomas A. 1998. "Français Cadien, Créole des Blancs et Créole des Noirs en Louisiane." In *Français d'Amérique: Variation, Créolisation, Normalisation*, edited by Patrice Brasseur, 205-15. Avignon: Centre d'Études Canadiennes, Université d'Avignon.
Klingler, Thomas A. 2000. "Louisiana Creole: The Multiple Geneses Hypothesis Reconsidered." *Journal of Pidgin and Creole Languages* 15 (1): 1-35.
Klingler, Thomas A. 2003a. *If I Could Turn My Tongue Like That: The Creole of Pointe Coupee Parish, Louisiana*. Baton Rouge: Louisiana State University Press.
Klingler, Thomas A. 2003b. *Language Labels and Language Use among Cajuns and Creoles in Louisiana*. https://repository.upenn.edu/pwpl/vol9/iss2/8/.
Klingler, Thomas A. 2005. "Le Problème de la Démarcation des Variétés de Langues en Louisiane: Étiquettes et Usages Linguistiques." In *Le Français en Amérique du Nord: État Present*, edited by Albert Valdman, Julie Auger, and Deborah Piston-Hatlen, 349-67. Saint-Nicolas, QC: Presses de l'Université Laval.
Klingler, Thomas A. 2009. "How Much Acadian Is There in Cajun?" In *Acadians and Cajuns: The Politics and Culture of French Minorities in North America*, edited by Ursula Mathis-Mosen and Günter Beschof, 91-103. Innsbruck: Innsbruck University Press.
Klingler, Thomas A. 2013. *Le Bijou sur le Bayou Teche*. Video recording. https://www.youtube.com/watch?v=QodpvU-Z2PI.
Klingler, Thomas A. 2014. "Variation Phonétique et Appartenance Ethnique en Louisiane Francophone." In *La Phonologie du Français: Normes, Périphéries, Modélisation: Mélanges pour*

Chantal Lyche, edited by Jacques Durand, Gjert Kristoffersen, and Bernard Laks, 289–305. Paris: Presses Universitaires de Paris Ouest.

Klingler, Thomas A., and Nathalie Dajko. 2006. "Louisiana Creole at the Periphery." In *History, Society, and Variation: Studies in Honor of Albert Valdman*, edited by Clancy J. Clements, Thomas A. Klingler, Deborah Piston-Hatlen, and Kevin J. Rottet, 11–28. Amsterdam: Benjamins.

Klingler, Thomas A., Michael Picone, and Albert Valdman. 1997. "The Lexicon of Louisiana French." In *French and Creole in Louisiana*, edited by Albert Valdman, 145–81. New York: Plenum.

Lane, George S. 1935. "Notes on Louisiana French II: The Negro-French Dialect." *Language* 11:5–16.

Lavergne, Remi. 1930. "A Phonetic Transcription of the Creole Negro's Medical Treatments, Superstitions, and Folklore in the Parish of Pointe Coupee." Master's thesis, Louisiana State University.

Maguire, Robert E. 1979. *Notes on Language Use among English and French Creole Speaking Blacks in Parks, Louisiana*. Saint-Nicolas, QC: Département de Géographie, Université Laval.

Marshall, Margaret M. 1987. "A Louisiana Creole Speech Continuum." *Regional Dimensions* 5:71–94.

Marshall, Margaret M. 1989. "The Origins of Creole French in Louisiana." *Regional Dimensions* 8:23–40.

Marshall, Margaret M. 1991. "The Creole of Mon Louis Island, Alabama, and the Louisiana Connection." *Journal of Pidgin and Creole Languages* 6 (1): 73–87.

Mayeux, Oliver. 2015. "New Speaker Language: The Morphosyntax of New Speakers of Endangered Languages." Master's thesis, University of Cambridge.

Mayeux, Oliver. 2017. "Agreement in Louisiana Creole: Quantitative Sociolinguistics in a Diachronic Corpus." Poster presented at the Language Sciences Symposium, University of Cambridge, November 21. http://www.academia.edu/35214652/Agreement_in_Louisiana_Creole_Quantitative_sociolinguistics_in_a_diachronic_corpus.

Mercier, Alfred. 1880. "Étude sur la Langue Créole en Louisiane." *Comptes-Rendus de l'Athénée Louisianais* 5:378–83.

Mercier, Alfred. 1881. *L'Habitation Saint-Ybars ; ou, Maîtres et Esclaves en Louisiane*. Introduction by Réginald Hamel. Montreal: Guérin, 1989.

Morgan, Raleigh, Jr. 1959. "Structural Sketch of Saint Martin Creole." *Anthropological Linguistics* 1 (8): 20–24.

Morgan, Raleigh, Jr. 1960. "The Lexicon of Saint Martin Creole." *Anthropological Linguistics* 2 (1): 7–9.

Morgan, Raleigh, Jr. 1970. "Dialect Leveling in Non-English Speech of Southwest Louisiana." In *Texas Studies in Bilingualism*, edited by Glenn G. Gilbert, 50–62. Berlin: De Gruyter.

Neumann, Ingrid. 1984. "Le Créole des Blancs en Louisiane." *Études Créoles* 6 (2): 63–78.

Neumann, Ingrid. 1985a. "Bemerkungen zur Genese des Kreolischen von Louisiana und seiner historischen Relation zum Kreolischen von Haiti." In *Akten des Ersten Essener Kolloquiums über Kreolsprachen und Sprachkontakte*, edited by Norbert Boretsky, Werner Enninger, and Thomas Stoltz, 87–113. Bochum: Brockmeyer.

Neumann, Ingrid. 1985b. *Le Créole de Breaux Bridge, Louisiane: Étude Morphosyntaxique, Textes, Vocabulaire*. Hamburg: Buske.

Neumann-Holzschuh, Ingrid, ed. 1987. *Textes Anciens en Créole Louisianais: Avec Introduction, Notes, Remarques sur la Langue et Glossaire*. Hamburg: Buske.

Neumann-Holzschuh, Ingrid, ed. 2011. *Morceaux Choisis du Folklore Louisianais: Matériaux pour l'Étude Diachronique du Créole de la Louisiane*. Hamburg: Buske.
Perret, Michael John. 1933. "A Study of the Syntax and Morphology of the Verb of the Creole Dialect of Louisiana." Master's thesis, Louisiana State University.
Read, William. 1931. *Louisiana-French*. Baton Rouge: Louisiana State University Press.
Ricard, Ulysses S., Jr. 1992. "The Pointe Coupee Slave Conspiracy of 1791." In *Proceedings of the Fifteenth Meeting of the French Colonial Historical Society, Martinique and Guadeloupe, May 1989*, edited by Patricia Galloway and Philip P. Boucher, 116–19. Lanham, MD: University Press of America.
Rottet, Kevin J. 1992. "Functional Categories and Verb Movement in Louisiana Creole." *Probus* 4 (3): 261–90.
Speedy, Karin. 1994. "Mississippi and Tèche Creole: A Demographic and Linguistic Case for Separate Genesis in Louisiana." Master's thesis, University of Auckland.
Speedy, Karin. 1995. "Mississippi and Tèche Creole: Two Separate Starting Points for Creole in Louisiana." In *From Contact to Creole and Beyond*, edited by Philip Baker, 97–111. London: University of Westminster Press.
Creole Heritage Center. 2010. *Time to Learn French Creole*. Video recording. https://www.youtube.com/watch?v=9E9iHs6S47w. Trappey, Adam Shelby Holmes. 1916. "Creole Folklore in Phonetic Transcription." Master's thesis, Louisiana State University.
U.S. Census Bureau. 2009–13. "American Community Survey Five-Year Estimate: Table B16001—Language Spoken at Home by Ability to Speak English for the Population Five Years and Older." https://factfinder.census.gov/faces/tableservices/jsf/pages/productview.xhtml?pid=ACS_13_5YR_B16001&prodType=table.
Valdman, Albert. 1979. "La Diglossie Français-Créole dans l'Univers Plantocratique." *Revue de Louisiane* 8:43–53.
Valdman, Albert. 1992. "On the Sociohistorical Context in the Development of Louisiana and Saint-Domingue Creoles." *Journal of French Language Studies* 2 (1): 75–95.
Valdman, Albert. 1993. "La Situation Actuelle du Créole en Louisiane." *Présence Francophone* 43:85–110.
Valdman, Albert. 1996a. "La Diffusion dans la Genèse du Créole Louisianais." *Études Créoles* 19 (1): 72–92.
Valdman, Albert. 1996b. "The Place of Louisiana Creole among New World French Creoles." In *Creoles of Color of the Gulf South*, edited by James Dorman, 144–65. Knoxville: University of Tennessee Press.
Valdman, Albert, ed. 1997. *French and Creole in Louisiana*. New York: Plenum.
Valdman, Albert, and Thomas A. Klingler. 1997. "The Structure of Louisiana Creole." In *French and Creole in Louisiana*, edited by Albert Valdman, 109–44. New York: Plenum.
Valdman, Albert, Thomas A. Klingler, Margaret M. Marshall, and Kevin J. Rottet. 1998. *Dictionary of Louisiana Creole*. Bloomington: Indiana University Press.
Wendte, N. A., Oliver Mayeux, and Herbert Wiltz. n.d. *Ti Liv Kréyòl: A Louisiana Creole Primer*. N.p. Available from the authors.
Wiltz, Herbert. 1991. "La Leson Kreyol." *Creole Magazine* 2 (6): 15.

CHAPTER 8

THE FUTURE OF FRENCH IN LOUISIANA

TAMARA LINDNER

The vernacular variety of French historically spoken in south Louisiana, commonly known as *Cajun French* or to linguists as *Louisiana Regional French* (Klingler 2003), is the unique product of the contact between varieties of French spoken by the colonists, immigrants, and Acadian exiles who populated the region. The Acadian influence on this Louisiana dialect of French is reflected in its common name, *Cajun French*, but the dialect is understood to be the product of "the French of the Acadians and the French of the earlier colonial period," which "merged and now live on in what may be considered a single language showing significant regional variation" (Valdman et al. 2010:xii). The language reflects various aspects of the dialects of French that played a part in its development as well as the influence of American English, with which it has coexisted in south Louisiana for hundreds of years. Brasseaux (1992:109) calls it "a linguistic hybrid including vocabulary drawn from Acadian French, Creole French, nineteenth-century Standard French, and English." Structurally, the dialect that developed in the Louisiana context is clearly a variety of French; as Ancelet (1988:347) has pointed out, "Cajun French does not differ from 'standard' French any more than do other regional variations of the French language among speakers of comparable social and cultural background."

Today, French is spoken mainly by elderly residents of a roughly triangular-shaped region made up of twenty-two civil parishes recognized as having a strong French cultural history. Known as Acadiana or the French Triangle (see figures 6.1, 11.1), this part of south Louisiana is celebrated as the home of Cajun culture, Cajun music, Cajun food, and Cajun French. The region is not homogeneous: the demographic composition of the parishes differs, and significant regional variation occurs in the varieties of French spoken by residents. The French of south Louisiana in fact consists of related dialects that may differ greatly from one part of Acadiana to another in details of pronunciation or lexicon, and this language was historically spoken by residents of the region both with and without Acadian ancestry. Although the term *Louisiana Regional French* most effectively reflects these facts, residents of the region most commonly refer to the local vernacular as *Cajun French*, though some prefer and promote the neutral term *Louisiana French*. In the context of this chapter, *Cajun French* should be understood to mean "Louisiana French, as spoken in Cajun, Creole, and American Indian communities" (Valdman et al. 2010:xi), effectively including the varieties of French spoken by all Louisiana francophones.

Louisiana French is, for the most part, a spoken language passed on within families and communities rather than through educational channels, and for much of its history, the dialect has not had a written standard. This language has a complicated history, as "the status and role of French in public life was a continual point of contention from the moment Louisiana became an American state in 1814" (Henry and Bankston 2002:156). Although French was used both in public and private life in Louisiana into the nineteenth century, English increasingly came to replace French in government, business, and other areas of official communication after statehood (Valdman et al. 2010:xii). According to Dubois, Leumas, and Richardson (2018:86), complex social, political, and economic pressures led to the "decline of bilingualism" within white and black francophone populations "after the profound transformation of Louisiana society after Reconstruction."

However, French generally remained the language of daily life in rural communities until the imposition of English-only education in 1921 as a consequence of legislation that "established English as the only official language in Louisiana" (Dubois and Melançon 1997:67). French was forbidden in educational settings, and francophone pupils were punished and ridiculed for their lack of mastery of the English language. As a result, "several generations of young Cajun pupils soon associated their native language and culture with social stigmatization; speaking local French was considered something well-raised people did not do in public" (Valdman et al. 2010:xii). English represented power and opportunity, and French came to be perceived as the language of an uneducated rural population; Henry and Bankston (2002:159) attribute this perception to the concentration of French speakers in rural areas, the relative prestige of English, and the lack of French education. As their language became stigmatized, Cajun parents began to actively avoid passing on their variety of French to their children.

A shift from French to English thus occurred in Cajun communities in the mid-twentieth century. According to Bernard (2003:xxi–xxii), although Louisiana's francophones had lived in relative isolation for the early part of the century, World War II constituted a turning point that led to rapid Americanization. Throughout the United States, the war effort fueled the construction of a common national identity, and francophone communities were exposed to more Anglo-American culture as workers came to military bases and oil fields from other parts of the country. As English and Anglo-American culture entered south Louisiana, the local variety of French began to lose ground, and the number of speakers of Louisiana French steadily declined through the twentieth century.

The long-term and large-scale language shift observed in south Louisiana has resulted in an increasingly English monolingual culture in the region. Nevertheless, the character of the area and its people are perceived as closely tied to their francophone heritage, particularly after several decades of activism on behalf of Louisiana French. This chapter examines how young people who live in this area relate to the particular linguistic situation of south Louisiana and considers how they perceive the role and importance of Louisiana French and the link between the language and the culture.

RESEARCH STUDIES

The information in this chapter comes from two separate studies of students in south Louisiana. Participants in the first study were high school students enrolled in French courses in various schools around Acadiana; the second study was conducted with university students enrolled in beginning and intermediate French courses in Lafayette (commonly considered the capital of Acadiana). For both studies, participants completed questionnaires that included a variety of items, including self-identification and experience with French as well as several series of questions and statements related to opinions about or attitudes toward Cajun French. For each opinion statement, participants responded on a five-point Likert scale on which they indicated their level of agreement from *Strongly Agree* to *Strongly Disagree*. Table 8.1 presents the statements used in the university study; the response options were to the right of the statements, and participants indicated their choice by marking the relevant box.

Calculating the proportion of respondents who chose each answer for a given item offers a picture of general trends among the groups surveyed. Also, assigning numeric scores (from 5 for *Strongly Agree* to 1 for *Strongly Disagree*) allows for a calculation of mean response scores for a given item. For example, if the average of all response scores for an item is 4.12, this score indicates general agreement in response to the item, whereas an average of 2.15 suggests general disagreement. Comparing intergroup mean response scores for an item may reveal subtle differences between the groups.

Table 8.1. Statements Used in University Study
Cajun French is very widely used in Louisiana nowadays.
Cajun French has very high status in Louisiana.
The Cajun French language is very strongly supported by institutions (such as the government, the mass media, and schools).
Cajun French will be stronger in ten years' time than it is today.
South Louisiana should be bilingual in Cajun French and English.
Cajun French can be revived as a common means of communication in south Louisiana.
More money should be spent on reviving Cajun French.
If nothing is done about it, Cajun French will disappear in the next generation or two.
No matter what anyone does, attempts to revive Cajun French are bound to fail.
The government should provide Cajun French instruction wherever people want it.
Government or educational actions on behalf of Cajun French are not important to me.
The government should encourage and support Cajun French language organizations.
Revitalizing (i.e., bringing back) Cajun French is important for south Louisiana.
The continued existence of Cajun French is unimportant for south Louisiana.
Cajun French is not useful for business or other modern professional pursuits.
Cajun French should be preserved for its cultural value (as in music and arts).
Most people see all things associated with Cajun French as too old-fashioned.

The questionnaires for both studies included a self-identification component. Participants were asked "What do you consider yourself?" and offered choices that included *American, Cajun, Cajun-American,* and *Creole* (adapted from Dubois and Melançon 1997:79). Participants could also choose to fill in a different specification in a blank marked *Other*. Cajun ethnicity may once have been determined by Acadian ancestry and the use of Cajun French, but today the question of who can claim to be Cajun often includes far more subjective factors. For the purposes of these studies, anyone who claimed to be Cajun or Cajun-American (or any other combination of labels that included the word *Cajun*) was accepted as Cajun. For the analysis of the study results, participants were divided into two groups, Cajun and Not-Cajun, to explore whether differences would emerge between Cajun-identified respondents and their Not-Cajun counterparts where questions of language and culture are concerned.

The first study was conducted in 2007 with 586 high school students from thirteen high schools in five parishes (Lindner 2008). Of these participants, 86.7 percent were born and raised in Louisiana, 8.7 percent were born outside Louisiana but had lived most of their lives in Louisiana, 3.2 percent were born and had lived most of their lives outside Louisiana, and 1.2 percent were born in Louisiana but had lived most of their lives elsewhere. For self-identification, 327 (55.8 percent) used the *Cajun* label (e.g., Cajun, Cajun-American, Cajun-Scottish-American, Cajun-Hispanic-American, Asian-Cajun), and 253 (43.2 percent) chose other options without the *Cajun* label.

The second study, conducted in the fall of 2010, involved 297 university students. The vast majority (91.9 percent) of those who completed the survey were from Louisiana; only 27 students (9.1 percent) were from other places, including Canada, Korea, Nigeria, the United Kingdom, Venezuela, and the US states of California, Hawaii, Mississippi, Oklahoma, and Texas. A strong regional presence was evident, with 90 students from Lafayette Parish and many others from nearby Acadiana parishes such as Acadia, St. Landry, St. Martin, and Vermilion. Although a student could theoretically have completed both the high school and university studies, there is no way to determine whether this was the case because both studies were anonymous. In terms of self-identification, 116 (39.1 percent) of the university participants self-identified as Cajun, Cajun-American, or various other combinations that incorporated the *Cajun* label, and the remaining 181 (60.9 percent) self-identified without the *Cajun* label.

ANALYSIS OF RESPONSES

The questionnaires used for the two studies were different, so the majority of the analysis addresses each student group separately. However, four statements related to the use and status of Cajun French in Louisiana appeared on both questionnaires, so the high school and university results can be compared (table 8.2). For the first statement, "Cajun French is very widely used in Louisiana nowadays," agreement rates were similar between the two groups, with 38.4 percent of all high school participants and 37 percent of all university respondents strongly agreeing or agreeing. In the remaining response options, however, the two groups began to differentiate themselves: a slightly higher proportion of high school participants chose the neutral response (31.4 percent) than selected the disagreement options (29.7 percent), whereas the university participants were more likely to disagree or strongly disagree (38.4 percent), and only 24.6 percent chose the neutral response. These differences suggest that the high school participants, with a mean of 3.15 (slightly on the positive side of the neutral or ambivalent response), were not really sure about how widely used Cajun French currently is in Louisiana. University students, conversely, tended toward disagreement, with a mean response score of 2.67. The response means were closer together for the statement "Cajun French has very high status in Louisiana," with both groups tending toward agreement.

Table 8.2. Vitality of Cajun French: Comparison

Statement		Strongly Agree (%)	Agree (%)	Neutral (%)	Disagree (%)	Strongly Disagree (%)	Mean
Cajun French is very widely used.	High School	10.1	28.3	31.4	25.6	4.1	3.15
	University	9.1	27.9	24.6	34.7	3.7	2.67
Cajun French has very high status.	High School	11.3	27.8	37.5	20.3	2.7	3.25
	University	11.1	33	27.6	25.6	3	3.21
Cajun French has strong institutional support.	High School	3.2	12.5	37.5	33.4	12.8	2.60
	University	2	11.4	21.5	42.8	22.2	2.27
Cajun French will be stronger in ten years.	High School	4.3	6.1	37.9	32.1	19.1	2.44
	University	1.4	8.9	22.5	40.3	27	2.02

Although a higher proportion of university students (44.1 percent) than high school students (39.1 percent) agreed or strongly agreed with this statement, the mean score for the high school group was again higher because a higher proportion of high school respondents chose the neutral option. The statement "The Cajun French language is very strongly supported by institutions (such as the government, the mass media, and schools)" prompted a very high proportion of negative responses from both groups of participants. Almost two-thirds of university respondents (65 percent) disagreed or strongly disagreed with this statement, as did nearly half (46.2 percent) of the high school respondents. Again, the high school group selected a higher proportion of neutral responses, resulting in a mean response score of 2.60, but the university students showed a stronger negative sentiment, with a mean of 2.27. Finally, the statement "Cajun French will be stronger in ten years' time than it is today" elicited little optimism. More than half of high school students (51.2 percent) disagreed or strongly disagreed, and even more university students (67.3 percent) selected those two options. The university mean of 2.02 illustrated clear disagreement with this statement, while the high school mean of 2.44 also showed the tendency toward disagreement.

Overall, then, the results suggest the perception among students that Cajun French has relatively high status as well as the knowledge that the language is no longer very widely spoken. To these young residents of south Louisiana, the language apparently no longer carries its previous stigma, but this change has not translated into an increase in usage. Study participants seem to believe

Table 8.3. Maintenance of Cajun French: High School Students	
Statement	**Mean**
Cajun French should be kept up for the sake of tradition.	4.16
Cajun French is part of our culture and should not be allowed to die.	4.14
It is important for my culture and community to keep Cajun French alive.	3.95

that Cajun French suffers from a lack of institutional support and do not seem to hold much hope for the future of the language. These relatively objective items help us understand students' perception of the vitality of Cajun French as a starting point for more subjective questionnaire items.

Turning to the high school study, two series of statements are relevant for the analysis. Table 8.3 presents the first three items, focused on the preservation of Cajun French. A large majority (80.9 percent) strongly agreed (40.8 percent) or agreed (40.1 percent) that "Cajun French should be kept up for the sake of tradition." A very small proportion of respondents (4.5 percent) disagreed (3.1 percent) or strongly disagreed (1.4 percent) with this statement, and the remainder (14.7 percent) selected the neutral response. The idea that "Cajun French is part of our culture and should not be allowed to die" also elicited positive responses: three-quarters of respondents strongly agreed (47.0 percent) or agreed (28.3 percent) with this statement. A smaller number of students were neutral (18.4 percent), and even fewer disagreed (4.2 percent) or strongly disagreed (2.1 percent). For the third statement, "It is important for my culture and community to keep Cajun French alive," the overall agreement rate was somewhat lower, with 37.4 percent of participants agreeing and 32.0 percent strongly agreeing. Nearly a quarter of respondents were neutral, and fewer than 6 percent disagreed or strongly disagreed.

Response patterns across these three items were consistent: high levels of agreement, relatively low levels of neutral or ambivalent responses, and very low levels of disagreement (less than 7 percent) were in evidence. Thus, these high school students apparently felt a certain connection with the French dialect of the region and recognize its role in the culture and traditions of local Cajun communities.

Despite the strong positive responses to the statements about the general maintenance of Cajun French, much more variation was evident in distribution of the responses to more specific statements about the relationship between Cajun French and Cajun culture (table 8.4). More than a third of respondents (35.1 percent) disagreed or strongly disagreed that "It's looking backward instead of forward to try to keep Cajun French alive," whereas only 25.1 percent agreed or strongly agreed with this statement. The highest proportion of responses (37.7 percent) fell in the middle, suggesting that many young people are ambivalent

Table 8.4. Cajun French and Cajun Culture: High School Students

Statement	Strongly Agree (%)	Agree (%)	Neutral (%)	Disagree (%)	Strongly Disagree (%)
Looking backward instead of forward	10.9	24.2	37.7	14.5	10.6
Cajun culture can go on just fine in English	7.8	22.7	37.5	23.5	6.5
Doesn't matter if Cajuns speak English, not CF	6.5	19.1	43.9	19.5	9.9
Far more useful things to spend time on than CF	6.0	12.6	40.1	24.9	14.5
Speaking CF isn't important for being Cajun	4.8	12.3	32.1	31.1	17.7
Waste of time to keep up Cajun French	3.6	7.2	26.1	36.5	25.3

toward this statement. They also seemed ambivalent when considering the idea that "Cajun culture can go on just fine in English": not only did 37.5 percent of respondents choose the neutral option, but 30.5 percent agreed and 30 percent disagreed. Whereas a quarter (25.6 percent) agreed or strongly agreed with the statement "It doesn't matter if all Cajuns speak English instead of Cajun French," 29.4 percent disagreed, and 43.9 percent opted for the neutral response. Agreement levels declined in response to the statement "There are far more useful things to spend time on than Cajun French," with only 18.6 percent of respondents choosing the agreement options and the remainder almost evenly divided between ambivalence (40.1 percent) and disagreement or strong disagreement (39.4 percent). "Speaking Cajun French isn't important for being Cajun" evoked stronger sentiments, with 48.8 percent of participants choosing the disagreement options, 32.1 percent neutral, and only 17.1 percent agreeing or strongly agreeing with the statement. Finally, the notion that "Everyone here speaks English, so it's a waste of time to keep up Cajun French," was met with strong (68.1 percent) disagreement from participants; 26.1 percent were neutral on this point, and only 10.8 percent agreed or strongly agreed with this statement.

Dividing the participants by Cajun identification reveals trends in their responses to these items. Table 8.5 presents the mean response scores for each statement for each group. In general, the results are similar between the two groups, though the Cajun-identified respondents seem to respond somewhat more strongly to these statements. For example, the members of the Cajun group, with a mean response score of 2.04, clearly disagreed with the idea that keeping up Cajun French is a waste of time, whereas their

Table 8.5. Cajun French and Cajun Culture: Cajun versus Not-Cajun Responses		
Statement	Cajun	Not-Cajun
Everyone here speaks English, so it's a waste of time to keep up Cajun French.	2.04	2.56
There are far more useful things to spend time on than Cajun French.	2.46	3.01
Speaking Cajun French isn't important for being Cajun.	2.49	2.61
It doesn't matter if all Cajuns speak English instead of Cajun French.	2.84	3.06
Cajun culture can go on just fine in English.	2.95	3.12
It's looking backward instead of forward to try to keep CF alive.	3.09	3.13

non-Cajun-identified counterparts, with a mean response score of 2.56, fell between ambivalence and disagreement. A similar gap between the two groups was revealed in that Cajun-identified participants (2.46) disagreed somewhat less strongly with the notion that there were more useful things to spend time on than Cajun French, whereas the Not-Cajun group was ambivalent about this statement (3.01).The groups were clearly quite similar, meaning that it is not possible to argue for an ideological divide, but the difference in the scores is interesting. The means were closer when the groups considered whether speaking Cajun French was important for being Cajun: disagreement with this statement was almost as strong among the Not-Cajun group (2.61) as it was for the Cajun-identified students (2.49). For the two statements regarding English replacing Cajun French, the Cajun group response mean fell just under the neutral score, and the Not-Cajun mean was just above it. Finally, the two groups were closest and both means displayed an ambivalence that tended toward agreement with regard to the notion that keeping Cajun French alive was a nostalgic notion.

High school students clearly maintained an attachment to Cajun French; even if they no longer grew up speaking the language, they were not ready to abandon it. However, a statement such as "Cajun culture can go on just fine in English" may pose a dilemma. If these young people consider themselves Cajun but speak only English, then Cajun culture is apparently being maintained to a certain extent without Cajun French playing an important role. As the generations of fluent francophone Cajuns disappear and are not replaced by new speakers, the continuation of the culture in English may be the reality that these students will face as they grow older.

The analysis now turns to the university study. Table 8.6 presents the responses of these students to a series of statements about the preservation or revitalization of Cajun French. Once again, respondents appeared to perceive a connection between Cajun French and the Cajun culture. An overwhelming

Table 8.6. Maintenance and Revitalization of Cajun French: University Students

Statement	Strongly Agree (%)	Agree (%)	Neutral (%)	Disagree (%)	Strongly Disagree (%)
Cajun French should be preserved for its cultural value.	57.9	33.3	7.0	1.0	0.7
Cajun French will disappear in the next generation or two.	49.2	33.7	10.1	5.4	1.7
Revitalizing Cajun French is important for south Louisiana.	36.1	45.6	15.2	2.4	0.7
The government should encourage and support Cajun French organizations.	26.6	51.2	20.5	1.7	—
The government should provide Cajun French instruction.	20.3	47.0	23.3	8.8	0.7
More money should be spent on reviving Cajun French.	20.3	41.9	27.4	8.1	2.4
South Louisiana should be bilingual in Cajun French and English.	21.1	38.1	26.5	10.2	4.1
Cajun French can be revived as means of communication.	14.1	41.4	25.6	15.5	3.4

majority (91.2 percent) agreed or strongly agreed that "Cajun French should be preserved for its cultural value (as in music and arts)." Almost as many (82.8 percent) agreed or strongly agreed that "If nothing is done about it, Cajun French will disappear in the next generation or two" and supported revitalization (81.7 percent). To this end, 77.8 percent believed that "The government should encourage and support Cajun French language organizations," and 67.3 percent agreed or strongly agreed that "The government should provide Cajun French instruction wherever people want it." A majority of participants (62.2 percent) also agreed or strongly agreed that "More money should be spent on reviving Cajun French." More than half of participants (59.2 percent) agreed or strongly agreed that "South Louisiana should be bilingual in Cajun French and English," while 26.5 percent chose the neutral response and 14.3 percent responded negatively. A little over half of respondents believed that "Cajun French can be revived as a common means of communication in South Louisiana,"

Table 8.7. Maintenance and Revitalization: Cajun versus Not-Cajun Responses

Statement	Cajun	Not-Cajun
Cajun French should be preserved for its cultural value.	4.66	4.35
If nothing is done about it, Cajun French will disappear in the next generation or two.	4.47	4.08
Revitalizing Cajun French is important for south Louisiana.	4.46	3.94
The government should encourage and support Cajun French language organizations.	4.23	3.89
The government should provide Cajun French instruction wherever people want it.	3.90	3.70
More money should be spent on reviving Cajun French.	4.03	3.48
South Louisiana should be bilingual in Cajun French and English.	4.00	3.37
Cajun French can be revived as a common means of communication in south Louisiana.	3.73	3.31

with more agreeing (41.4 percent) than strongly agreeing (14.1 percent). Again, approximately a quarter of respondents were neutral, and a smaller proportion disagreed (15.5 percent) than strongly disagreed (3.4 percent).

As was the case for high school students, a comparison between the Cajun-identified and Not-Cajun-identified university participants reveals differences (table 8.7). For each item, the mean response score for Cajun-identified participants was higher than that for their non-Cajun-identified counterparts. In some cases, however, the mean scores for the two groups were not very far apart; for example, in the case of "The government should provide Cajun French instruction," the mean score of 3.90 for the Cajun-identified group indicated somewhat higher agreement than the mean score of 3.70 for the Not-Cajun group, but the two scores fell relatively close together on the positive end of the scale. Similarly, the idea that Cajun French should be preserved for cultural value received relatively strong support from both groups, though the Cajun-identified group delivered a more enthusiastic response (4.66) than the non-Cajun group (4.35). Cajun-identified respondents were more optimistic about the possibility of language revival and clearly agreed with government support for Cajun French language organizations (4.23), whereas the non-Cajun-identified participant mean response score (3.89) approached but did not quite reach general overall agreement. The mean scores likewise moved farther apart regarding the question of whether language revitalization was important; the Cajun-identified group, with a mean response score of 4.46, seemed to believe strongly in revitalization, whereas the Not-Cajun group, with a mean response score of 3.94, was just shy of collective agreement. On the issue of spending more money on language revitalization, the Cajun response

Table 8.8. Negative Statements: University Students

Statement	Strongly Agree (%)	Agree (%)	Neutral (%)	Disagree (%)	Strongly Disagree (%)
The continued existence of Cajun French is unimportant.	3.7	7.4	14.1	35.7	39.1
Attempts to revive Cajun French are bound to fail.	1.0	5.4	26.7	45.6	21.3
Actions on behalf of Cajun French are not important to me.	2.4	10.8	24.2	39.4	22.9
Things associated with Cajun French are too old-fashioned.	6.1	21.9	34	28.6	9.4
Cajun French is not useful for business or professional purposes.	6.1	18.5	38.7	28.6	8.1

mean again indicated agreement, even if, at 4.03, it was slightly lower than for the previous items, but the Not-Cajun response mean of 3.48 indicated general sentiments that fell between neutrality and support. Finally, the Not-Cajun group was more hesitant to embrace the idea that south Louisiana should be bilingual in Cajun French and English (3.37) than was the Cajun-identified group (4.00). The relatively high mean scores for this item may have resulted in part from the fact that all of these students were enrolled in a French class at the time of the survey, which might have made them more open to the possibility than would otherwise have been the case.

The survey also included some similar statements phrased in negative terms (table 8.8). Reflecting the response trends discussed previously, the statement "The continued existence of Cajun French is unimportant for South Louisiana" drew a decidedly negative response, with 74.7 percent of participants disagreeing or strongly disagreeing. Optimism also prevailed in that 66.9 percent of respondents disagreed or strongly disagreed with the statement "No matter what anyone does, attempts to revive Cajun French are bound to fail," and just 6.4 percent agreed or strongly agreed. These students supported efforts on behalf of Cajun French, with 62.3 percent choosing the disagreement options in response to the statement "Actions on behalf of Cajun French are not important to me," and only 13.2 percent uninterested in such efforts. Levels of disagreement were substantially lower for the statements that "Most people see all things associated with Cajun French as too old-fashioned" and that "Cajun French is not useful for business or other modern professional pursuits."

Table 8.9. Negative Statements: Cajun versus Not-Cajun Responses		
Statement	Cajun	Not-Cajun
The continued existence of Cajun French is unimportant for south Louisiana.	1.77	2.17
No matter what anyone does, attempts to revive Cajun French are bound to fail.	2.07	2.27
Actions on behalf of Cajun French are not important to me.	1.94	2.53
Most people see all things associated with Cajun French as too old-fashioned.	2.85	2.87
Cajun French is not useful for business or other modern professional pursuits.	2.70	2.96

Table 8.9 compares Cajun and Not-Cajun response means for these items. The increases in mean scores of the Not-Cajun group align with the ranking of the statements in table 8.7, whereas the Cajun response means do not. For both groups, the strongest disagreement was elicited by the idea that Cajun French is unimportant to the region: both Cajun-identified and Not-Cajun-identified participants clearly felt that this was not the case. For the Cajun group, the statement about actions on behalf of Cajun French provoked stronger disagreement (1.94) than did the notion that revitalization efforts are destined to fail (2.07). In contrast, the Not-Cajun group felt more strongly about the second statement (2.27) than the first (2.53). The two groups converged in their assessment of Cajun French as old-fashioned, with means of 2.85 for the Cajun-identified respondents and 2.87 for the Not-Cajun group. However, members of the Cajun group, with a mean of 2.70, seemed to resist the idea that Cajun French was not useful for modern pursuits, whereas the Not-Cajun participants, with a mean of 2.96, seemed rather ambivalent about this statement.

A final series of opinion items on the university questionnaire addressed how specific language skills in Cajun French relate to an understanding of the culture (table 8.10). The strongest pattern emerged in response to the idea that "to really understand Cajun culture, one must know a little Cajun French," with 57.7 percent of participants agreeing or strongly agreeing. Disagreement prevailed in response to the idea that "one must speak and understand Cajun French," with 42.9 percent of respondents disagreeing or strongly disagreeing and only 28 percent believing fluency necessary for a true understanding of Cajun culture. However, 40.9 percent disagreed or strongly disagreed with the idea that "it is not necessary to know any Cajun French." The necessity of understanding Cajun French garners slightly more positive (33.1 percent) than negative (29.1 percent) responses, but the percentage of neutral responses (28 percent) is also similar: these young people did not seem to feel very strongly about this aspect of linguistic competence. The idea that "one must know Cajun

Table 8.10. Culture and Language: University Students

To really understand Cajun culture,	Strongly Agree (%)	Agree (%)	Neutral (%)	Disagree (%)	Strongly Disagree (%)
...one must know Cajun French.	7.4	29.7	29.1	31.1	2.7
...one must speak and understand Cajun French.	5.7	22.3	29.1	38.2	4.7
...one must understand Cajun French.	6.8	33.1	28.0	29.1	3.0
...one must know a little Cajun French.	9.2	48.5	23.4	17.3	1.7
...it is not necessary to know any Cajun French.	6.1	25.6	27.3	33.4	7.5

French" presents almost the same response pattern in the opposite direction, with similar numbers disagreeing (31.1 percent), agreeing (29.7 percent), and expressing neutrality (29.1 percent). The results thus reveal no strong consensus about the importance of knowing Cajun French for understanding Cajun culture.

A comparison of the response means of the two identification groups (table 8.11) reveals that the Cajun-identified and Not-Cajun-identified respondents have rather similar opinions. Contrary to the data in the previous comparisons, in which the differences in response means ranged from just a few points to a high in the range of .60, the response mean scores were very close for all of these items. Furthermore, the only item for which the Cajun response mean was higher than the Not-Cajun response mean was that one must know a little Cajun French to really understand Cajun culture. Given that "a little" is open to interpretation, possibly signifying for some respondents a basic communicative ability but for others simply knowledge of a few words (potentially even those commonly used in English in the region, such as *lagniappe, boudin,* or *couillon*), it was not surprising that this statement elicited the most agreement. For Cajun-identified participants, the phrasing of this item allowed the claim of a direct association with French even if they knew only a handful of Cajun French words. At the other end of the scale, the notion that one must speak and understand Cajun French, which does suggest a reasonable level of fluency, garnered a less positive response, with means for both groups falling just below the neutral score. Both groups were neutral regarding the idea that it is not necessary to know any Cajun French, though the data do not permit a determination of whether they were unsure of or unwilling to concede the relevance of Cajun French for the culture. Participants' responses to the requirement of understanding Cajun French also fell right around the middle score, and the

Table 8.11. Culture and Language: Cajun versus Not-Cajun Responses		
To really understand Cajun culture,	Cajun	Not-Cajun
. . . one must know a little Cajun French.	3.46	3.33
. . . it is not necessary to know any Cajun French.	3.01	3.03
. . . one must understand Cajun French.	2.99	3.04
. . . one must know Cajun French.	2.91	2.99
. . . one must speak and understand Cajun French.	2.73	2.82

notion that one must know Cajun French elicited slightly more disagreement from the Cajun-identified group, though without pulling the score very far from the neutral mean. This response pattern suggests the reality of south Louisiana at present: once an essential element of the culture, speaking Cajun French is becoming less salient. Although disagreement with these language ability requirements was not particularly strong, the fact that these statements did not elicit general overall agreement is telling.

For this series of items, it is notable that the Not-Cajun respondent group had slightly higher means, indicating slightly more agreement, for each of these statements except the first one. How and why would these community outsiders be more attached to the French language as part of the culture than their Cajun-identified counterparts? This result could stem from personal experience for students from outside south Louisiana who have encountered unfamiliar expressions or cultural artifacts that are (or seem to be) in Cajun French. In other cases, conceptualizations of Cajun communities, whether based on direct experience or not, may carry automatic associations with Cajun French. For Cajun-identified participants, responses may have been influenced by their knowledge (or lack of knowledge) of Cajun French; respondents may tend to disagree with items that do not correspond to their own level of familiarity with the language.

DISCUSSION AND CONCLUSIONS

Cajun French clearly plays a complicated role in Cajun culture for young people growing up in the context of this language shift environment. Students willingly claim the once-stigmatized Cajun ethnicity but are generally monolingual in English. Thus, their relationship to the traditional language of their ethnic group may be somewhat tricky: if they consider themselves Cajun but do not speak Cajun French, then claiming the language as a necessary part of the culture undermines their self-identification. The apparently simple questions and statements used for these studies in fact address a negotiation on the part of Cajun-identified students about how to reconcile their identity as Cajun with the reality that they lack mastery of the traditional vernacular language associated with this identity. Facing the fact that the language of their grandparents is no longer the language of their daily lives does not, however, mean that they are ready to give up the idea that the language remains linked to the culture.

Attitudes toward Cajun French—often referred to as "broken French" by its speakers—obviously have changed insofar as the participants in these studies reflected the perception that the language has relatively high status rather than the low status previously associated with it. Nevertheless, greater appreciation for the local dialect and French educational initiatives have not significantly affected the continuing decline of the language. Both high school and university students were aware that Cajun French is in peril, however, and they perceived a lack of institutional support and had a relatively pessimistic view of the future of the language. Nevertheless, they seemed to support the notion of language revitalization. Given these young people's positive attitudes, educational and social efforts aimed at this age group may be particularly beneficial. A variety of Cajun French–based courses are available at Louisiana State University in Baton Rouge, the University of Louisiana at Lafayette, and Tulane University in New Orleans, offering contact and familiarity with the language for students who are motivated to seek them. The Council for the Development of French in Louisiana (CODOFIL) and the Center for Cultural and Eco-Tourism at the University of Louisiana at Lafayette also regularly offer French events, many of them focused on the local culture and language. The existence of such educational and social activities may help interested persons develop their interest in and familiarity with Cajun French.

Overall trends in the data illustrated support for general notions such as language revitalization and the continued existence of Cajun French, and participants seemed to feel that official entities such as the government should provide and support efforts on behalf of the language. They clearly believed in the cultural and traditional value of Cajun French, though addressing questions of the use of the language and its current role in the maintenance of the culture underscores the state of the language in the community at present. Neither self-identification group strongly associated language ability in Cajun French (beyond knowing "a little") with an understanding of the culture in spite of the fact that disagreement was in evidence when they considered the notion that speaking Cajun French was not important for being Cajun. The fact that English dominates the linguistic landscape of south Louisiana and the daily lives of these students challenges the notion of the importance of French, but participants were not ready to concede that Cajun culture could go on just fine in English. Reconciling the (English) reality with the conceptualization of a culture that is closely tied to French is obviously a challenge.

According to Valdman (2007:1220), the situation of Cajun French in Louisiana is not unique: one often finds that in the United States, "endogenous varieties of French ... no longer assume functional roles: they serve mainly an emblematic function as symbols of an ethnic identity that distinguishes members of these communities from mainstream Americans." The language may continue to be associated with the culture, although "the linguistic criterion is ... removed from its objective basis, that is whether people actually know or speak the language" (Henry and Bankston 2002:149). This assessment should not however, discourage efforts to preserve of Cajun French. Young people are clearly attached to and interested in the traditional French language of their communities, and they should be encouraged and offered opportunities to pursue this interest.

WORKS CITED

Ancelet, Barry Jean. 1988. "A Perspective on Teaching the 'Problem Language' in Louisiana." *French Review* 61:345–56.

Bernard, Shane K. 2003. *The Cajuns: Americanization of a People*. Jackson: University Press of Mississippi.

Brasseaux, Carl A. 1992. *Acadian to Cajun: Transformation of a People, 1803–1877*. Jackson: University Press of Mississippi.

Dubois, Sylvie, Emilie Gagnet Leumas, and Malcolm Richardson. 2018. *Speaking French in Louisiana, 1720–1955: Linguistic Practices of the Catholic Church*. Baton Rouge: Louisiana State University Press.

Dubois, Sylvie, and Megan Melançon. 1997. "Cajun Is Dead—Long Live Cajun: Shifting from a Linguistic to a Cultural Community." *Journal of Sociolinguistics* 1 (1): 63–93.

Henry, Jacques M., and Carl L. Bankston III. 2002. *Blue Collar Bayou: Louisiana Cajuns in the New Economy of Ethnicity*. Westport, CT: Praeger.

Klingler, Thomas A. 2003. *Language Labels and Language Use among Cajuns and Creoles in Louisiana*. https://repository.upenn.edu/pwpl/vol9/iss2/8/.

Lindner, Tamara. 2008. "Attitudes toward Cajun French and International French in South Louisiana: A Study of High School Students." PhD diss., Indiana University.

Valdman, Albert. 2007. "Vernacular French Communities in the United States: A General Survey." *French Review* 80:1218–34.

Valdman, Albert, Kevin J. Rottet, Barry Jean Ancelet, Richard Guidry, Amanda LaFleur, Thomas A. Klingler, Tamara Lindner, Michael D. Picone, and Dominique Ryon. 2010. *Dictionary of Louisiana French: As Spoken in Cajun, Creole, and American Indian Communities*. Jackson: University Press of Mississippi.

CHAPTER 9

THE INSTITUTIONALIZATION OF FRENCH IN LOUISIANA: HISTORY, SUCCESSES, AND CHALLENGES FOR THE FUTURE

ALBERT CAMP

The popular perspective that Louisiana French is reserved for the remote bayous and far-flung sugarcane fields and constitutes a purely oral language that evolved in isolation from the institutionalized Standard French found in the rest of the francophone world is simply not accurate. It may be true that most of the native speakers of Louisiana varieties of French today were raised in an environment where French literacy was rare and interactions with speakers from other parts of the francophone world were even rarer, but throughout most of the nearly 350 years of Louisiana's history, which began with the arrival of the first Europeans at the mouth of the Mississippi in 1682, French has played an almost constantly significant role in one or more of the official institutions of the area.

During the French colonial period, from 1682 to 1763, French was the official language of the two main institutions that governed the daily lives of people in Louisiana, the Roman Catholic Church and the French Crown. While the church as an institution may have had Latin as its official language, the vast majority of religious and priests who served in Louisiana came from New France (modern-day Canada) and France. As such, with the exception of saying Mass, most daily interactions of the church occurred in French. Yet "the early residents of this area would have found our distinction between political and religious matters strange and unintelligible. War, a business or marriage contract, and a baptismal ceremony were both sacred and secular" (Nolan 1976:XIX.). For example, in 1724 Louis XV issued an updated version of the *Code Noir* for the Louisiana colony that decreed that all residents, slave or free, had to be baptized and instructed in the Catholic faith, allowed a Catholic marriage (with the permission of their masters if enslaved), and buried in a Catholic cemetery. These laws, though enforced to varying degrees, necessitated that the church work hand in hand with the Crown as an institution.

Thus, when Louisiana shifted from an officially French colony to an officially Spanish one in 1763, the vital institution of the Louisiana Catholic Church remained mostly intact. According to Dubois, Leumas, and Richardson (2018:13),

> The idea of monolingual Spanish priests at the parish level in colonial Louisiana is absurd and against the Church practice of accommodation to reach the local populace. French priests were therefore needed and retained in the diocese for the transition in the 1760s and later. French and Spanish entries go back and forth in the parish registers. Parishioners' signatures in Spanish in a Spanish register did not mean that a parishioner knew the language any more than he knew Latin when reciting Latin. Most obviously, Spanish priests had to know French in order to serve the native and incoming French Catholics.

Furthermore, demographic shifts in the colony throughout the Spanish period increased rather than diminished the French language's importance.

Spanish immigration policy in colonial Louisiana generally sought not to replace the native French-speaking population but rather to increase the population by any means necessary. The Spanish inherited a colony that was massively underpopulated at approximately eleven thousand residents (Din 1998:12). Thus, immigrants from many different linguistic and cultural backgrounds were welcomed—as long as they were Catholic. Roughly twenty-six hundred French settlers in Acadia (modern-day Nova Scotia) who were expelled after the Treaty of 1763 ceded Canada to Britain made their way to Louisiana between 1765 and 1785 (Brasseaux 1990:1:xii). In contrast, the only major influx of Spanish immigrants involved fewer than two thousand people from the Canary Islands (Din 1988:15–25). Many other arrivals during this period sought to escape the growing unrest in France and Saint-Domingue (Haiti). This numerical discrepancy meant that French remained the language of daily life and business for most in Louisiana, including the church, which had even less motivation to replace the French language with Spanish than did the Spanish Crown.

Even if the period of Spanish rule had little impact on the use of French and the second period of French rule was too brief to have any lasting effect, the Louisiana Purchase would be expected to have had a major effect on language use. Indeed it did, though not necessarily the effect that might be predicted. Most sources estimate Louisiana's population at around 60,000 at the time of the Louisiana Purchase (1803). Most of that population would certainly have been Catholic and French-speaking (Dubois, Leumas, and Richardson 2018).

By 1810, the population had increased to 76,566 (Forstall 1996:4). However records show that the rebellion in the French colony of Saint-Domingue led to an influx of more than 10,000 French-speaking refugees (Lachance 1988:111).

Anglo-American immigration also had a major impact on the linguistic landscape. Americans had been migrating to Louisiana since colonial times, but the level of immigration increased dramatically after the Louisiana Purchase and statehood in 1812. In 1820, the state's population had nearly doubled, reaching 153,407 (Forstall 1996:4). Although the pace of growth did slow, the population continued to increase steadily throughout the decades with immigration from other parts of America as well as other parts of the world. Nevertheless, Louisiana remained a destination of choice for tens of thousands of French immigrants, particularly during that country's early nineteenth-century political turmoil (Brasseaux 1990).

Despite the Americanization of Louisiana, French enjoyed a privileged status in business and politics, de facto at first and then de jure. However, ideological views about the link between speaking English and being American significantly affected antebellum language use, and political considerations fundamentally changed the legal status of French in the Reconstruction period. Yet one Louisiana institution continued to use and even indirectly to promote French throughout the nineteenth century. The Catholic Church continued to offer French a level of institutional legitimacy.

Although the Catholic Church lost its status as a legal authority after the colonial era, the fact that the vast majority of the state's population followed the faith meant that its institutional place in Louisianans' lives continued. Every important event in the life of a Catholic involves not only a church ceremony but also an official written record of the event. So from an infant's baptism to an individual's marriage and eventual death, the institution of the church both participates in and records the event in a particular language. Studies have shown that Catholic Church registers in south Louisiana continued to use French well into the twentieth century, with a median date of 1916 for the shift to English (Dubois, Leumas, and Richardson 2007). Throughout the nineteenth century, the Church in Louisiana was dominated by priests and bishops from France, and well into the twentieth century, the major life events of people in south Louisiana were conducted in and recorded in the more standardized European French of these priests. One rough estimate puts the number of Catholics in south Louisiana at 75 percent of the population between 1906 and 1916 (Dubois, Leumas, and Richardson 2018:137). Standard varieties of French thus remained a part of Louisiana institutions into the early twentieth century.

Demographic, political, and ideological pressure unfortunately ensured that by the mid-1900s, neither state institutions nor the Catholic Church continued to use French in an official capacity. Though Census data are not very specific or reliable, Louisiana appears to have had at least a few hundred thousand French speakers in 1940. In 1968, the state government gave French an institutional status by creating the Council for the Development of French in Louisiana (CODOFIL) to revitalize the language. Nevertheless, current estimates put the French-speaking population somewhere between one hundred thousand and two hundred thousand, and most of these people are elderly. This chapter evaluates the institutionalization of language revitalization efforts in Louisiana and the ways in which ideological and political considerations have affected the role of public education in Louisiana's French revitalization movement.

THE ROLE OF THE STATE IN FRENCH REVITALIZATION

The legal status of French in the state of Louisiana has had a rather mixed history. The first Louisiana Constitution (1812) required that all laws be written and disseminated in English. However, this clause was inserted only to appease the US Congress, which had previously mandated that all legal affairs in the Territory of Orleans be written in English (Ward 1997). In reality, all acts of the Louisiana legislature were recorded and promulgated in French and English from 1812 to 1867. The Reconstructionist Louisiana Constitution of 1868 forbade any laws requiring judicial processes from being made available in a language other than English and required that free public education for all be offered only in English (Ward 1997).

The Louisiana Constitution of 1879 restored the legal status of French by requiring the promulgation of laws in French and allowing public schools to use the language. By this time, however, the French language had already begun to develop a pariah status, and the 1921 Louisiana Constitution again removed all references to the French language and required English-only education (Ward 1997). Finally, in 1968, one hundred years after Louisiana law first removed French from state institutions, Act 409 of the Louisiana legislature restored the language's legal institutional status and created CODOFIL to "do any and all things necessary to accomplish the development, utilization, and preservation of the French language as found in Louisiana for the cultural, economic and touristic benefit of the state" (Act 409, sect. 1). Act 408, also passed in 1968, required Louisiana children to learn French for a number of years.

These laws and CODOFIL owe their existence to a populist movement known as the Cajun Renaissance that had been taking place in Louisiana for at least a decade. Social activists, musicians, and politicians such as Dudley LeBlanc had been organizing public events to promote Cajun heritage, ethnicity, and language. The 1960s also saw a change in public attitudes toward Louisiana's French-speaking population, though it is unclear whether this change was a cause or effect of the Cajun Renaissance. The laws essentially constituted a reaction to the Cajun Renaissance and the realization that Louisiana's French-speaking population was disappearing rapidly. By requiring "preservation" of the French language, the Louisiana legislature signaled its acknowledgment that institutional intervention was needed to slow or reverse the language shift away from French.

Loopholes in Act 408 meant that it was completely unenforceable: schools and parents could simply request and receive exemption from the law. In 1972, only ninety-five schools in twenty parishes had French programs (Henry 1997:192). In 1975, the legislature repealed Act 408 and passed Act 714, which allowed parishes to establish their own second-language programs, provided state funding for these programs, and allowed parents to request that schools offer particular second-language programs. This law met with some success, and by 1977, thirty-six parishes were providing French-language education to 42,644 students (Henry 1997:193). In 1985, the Louisiana Board of Elementary and Secondary Education mandated second-language education for students from the fourth to eighth grade (Egéa-Kuehne 2006:121). This mandate had an important impact on CODOFIL's role in French education.

James Domengeaux, CODOFIL's first director, met with French president Georges Pompidou in 1969, and the Louisiana Department of Education subsequently signed formal accords with the French government and later with the governments of Belgium and Quebec (Egéa-Kuehne 2006:123). CODOFIL created the Foreign Associate Teacher (FAT) program to bring French teachers from other French-speaking countries into Louisiana's public schools. While the state still had a sizable population of French speakers in the 1960s and 1970s, very few were qualified to teach, and for more than a decade, most of Louisiana's French teachers came from other countries via this program. However, the 1985 Board of Elementary and Secondary Education mandate to provide second-language education in all schools changed this dynamic.

Because the board placed responsibility for implementing second-language education on local school boards in the 1980s, the model of a centralized supply of French teachers changed. Second-language education programs began to look more and more like their equivalent programs in other states that do not have an organization like CODOFIL. Schools began to advertise job openings and conduct interviews with eligible candidates. This new system led to a significant increase in the number of students studying French as a second language. Whereas 95 schools offered French in 1972, that number had risen to 536 schools offering French to 77,924 students in the 1991–92 school year (Henry 1997:193). However, since then the number of students studying French has actually decreased. A 2010 report by the French Education Project at Louisiana State University found only 56,454 students studying any foreign language in the 2009–10 school year (Egéa-Kuehne 2010). Of those students, only 31,468 were studying French, and most of the others were studying Spanish.

With schools less dependent on CODOFIL to supply foreign-language teachers in the 1980s, the agency shifted its focus to French immersion education. Unlike traditional foreign-language instruction, students in French immersion schools not only study French as a language but also learn other subjects such as science, math, and social studies in French. Following a Canadian trend, French immersion programs and entire schools were founded throughout south Louisiana with CODOFIL's assistance. By the second decade of the twenty-first century, the United States had 114 French immersion programs, 28 of them in Louisiana, more than any other state (Center for Applied Linguistics 2011). CODOFIL is largely responsible for the success and rapid growth of French immersion programs in Louisiana, which have become the agency's main focus. Although CODOFIL provides some funding and support for other programs, the organization primarily serves as an intermediary between immersion programs and the foreign governments whose citizens constitute most of the French immersion teachers.

Until recently, school principals had to request the creation of immersion programs, with permission dependent on local school boards, which often denied these requests for various reasons. In some areas, immersion magnet programs have been used as a tool for desegregation (Beal 2008), while at other times, these programs placed a cohort of high-performing children in an underprivileged school to artificially boost its overall test scores (Tornquist 2000:96). These behaviors not only pose ethical questions but create unnecessary barriers to CODOFIL's legally defined mission and to everyone involved in the French revitalization movement.

In 2013, Act 361, the Immersion School Choice Act, began requiring any school that receives a written request from the guardians of at least twenty-five kindergarten children to form an immersion program beginning with the school year 2014–15. It is not yet clear whether this change will increase the availability of French immersion education. However, CODOFIL is actively working to encourage parents to request immersion programs.

According to CODOFIL, most "teachers of French are Louisiana natives, thanks largely to the efforts of CODOFIL and the state's educational system. Today, almost 100,000 students across Louisiana study French, and there are 26 French immersion schools in eight parishes" (CODOFIL n.d.b). While these numbers appear misleading given that CODOFIL now focuses almost exclusively on immersion schools where the overwhelming majority of teachers are foreign, these statements clearly reflect the ideological views that the agency seeks to promote. CODOFIL wants the people of Louisiana to believe that

French immersion education leads to economic opportunities. Clearly, becoming a French teacher is an economic opportunity.

CODOFIL's 2014 annual report includes nine goals for fiscal year 2015:

1. Consolidate all recent CODOFIL legislative mandates into several clusters of public-private "spheres of activity" for more efficient development of best practices that may be duplicated for the benefit of Louisiana stakeholders at large.
1. [*sic*] Increase number of Louisiana teachers of French.
2. Engage youth. Assure that a minimum of 12% of the products of French Immersion (former students) are actively engaged in "living, working and playing" in French in Louisiana.
3. Grow career paths through French, especially in tourism.
4. Develop a program for articulating Louisiana French to military communities.
5. Increase number of scholarships.
6. Improve Louisiana's standing with the Organisation Internationale de la Francophonie.
8. Increase presence of Louisiana French in the media. (CODOFIL 2014:6)

The goals of increasing the number of Louisiana teachers of French, assuring 12 percent of immersion students "work" in French, and growing career paths offer significant insight into CODOFIL's linguistic ideology.

While more and more Americans and specifically Louisianans have been hired to teach French as a second language in Louisiana, teaching in French immersion schools remains a largely foreign job. In the 2008–9 school year, the Louisiana Department of Education reported that 125 of the state's 160 immersion teachers were participants in the FAT program (Barnett 2010:32). However, even those 35 teachers who were not currently members of the program might have previously participated but now had permanent visa status (32). My research in Louisiana's French immersion schools has found that it is common for participants in the FAT program to change their visa status and remain, whether through marriage to an American or through some other means. Among administrators from eight immersion schools throughout south Louisiana, only one remembered having an American work in their French immersion program. Thus, although CODOFIL and grassroots organizations focus primarily on French immersion schools as a means of revitalizing French in Louisiana, Louisianans are largely excluded from working there. Despite their immense success in helping students learn French, the immersion schools have been hindered by ideological and institutional hurdles.

LINGUISTIC IDEOLOGY AND FRENCH IMMERSION SCHOOLS

CODOFIL was born out of the so-called Cajun Renaissance, and its purpose was and still is to prevent the decline of French in Louisiana and hopefully revitalize it. The fact that the state of Louisiana has had a government agency devoted to the revitalization of French for more than fifty years indicates a level of support for this minority language that is probably unparalleled in any other state. Nevertheless, ideological hurdles continue to stall the progress that French immersion schools might make toward that revitalization. As one linguist said, "Linguistic revitalization starts first at the psycholinguistic level, that is to say at the level of linguistic representations, for speakers (or semispeakers or passive speakers), language experts, and educators" (Ryon 2002:282–83). These ideological perspectives have a concrete influence on the planning and practice of language revitalization. In the words of Albert Valdman (1998:290), "The choice of objectives for the teaching of foreign languages in schools and universities depends to a large extent on the interested parties: the political powers, the various community representatives, the educational administration, and the students themselves." Many studies of language attitudes in Louisiana have focused on the variety of French used in schools and particularly on the choice to use a standardized version of international French rather than a more local vernacular such as the Cajun or Creole varieties. While this debate may have had some impact on parents' and communities' decisions in the early years of CODOFIL's existence, the use of standardized international French remains the only realistic option for immersion schools.

However, the crucial ideological question for French immersion schools and the French revitalization movement as a whole is why these children should learn French at all. French immersion schools definitely have a place in CODOFIL's mission to "accomplish the development, utilization, and preservation" of French. Yet the reasons why teachers and administrators participate in expanding French education have remained far less clear until recently. For example, the reasons why Louisianans decide to become French teachers may have nothing to do with language revitalization. Similarly, the school administrators who run these programs may not see themselves as part of a revitalization movement. The ideology of those working toward language revitalization will have a profound impact on the success or failure of the revitalization movement.

Traditionally, Louisianans who wanted to become French teachers first needed to acquire the requisite education and legal certification. In 2014, I conducted a study of undergraduate students at south Louisiana's four largest universities—McNeese State University, Louisiana State University, Tulane

University, and the University of Louisiana at Lafayette. I asked faculty to identify every student majoring or minoring in French who was planning to become a French teacher and would be graduating within two years. Only ten students—all at Tulane or Louisiana State—met these criteria. I interviewed nine of them, created sociobiographic profiles for each of them, and explored their linguistic ideologies.

All were white, and seven were female. All came from relatively high socioeconomic classes and had at least one parent with a college degree, characteristics that reflect the general demographics of these two universities. However, only about half of the interviewees had parents from Louisiana, and only one had any familial connection to Louisiana's French-speaking population (Camp 2015:78). If this sample is consistent with the general population of Louisiana's future French teachers, then it would suggest that the children and grandchildren of Louisiana's Cajun and Creole French speakers are not generally interested in teaching French.

Eight of the nine students were either open to or preferred the idea of teaching in French immersion schools; the only exception was the one student who had Cajun French–speaking family, who did not believe that her French was fluent enough. All of them wanted to teach simply because they liked French and liked teaching. Thus, while almost all of them would be happy to work in a French immersion school, none were motivated by a desire to revitalize French (Camp 2015:82).

I also interviewed nine administrators from immersion schools throughout south Louisiana to compile sociobiographic and ideological profiles that could be compared with those of the students. Five of the nine administrators were white females, two were black females, and two were white males. Unlike the students, these administrators generally came from lower socioeconomic classes, and only one had college-educated parents (Camp 2015:88). In addition, eight of the nine administrators claimed to be ethnically Cajun, Creole, or French, the same number that had French-speaking family (89–90). Paradoxically, only two of the administrators spoke French, and all ended up administering immersion programs by chance rather than by desire. If this sample of administrators is typical as well, then neither Louisianans who run immersion programs nor those who desire to teach in them do so for reasons that mesh with CODOFIL's mission to "accomplish the development, utilization, and preservation" of French.

From an ideological standpoint, both groups either supported or were ambivalent to the idea of the state government working to revitalize French. The aspiring teachers who generally lacked a familial connection to Louisiana French believed that preserving and promoting Louisiana's French heritage constituted the main benefit of French education. The administrators tended to be more practical, seeing cognitive benefits, job opportunities, and economic benefits as the main advantages. Consequently, the administrators also tended to see any second language, not particularly French, as equally beneficial for Louisiana students (Camp 2015).

The linguistic ideology of these administrators seems to mirror CODOFIL's goals, which, in turn, mirror its leaders' ideological positions. CODOFIL leaders have described the long-term goals of the immersion programs as "critical to the revitalization of French in Louisiana. Not only can the immersion help to create a population identifying with French, it also improves education and creates pathways to careers for students" (Haskins 2015:32–33). In addition, the administrators claim that "parents and students see the benefits of bilingualism and aren't necessarily participating for the Louisiana French aspect.... [P]arents of current immersion students are younger than the parents of immersion students when the programs were created and they're less concerned with the emphasis on Louisiana French" (33). Based on her interviews with CODOFIL officials, researcher Meredith Haskins believes that "the focus is more on a diverse and global approach that promotes functional bilingualism and enhances employment opportunities outside of Louisiana than an actual attempt at revitalizing Louisiana French varieties" (35).

THE CURRENT STATUS OF LOUISIANA'S FRENCH IMMERSION SCHOOLS AND ESCADRILLE LOUISIANE

As of 2016, Louisiana's public schools had twenty-nine French immersion programs. Almost all of the teachers in these French immersion programs either are or were participants in the FAT program. According to Brian Barnett's (2010:83) survey, only seven of eighty-five French immersion teachers in Louisiana public schools were native-born Americans, and only four were from Louisiana. Despite CODOFIL's emphasis on the economic and job opportunities that learning French can provide, these immersion school teacher jobs have not traditionally been available for Louisianans. Today, institutional legal hurdles stand in the way of Americans who want to teach in French immersion schools.

The Board of Elementary and Secondary Education requires school districts to hire, with priority, all qualified Louisiana teachers to teach French or in French immersion schools (Egea-Kuehne 2006:10). Only then can schools hire FATs provided by CODOFIL. Yet, for many years, schools have had a financial incentive to hire FATs rather than American teachers. Multiple immersion school principals told me that they would prefer to have immersion teachers from Louisiana, but hiring them rather than FATs would be foolish because the schools would lose money: the Louisiana legislature contributes twenty thousand dollars to offset the cost of each FAT's salary. Teachers in French immersion programs are paid the same state-mandated salaries as any other teacher in a particular area. During the 2014 regular session, the Louisiana Senate adopted Concurrent Resolution 55, which provides:

> Any city, parish, or other public school system or school employing a Foreign Language Associate or a graduate of the Escadrille Louisiane program shall receive a supplemental allocation from State Board of Elementary and Secondary Education of $21,000 per teacher. The state shall maintain support of the Foreign Language Associate program at a maximum of 300 Foreign Language Associates employed in any given year. These teachers shall be paid by the employing city, parish, or other local public school system or school at least the state average classroom teacher salary.... Of the $21,000 allocation, $20,000 shall be allocated to the school where the teacher is employed and the funds used to support the total cost of the teacher salary, and the remaining amount shall be associated with costs of VISA sponsorship pursuant to State Board of Elementary and Secondary Education regulations. (Appel 2014)

No doubt, these allocations were originally intended to provide schools with an incentive to open language immersion programs that might otherwise be seen as too costly. Until recently, any Americans who might have wanted to work in immersion schools would have to overcome the financial incentives not to hire them.

Although there appeared to be no evidence that a Louisianan had ever been denied a job for this reason, the situation remained problematic. However, to address this problem and the general lack of Louisianans teaching French immersion, CODOFIL and the French government partnered in 2011 to create the Escadrille Louisiane (Louisiana Squadron) program. The name is a reference to two hundred Louisiana pilots who flew planes for the French army in World War I, and the program seeks to train two hundred Louisianans to teach in French immersion schools over the next twenty years by sending them to study in France. Students from Louisiana would spend a year working in France as English teachers through the French government's long-established TAPIF program. In addition, students would also take classes at the University of Rennes, credits that would apply toward a master's degree in teaching and teacher certification from Shreveport's Centenary College.

In exchange for grants and stipends that cover their education and expenses, Escadrille Louisiane graduates will be asked to commit to teaching in Louisiana

Table 9.1. Escadrille Louisiane Enrollment and Placement, 2011–2018

Iteration	Enrolled	Teaching Immersion	Teaching French as Foreign Language	Not Teaching French
1 (2011–13)	6	0	3	3
2 (2012–14)	7	0	3	4
3 (2013–15)	6	1	1	4
4 (2014–16)	3	1	0	2
5 (2015–17)	8	3	3	2
6 (2016–18)	9	7	7	2

Source: Rodriguez 2019

French immersion schools for at least three years. Schools that hire graduates of the Escadrille program are entitled to the same twenty-thousand-dollar supplemental allocation as schools that hire FATs. In theory, this seems like a practical solution to the lack of Louisiana French immersion teachers. In practice, however, one immersion school administrator confided in 2014 that it was impossible to find American teachers with the necessary fluency and certification in a second subject to work in an immersion program. The idea of Escadrille is that a year in France would provide Louisianans the necessary fluency, and their degree from Centenary College would provide them the necessary certifications.

CODOFIL had sought to have ten students per year participate in the Escadrille program (Haskins 2015:31), but low enrollment has been a problem, as table 9.1 shows. While CODOFIL has yet to achieve its goal of ten students per year returning to teach French immersion, the numbers are improving significantly. After six years, Escadrille Louisiane has produced only twelve French immersion teachers, but that number may actually represent more actual Louisianan French immersion teachers than ever before. One of the problems with all of these numbers is deciding who qualifies as a Louisianan, since Louisiana issues no passports and does not actually have citizens, only residents. Even if this pattern continues, it will be quite some time before Louisianans comprise a significant number of French immersion teachers.

Enrollment in the Escadrille program may be hindered by its location. After the year in France, students must spend two more years at Centenary College in Shreveport, a small private Methodist College that is three to five hours away from most of Louisiana's French immersion schools. Since most south Louisiana students who wish to become French teachers attend Louisiana State University or Tulane, a program based geographically closer to students' homes might be more attractive.

According to two CODOFIL employees, "even if the number of native Louisiana French speakers were to increase, . . . they would not ever completely replace the foreign associate teachers . . . for several reasons." First, CODOFIL has "establish[ed] good working relationships with educational organizations in francophone countries due to the hiring of foreign associate teachers." Second, FATs have the "ability to offer a cultural mix" that benefits students, who "learn more than if they were learning from teachers who all came from the same place." These administrators believe "that a better balance between Louisiana teachers and foreign associate teachers would be ideal" (Haskins 2015:30–32). Thus, the Escadrille Louisiane program clearly does not seek to replace the FATs in French immersion programs but rather is geared toward redressing the extreme imbalance that has existed for some time.

It is difficult to assess what progress has resulted from CODOFIL's creation half a century ago and from the funds that the state has directed toward the agency's efforts to preserve and promote French. According to a well-known CODOFIL slogan, usually attributed to its first president, James Domengeaux, "The schools destroyed French; the schools must restore it." There are certainly many more Louisiana students studying French today than there were fifty years ago. However, it is unclear what level of fluency they generally achieve. Those who go through elementary and/or middle school French immersion programs undoubtedly achieve a relatively high level of fluency by necessity: as of 2014, forty-five hundred students were enrolled in French immersion and about twenty thousand adults had graduated from immersion programs (Haskins 2015:34), meaning that CODOFIL had increased the population of people who speak at least semifluent French by nearly twenty-five thousand. However, Louisiana has probably lost more than five times as many elderly French speakers in the past twenty years. Numbers thus are probably not the best measure of success or failure for CODOFIL and the French revitalization movement in general. The fact that Louisiana has a government institution devoted to promoting and preserving French is a unique and important achievement.

To ensure the continued success of the French revitalization movement and particularly CODOFIL, greater efforts need to be made to remove the institutional and ideological hurdles that prevent Louisianans from engaging with French immersion schools. One administrator at a French immersion school informed me that "all of our teachers are native speakers; we would not hire an American with a degree in that language." Being American and speaking French—or any language other than English—must no longer be seen as contradictory. The administrator also said, "Every day they sing a patriotic song, even though this is a school that focuses on other languages, we want the children to understand their heritage and be proud of being American." Such a linguistic ideology, pervasive in Louisiana, truly hinders the French revitalization movement.

While changing people's attitudes may be difficult, eliminating institutional hurdles should be more straightforward. To put more Louisianans in French immersion classrooms, the Escadrille Louisiane program must increase its numbers. Perhaps the program needs to be moved or expanded to include other university partners or simply needs to be better advertised. Changing the laws so that hiring an American who did not go through Escadrille would not cost a school twenty thousand dollars might also help if other pathways to gaining French fluency and certification can be opened. CODOFIL's existence is a noteworthy achievement, but French must occupy an expanded place in other Louisiana institutions if it is to survive.

WORKS CITED

Appel, Conrad. 2014. "Senate Concurrent Resolution No. 55." Regular Session, 2014. https://www.louisianabelieves.com/docs/default-source/minimum-foundation-program/2014-15-circular-no-1156-senate-concurrent-resolution-55.pdf?sfvrsn=4.

Barnett, Brian. 2010. "French Immersion Teachers' Attitudes toward Louisiana Varieties of French and the Integration of Such Varieties in Their Classroom: A Quantitative and Qualitative Analysis." PhD diss., Indiana University.

Beal, Heather K. Olson. 2008. "Speaking the Language of Integration: A Case Study of South Boulevard Foreign Language Academic Immersion Magnet." PhD diss., Louisiana State University.

Brasseaux, Carl A. 1990. *The "Foreign French": Nineteenth-Century French Immigration into Louisiana*. 3 vols. Lafayette: Center for Louisiana Studies, University of Southwestern Louisiana.

Camp, Albert. 2015. "L'Essentiel ou Lagniappe: The Ideology of French Revitalization in Louisiana." PhD diss., Louisiana State University.

Center for Applied Linguistics. 2011. *Directory of Foreign Language Immersion Programs in U.S. Schools.* http://webapp.cal.org/Immersion/.

CODOFIL. N.d.a. *About/À Propos.* https://www.crt.state.la.us/cultural-development/c`1odofil/about/index.

CODOFIL. N.d.b. "Programs/Programmes: French Immersion." https://www.crt.state.la.us/cultural-development/codofil/programs/french-immersion/index.

CODOFIL. 2014. "Annual Report." September 5. https://www.crt.state.la.us/Assets/OCD/codofil/reports/CODOFIL%20Annual%20Report_September%202014%20(2).pdf.

Din, Gilbert C. 1988. *The Canary Islanders of Louisiana.* Baton Rouge: Louisiana State University Press.

Dubois, Sylvie, Emilie Gagnet Leumas, and Malcolm Richardson. 2007. *Spatial Diffusion of Language Practices within the Catholic Church in Louisiana.* https://repository.upenn.edu/pwpl/vol13/iss2/5/.

Dubois, Sylvie, Emilie Gagnet Leumas, and Malcolm Richardson. 2018. *Speaking French in Louisiana, 1720–1955: Linguistic Practices of the Catholic Church.* Baton Rouge: Louisiana State University Press.

Egea-Kuehne, Denise. 2006. "L'Enseignement du Français en Louisiane: Préserver un Héritage." In *Mémoires Francophones: La Louisiane*, edited by Guy Clermont, Michel Beniamino, and Arielle Thauvin-Chapot, 115–61. Limoges: Pulim.

Egea-Kuehne, Denise. 2010. "The French Education Project, School of Education, Louisiana State University, Baton Rouge, Louisiana." Unpublished report.

Forstall, Richard L., ed. 1996. *Population of States and Counties of the United States: 1790–1990*. https://www.census.gov/population/www/censusdata/PopulationofStatesandCountiesof theUnitedStates1790-1990.pdf.

Haskins, Meredith. 2015. "French Immersion in Louisiana: Instructor Perceptions and Practices." Master's thesis, University of Alabama.

Henry, Jacques. 1997. "The Louisiana French Movement." In *French and Creole in Louisiana*, edited by Albert Valdman, 183–214. New York: Plenum.

Lachance, Paul. 1988. "The 1809 Immigration of Saint-Domingue Refugees to New Orleans: Reception, Integration, and Impact." *Louisiana History* 29 (2): 109–41.

Nolan, Charles. 1976. *A Southern Catholic Heritage*. New Orleans: Archdiocese of New Orleans.

Rodriguez, Jennifer. 2019. Personal communication, February 1.

Ryon, Dominique. 2002. "Cajun French, Sociolinguistic Knowledge, and Language Loss in Louisiana." *Journal of Language, Identity, and Education* 1 (4): 279–93.

Tornquist, Lisa L. 2000. "Attitudes Linguistiques vis-à-vis du Vernaculaire Franco-Louisianais dans les Programmes d'Immersion en Louisiane." PhD diss., University of Louisiana at Lafayette.

Valdman, Albert. 1998. "Revitalisation du Cadien et Enseignement du Français Langue Étrangère aux Etats-Unis." In *Français d'Amérique: Variation, Créolisation, Normalisation*, edited by Patrice Brasseur, 280–92. Avignon: Centre d'Études Canadiennes, Université d'Avignon.

Ward, Roger. 1997. "The French Language in Louisiana Law and Legal Education: A Requiem." *Louisiana Law Review* 57 (4): 1283–1324.

CHAPTER 10

FRENCH EDUCATION IN NEW ORLEANS

ROBIN WHITE

Contemporary French education in New Orleans is tied both to the history of French in the state and to changes in public education in the city. The rising popularity of French education in New Orleans today is emerging amid irony, given that French is in decline in Louisiana. Moreover, New Orleans boasts the majority of Louisiana's immersion schools despite being located in what is arguably the least francophone of Louisiana's formerly French-majority parishes.

Well into the twentieth century, New Orleanians spoke French. In 1931's *Louisiana-French*, William A. Read (xii) thanked forty-three consultants, two of whom lived in New Orleans. In addition, Read counted Orleans Parish as one of the places where "French is still spoken by many residents" (xxiii). Nonetheless, by 1920, only one New Orleans school offered an education conducted entirely in French. That school was operated by L'Union Française, a francophone society, which had opened a girls' school at 928 N. Rampart Street in 1887. The school became coeducational in 1920 (L'Union Française 2016). That address was also the home of the Athénée Louisanais, a society established in 1878 to honor and offer space for francophone authors (*Times-Picayune Guide* 1917). The Athénée published a journal between one and four times a year from 1876 until its demise in 1975. Notable New Orleanians who were francophone advocates and members of the Athénée included author Alcée Fortier (1856–1914) and General P. G. T. Beauregard (1818–93)(Athénée Louisianais Records n.d.). Despite the efforts of such societies and notable francophones, immersive French education came to a standstill between 1952, when the school sponsored by the Athénée Louisianais closed, and 1986, when the Audubon French School was established.

Nearly seventy years after the closing of the Union Française girls' school, it is virtually impossible to find a native New Orleanian French speaker, but many schools are again offering French immersion education. The city had three French immersion programs—two public, one private—when Hurricane Katrina hit on August 29, 2005. None of the schools went beyond eighth grade. In 2003, however, Louisiana's Board of Elementary and Secondary Education had laid the groundwork for the unlikely rise in the number of elementary school French immersion programs in New Orleans by assuming control of most of the city's public schools and allowing the establishment of a large charter school system. French immersion schools became easier to establish than might have been the case prior to the storm.

Consequently, New Orleans is now home to more French language elementary schools per capita than in any other American city. But despite its history, the city provides few meaningful opportunities to use French in familial, professional, or social communities. This chapter details the history of French use and education in New Orleans in the nineteenth century, the disappearance of French, and the unexpected reemergence of French education after 2005.

OÙ SONT LES ÉCOLES D'ANTAN?

When French colonists founded and built New Orleans from 1718 to 1762 and under Spanish rule from 1762 to 1800, residents largely spoke, read, and wrote in French. Though religious and governmental records were kept in Spanish during that country's control, Spaniards tended to marry francophones, and French remained dominant. The dominance of French is evidenced by the fact that little Spanish-language legacy remains other than street names.

Despite the hegemony of French, New Orleans public spaces must have been a polyglot bustle in the eighteenth and nineteenth centuries, given the busy port and the waves of immigrants (voluntarily and involuntarily) arriving there. The largest and most easily identifiable language groups were European—German, Spanish, English (especially via American and Irish immigration), and later Italian. A Jewish population likely brought Yiddish speakers into the mix. Louis Armstrong, born on the cusp of the twentieth century, was familiar with Yiddish, which he heard while he was employed and befriended by a Lithuanian family, the Karnofskys. In the nineteenth century, several Yiddish-speaking families lived on S. Rampart, a place sometimes associated with the birth of jazz (Fertel 2011). The large early nineteenth-century Irish immigration conceivably featured some Irish speakers. As an important slave market, New Orleans hosted Africans brought directly from their home continent before 1807: they would have spoken more than fifty African languages (Midlo-Hall 1992). Yet French remained the dominant language of this Tower of Babel.

In 1803, the United States purchased the Louisiana Territory, and nine years later, Louisiana became a state. New Orleans sluggishly began to Americanize and adopt the English language during this era; paradoxically, however, francophone New Orleans also experienced its second golden age. From 1803 to about 1860, a steady stream of people made their way from France to Louisiana, escaping service in the Napoleonic army, fleeing poverty, or evading the aftermath of the 1848 revolution. In addition, thousands of free and enslaved French-speaking immigrants fleeing the revolution in Saint-Domingue (modern Haiti) poured in on the eve of statehood. Louisiana's 1845 constitution recognized French language rights, and an 1847 law authorized bilingual instruction in the state's public schools (DeVore and Logsdon 1991).

In 1850, one in five immigrants to New Orleans was born in France (Bankston 2007:26). As New Orleans became a part of America, the city's African-heritage population doubled, while its francophone population increased as well. New Orleans residents, whether established or newly arrived, conducted private and public business in French.

Many newspapers, church records, and court documents continued to be written in French. From the end of the Spanish period until 1959, the city had more than one hundred French-language newspapers (LSU Special Collections 2009). The longest-lasting of these papers was *L'Abeille de la Nouvelle-Orléans* (the New Orleans Bee), which was published from 1827 to 1923). *Le Courrier de la Nouvelle-Orléans* (the New Orleans Courier), though established later, outlived *l'Abeille*, lasting until 1955. Many of these papers had French and English columns side-by-side and must have served an educated francophone public.

People learned to read and write mostly with the help of private tutors, by attending small private schools or French Catholic schools, or by going to study in France. Some Creoles with the means furthered their studies in France (Read 1931; Brasseaux 2005). A handful of people of color, including the playwright Victor Séjour, went to France in search of artistic and other freedoms denied to them in Louisiana (O'Neill 1995).

French education dates to the early years of the colony. Most famously, in 1752, Ursuline nuns established a convent and what became Ursuline Academy, now the oldest extant girls' school in the United States as well as the nation's oldest integrated school; since the school's inception, girls of European, African, and Native backgrounds have studied with the Ursulines. And for at least a century, they did so in French.

In antebellum Louisiana, unlike elsewhere in the United States, free people of color were afforded some of the same educational opportunities as their white counterparts. A small group of free people of color published the country's first collection of poems by African Americans, *Les Cenelles* (1845); it was written in French (Lanusse 1845). Some researchers have claimed that by 1850, four-fifths of New Orleans's free people of color were literate and that more than a thousand of their children attended schools (Brosman 2013:23).

Not all formal education conducted in French was Catholic or private. The early nineteenth century saw Louisiana's first public institution of higher education, the short-lived Collège d'Orléans (1811–23), which was a public school that sought to educate both the francophone and anglophone populations. It stood where St. Augustine Church was later erected, in the neighborhood known today as the Tremé.

One of the early directors of the Collège, Joseph Lakanal, had been an original member of the Institut de France, a French academic umbrella institution that included the Académie Française, the French council that oversees French-language issues. Lakanal came to the Collège d'Orléans in 1818, and the school may have closed its doors because of him. Lakanal, who later became president of what is now Tulane University, was an ex-priest turned atheist. According to a colorful description in the 1903 *Picayune's Guide to New Orleans* (45), pious mothers did not want their sons entrusted to and educated by a supporter of revolutionary regicide (Deléry 1950).

Three decades after Louisiana had ceased to be a French colony, French remained the language of everyday communication. Yet the state's francophone youth realized the urgency and utility of learning English. In 1838, Séverin Landry, an Assumption Parish man who conducted business in New Orleans, wrote (in French) to his sweetheart to explain why he had left Louisiana to study English in Missouri:

> Je suis placé depuis quelques temps dans une maison de commerce où je pense que ce sera pour moi une [sic] avantage pour apprendre l'anglais et je ferai tout ce qui dépendra de moi afin d'en remporter tous les avantages possibles car je m'aperçois plus que jamais de quelle utilité est la langue anglaise pour un pays tel que le notre [sic].

> I have been working for some time in a business where I think it will be an advantage for me to learn English and I will do all that I can to gain from it all the benefits possible because I realize more than ever the usefulness of the English language for a country such as ours. (translation by author)

The establishment of public schools in 1841 raised debate as to what the language of instruction should be. In 1836, the city had divided itself into three municipalities. The First Municipality (roughly today's French Quarter) was the oldest, most francophone section, while many incoming Anglo-Americans settled in the Second Municipality, on the upriver side of Canal Street (now the Central Business District). The Third Municipality consisted of the Faubourgs Tremé and Marigny (sometimes called the Creole Faubourgs). From this period until after the Civil War, public schools in the First and Third Municipalities

Table 10.1. Mother Tongues of School-Age Children, First Municipality (School District 2), New Orleans, 1852 and 1853

	1852	1853
French	1,288 (52%)	1,122 (41%)
English	968 (39%)	1,109 (40%)
German	141 (6%)	446 (16%)
Spanish	42 (2%)	44 (2%)
Italian	40 (2%)	27 (1%)
TOTAL	2,479	2,748

Note: Because of rounding, totals may not equal 100%.
Source: Adapted from DeVore and Logsdon 1991:29 (Minutes School District 2, May 17, 1852, December 19, 1852), with permission from the University of Louisiana at Lafayette Press.

offered bilingual French and English instruction, while public schools in the Second Municipality had English-only instruction, though French was required for all high school students (DeVore and Logsdon 1991; Reinders 1964).

The private Catholic school sector also continued to grow during this era, with French clergy founding the Holy Cross School (1849), Brother Martin High School (1869), and the Sacred Heart Academy (1886). The language of instruction is not known. The Jesuits, who had arrived as missionaries when Louisiana was a French colony and were then expelled under Spanish rule, returned and launched both the College of the Immaculate Conception (1847), which became Jesuit High School, and Loyola College (1886), which is now Loyola University.

According to DeVore and Logsdon (1991:25), French education in the public schools failed after the Civil War as a consequence of the dearth "of well-trained bilingual teachers and no easy access to textbooks in both languages." In spite of the declining number of New Orleans French speakers (table 10.1), First Municipality residents sought to maintain public French education. In response to the "desperate need for competent bilingual teachers" (30) French speakers established schools to train teachers. By 1853, more than twenty-five teachers equipped to teach in French and English had graduated from the girls' high school in the in the First Municipality, the Creole part of the city (29–30). Jumonville (1997:127 n.11) notes, however, that "curiously, no bilingual Louisiana studies text appeared." With just a few bilingual teachers and no bilingual textbooks or manuals, the future of parallel French and English education was grim.

During and after the Civil War, former slaves had some limited opportunities to educate themselves and their children in New Orleans, an enterprise that parents, educators, and the children themselves took very seriously even when resources were lacking (Mitchell 2008). The few educational establishments for children of color included the Institut Catholique, founded in the Faubourg Marigny in the 1840s. Marie Couvent, a wealthy free African American widow, funded and established the Institut to teach young boys in both English and French. A public school in the neighborhood still bears Couvent's name on its lintel, although the school's name was subsequently changed first to honor Alexandre Pierre Tureaud and later to honor Homer Plessy, both of whom were New Orleanians from francophone backgrounds who were involved in civil rights.

Louisiana's *francophonie*[1] began to decline more precipitously after the Civil War, which is frequently noted as the beginning of the end for French in New Orleans because of the Union army occupation (1862–65) and subsequent shifts in the city's economy and legal system that permanently transformed the city. Later language legislation further complicates the story. Both French and English were official languages until the Louisiana Constitution of 1868, which not only mandated publication of official acts solely in English but also required schooling to take place only in that language. The 1879 Constitution subsequently restored the legality of publishing official documents in both languages and returned to a sort of tolerance of the language in arenas (such as education) where French was permitted if it did not add additional costs. French teachers and materials were, however, regarded as extra expenses. The respite from legislative attacks lasted until 1921, when public schools were required to provide instruction only in English. This requirement is generally credited with causing the precipitous decline of French in the twentieth century.

However laws surrounding public education changed, people's language habits did not change with them, as an 1868 advertisement in the *Abeille de la Nouvelle-Orléans* illustrates:

Collège de la Louisiane
Dirigé par M. le colonel A. Ferrier Pensionnat et externat
Les cours de cette institution sont en pleine activité. Les classes supérieures confiées à des professeurs de premier mérite, comprennent: le Latin, le Grec, les Mathématiques, Algèbre et Géometrie—et les cours de Rhétorique et de Philosophie en Anglais et en Français. ("Collège de la Louisiane" 1868)

College of Louisiana
Led by Colonel A. Ferrier Boarding and Day School
The courses in this institution are currently in session. The upper classes, assigned to the best teachers, include: Latin, Greek, Mathematics, Algebra and Geometry—and Rhetoric and Philosophy courses in English and French. (translation by author)

Advertisements for bilingual schools appeared frequently in newspapers through the 1860s but subsequently became scarcer. But many late-nineteenth-century New Orleans residents understood the utility of multilingualism and sought language instruction. In Kate Chopin's *The Awakening* (1899:10), Robert's professional value is measured by his linguistic ability: "Meanwhile he held on to his modest position in a mercantile house in New Orleans, where an equal familiarity with English, French and Spanish gave him no small value as a clerk and correspondent." Some New Orleanians educated their children primarily in French at private schools until the closure of the Union Française school in 1952.

FRENCH EDUCATION IN NEW ORLEANS TODAY

French remains alive as a home language in greater New Orleans, largely as a result of immigration from elsewhere in Louisiana and from francophone countries; however, there are very few of these francophones. According to the MLA Language Map, between 0.22 percent and .68 percent of the population of Orleans Parish speaks French (Modern Language Association n.d.). Other estimates hover around 1.5 percent (Eble 2009). The US Census Bureau (2015) put the percentage at about .093 for Orleans and Jefferson Parishes. Just fifty miles from metropolitan New Orleans, in Lafourche Parish, as much as 18 percent of the population is francophone (Modern Language Association n.d.). But despite the lack of home speakers, French heritage has remained a key source of cultural identity in New Orleans, with French terms used frequently in business names and in other public discourse (Dajko 2018). The rise of contemporary French education in the city is a story shaped by governmental programs, school failures, natural disasters, an influx of residents, and history.

The result is one of the largest numbers of French immersion schools in the nation, with at least fourteen schools offering either full immersion of intensive training in French. Atlanta, which has a population approximately four times larger than that of New Orleans and has double the percentage of native francophones (Modern Language Association n.d.), has just one-third as many French immersion schools and classes as New Orleans. This phenomenon demonstrates the ongoing importance of the state's French heritage as well as the influence of the charter school movement, Hurricane Katrina, and an influx of new residents ready to embrace the New Orleans French legacy.

The pre-Katrina rebirth of French education is tied to the state's larger French history and to the French revitalization movement (Valdman 1997:185), which led to the 1968 establishment of the Council for the Development of

French in Louisiana (CODOFIL). Charged with doing "all things necessary to accomplish the development, utilization, and preservation of the French language as found in Louisiana for the cultural, economic and touristic benefit of the state," CODOFIL led directly to the establishment of French-language programs throughout the state, including the Audubon French School (now renamed the French program at Audubon Charter School), a publicly funded immersion program.

The Audubon Montessori School began its French immersion program in 1986, and it remained the only one in the city until the establishment of the private École Bilingue in 1998. Both schools follow the French national curriculum, and Audubon is accredited by the Agence de l'Enseignement de Français à l'Étranger (Agency for French Education Abroad). Founded in 2000, the International School of Louisiana offers a standard Louisiana curriculum in French, Spanish, and Mandarin immersion. Those three French immersion programs were the only ones available before Hurricane Katrina, although other schools offered intensive language training.

By 2015, however, six other public or charter schools had joined their predecessors in offering either French immersion or highly intensive language programs in either Orleans or neighboring Jefferson Parish:

- Le Lycée Français de la Nouvelle-Orléans (2010), which offers the French national curriculum and plans to add French education at the secondary level
- International High School of New Orleans, which uses English as the language of instruction but offers the International Baccalaureate program and intensive language instruction with the goal of achieving fluency in one of four languages
- Hynes Charter School, which offers an immersion program alongside an English-based curriculum
- Haynes Academy for Advanced Studies (Metairie, Jefferson Parish)
- J. C. Ellis Elementary (Jefferson Parish)
- Ben Franklin High School (a selective-admission public school)

Intensive and advanced French curricula have long been available at private and parochial schools including Academy of the Sacred Heart, Louise S. McGehee School, and Isidore Newman School, all of which offer Advanced Placement French courses. Metairie Park Country Day School, McGehee, and Newman provide French instruction beginning in Pre-K, and McGehee organizes trips to France for high school students.

The number of public and charter programs began growing in 2003, when the state took over many failing schools and opened a path for parents and groups to operate schools under focused pedagogical charters. The charter school movement took off, and New Orleans became the first city in the nation to have a majority of public schools operating as charter schools (Zernike 2016); by 2014, 91 percent of New Orleans's schools were charters (National Alliance for Charters 2014).

Much of this growth resulted from Hurricane Katrina's hollowing out of New Orleans's institutional landscape and the subsequent influx of new residents from out of state (Campbell 2014). The city's post-Katrina population includes higher numbers of Latinos, a higher percentage of whites, and a lower percentage of African Americans than before the storm (Shrinath, Mack, and Plyer 2014; Waller 2013). In some cases, the new residents champion new programs or schools. Some of the newly arrived embrace New Orleans French with the fervor of religious converts, establishing Mardi Gras krewes with seemingly local names like Krewe de Lune (2010) and 'tit Rəx (est. 2011) (*'tit* [*tee*] is the abbreviation of *petit*). Even English-speaking schools that do not have French programs may co-opt the French language, as in the English-language Bricolage Academy (2013) (see Camp, this volume).

PARENTS, CHILDREN, AND FRENCH-LANGUAGE EDUCATION

To investigate the foundations of the boom in French education, I attended school meetings and Alliance Française cultural events between 2012 and 2014. I also interviewed seven parents whose children attended Audubon Charter, the International School of Louisiana, Le Lycée Français de la Nouvelle Orléans, J. C. Ellis, and the École Bilingue; two principals (Melanie Tennyson, CEO/head of school/principal of the Camp Street Campus of the ISL; Jean-Jacques Grandière, formerly of the Lycée Français); and several French teachers in the immersion schools. In addition, I was interviewed for an immersion French position and reviewed press reporting on the schools, particularly the *Uptown Messenger* and the *Lens*, which thoroughly covered the tumultuous founding of the Lycée Français.

I have learned that the New Orleans parents who prioritize French study by sending their children to schools that emphasize French or offer French immersion are not typically native French speakers, nor do they always have French as a heritage language (although some do). Parents want their children to study French for different reasons: opportunities to travel, to speak with French people, to read French literature, to improve cognition, and to improve their chances for college admission. For non-French-nationals, the impression of French as a sophisticated language appears to influence school selection more than does the historical importance of French in Louisiana. Only two parents (one whose children attended the ISL, and one whose children attended École Bilingue) were seeking to reclaim a lost family heritage.

Their children and the others in these schools—the new New Orleans francophones—are comparable to a species that is extinct in its natural habitat but can be kept alive in controlled environments. In other words, while the French language is still taught, learned, understood, written, spoken, and read in New Orleans French immersion schools, no researcher would say the language thrives. Children speak English among themselves on playgrounds, and some school administrators do not speak French and thus must communicate in English. Parents often struggle to understand their children's newly acquired language. Beyond the Alliance Française, a consular office, and a handful of French-owned businesses, New Orleans offers few meaningful opportunities to use French. One parent lamented that the children used English during recess and that French had come to represent classroom drudgery (Durocher 2015).

In 2010, I participated in a pilot series of French storybook readings sponsored by the Louisiana Endowment for the Humanities and the French Consulate of New Orleans as part of the Endowment's Prime Time literacy program. I was engaged as the bilingual humanities scholar who would lead a discussion in French with parents and children; the intended audiences were parents and guardians considered less likely to read a bedtime story to their children. I observed fifteen children who attended either ISL or Audubon and their mostly monolingual English-speaking parents, who came from a variety of backgrounds and included native New Orleanians, New Yorkers, and a French expatriate. Concurrently, I worked in Terrebonne Parish with five families that were nearly universally monolingual English-speaking and in which the children did not attend French immersion programs. The children's grandparents and great-grandparents (not present at the event), however, had retained some ability to speak Louisiana French. In Terrebonne, the storyteller was a Louisiana French speaker, and both adults and children discussed the storybooks in English. In New Orleans, the discussions took place in French, but the parents did not participate, partially defeating the purpose of the program. The Prime Time pilot thus was not successful in either Orleans or Terrebonne: the children's natural language environment is clearly English, and they cannot join with their families using French as a home language.

FRAGMENTED FRENCH REVITALIZATION

The French that is taught in New Orleans schools is Reference French. Three of the immersion schools (Audubon Charter, the École Bilingue, and the Lycée Français de la Nouvelle-Orléans) are accredited by the French ministry of education and follow the French national curriculum. In other francophone cities such as Montreal or Kinshasa—arguably the second-largest francophone city in the world—students learn local varieties of French. Rural Louisiana has its own French, with a local lexicon (a *cyprière* is a cypress tree marsh; a *chaoui* is a raccoon) and its own dictionary. But the Louisiana lexicon is not used in immersion schools in New Orleans. French is taught by teachers who neither know Louisiana dialects nor are equipped with a curriculum in Louisiana French. Historically (at least in the nineteenth century), New Orleans was home to a prestige dialect close to modern Reference French. This practical justification for *French* French in New Orleans has greater cultural-linguistic ramifications, however. The teaching of Reference French in a formerly French-dominant state in which at least two varieties of the language (Louisiana Regional French and Creole) remain extant has occasionally drawn criticism. Some of the state's academics, francophone community members, and language activists have reproached CODOFIL for promoting "standard," metropolitan, or "French French" (Gold 1979). Reporting on the publication of Donald Faulk's *Cajun French I: The First Written Record and Definitive Study of the Cajun Language as Spoken by the People in Vermilion and Surrounding Parishes* (1977), the *New York Times* (1977) wrote that "some Cajuns grumbled that the modern French their children were learning was not true Cajun. For example the French '*je bois*,' or 'I drink,' becomes '*j'bwo*' in Cajun. They feared the culture was only being further eroded by the French lessons." According to the article, Faulk claimed that "nobody wanted to take standard French." A priest, Jules Daigle, wrote and published *A Dictionary of the Cajun Language* (1984), followed by *Cajun Self-Taught* (1992), both of which went through many editions and included cassettes and CDs, and Raymond Landreneau published *La Langue Cadjinne Française* (1989). While these resources exist, however, none are really functional for instruction for various reasons. The push to include Louisiana French in the curriculum continues. Richard Guidry, the Louisiana Department of Education's coordinator of foreign languages and bilingual education around the Lafayette area, promoted Louisiana French and introduced varieties of the language to the classroom, and teachers Kirby Jambon and Ashley Michot continue the tradition of promoting local French in their nonimmersion classrooms. French native and former Lafourche Parish CODOFIL teacher Céline Doucet pursued a doctorate in linguistics while teaching in Louisiana and has presented a conference paper on the importance of transmitting Louisiana French (Doucet 2014). But these individual efforts have not resulted from widespread teacher training or production of curriculum materials.

Solving the problem is far from easy. CODOFIL has grown to recognize the importance of rural Louisiana French language and culture but has not been able to create a cadre of native Louisiana French teachers. In the 1960s and 1970s, when CODOFIL began to promote French instruction in schools, local French speakers generally not only lacked the requisite professional credentials but also did not possess French literacy. In 2015, New Orleans had no native Louisiana francophones teaching French in immersion schools.

Indeed, immersion schools in New Orleans pride themselves on having native French speakers, not native Louisiana French speakers. According to the Audubon Charter School (2015) website, "Our full time French faculty is composed of certified teachers who speak French as their first language." Given that there are no longer very many Louisianans (and virtually no New Orleanians) who fit such criteria, the school's hiring practices do not encourage locals to become French teachers. In contrast, the structure of the Teachers of English to Speakers of Other Languages actively seeks to empower nonnative speakers to become teachers of English as a second language (Bernat 2008). This approach does not appear to be an emphasis in Français Langue Étrangère pedagogy, the rough equivalent of English as a Second Language. As a result, French-language training in Louisiana cannot lead to jobs in New Orleans schools, since the schools seek first-language French speakers, who are not likely to be from Louisiana.

This incongruous state of affairs is in some ways reflected in the opportunities offered by postsecondary institutions. Most notably, Louisiana State University's Department of French Studies houses the Center for French and Francophone Studies and offers a Cajun studies program including language classes that results in a minor in Cajun French. Courses in Louisiana French and Creole are also available at the University of Louisiana at Lafayette, which is home to an impressive archive of recordings and more at the Center for Louisiana Studies. Tulane University's Department of French and Italian offers a course in linguistic field methods that sends students out to the Louisiana countryside to learn and document the language by interviewing speakers. Although Shreveport is not historically French-speaking, the city's Centenary College, a selective private school, has since 2011 hosted the Escadrille Louisiane. In partnership with CODOFIL and the Université de Rennes, Centenary offers a master's degree in teaching to Louisiana students who wish to study and teach French in the state. Centenary also houses the only French-language publishing house in the United States, Les Éditions Tintamarre. (For more on French education in Louisiana, see Camp, this volume.)

New Orleans stands out in the United States for its opportunities for French immersion education. Nevertheless, it is not yet clear whether new francophones are being created in New Orleans. In spite of decreasing funding and a lack of native francophones, French immersion education has blossomed in the city as well as beyond: Louisiana now has more than thirty French immersion schools and programs (see Camp, this volume). One logical step has been that Louisiana in 2018 joined the Organisation Internationale de la Francophonie with "observer status," thereby becoming part of an international cohort of French speakers and French educators. An international affiliation should benefit not only budding New Orleans francophones but also those from regions of the state where the language is not yet gone. Louisiana also needs a university-based French immersion program. Such a setting might permit students to become completely competent to teach or engage in any profession using French as well as increase transparency regarding the question of what a student would do with French fluency.

The rather dreary fact that the French language has been threatened in New Orleans for more than one hundred years does not seem to reduce the tenacity of individuals who work to keep French alive. In the future, linguists, sociologists, anthropologists, and hopefully literary scholars will focus on the emergent bilinguals who will have graduated from French immersion programs. Time will tell whether the youth who gain French fluency and a francophone identity through formal immersion environments constitute the nascent bilingual community that will create a new New Orleans *francophonie*.

NOTES

Mille mercis to the families, colleagues, administrators, schools, students, friends, and scholars who helped me in my research relating to yesterday and today's French education in New Orleans.

1. The term *francophonie* was coined in 1880 by geographer Onésime Reclus (1837–1916), whose brother, Élisée Reclus (1830–1905) published *Fragment d'un Voyage à la Nouvelle-Orléans* (1860) after having served as the private tutor for the Fortier family at Felicity Plantation in St. James Parish, Louisiana (Deniau 1992:11–13; Clark 1993–94).

WORKS CITED

L'Athénée Louisianais Records, 1834–1987. N.d. LaRC/Manuscripts Collection 108, Tulane University Special Collections, New Orleans.
Audubon Charter School. n.d. "About our School: French Program." http://www.auduboncharter.org/thefrenchschool.aspx/.
Bankston, Carl. 2007. "New People in the New South: An Overview of Southern Immigration." *Southern Cultures* 13 (4): 24–44.
Bernat, Eva. 2008. "Towards a Pedagogy of Empowerment: The Case of the Imposter Syndrome among Pre-Service Non-Native Teachers of TESOL." *English Language Teacher Education and Development* 11 (28): 1–8.

Brasseaux, Carl. 2005. *French, Cajun, Creole, Houma: A Primer on Francophone Louisiana.* Baton Rouge: Louisiana State University Press.
Brosman, Catharine Savage. 2013. *Louisiana Creole Literature: A Historical Study.* Jackson: University Press of Mississippi.
Campbell, Alexia Fernández. 2014. "New Orleans' Post-Katrina Identity Crisis." *National Journal Online*, October 20. http://www.nationaljournal.com/next-america/population-2043/new-orleans-post-katrina-identity-crisis-20141020.
Chopin, Kate. 1899. *The Awakening.* New York: Avon, 1972.
Clark, John. 1993–94. "Putting Freedom on the Map: The Life and Work of Élisée Reclus." http://dwardmac.pitzer.edu/anarchist_archives/bright/reclus/voyage.html.
"Collège de la Louisiane." 1868. *L'Abeille de la Nouvelle-Orléans*, January 3. http://nobee.jefferson.lib.la.us/Vol-062/01_1868/1868_01_0007.pdf.
Daigle, Jules. 1984. *A Dictionary of the Cajun Language.* Ann Arbor: Edwards.
Daigle, Jules. 1992. *Cajun Self-Taught.* Welsh, LA: Daigle.
Dajko, Nathalie. 2018. "The Continuing Symbolic Importance of French in Louisiana." In *Language Variation in the New South: Contemporary Perspectives on Change and Variation*, edited by Jeffrey Reaser, Eric Wilbanks, Karissa Wojcik, and Walt Wolfram, 153–74. Chapel Hill: University of North Carolina Press.
Deléry, Simone de la Souchère. 1950. "Alphabet, Modèle 1829." *French Review* 23 (4): 300–303.
Deniau, Xavier. 1992. *La Francophonie.* Paris: Presses Universitaires de France.
DeVore, Donald E, and Joseph Logsdon. 1991. *Crescent City Schools: Public Education in New Orleans, 1841–1991.* Lafayette: Center for Louisiana Studies, University of Southwestern Louisiana.
Doucet, Céline. 2014. "Language Maintenance and Transmission: The Case of Cajun French." Paper presented at the Language as a Social Justice Issue Conference, Perth, Australia, November 26. http://ro.ecu.edu.au/lsjic/8/.
Durocher, Dennis. 2015. Personal communication, January 21.
Eble, Connie. 2009. "French in New Orleans: The Commodification of Language Heritage." *American Speech* 84 (2): 211–15.
Faulk, James Donald. 1977. *Cajun French I: The First Written Record and Definitive Study of the Cajun Language as Spoken by the People in Vermilion and Surrounding Parishes.* Crowley, LA: Cajun.
Fertel, Randy. 2011. *Gorilla Man and the Empress of Steak: A New Orleans Family Memoir.* Jackson: University Press of Mississippi.
Gold, Gérald L. 1979. *The Role of France, Quebec, and Belgium in the Revival of French in Louisiana Schools.* Toronto: Department of Anthropology, York University.
Hall, Gwendolyn Midlo. 1992. *Africans in Colonial Louisiana: The Development of Afro-Creole Culture in the Eighteenth Century.* Baton Rouge: Louisiana State University Press.
Jumonville, Florence M. 1997. *Creating and Transmitting the Louisiana Memory: Teaching Louisiana Studies in the Schools.* New Orleans: University of New Orleans Press.
Landreneau, Raymond Lee. 1989. *La Langue Cadjinne Française.* Atlanta: Chicot.
Landry, Severin. 2007. Landry Family Papers. http://www.lib.lsu.edu/sites/default/files/sc/findaid/0731.pdf.
LSU Special Collections. 2009. "Louisiana French Newspapers by Dates." https://www.lib.lsu.edu/sites/all/files/sc/lnp/lnp_french.pdf.
Lanusse, Armand, ed. 1845. *Les Cenelles: Choix de Poésies Indigènes.* New Orleans: Fauve.

Mitchell, Mary Niall. 2008. *Raising Freedom's Child: Black Children and Visions of the Future after Slavery*. New York: New York University Press.

Modern Language Association. N.d. *MLA Language Map*. http://arcgis.mla.org/mla/default.aspx.

National Alliance for Charters. 2014. *A Growing Movement: America's Largest Charter School Communities*. https://www.publiccharters.org/publications/growing-movement-americas-largest-charter-public-school-communities.

New York Times. 1977. "Cajun Language Textbook Seen as Helping Preserve Culture." June 25.

O'Neill, Charles F. 1995. *Séjour: Parisian Playwright from Louisiana*. Lafayette: Center for Louisiana Studies, University of Southwestern Louisiana.

The Picayune's Guide to New Orleans. 1903. http://hdl.loc.gov/loc.gdc/scd0001.00145449273.

Read, William A. 1931. *Louisiana-French*. Baton Rouge: Louisiana State University Press.

Reclus, Élisée. 2004. *A Voyage to New Orleans: Anarchist Impressions of the Old South*. Thetford, VT: Glad Day.

Reinders, Robert C. 1964. "New England Influences on the Formation of Public Schools in New Orleans." *Journal of Southern History* 30 (2): 181–95.

Shrinath, Nihal, Vicki Mack, and Allison Plyer. 2014. "Who Lives in New Orleans and Metro Parishes Now?" October 16. http://www.datacenterresearch.org/data-resources/who-lives-in-new-orleans-now/.

The Times-Picayune Guide to New Orleans. 1917. https://archive.org/details/timespicayuneguio1newo.

"L'Union Française." 2016. http://lunionfrancaise.org/.

US Census Bureau. 2015. "Detailed Languages Spoken at Home and Ability to Speak English for the Population 5 Years and Over for Core-Based Statistical Areas (CBSAs): 2009–2013." http://www.census.gov/data/tables/2013/demo/2009-2013-lang-tables.html.

Valdman, Albert. 1997. *French and Creole in Louisiana*. New York: Plenum.

Waller, Mark. 2013. "Hurricane Katrina Eight Years Later: A Statistical Snapshot of the New Orleans Area." *New Orleans Times-Picayune*, August 28. http://www.nola.com/katrina/index.ssf/2013/08/hurricane_katrina_eight_years.html.

Zernike, K. 2016. "New Orleans Plan, Charter Schools with a Return to Local Control." *New York Times*, May 9. http://www.nytimes.com/2016/05/10/us/charter-driven-gains-in-new-orleans-schools-face-a-big-test.html.

SECTION III

English in Louisiana

NATHALIE DAJKO AND SHANA WALTON

English has been spoken in Louisiana for hundreds of years, though not until the late twentieth century did it become predominant throughout even the former French strongholds of Acadiana. Today, for example, more than 90 percent of New Orleans residents report being monolingual anglophones (US Census 2010). Increasingly, Louisiana is a strikingly English place.

Significant numbers of English speakers first arrived with the influx of Americans following statehood in 1812, with another wave coming during the massive Irish immigration that peaked in the 1820s and 1840s. While at least some of the Irish immigrants likely spoke Gaelic, the strong likelihood of their literacy (Kelley 2004:45–46) serves as solid evidence for the fact that by and large they spoke English. English speakers mixed with francophones, speakers of African languages, and German speakers who arrived alongside the Irish as well as with Italian immigrants at the turn of the twentieth century. While French has clearly had a significant impact on English spoken in south Louisiana, in New Orleans, and especially in the countryside, the effects of other languages have yet to be fully investigated. German and Italian immigrants seem to have shifted rapidly to English (or French, in the case of earlier/more rural German populations), leaving little to no obvious trace of their passing save perhaps an isolated lexical item—for example, the use of *Christine* (from the German *krist kind* [Santa Claus]) in the French spoken in Terrebonne and Lafourche Parishes or the use of *by* to mean *at* (as in *I'm by my Mama's house*) in New Orleans English (Reinecke 1985). Some observers have suggested that the striking similarity between New Orleans's working-class white dialect and the working-class dialect spoken in New York City results from the influence of similar immigrant populations in the two cities (Mucciaccio 2009) or from the presence of Maritime English in such port cities (Dillard 1985). Others scholars, however, have suggested that the similarities instead result from significant contact between the two cities (Labov 2007; Becker and Carmichael 2014; Carmichael and Becker 2016).

Despite the predominance of English, relatively little research has as yet been conducted on the language in Louisiana. Cajun English has received the most attention to date, with a number of articles documenting the effect of French on that dialect (e.g., Dubois and Horvath 1998, 2000, 2002; Cheramie and Gill 1992; Cox 1992; Scott 1992) or examining the stylistic use of the dialect (Walton 1994, 2002; Carmichael 2013). Dubois and Horvath (2003) have studied Creole English. This volume contributes to this literature with Katie Carmichael's overview of the study of Cajun English and her analysis of its metalinguistic function through its use in joke telling.

English outside of Acadiana and New Orleans is most often classified by its similarity to other Southern Englishes, though this classification is the result of sparse documentation in the *Linguistic Atlas of the Gulf States* (n.d.) more than twenty years ago. The state's largest speech region subsequently has had virtually no published accounts testing its participation in changes occurring in the rest of the South or describing searches for varieties within the area. Most recently, researchers have undertaken preliminary attempts to study English spoken in Independence, Louisiana, (Abdalian 2016; Dajko 2016; Sprowls 2016; Sprowls and Abdalian forthcoming). In this volume, Lisa Abney's offers preliminary results from her effort to restart the *Linguistic Atlas* studies across the northern part of the state.

Perhaps the most glaring lacuna in the field, however, is that of New Orleans. Though the city is home to at least two and possibly three or more dialects (the matter has not been settled; its speech remains woefully understudied. Most completed studies are master's theses or doctoral dissertations (e.g., Reinecke 1951; Douglas 1969; Malin 1972; Brennan 1982; Aubert-Gex 1983; Mucciaccio 2009; White-Sustaíta 2012; Schoux Casey 2013; Carmichael 2014) or are the work of laypeople (e.g., Smith 1996). Brief examinations of the working-class white dialect known as Yat (Coles 1997, 2001) and a handful of encyclopedia entries and overview articles (Blanton 1989; Eble 2009) constitute the largest body of research beyond theses and dissertations. The good news is that scholarly interest in both New Orleans English and Louisiana English in general is on the rise. Katie Carmichael and Nathalie Dajko are currently conducting a major study of the city funded by the National Science Foundation (BCS 1749217 and 1749257, respectively), focusing on both documenting variation and examining its correlation with place- and ethnic-based identity. At least three graduate students at three different institutions are currently documenting aspects of New Orleans English, focusing on populations long neglected by linguists: Hispanics, upper-class whites, and African Americans. These studies will surely add pieces to the puzzle of New Orleans English. Recent work by

Christina Schoux Casey, Katie Carmichael, and Nathalie Dajko continues this push to involve New Orleans in the canon of American English dialects. Schoux Casey's chapter here takes a general look at speech in the city, focusing on both particular characteristics and the commodification of the language.

WORKS CITED

Abdalian, Andrew. 2016. "The History and Language of Independence, LA." Video recording. https://www.youtube.com/watch?v=3UWAc66Z7eY.

Aubert-Gex, Madeleine. 1983. "A Lexical Study of the English of New Orleans Creoles." Master's thesis, University of New Orleans.

Becker, Kara, and Katie Carmichael. 2014. "'That Hoboken Near the Gulf of Mexico': What (r) Can Tell Us about English in New York City and New Orleans." Paper presented at New Ways of Analyzing Variation, Chicago, October 25.

Blanton, Mackie J. V. 1989. "New Orleans English." In *The Encyclopedia of Southern Cultures*, edited by William Ferris and Charles Wilson, 780–81. Chapel Hill: University of North Carolina Press.

Carmichael, Katie. 2013. "The Performance of Cajun English in Boudreaux and Thibodeaux Jokes." *American Speech* 88 (4): 377–412.

Carmichael, Katie. 2014. "'I Never Thought I Had an Accent until the Hurricane': Sociolinguistic Variation in Post-Katrina Greater New Orleans." PhD diss., Ohio State University.

Carmichael, Katie, and Kara Becker. 2016. "Raised BOUGHT in New Orleans and New York City: It's Not What You THOUGHT." Paper presented at the annual meeting of the American Dialect Society, Washington, DC, January 8.

Cheramie, Deany M., and Donald A. Gill. 1992. "Lexical Choice in Cajun Vernacular English." In *Louisiana English Journal*, edited by Ann Martin Scott, 38–55. Lafayette: University of Southwestern Louisiana.

Coles, Felice Anne. 1997. "Solidarity Cues in New Orleans English." In *Language Variety in the South Revisited*, edited by Cynthia Bernstein, Thomas Nunnally, and Robin Sabino, 219–24. Tuscaloosa: University of Alabama Press.

Coles, Felice Anne. 2001. "The Authenticity of Yat: A 'Real' New Orleans Dialect." *Southern Journal of Linguistics* 25 (1–2): 74–86.

Cox, Juanita. 1992. *A Study of the Linguistic Features of Cajun English*. http://files.eric.ed.gov/fulltext/ED352840.pdf.

Dajko, Nathalie. 2016. "Patterns of (r) in Independence." Paper presented at the Southeastern Conference on Linguistics, New Orleans, March 30.

Dictionary of American Regional English. N.d. Linguistic Atlas Project Online. http://dare.wisc.edu

Dillard, J. L. 1985. "Language and Linguistic Research in Louisiana." In *Louisiana Folklife: A Guide to the State*, edited by Nicholas R. Spitzer. http://www.louisianafolklife.org/LT/Virtual_Books/Guide_to_State/creole_book_guide_to_state.html.

Douglas, Connie. 1969. "A Linguistic Study of the English Used by New Orleans Speakers of Creole." Master's thesis, University of New Orleans.

Dubois, Sylvie, and Barbara Horvath. 1998. "Let's Talk about Dat: Interdental Fricatives in Cajun English." *Language Variation and Change* 10:245–61.

Dubois, Sylvie, and Barbara Horvath. 2000. "When the Music Changes, You Change Too: Gender and Language Change in Cajun English." *Language Variation and Change* 11:287–313.

Dubois, Sylvie, and Barbara Horvath. 2002. "Sounding Cajun: The Rhetorical Use of Dialect in Speech and Writing." *American Speech* 77:264–87.

Dubois, Sylvie, and Barbara Horvath. 2003a. "Creoles and Cajuns: A Portrait in Black and White." *American Speech* 78:192–207.

Dubois, Sylvie, and Barbara Horvath. 2003b. "The English Vernacular of the Creoles of Louisiana." *Language Variation and Change* 15:253–86.

Eble, Connie. 2009. "French in New Orleans: The Commodification of Language Heritage." *American Speech* 84:211–15.

Kelley, Laura D. 2004. "Erin's Enterprise: Immigration by Appropriation: The Irish in New Orleans." PhD diss., Tulane University.

Labov, William. 2007. "Transmission and Diffusion." *Language* 83 (2): 344–87.

Linguistic Atlas of the Gulf States. N.d. Linguistic Atlas Project Online. http://www.lap.uga.edu/Site/LAGS.html.

Malin, Helen Rahm. 1972. "A Questionnaire of Lexical Items Used by New Orleans English Speakers." Master's thesis, University of New Orleans.

Mucciaccio, Francesca. 2009. "'A Gaggle a' Y'ats' and Other Stories: Tracing The Effects Of Ideology on Language Change through Indexical Formation in Y'at." Honors thesis, Reed College.

Reinecke, George F. 1951. "New Orleans Pronunciation among School Children and Educated Adults." Master's thesis, Tulane University.

Schoux Casey, Christina. 2013. "Postvocalic /r/ in New Orleans: Language, Place, and Commodification." PhD diss., University of Pittsburgh.

Scott, Ann Martin. 1992. "Some Phonological and Syntactic Characteristics of Cajun Vernacular English." In *Louisiana English Journal*, edited by Ann Martin Scott, 26–37. Lafayette: University of Southwestern Louisiana.

Smith, Darrlyn. 1996. *The New Orleans 7th Ward: Nostalgia Dictionary, 1938–1965*. Seattle: JADA.

Sprowls, Lisa. 2016. "Independence English: Careful Speech Analysis." Paper presented at the Southeastern Conference on Linguistics, New Orleans, March 30.

Sprowls, Lisa, and Andrew Abdalian. Forthcoming. "A little Southern" in Little Italy: Production and perception of local speech in Independence, Louisiana. *Southern Journal of Linguistics*.

Walton, Shana. 1994. "Flat Speech and Cajun Ethnic Identity in Terrebonne Parish, Louisiana." PhD diss., Tulane University.

Walton, Shana. 2002. "Not with a Southern Accent: Cajun English and Ethnic Identity." In *Language Diversity in the South: Changing Codes, Practices, and Ideology*, edited by Margaret Bender, 104–19. Athens: University of Georgia Press.

White-Sustaíta, Jessica. 2012. "Socio-Historical Perspectives on Black and White Speech Relations in New Orleans." *Southern Journal of Linguistics* 36 (1): 45–60.

CHAPTER 11

CAJUN ENGLISH: A LINGUISTIC AND CULTURAL PROFILE

KATIE CARMICHAEL

Louisiana's cultural and linguistic heritage has always presented a gumbo of mixed influences (Picone and Valdman 2005; Melançon 2006), with the undeniable role of French, among other languages, playing a part. The influence of French is particularly apparent in the varieties of English spoken throughout Acadiana, or francophone Louisiana. Acadiana consists of twenty-two Louisiana parishes (the equivalent of counties) that exhibit "strong French Acadian cultural aspects" (Louisiana House of Representatives 1971) (fig. 11.1). The number of fluent French speakers in these regions of "French" Louisiana is dwindling, though there is evidence that the cultural and linguistic uniqueness of these areas carries on through English (Trépanier 1991; Dubois and Horvath 2000; Carmichael 2013). This chapter provides an introduction to Cajun English as a distinctive linguistic entity in its own right as well as an element of Louisiana's cultural heritage.

Cajun English interests linguists in part because of the particular linguistic patterns that have emerged as a result of long-term contact between French and English. And indeed, as more speakers shift to English, documenting these features becomes all the more urgent. Studying the structural effects of this historical contact and current linguistic shift can inform theories about how languages are organized in the brain and how social and political forces can affect linguistic choices and patterns (Winford 2003). Linguists also study Cajun English because of its role in the cultural revival of Cajunness, as both French and English have become commodified in the process of revalidating all things Cajun in Louisiana (Bankston and Henry 1998; Dubois and Horvath 2000). Commodification represents the transformation of cultural and linguistic heritage into sellable goods, a process that can sometimes produce problematic results for the language or culture in question. Finally, Cajun English represents

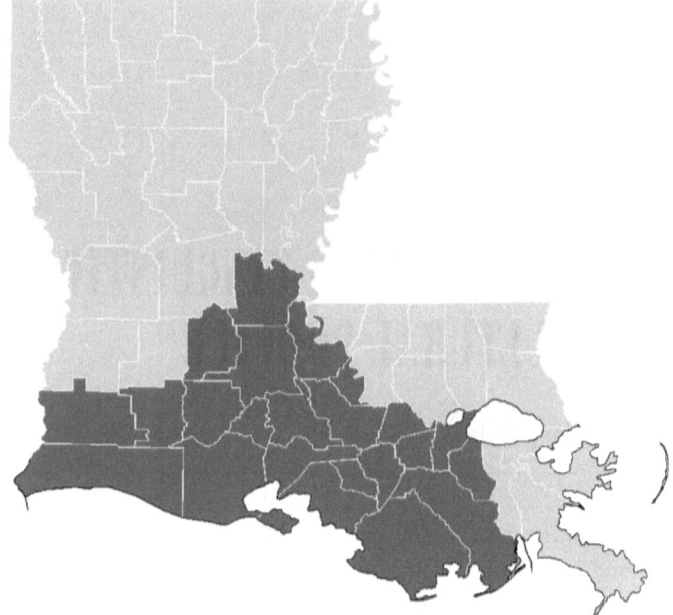

Figure 11.1. Parishes of Acadiana. Map from Wikimedia commons: https://commons.wikimedia.org/wiki/File:Acadiana_parishes_map.png.

a dialect with connections to both regional and ethnic identities within Louisiana, making it worthy of examination in terms of how individuals express parts of their identity linguistically.

THE FRENCH UNDERPINNINGS OF CAJUN ENGLISH

Historically, the presence of French in Louisiana preceded English. (And of course, Native American languages such as Houma and Tunica were spoken in the region before any European languages.) (For the history and development of Louisiana French, see Dajko, this volume; Klingler, this volume.) Linguists have recognized at least three varieties of French spoken in Louisiana, of which only two varieties—Cajun French and Louisiana Creole—currently survive, and both are in severe danger of disappearing in the next generation or two (Trépanier 1991; Rottet 2001; Klingler 2003; Dajko 2009; Carmichael 2017b). Most modern-day French speakers reside in Acadiana, particularly along the eastern edge of the Atchafalaya Basin, in Terrebonne and Lafourche Parishes, and in southwest prairie communities surrounding Lafayette. Additional speakers live outside of Acadiana in Louisiana and into Mississippi and Texas (Blyth 1997). Prevailing ideologies suggest that Cajun French speakers are white, while Louisiana Creole speakers are black (or Creole, meaning mixed race in this context), though this assumption does not bear out.

For example, many Native Americans and self-identified Creoles speak Cajun French (Carmichael 2017b; Dajko 2009) and a number of white Louisianans, who generally identify as Cajun, speak Creole (Klingler 2003; Picone and Valdman 2005). Despite the racial associations with Cajun French and Louisiana Creole, these varieties of French in fact encompass a broad population of speakers across demographic backgrounds, with speakers tending to label their language in accordance with their ethnic and/or racial self-identification (Klingler 2003). An additional complication is that these two varieties of French are very similar to each other, making it difficult to tease apart the influence of one variety versus the other (Klingler, this volume). Given these issues, in this chapter I use *Cajun French* in the same way speakers do: to reference French of any variety when spoken by people who identify as Cajun. Though French was once widely spoken across south Louisiana, these regions are now dominated by English.

The Shift from Francophone to Anglophone Louisiana

The decline of French in Louisiana began with the Louisiana Purchase in 1803. While Louisiana had been under Spanish rule for a brief period leading up to the purchase of the territory by the United States, Spain did not push residents to learn Spanish, so this change in power had little linguistic effect (Griolet 1986). In contrast, when Louisiana achieved statehood in 1812, the United States expected English to become the primary language (see Camp, this volume; White, this volume). During early statehood, waves of anglophone settlers descended on Louisiana, constituting 70 percent of Louisiana's population by 1860 (Brasseaux 1992). In addition, the prohibition on the importation of enslaved Africans meant that any newly arrived enslaved people in the state would be coming from anglophone areas within the South (Picone 2003). By the end of the Civil War, most of the upper crust of French-speaking Louisiana had been ruined financially, thereby ensuring their assimilation into anglophone society since they could no longer afford trips to France to retain connections with their French-speaking ancestry (Picone and Valdman 2005).

French retained some strongholds in rural Louisiana until 1921, when the state constitution was revised to make English the sole language of instruction in schools (Blyth 1997). Many students during this era encountered harsh discipline if they were overheard speaking French. This policy led rates of French fluency to drop precipitously during the first half of the twentieth century (Lindner, this volume).

The 1960s and 1970s brought the Cajun Revival, which began to gain momentum with the establishment of the Council for the Development of French in Louisiana (CODOFIL) in 1968 (CODOFIL 2009). The revaluing of all things

Cajun has had positive effects on the cultural preservation of traditions but may have come too late to save the French language, which has continued to decline in usage. That said, the presence of French in Louisiana has clearly affected the varieties of English throughout the state and particularly Cajun English (Dubois and Horvath 2000; Eble 1993).

VARIETIES OF ENGLISH IN LOUISIANA

While this chapter focuses on Cajun English, speakers of this language variety are in contact with speakers of other dialects such as African American English, Southern English, and New Orleans English(es), among other language varieties. A closer look at the geographic and demographic distribution of these dialects helps situate Cajun English within the region as a whole.

Very little research has examined African American English in Louisiana, and most research to date has centered on varieties spoken in New Orleans (Brennan 1983; Charity 2007; Schoux Casey 2016)[1] despite the fact that the vast majority of black Louisianans live outside the city limits (US Census Bureau 2010). Evidence shows both that New Orleans African American English is more vernacular—or nonstandard—than other regional varieties of African American English (Charity 2007) and that it does not differ significantly from white varieties of English in New Orleans in terms of certain linguistic features (Brennan 1983; Schoux Casey 2016). These studies suggest that white dialects of English in New Orleans may also be particularly vernacular.

Creole African American English as described by Dubois and Horvath (2003a) is similar structurally to other varieties of African American English, with some distinctive Creole French–influenced qualities, such as glide reduction on vowels (pronouncing /o/ and /e/ in a shorter or "purer" way, without the off-glide) and nonaspiration of initial /p, t, k/ (pronouncing word-initial /p, t, k/ without the puff of air typical in most varieties of English). Some features that Creole African American English shares with both African American English and Cajun English include *th*-stopping (pronunciation of *this thing* as *dis ting*), *r*-lessness (pronouncing *car* as *cah*), and monophthongal /aɪ/ (deleting the final portion of the /aɪ/ sound, such that *time* is pronounced more like *tom*) (Dubois and Horvath 2003a; Wroblewski, Strand, and Dubois 2009).

Southern White English is spoken primarily in north Louisiana and the Florida parishes north of Lake Pontchartrain. The defining feature of this dialect is participation in the southern vowel shift (Labov, Ash, and Boberg 2006), the set of vowel characteristics found throughout the American South that gives the "Southern drawl" its distinctive flavor. In addition to the southern vowel shift, north Louisiana features significantly less French influence than

Table 11.1. Varieties of English in Louisiana

Dialect	Who speaks it	Sounds like
African American English	African American residents of Louisiana from throughout the state	African American English spoken throughout the United States
Creole African American English	Creole or mixed-race residents throughout Louisiana but primarily in rural south Louisiana	African American English with Creole French influences
Southern White English	primarily white speakers from north Louisiana and the Florida parishes	drawls throughout the American South
New Orleans English/Yat	the white working-class population of New Orleans (though many other dialects are present within city limits)	a Brooklyn or Bronx accent with some southern influences
Cajun English	primarily Cajun-descended people throughout Acadiana	French-influenced Southern English

south Louisiana, since French was not historically spoken in regions north of the Red River (Marcotte 1992). Many of the words and pronunciations found in Cajun English thus are not present in regions of Louisiana where Southern White English dominates.

In contrast with Southern White English, most varieties of New Orleans English do not participate in the southern vowel shift (Labov, Ash, and Boberg 2006). That said, some southern linguistic features, such as monophthongal /aɪ/, can be found in New Orleans (Carmichael 2014). Among the diverse dialects of English in New Orleans, linguistic research has tended to focus on the city's white, working-class dialect sometimes referred to as *Yat* (Coles 1997; Eble 2003, 2006; Mucciaccio 2009). Yat is known for sounding more like a Brooklyn or Bronx accent than a southern dialect of English (Lyman 1978). Recent studies have indicated, however, that many of these distinctive New York–flavored features of Yat are in decline (Schoux Casey 2016; Carmichael 2014, 2017a).

Cajun English is spoken throughout French Louisiana, and many speakers are not fluent in French. French-influenced features, however, are found even in the speech of monolingual English speakers in Acadiana (Dubois and Horvath 2000). Defining features of Cajun English include French-influenced pronunciations and grammatical constructions, along with some Southern English qualities, such as use of *y'all* to indicate second-person plural and monophthongal /aɪ/. Speakers of Cajun English exhibit some southern linguistic features but do not participate in the southern vowel shift, a phenomenon that accounts in part for Cajun English's distinctiveness within the American South.

Table 11.1 summarizes Louisiana's dialects of English. While English has supplanted French as the primary language of communication in Louisiana, no single variety of English dominates.

CAJUN ENGLISH: LINGUISTIC FEATURES

Phrases and Terms

One of the most distinctive features of Cajun English is the number of French-influenced terms and phrases that are common even in the speech of monolingual English speakers. In this complex bilingual situation, there has been much debate about the line between code-switches and borrowings (Brown 1986, 2003; Dajko and Carmichael 2014; Picone 1994, 1997a). According to some definitions, a code-switch occurs when a speaker alternates between two or more languages, while borrowing is a process by which terms and phrases are adopted from one language into another (Myers-Scotton 1993; Winford 2003). In the case of French and English in Louisiana, the question is whether a given speaker is truly switching between the two languages or using one language with a number of words and phrases borrowed from another. I do not differentiate between the two here, though I acknowledge that aside from these words and set phrases, bilingual Cajun English speakers commonly switch into French for full, novel sentences (as opposed to set phrases) or even entire stories.

Some words used in Cajun English that have been taken directly from French include *lagniappe* (a little something extra), *fais do-do* (family dance),[2] and *boudin* (sausage casing filled with rice, meat, and spices). Two particularly iconic Cajun English terms from French are *cher* (darling; pronounced *shah* [ʃæ]) and *mais* (but; pronounced *may* [me]). As a term of endearment, *cher* occurs most commonly at the end of a phrase. *Mais* (when not in its primary function as a contrastive conjunction) is used somewhat like *well* in English—introducing a turn, for example (Dajko and Carmichael 2014). Thus these terms are used throughout conversation to organize discourse as well as in longer tracts of speech. Like other discourse markers, they do not add much content or change the literal meaning of the utterance, though they may add some social information—for example, that the speaker seeks to indicate that he or she is Cajun or considers the listener an intimate friend. For this reason, *mais* and *cher* may be used liberally throughout an interaction. In contrast, other French words present in Cajun English carry more content, reflecting regional traditions and legends in the region. One such example is *rougarou* (werewolf), a key villain in horror stories told on the bayous of south Louisiana.

Not all distinctive Cajun English terms have French origins. Some terms in Acadiana are of African origin—for example, *okra* and *jazz* (Condon and Pittman 1992). Other terms have unclear origins. For example, many Cajun English speakers pronounce *ask* as *ax* [æks], which is also common in dialects of African American English and some other regional varieties of English (Scott

1992). Similarly, the label *coonass*, which has come to mean something like an authentic Cajun who does not care what others think of his or her lifestyle, has been the site of controversy as to its source. Some have postulated the French term *connasse* (idiot [fem.]),[3] while others have examined the possibility of English roots (Marcotte 1992). This term is also controversial in its usage, with some individuals asserting that the term degrades Cajun people and others seeing it as a source of pride (Bankston and Henry 1998; Zaragovia 2014).

In addition to particular Cajun English words, certain phrases, many derived from French, are associated with Cajun English. While some bilingual speakers do indeed switch to French for longer tracts of speech, the widespread shift from French to English has resulted in French phrases used in Cajun English more commonly consisting of set phrases or clichés that may be employed regardless of fluency in French. For example, *Lâche pas la patate* (Don't drop the potato) derives from the game of hot potato but is used to mean "Don't give up!" sometimes in the context of not giving up Cajun traditions. Another example is the greeting *Qui/Quoi ça dit?* (What do you say?), with the use of *qui* or *quoi* depending on the specific region of Acadiana (Cheramie and Gill 1992; see also Dajko, this volume).

Grammar

French influence on Cajun English grammar can be seen both in how sentences are structured (syntax) and in how words are constructed and inflected (morphology). Some phrases that may sound odd to people outside of Acadiana are calques—that is, words that are direct translations of French phrases. For example, *make twelve* (to turn twelve on a birthday) comes from the French *faire*, which can be translated as *to make* but is also used to indicate achieving an age. Other calques include *pass by your house* (stop in for a visit at your house), and *come see* (come over here), which come from *viens voir* (lit. come see) (Cheramie and Gill 1992; Scott 1992). Another feature of Cajun English syntax that appears to be French-influenced is emphatic repetition of pronouns at the beginning or end of sentences, as in "Me, I don't like that much" or "He went to the store, him" (Carmichael 2013; see also Picone 2003, 2014), which may derive from pronoun repetition in Cajun French (Rottet 1995, 1996; Carmichael and Gudmestad 2018). Markers of agreement or negation may also follow this process at the ends of sentences, as in "He don't watch that show, no," or "I'm goin' pass by your house later, yeah" (Scott 1992). Finally, question formation is highly influenced by Cajun French question structure, which does not feature subject-verb inversion. In Cajun English, "What is that?" is more likely to be structured as "What that is?," without inversion (Scott 1992).

Not all Cajun English grammatical features are unique to French-influenced dialects. A grammatical construction found in Cajun English that is also present in other nonstandard regional dialects is *was* leveling, or the use of *was* throughout the verb paradigm (e.g., "I was walking," "you was walking," "we was walking," and so on) (Dubois and Horvath 2003b, 2002). This feature is also typical of Appalachian English. A grammatical structure shared with African American English is copula absence, or the lack of conjugated *to be* in some contexts (e.g., "They on the way"; "You stupid") (Dubois and Horvath 2002, 2003b).

Pronunciation

Many phonetic (or pronunciation-related) features of Cajun English appear to be influenced by Cajun French, though even people who speak no French may exhibit these pronunciations (Dubois and Horvath 2000). Most research on Cajun English pronunciation is quite recent, likely due to advances in technology for examining phonetic variation (variation in how sounds are produced).

Phonetic features of Cajun English can be organized into consonantal features (table 11.2) and vocalic (or vowel) features (table 11.3). *Th*-stopping and deletion of /r/ (also called *r*-lessness) are common in many nonstandard English varieties, including African American English (Green 2002) and some varieties of New Orleans English (Schoux Casey 2016; Carmichael 2017a). Nonaspiration of /p, t, k/, syllable-initial deletion of /h/, and rolled or tapped /r/ are more clearly traceable to French influence. Vowel features of Cajun English have received less attention than consonantal features. While monophthongal tense vowels and heavy vowel nasalization clearly correspond to more French-like pronunciations, monophthongal /aɪ/ is present in neighboring varieties of English such as Southern English (Labov, Ash, and Boberg 2006) and New Orleans English (Carmichael 2014).

Note that these phonetic features do not appear across the board for all Cajun English speakers. Indeed, Cajun English has changed over time, with more French-like pronunciations such as nonaspiration of /p, t, k/ and heavy vowel nasalization becoming less common among younger Cajun English speakers, while features common in other surrounding dialects, such as *th*-stopping or monophthongal /aɪ/, have increased in rates of usage over time (Dubois and Horvath 2000; Coyne 2008; Carmichael 2013). Just as speakers of different ages vary in their usage of Cajun English features, variation also occurs across types of speakers within Acadiana. For example, the individuals who show the highest frequency of Cajun English linguistic features in the youngest cohort are men, particularly those with open social networks, meaning that they frequently deal with individuals from outside their community (Dubois and Horvath 2000).

Table 11.2. Consonantal Features of Cajun English

Feature	Description
Th-stopping (Rubrecht 1971; Scott 1992; Walton 1994; Dubois and Horvath 1998a, b, 2000, 2002; Coyne 2008; Carmichael 2013)	Pronunciation of *th* in words like *this* or *thing* as the stops [d] or [t]; *this thing* pronounced *dis ting*
Nonaspiration of /p, t, k/ (Rubrecht 1971; Walton 1994; Dubois and Horvath 2000, 2002; Coyne 2008; Carmichael 2013)	Pronunciation of syllable-initial /p, t, k/ without the puff of air typical in most varieties of English; *pan* sounds more like *ban* to English speakers
Syllable-initial deletion of /h/ (Dubois and Horvath 2000, 2002; Coyne 2008)	Deletion of the *h* sound as the beginning of words or syllables; *hair* sounds more like *air*
Variability in pronunciation of /r/ (Walton 1994; Dubois and Horvath 2002; Coyne 2008)	Pronunciation of *r* sounds as a roll/tap (similar to Spanish) or deletion of *r* entirely; *car* pronounced *cah*

Table 11.3. Vowel Features of Cajun English

Feature	Description
Monophthongal tense vowels (Rubrecht 1971; Walton 1994; Dubois and Horvath 2002; Wroblewski, Strand, and Dubois 2009; Carmichael 2013)	Shortening of tense vowels /i, e, o, u/; words such as *boat* and *beet* pronounced with shorter or more French-like vowels
Monophthongal /aɪ/ (Scott 1992; Dubois and Horvath 1998a; Coyne 2008)	Shortening of /aɪ/ by deletion of off-glide [ɪ]; *time* pronounced more like *tom*
Heavy vowel nasalization (Dubois and Horvath 1998a; Walton 1994)	Nasalizing (pushing more air through the nose) vowels that occur before nasal consonants in words such as *pan* or *foam*

Moreover, use of Cajun English features can be exploited in performances, which include subconscious "deepening" while storytelling (Walton 1994) as well as intentional, self-aware displays of Cajunness while telling jokes (Dubois and Horvath 2002; Carmichael 2013). Some of these instances of variation may be explained as identity expression through language.

CAJUN ENGLISH AND IDENTITY

Many current attitudes and opinions about Cajun English—and, indeed, Cajuns in general—have developed from the particular history of French in Louisiana. For example, the policies forbidding French in schools have affected how Louisianans view the education and intelligence of French speakers, and of Cajuns on the whole (Brown 1993; Picone 1997b; Blyth 1997; Cheramie 1998). Indeed, one negative stereotype holds that Cajuns are ignorant or unworldly (Condon and Pittman 1992). Outside observers can spot such stereotypes by examining ethnic humor that pokes fun at Cajunness (Ancelet 1989; Bankston and Henry 1998; Dubois and Horvath 2002; Carmichael 2013). The genre of Boudreaux and Thibodeaux jokes features two stereotypical Cajuns bumbling through improbable scenarios in stories that generally highlight their lack of intelligence. Joke tellers have been found to exaggerate their Cajun English accents while telling Boudreaux and Thibodeaux jokes, reflecting the implicit associations between Cajun linguistic features and ignorance or lack of education (Carmichael 2013).

Not all stereotypes about Cajuns are negative, however. They are often portrayed as fun-loving, good-natured individuals with a fine appreciation of good food and music (Blyth 1997; Condon and Pittman 1992). These sorts of stereotypes have been commodified since the Cajun Revival (Bankston and Henry 1998). "Cajun" spices and "Cajun" music albums have created a specific identity for Acadiana, attracting tourism and money to this historically poor region of Louisiana. Some of this tourism, however, depends on the reproduction and continued circulation of dated stereotypes about Cajuns as simple, French-speaking fishermen, which presents a problem when fewer and fewer self-identified Cajuns speak French or take part in such traditional careers (Dubois and Melançon 1997; Bankston and Henry 1998; Carmichael 2008; Dajko 2009).

As Cajun French use continues to steadily decline, many residents of south Louisiana identify linguistically with their ethnic heritage through use of Cajun English features. While older Cajuns experienced their ethnic identity as a source of shame, younger generations of Cajuns have grown up celebrating Cajunness. Members of this generation use higher rates of Cajun English linguistic features than do their parents (Dubois and Horvath 2000) and are more likely to self-identify as Cajun (Dubois and Melançon 1997). Furthermore, these younger speakers display more favorable perceptions of Cajun French and Cajun English than do older generations (Condon and Pittman 1992). Thus, a number of factors—social, historical, and political—have shaped the linguistic situation in south Louisiana, with Cajun English ultimately standing in as the primary linguistic means of marking Cajun identity.

CONCLUSION AND FUTURE DIRECTIONS

Because Cajun English represents a relatively "young" dialect (Dubois and Horvath 2002), much remains to be done to document and understand this linguistic system. For example, only a handful of phonetic studies using acoustic analysis have examined the sound qualities of certain consonants and vowels (Wroblewski, Strand, and Dubois 2009; Carmichael 2013). One area that acoustic analysis may illuminate is prosody, or the rhythm and intonation of the dialect. While Cajun English prosody has been noted as aberrant, with a characteristic staccato rhythm that is generally attributed to French influence (Smith 1992; Walton 1994), the particular dimensions that distinguish Cajun English prosody have not yet been identified. Continuing acoustic research may further clarify the dialect's relationship with French as well as with other regional Englishes within south Louisiana.

Linguistic scholarship has also explored how ethnic identity may be performed linguistically (Dubois and Horvath 2002; Carmichael 2013). As the issues of speaker agency and the role of style-shifting in producing sociolinguistic meaning become more prominent in sociolinguistic research (Eckert 2012), the situation of Cajun English in Louisiana provides an opportunity to better understand the complex relationship between language and identity. Similarly, it will be crucial to analyze how linguistic commodification and tourism promote the propagation of Cajun English features beyond their current realms. (For the commodification of French in Louisiana, see Eble 2009.)

Finally, future research on Cajun English must address variation across regions of south Louisiana. Cajun English has generally been examined as a single monolithic dialect, although it is well established that Cajun French varies from the east to the west (Valdman et al. 2009) and even within a given parish (Dajko 2009, this volume). Furthermore, indications show that phonetic variation within Cajun English may have geographic correlates (Carmichael 2013). Thus, speech samples from across Acadiana should be compared to determine the similarities among Cajun English dialects throughout French Louisiana.

While the future of Cajun French in Louisiana is unsure, the use of French-influenced linguistic features in Cajun English provides a way to express Cajunness through language (Dubois and Horvath 2000). The complex linguistic and cultural situation of Cajun English also represents a central site for continued linguistic research on language and identity in a situation of language shift, as inquiries into these issues in Acadiana will no doubt continue to expand.

NOTES

1. One notable exception is Dubois and Horvath's (2003a) work on Creole African American English, which they argue is a distinct dialect in its own right.

2. *Fais do-do* literally translates as "make or cause to sleep" and is a way of telling children to nap. During Cajun dances, children traditionally were brought along and put in a separate room to sleep while the adults danced into the night (Cheramie and Gill 1992).

3. *Connasse* is considered a strong insult in France.

WORKS CITED

Ancelet, Barry Jean. 1989. "The Cajun Who Went to Harvard: Identity in the Oral Tradition of South Louisiana." *Journal of Popular Culture* 23 (1): 101–15.

Bankston, Carl L., and Jacques M. Henry. 1998. "The Silence of the Gators: Cajun Ethnicity and Intergenerational Transmission of Louisiana French." *Journal of Multilingual and Multicultural Development* 19 (1): 1–23.

Blyth, Carl. 1997. "The Sociolinguistic Situation of Cajun French: The Effects of Language Shift and Language Loss." In *French and Creole in Louisiana*, edited by Albert Valdman, 24–46. New York: Plenum.

Brasseaux, Carl A. 1992. *Acadian to Cajun: Transformation of a People, 1803–1877.* Jackson: University Press of Mississippi.

Brennan, Pamela. 1983. "Postvocalic /r/ in New Orleans." Master's thesis, University of New Orleans.

Brown, Becky. 1986. "Cajun/English Code-Switching: A Test of Formal Models." In *Diversity and Diachrony*, edited by David Sankoff, 399–406. Amsterdam and Philadelphia: John Benjamins.

Brown, Becky. 1993. "The Social Consequences of Writing Louisiana French." *Language in Society* 22:67–101.

Brown, Becky. 2003. "Code-Convergent borrowing in Louisiana French." *Journal of Sociolinguistics* 7 (1): 3–23.

Carmichael, Katie. 2008. "Language Death and Stylistic Variation: An Intergenerational Study of the Substitution of /h/ for /ʒ/ in the French of the Pointe-au-Chien Indians." Master's thesis, Tulane University.

Carmichael, Katie. 2013. "The Performance of Cajun English in Boudreaux and Thibodeaux Jokes." *American Speech* 88 (4): 377–412.

Carmichael, Katie. 2014. "'I Never Thought I Had an Accent until the Hurricane': Sociolinguistic Variation in Post-Katrina Greater New Orleans." PhD diss., Ohio State University.

Carmichael, Katie. 2017a. "Displacement and Variation: The Case of R-lessness in Greater New Orleans." *Journal of Sociolinguistics* 21 (5): 696–719.

Carmichael, Katie. 2017b. "Stylistic Variation and Dialect Contraction: The Case of /ʒ/ and /h/ in Louisiana French." *Fleur de Ling: Tulane University Working Papers* 3 (1): 72–89.

Carmichael, Katie, and Aarnes Gudmestad. 2018. "Language Death and Subject Expression: First-Person Singular Subjects in a Declining Dialect of Louisiana French." *Journal of French Language Studies* 29(1): 67-91. https://doi.org/10.1017/S0959269518000236.

Charity, Anne H. 2007. "Regional Differences in Low SES African-American Children's Speech in the School Setting." *Language Variation, and Change* 19:281–93.

Cheramie, Deany M. 1998. "'Glad You Axed': A Teacher's Guide to Cajun English." *Louisiana English Journal* 5 (1): 72–81.

Cheramie, Deany M., and Donald A. Gill. 1992. "Lexical Choice in Cajun Vernacular English." In *Cajun Vernacular English: Informal English in French Louisiana*, edited by Ann Martin Scott, 38–55. Lafayette: University of Southwestern Louisiana Press.

CODOFIL. 2009. *Conseil pour le Développement du Français en Louisiane*/Council for the Development of French in Louisiana. http://www.codofil.org/.

Coles, Felice Anne. 1997. "Solidarity Cues in New Orleans English." In *Language Variety in the South Revisited*, edited by Cynthia Bernstein, Thomas Nunnally, and Robin Sabino, 219–24. Tuscaloosa: University of Alabama Press.

Condon, Sherri L., and Pamela T. Pittman. 1992. "Language Attitudes in Acadiana." In *Cajun Vernacular English: Informal English in French Louisiana*, edited by Ann Martin Scott, 56–72. Lafayette: University of Southwestern Louisiana Press.

Coyne, Amanda Louise. 2008. "Intergenerational Patterns of Phonological Features and Linguistic Attitudes of Cajun English Speakers." Master's thesis, Southern Illinois University.
Dajko, Nathalie. 2009. "Ethnic and Geographic Variation in the French of the Lafourche Basin." PhD diss., Tulane University.
Dajko, Nathalie, and Katie Carmichael. 2014. "But *Qui C'Est la Différence*? Discourse Markers in Louisiana French: The Case of 'But' vs. 'Mais.'" *Language in Society* 43:159–83.
Dubois, Sylvie, and Barbara M. Horvath. 1998a. "From Accent to Marker in Cajun English: A Study of Dialect Formation in Progress." *English World-Wide* 19 (2): 161–88.
Dubois, Sylvie, and Barbara M. Horvath. 1998b. "'Let's Tink about Dat': Interdental Fricatives in Cajun English." *Language Variation and Change* 10 (3): 245–61.
Dubois, Sylvie, and Barbara M. Horvath. 2000. "'When the Music Changes, You Change Too': Gender and Language Change in Cajun English." *Language Variation and Change* 11 (3): 287–313.
Dubois, Sylvie, and Barbara M. Horvath. 2002. "Sounding Cajun: The Rhetorical Use of Dialect in Speech and Writing." *American Speech* 77 (3): 264–87.
Dubois, Sylvie, and Barbara M. Horvath. 2003a. "Creoles and Cajuns: A Portrait in Black and White." *American Speech* 78 (2): 192–207.
Dubois, Sylvie, and Barbara M. Horvath. 2003b. "Verbal Morphology in Cajun Vernacular English: A Comparison with Other Varieties of Southern English." *Journal of English Linguistics* 31 (1): 34–59.
Dubois, Sylvie, and Megan Melançon. 1997. "Cajun Is Dead: Shifting from a Linguistic to a Cultural Community." *Journal of Sociolinguistics* 1:63–93.
Eble, Connie. 1993. "Prolegomenon to the Study of Cajun English." *SECOL Review* 17:164–77.
Eble, Connie. 2003. "The Englishes of Southern Louisiana." In *English in the Southern United States*, edited by Stephen Nagle and Sara Sanders, 173–88. Malden, MA: Blackwell.
Eble, Connie. 2006. "Speaking the Big Easy." In *American Voices: How Dialects Differ from Coast to Coast*, edited by Walt Wolfram and Ben Ward, 42–48. Malden, MA: Blackwell.
Eble, Connie. 2009. "French in New Orleans: The Commodification of Language Heritage." *American Speech* 84 (2): 211–15.
Eckert, Penelope. 2012. "Three Waves of Variation Study: The Emergence of Meaning in the Study of Variation." *Annual Review of Anthropology* 41:87–100.
Green, Lisa J. 2002. *African American English: A Linguistic Introduction*. Cambridge: Cambridge University Press.
Griolet, Patrick. 1986. *Cadjins et Creoles en Louisiane: Histoire et Survivance d'une Francophonie*. Paris: Payot.
Klingler, Thomas A. 2003. *If I Could Turn My Tongue Like That: The Creole Language of Pointe-Coupée Parish, Louisiana*. Baton Rouge: Louisiana State University Press.
Labov, William, Sharon Ash, and Charles Boberg. 2006. *The Atlas of North American English: Phonetics, Phonology, and Sound Change*. New York: Mouton de Gruyter.
Louisiana House of Representatives. 1971. House Concurrent Resolution No. 496. June 6.
Lyman, Tim. 1978. "An Introduction." In *F'Sure! Actual Dialogue Heard on the Streets of New Orleans*, edited by Bunny Matthews, i–x. New Orleans: Neetof.
Marcotte, Mary. 1992. "North and South Louisiana: Are We Really So Different?" In *Cajun Vernacular English: Informal English in French Louisiana*, edited by Ann Martin Scott, 73–84. Lafayette: University of Southwestern Louisiana Press.
Melançon, Megan E. 2006. "Stirring the Linguistic Gumbo (Cajun English)." In *American Voices*, edited by Walt Wolfram and Ben Ward, 238–43. Malden, MA: Blackwell.
Mucciaccio, Francesca. 2009. "'A Gaggle a' Y'ats' and Other Stories: Tracing the Effects of Ideology on Language Change through Indexical Formation in Y'at." Honors thesis, Reed College.

Myers-Scotton, Carol. 1993. *Social Motivations for Codeswitching: Evidence from Africa*. Oxford: Clarendon.

Picone, Michael D. 1994. "Code-Intermediate Phenomena in Louisiana French." In *CLS 30-I: Papers from the Thirtieth Regional Meeting of the Chicago Linguistic Society, Volume 1: The Main Session*, edited by Katie Beals, Jeannette Denton, Bob Knippen, Lynette Melnar, Hisami Suzuki, and Erika Zeinfeld, 320–34. Chicago: Chicago Linguistic Society.

Picone, Michael D. 1997a. "Code-Switching and Loss of Inflection in Louisiana French." In *Language Variety in the South Revisited*, edited by Cynthia Bernstein, Thomas E. Nunnally, and Robin Sabino, 152–62. Tuscaloosa: University of Alabama Press.

Picone, Michael D. 1997b. "Enclave Dialect Contraction: An External Overview of Louisiana French." *American Speech* 72 (2): 117–53.

Picone, Michael D. 2003. "Anglophone Slaves in Francophone Louisiana." *American Speech* 78 (4) : 404–33.

Picone, Michael D. 2014. "Literary Dialect and the Linguistic Reconstruction of Nineteenth-Century Louisiana." *American Speech* 89:143–69.

Picone, Michael D., and Albert Valdman. 2005. "La Situation du Français en Louisiane." In *Le Français en Amérique du Nord: Etat Présent*, edited by Albert Valdman, Julie Auger, and Deborah Piston-Hatlen, 143–65. Saint-Nicolas, QC: Presses de l'Université Laval.

Rottet, Kevin J. 1995. "Language Shift and Language Death in the Cajun French-Speaking Communities of Terrebonne and Lafourche Parishes, Louisiana." PhD diss., Indiana University.

Rottet, Kevin. 1996. "Language Change and Language Death: Some Changes in the Pronominal System of Declining Cajun French." *Plurilinguismes* 11:117–52.

Rottet, Kevin. 2001. *Language Shift in the Coastal Marshes of Louisiana*. New York: Lang.

Rubrecht, August Weston. 1971. "Regional Phonological Variants in Louisiana Speech." PhD diss., University of Florida.

Schoux Casey, Christina. 2016. "Ya Heard Me? Rhoticity in Post-Katrina New Orleans English." *American Speech* 91:166–99.

Scott, Ann Martin. 1992. "Some Phonological and Syntactic Characteristics of Cajun Vernacular English." In *Cajun Vernacular English: Informal English in French Louisiana*, edited by Ann Martin Scott, 26–37. Lafayette: University of Southwestern Louisiana Press.

Smith, R. Mark. 1992. "A Brief History of the Acadian Migration to Louisiana and the Development of Cajun English." In *Cajun Vernacular English: Informal English in French Louisiana*, edited by Ann Martin Scott, 15–25. Lafayette: University of Southwestern Louisiana Press.

Trépanier, Cécyle. 1991. "The Cajunization of French Louisiana: Forging a Regional Identity." *Geographical Journal* 157 (2): 161–71.

US Census Bureau. 2010. Census Summary generated using American FactFinder. http://factfinder2.census.gov.

Valdman, Albert, Kevin J. Rottet, et al. 2009. *Dictionary of Louisiana French as Spoken in Cajun, Creole, and American Indian Communities*. Jackson: University Press of Mississippi.

Walton, Shana L. 1994. "Flat Speech and Cajun Ethnic Identity in Terrebonne Parish, Louisiana." PhD diss., Tulane University.

Winford, Donald. 2003. *An Introduction to Contact Linguistics*. Malden, MA: Wiley-Blackwell.

Wroblewski, Michael, Thea Strand, and Sylvie Dubois. 2009. "Mapping a Dialect 'Mixtury': Vowel Phonology of African American and White Men in Rural Southern Louisiana." In *African American English Speakers and Their Participation in Local Sound Changes: A Comparative Study*, edited by Malcah Yaeger-Dror and Erik R. Thomas, 48–72. Durham: Duke University Press.

Zaragovia, Veronica. 2014. "Cajuns Are Fiercely Proud of Their Culture, but They're Divided over the Word 'Coonass.'" October 1. http://www.pri.org/stories/2014-10-01/cajuns-are-fiercely-proud-their-culture-theyre-divided-over-word-coonass.

CHAPTER 12

DO YOU KNOW WHAT IT MEANS? NEW ORLEANS ENGLISH

CHRISTINA SCHOUX CASEY

Do you know what it means to miss New Orleans,
And miss it each night and day?
I know I'm not wrong, this feeling's getting stronger
The longer I stay away
—EDDIE DELANGE AND LOUIS ALTER,
"Do You Know What It Means to Miss New Orleans?" (1947)

"Do You Know What It Means to Miss New Orleans," a song made iconic by Louis Armstrong in the 1947 movie *New Orleans*, articulates the idea of New Orleans as an object of romantic nostalgia. The lyrics exemplify the broad narrative that paints New Orleans as both a place and an exotic fantasy that was the deliberate creation of businessmen, architectural preservationists (Stanonis 2006; Souther 2006), and writers and artists, particularly George Washington Cable, Lafcadio Hearn, Lyle Saxon, and Alice Dunbar Nelson (Woodland 1987; Stanonis 2001; Hearn 2001; Burnett 2009; Picone 2014). These writers worked within the regionalist literature tradition that blossomed after the Civil War, focusing on what they described as the unique customs, local color, and language of New Orleans, all of which were contrasted to a perceived national homogeneity caused by urbanization and industrialization. But rather than documenting traditional culture, southern literature scholar Katherine Burnett argues, the New Orleans and other regional writers "were, in fact, *creating* it through nostalgic language and the repeated use of romantic images to symbolize a lost culture" (2009:69). Most regional writers depicted New Orleans as a foreign, romantic, and timeless place, ignoring the presence of industrialization and other modern developments, erasing African Americans from the narrative, and instead focusing on an imagined antebellum vision of a flamboyant Creole population (Thomas 2009). In books, poems, newspaper columns, and state travel guides, writers circulated romantic visions of the city to a national, middle-class, largely white audience.

Businessmen and city officials capitalized on the popular literary representations and worked to make New Orleans culture convenient for white tourists. For example, city leaders developed and then promoted Mardi Gras, the pre-Lent Carnival, as an exotic but still easily accessible winter-vacation-timed public spectacle for tourists (Stanonis 2006). Efforts to encourage tourism had enormous success, causing historian Michael Mizell-Nelson to suggest that "to understand New Orleans' precarious existence before and after Hurricane Katrina one must examine tourism's role in misshaping its economic destiny as well as the perceptions of outsiders" (2008:232). Even the apparent rupture of the fantasy of New Orleans by the clearly race- and class-based failure of the 2005 evacuation of the city has been woven into the tourist narrative, with "Hurricane Katrina" or "post-Katrina" bus tours becoming popular activities for tourists (Pezzullo 2009; Thomas 2014) The dominance of the tourist-oriented romantic narrative means that New Orleans exists as both a geographical place and a collective imaginary.

As an imaginary, New Orleans is a global icon of jazz, Mardi Gras, and hedonistic Otherness. The appeal of the fantasy of New Orleans is demonstrated by the nearly eleven million tourists who visited the city in 2017. The fantasy of New Orleans generates cash: those visitors spent more than seven billion dollars (Brasted 2018), making tourism-related enterprise, from hotels to music venues to cemetery tours, the largest sector of the city's economy. This means that the city's 390,000 residents (US Census Bureau 2018), who live in the physical place of New Orleans, are constantly interacting with the imaginary construct of New Orleans. Embodying New Orleanianness is a commodifiable enterprise, from restaurateurs who cook Creole food to Mardi Gras Indians who are paid to appear at corporate events to tour guides who perhaps exaggerate their accents while taking tourists on mule-drawn carriage rides (see Dubois and Melançon 1997; Regis 1999; Regis and Walton 2008; Perry 2015). The intangible, discursively created imaginary of New Orleans and the people who live in the geographic reality of New Orleans are mutually constitutive, shaping and being shaped by one another.

The interconnectedness of New Orleans as a place and as an idea complicates and undermines the possibility of determining what counts as real or authentic local language. In a city whose culture is built largely on the performance of itself, determining whether a particular language feature is part of an authentic speech variety is not germane. Relatedly, the act of naming speech varieties—labeling them *Garden District*, *Yat*, or *Creole English*, for example—represents them as real, independent objects in the world. But languages and dialects are abstract concepts, and descriptions of all speech varieties are generalizations, artifacts of research (Johnstone 2009). Further, individual speakers manifest more idiosyncrasy and diversity than a formal description can express. In an interview, one young New Orleanian noted the idiosyncratic nature of language in use: "My aunt, she says *erl* [ɚl; oil] and *my-nez* [ˈmaɪ nɛz; mayonnaise], but my mom says *oil* [ɔɪl] and *my-nez* [ˈmaɪ nɛz], so you kind of—I won't say pick and choose, but it's a lot more open. . . . It's weird. It's so fractured."[1] Individual speakers, even those raised in the same house, do not use all the features associated with a particular variety, nor do they express one variety categorically; rather, they generally switch between more vernacular styles and more formal styles depending on context and audience. Variation within individual speakers and between speakers is the rule rather than the exception (Kretzschmar 2009).

Yet abstract generalizations about speech varieties and stereotypes about their speakers are powerful. New Orleanians frequently discuss features of local speech and ascribe social meanings to them, both in private conversation and public settings. A series of New Orleans Jazz and Heritage Festival panel discussions led by anthropologist Shana Walton (1996, 1999, 2000, 2001) consists of interviews with New Orleanians discussing differences in local speech, with audience members sharing stories about local talk. For both New Orleanians and outsiders, some features of local talk can index social stereotypes.

This chapter presents an overview of New Orleans English, keeping in mind the fact that New Orleans is an imaginary, with inhabitants who perform localness through speech, and that speech varieties themselves are useful fictions. The discussion here is preliminary because, as linguist—and New Orleans native—Connie Eble (2003:43) states, "Next to nothing based on scholarly research has been published on the speech of New Orleans." The exceptions include the works of Cooke and Blanton (1981), Dillard (1985), Reinecke (1951), Douglas (1969), Malin (1972), Brennan (1983), Aubert-Gex (1983), and DePascual et al. (1994). Researchers have also begun filling in these gaps, including Carmichael (2012, 2014, 2015, 2017), Carmichael and Becker (2016), Coles (1997, 2003, 2012), Dajko et al. (2012), Eble (2003, 2009, 2012, 2016), Schoux Casey (2012, 2013, 2016, 2018), and White-Sustaíta (2012), but knowledge about the city's speech remains partial. The chapter begins with a brief history of the city, followed by discussions of the term *Creole* and the impact of the 2005 flooding after Hurricane Katrina. The remainder of the chapter describes features of local speech, using examples from previously published research and from fieldwork conducted between 1993 and 1995 and 2009 and 2015.

NEW ORLEANS

New Orleans English is unique among American Englishes because the city was international, Catholic, and francophone for eighty years before the 1803 Louisiana Purchase. France founded the colony of New Orleans in 1718 on land used as a depot and market by several Native American groups. Enslaved Africans were brought to the city from its inception, and sailors and traders from many countries further contributed to an intensely diverse urban environment (Hirsch and Logsdon 1992; Campanella 2006). The original population—largely Native American, African, French, and Spanish—was augmented by European Americans after 1803. These anglophone Americans flooded the city, ensuring the erosion of French. But in 1809, almost ten thousand francophone colonists and enslaved Africans from Saint-Domingue (now Haiti) settled in the city, doubling the population and reinvigorating New Orleans as a French-speaking city.

Harriet Martineau's (1838:129) account of a mass at St. Louis Cathedral describes the diversity:

> Kneeling on the pavement may be seen a multitude, of every shade of complexion, from the fair Scotchwoman or German to the jet-black pure African. The Spanish eye flashes from beneath the veil; the French Creole countenance, painted high, is surmounted by the neat cap or the showy bonnet; while between them may be thrust a grey-headed mulatto, following with stupid eyes the evolutions of the priest; or the devout negro woman telling her beads,—a string of berries—as if her life depended on it.

In addition to its racist stereotypes, the description suggests linguistic diversity, which was further expanded when a new wave of African American residents arrived after emancipation in 1863. Large numbers of Irish, Germans, and Italians also came to the city in the nineteenth and early twentieth centuries, as did smaller groups of Greeks, Jews, Cubans, Hondurans, Croatians, Chinese, and more recently Vietnamese and Mexicans (Cooke and Blanton 1981; Campanella 2006). In addition, New Orleans's port has been a continuous source of linguistic diversity. Many New Orleanians trace their ethnic heritage to sailors who settled there after leaving countries including Cuba, Belize, Norway, Greece, and the former Yugoslavia. The mix of ethnicities and languages gave rise to an urban culture that, in the words of New Orleans linguist and city native George Reinecke (1985:55), was the "synthesis of the various cultures in the unique New Orleans melting pot as they interacted one by one with the original French, Franco-American or Afro-French population." Further, according to Reinecke, "Until the mid-nineteenth century,

Figure 12.1. Mardi Gras Indian with Yat-costumed assistant, 2013. Photo by the author.

[immigrant groups] were for the most part easily absorbed into the group of French speakers in the city, but even long after this language-group was in turn swallowed up by English, the New Orleans lifestyle, common in large measure to black and white, remains markedly distinct from other American places." (55) This "markedly distinct" local culture is evident everywhere—in music, food, and culture (figure 12.1)—and is evident in the city's speech. French colonial roots and sustained ethnic diversity created the synthesized civic culture and speech of New Orleans. Many scholars have called this synthesizing process creolization (e.g., Munro and Britton 2012; Baron and Cara 2011; Sublette 2008). At the same time, the fact of America as a racial democracy that subjugates nonwhite people (Omi and Winant 1994) means that the life experiences of white and nonwhite New Orleanians have always been different (see, e.g., Troutt 2006). Sociologist Daphne Spain (1979) calls the dissonance in the relationship between white and black New Orleanians "two centuries of paradox." The controversy over the term *Creole* instantiates the fundamental racial trouble of America—the tension between ethnoracial synthesis and cultural complexity on the one hand and white supremacy and cultural oversimplification on the other.

Creole

Given America's fundamental racial problems, it is unsurprising that the term *Creole* remains contentious in New Orleans. At the city's founding, *Creole* referred to those born in the colony, whether free or enslaved, European, African, or mixed (Dominguez 1977, 1986). Later colonial New Orleans used an ethnoracial system that named very fair-skinned people *Creoles*, less fair-skinned people *Creoles de Couleur*, and generally dark-skinned enslaved or free people *Nègres* (Brasseaux 2005; Dominguez 1977, 1986; G. Hall 1992; Dorman 1996; Valdman 1997; Kein 2000; Gaudin 2005; Eble 2008). In the late 1800s, nearly a century of American statehood had asserted the primacy of the binary black/white American racial construct. Responding to this binarity, some Creoles sought to distinguish themselves from darker-skinned Creoles by claiming "pure" European ancestry and stopped speaking French to promote identification with English-speaking white Americans (Dominguez 1977). Disagreements persist to this day about what *Creole* encompasses in New Orleans, as there are Creoles who claim solely European ancestry and are overwhelmingly English-monolingual, and Creoles who claim European and African or Native American ancestry and often speak some French. Further, the term *Creole* is widely used for many items claimed as native to New Orleans and south Louisiana, from food (e.g., *Creole tomato*) to architecture (e.g., *Creole cottage*).

From synonym for *indigenous* to the possession of pre-statehood ancestry, the definition of *Creole* in New Orleans remains a matter of debate. I use the term here to describe New Orleanians who claim French-speaking ancestors and European and African or Native American heritage (following Dominguez 1977:595). However, most self-identified Creole New Orleanians also identify themselves as African Americans, a legacy of the pressure of racial binarity and the civil rights movement (see Hirsch and Logsdon 1992; Hirsch 2007; Gaudin 2005). Consequently, it is unlikely that a contemporary New Orleans Creole English exists that is wholly distinct from a New Orleans African American English.

As the contested definition of *Creole* demonstrates, the population of New Orleans has historically occupied a border that reveals the artificiality of the constructs *black* and *white*. Linguist Mackie Blanton (1989:780) notes that it is "imprecise to speak of 'white' or 'black' as discrete varieties of American English in the South, and the lack of precise rubrics is even more noticeable in referring to the English of the New Orleans areas." Linguistically, New Orleans has occupied a liminal space, but the response to the flooding after the levees broke in 2005 made the entrenched and profound racial inequalities in the city plain for the world to see.

Flooding

On August 29, 2005, Hurricane Katrina hit New Orleans, and subsequent levee failures caused water from Lake Pontchartrain to pour into the city. Eighty percent of the city was flooded, with only stretches of high ground along the Mississippi River and scattered elsewhere in the city remaining dry. Flooded sections of the city lay under an average of six to nine feet of water for more than three weeks. Nearly the entire population of 450,000 was forced to leave.

The extended disaster of the evacuation and the continuing delays and inequities in reconstruction made New Orleans's race, gender, and class disparities visible internationally (see, e.g., Hartman and Squires 2006; Adams 2013). After the floodwaters receded, African American residents struggled to return because of racially discriminatory city, state, and federal policies (Seicshnaydre et al. 2018; Olshansky and Johnson 2017; Troutt 2015; Bullard and Wright 2009; Herscher 2006). One example of biased policy is the Road Home program, a state effort that gave federal money to homeowners for rebuilding. The program used the preflood value of houses rather than the estimated cost of rebuilding to calculate payouts. Because property value is indexed to race (white neighborhoods tend to be more expensive), white New Orleanians received more money than African American and other nonwhite homeowners. Fair housing advocates sued, and in 2010 the courts ordered the program to change its payment formula. However, many African Americans who wanted to return to New Orleans had already created new lives elsewhere.

The US Census estimated New Orleans's 2017 population at 391,000, 15 percent smaller than before Katrina. The bulk of the missing population consists of African Americans who were unable to return to the city as a consequence of biased policies, some of them centuries-old (Spain 1979; Campanella 2014) and some far more recent. In the words of author Fatima Shaik (2015), a New Orleans native, "We are approximately 100,000 black people poorer since the storm." The city is now 59 percent African American and 31 percent white (versus 67 percent African American and 28 percent white in 2005). Latinx and Asian Americans, primarily Vietnamese, make up 6 percent and 3 percent of the population, respectively, close to pre-Katrina percentages (Data Center 2018). Since 2005, the city has received an influx of new residents, particularly Hondurans and Mexicans as well as Americans from other states, who have created a "brain gain" of educated professionals . The poverty rate, however, is 25 percent, almost unchanged from the 27 percent rate in 2000 (US Census 2018).

Neighborhoods remain profoundly disturbed. The flooding destroyed nearly 40 percent of residences, and almost every neighborhood suffered catastrophic damage. Some neighborhoods are now less densely populated than they were pre-Katrina, and many people no longer live in the communities where they were raised. More than a decade after the flooding, many neighborhoods—particularly those that previously were largely African American—have not recovered (Data Center 2017). Further, gentrification of neighborhoods that have recovered has caused real estate prices to increase, causing more neighborhood changes as residents are priced out of the market. Neighborhood and school social networks are critical to the development and maintenance of speech varieties (see, e.g., Labov 2006), so these changes mean that local speech is certain to change in the future.

Another result of the destruction in 2005 has been the amplification of the performative aspect of local language. Katrina was a televised crucible that forced every New Orleanian to reflect and make decisions. Each adult who returned to live in New Orleans chose to do so, causing some residents to say that the city has a "100 percent volunteer" population. One intangible legacy is a new or renewed commitment by both native New Orleanians and newcomers to sustain many aspects of local culture. This change has caused a revalorization of local language, which has become seen as a beloved part of the lived experience of the city before the storm, a cultural practice that people want to revitalize and perpetuate. This post-Katrina affective valorization of the local, together with the commodified value of sounding local for tourism, affects local language.

English Varieties

For decades, French and English competed as official languages in New Orleans (Lief 2012), and although the city gradually became predominantly English monolingual, French reflexes remain scattered through the local lexicon. In the early twentieth century, as French eroded, a vernacular variety of New Orleans English emerged. According to the *Atlas of North American English* (Labov, Ash, and Boberg 2006:260), "The New Orleans dialect has been shown to be marginal to the South in many respects." Settlement patterns and long-standing commercial and social ties between northern cities and New Orleans (A. Hall 1851; Labov 2007) may have contributed to similarities between northeastern and New Orleans speech. Reinecke suggests that the arrival of New England merchants in the nineteenth century caused New Orleanians to adopt the speech of the socially prominent newcomers (Kent 1979). These features included the reversal of the pronunciation of the sounds [ɔɪ] and [ɚ] (*coil* is pronounced *curl* [kɚl], and *curl* is pronounced *coil* [kɔɪl]), *th*-stopping (*that* is pronounced *dat*), and possibly *r*-lessness (*car* pronounced *cah*), all of which are found in older New York City English (Babbitt 1896). The variety became known as *Yat* (from the expression *Where y[ou] at?*), or *Ninth Ward* speech, from one of its neighborhoods of origin. *Yat* refers to both the dialect and its speakers. A popular folk dictionary (Lemotte 1985:5) claims that most people "in the New Orleans area talk some form of Yat. Virtually all working class and lower middle class whites grow up speaking it.... Many Downtown Blacks also talk Yat, particularly in the Creole Seventh Ward." A 1994 Loyola University monograph similarly describes Yat English as widespread and non-upper-class (DePascual et al. 1994:21). In 1979, Reinecke claimed that Yat English "is now spoken by nine-tenths of the people in New Orleans" (Kent 1979:C1). These accounts suggest that Yat was a citywide dialect spoken by a majority of New Orleanians.

Yat is the best known variety of New Orleans speech. However, population shifts as a consequence of World War II–era housing development and racist white flight to the suburbs after desegregation in the 1960s has resulted in many fewer urban Yat speakers. DePascual et al. (1994:39) noted twenty-five years ago that Yat was "quickly disappearing" from its neighborhoods of origin. Yat is now predominantly a suburban variety, even as Coles (1997:224) finds that Yat is a symbol of being "truly native" to New Orleans (see Carmichael and Dajko 2016). Yat English is featured in many media, including television segments, books, and magazine and newspaper features (e.g., Brite 2004; Champagne 2012; Higgins 2007; Schneider 1996; Virgets 1997; Lind 2005, 2006; Lorando 2007), that circulate the idea of Yat as the authentic New Orleans variety. Carmichael (2014) uses the term *Chalmatian English*, taken from the town of Chalmette in suburban St. Bernard Parish, emphasizing the variety's current suburban and white location. The state of Yat English in the city of New Orleans is analogous to that of Dixieland jazz: while iconically associated with the city, it is now played by a small minority of local musicians.

Yat English in New Orleans, although more widely discussed and celebrated than ever before, is now an object of nostalgia that has been heightened by the city's near destruction in 2005. T-shirts, coffee mugs, note cards, and other merchandise printed with stereotypical phrases such as *makin' groceries* (grocery shopping) and *Where Y'at?* (How are you?) are popular. This genre of merchandise featuring local language and imagery exemplifies the nostalgia that suffuses Yat English in the city (Carmichael and Dajko 2016).

While very little research has focused on New Orleans English beyond Yat, linguist Jessica White-Sustaíta (2012:48) proposes five major varieties: Yat English, New Orleans African American English, Creole English, Southern White English, and Mainstream American English. Many New Orleans residents suggest additional microvarieties, finding distinctions in the speech of Uptown neighborhoods lying closer to or further from the Mississippi River and in the speech of those who attended particular parochial and private high schools. Comments such as "I could tell he went to St. Aloysius" (or other schools, including St. Augustine, Jesuit, and Holy Cross) are common. This may be because generations of families often attend the same high school, creating strong social and linguistic cues associated with schools. Some New Orleanians also identify differences in pronunciation between Uptown and Downtown neighborhoods. No research to date has substantiated these folk claims, but city residents frequently discuss differences in neighborhood varieties.

The pronunciation of the city's name is itself a local shibboleth. Pronouncing *New Orleans* as "nyoo AW lee unz" [nju ˈɔ: li ənz] or "nyoo OI ee unz" [nju ˈɔɪ ijənz], with four distinct syllables, tends to identify a speaker as belonging to a family with deep roots in New Orleans, while the pronunciation "nu AH linz" [nuˈa lɪnz], with three syllables, is the most common. Mainstream American English speakers also use "nu OR linz" [nu ˈɔɹ lɪnz]. The pronunciation "nu or LEENZ" [nu ɔɹ ˈlinz] is restricted to song lyrics and people unfamiliar with the city.

Vocabulary

The area of greatest agreement and overlap between speakers in New Orleans today is local vocabulary. The city abounds with vocabularies associated with all aspects of city life. (For extensive distribution analyses of local terms, see Malin 1972; Aubert-Gex 1983). All New Orleanians use some portion of the local lexicon, and the continuing vitality of local words is shown by the fact that newcomers import many terms into their speech.

Because the Mississippi River curls around New Orleans (forming the crescent of the Crescent City) so that the east and west banks of the river are actually north and south of one another, the river itself serves as the point of orientation for cardinal directions (see figure 12.2). *Upriver* and *downriver* are used, together with *lakeside* and *riverside* to designate positions closer to Lake Pontchartrain to the north or to the river roughly to the south. Other quotidian terms include *neutral ground* (street median), listed in the *Dictionary of American Regional English* (Cassidy and Hall 1985–2013:3:779) as found only in New Orleans; *brake tag* (car inspection sticker); *streetcar* (trolley); and *Page fence* (chain link fence—made by the Page company). The pronunciation of street names is also shared local knowledge. From Native American words (*Tchoupitoulas* [t͡ʃɔ pəˈtu ləs]) to Greek (*Calliope* [ˈkæ li oʊp] or [kə ˈli ə pi]) to French (*Burgundy* [bɚɹ ˈɡʊn di]), local pronunciations are not predictable and serve as tourist shibboleths. Figure 12.3 shows an image that appears on a T-shirt with the tag line, "If you can read this then you are local."

The city's cultural traditions also have developed extensive vocabularies. The most well-known tradition, Mardi Gras, has been celebrated in New Orleans since the late eighteenth century. A few Carnival terms include *flambeaux* (torches; French), used to refer to both the gas torches and the African

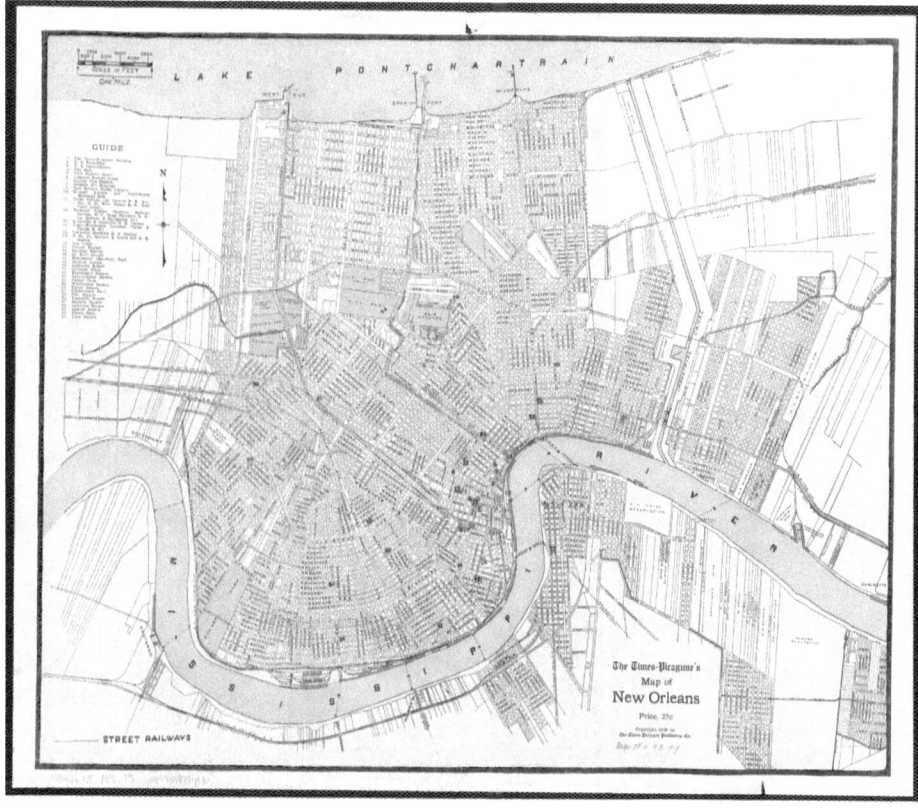

Figure 12.2. New Orleans, 1919. The Mississippi River curls around the city at the bottom of the map, while at the top, Lake Pontchartrain forms the city's northern boundary. Map by New Orleans Times-Picayune, 1919.

American men who carry them during evening parades (a practice called *totin' fire*). Flambeaux *skylark* (twirl torches) for tips from spectators. *Throws* are trinkets—beads, plastic cups, doubloon coins, and toys—that riders on Mardi Gras floats throw to parade-watchers lining the streets, a practice originating in civic efforts to make Mardi Gras more engaging for tourists.

Krewe is the generic term for all Mardi Gras organizations, membership-based groups that pay for floats, throws, and parade permits and for the privilege of riding the floats and attending balls. *Krewe* was coined in 1857 when a group of white American businessmen decided to form a Mardi Gras club, choosing the antique English-sounding name Mistick Krewe of Comus (Gill 1997). Other Mardi Gras terms include *skeletons* (Creole and African American men who dress as skeletons to frighten children into good behavior and remind spectators of their mortality, and *baby dolls* (traditionally Creole and African American women who mix baby clothes and accessories with tropes

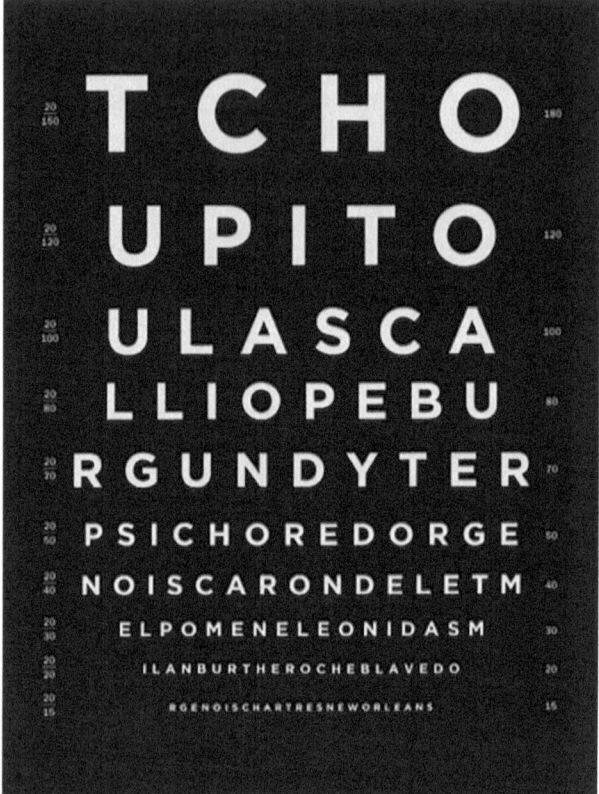

Figure 12.3. Street name eye chart T-shirt. From http://dirtycoast.com/products/if-you-can-read-this-then-you-are-local-black-1155.

on masculine stereotypes, including cigars and the showy use of money, in transgressive performances of femininity) (see, e.g., Vaz 2013). The verb for costuming at Mardi Gras is *mask* (e.g., "I couldn't let my family know I was maskin' as a baby doll").

The most famous maskers in New Orleans are Mardi Gras Indians, who have created a large lexicon. Mardi Gras Indians are groups of Creoles and African Americans who, since at least the nineteenth century, have celebrated ties to Native Americans and resistance to racism and injustice by creating elaborate costumes and performing stories of Native American and African American mutual aid, cultural survival, personal brilliance, and family history (M. Smith 1994, 2003). Indians rehearse and sew costumes all year but appear in public on only a few occasions, including Mardi Gras Day, Super Sunday, and St. Joseph's Night.

Mardi Gras Indian group members include the Big Chief, the male head of the tribe; the Big Queen, the female head (figure 12.4); Second and Trail Chiefs and Queens; a Spy Boy or Girl, who runs ahead of the tribe to keep an eye out for other Indians; a Flag Boy or Girl, who carries the tribe's banner and

Figure 12.4. Educator, activist, and filmmaker Cherice Harrison-Nelson, Big Queen of the Guardians of the Flame Maroon Society, 2012. Photo by Jeffrey David Ehrenreich.

communicates with the Spy Boy; and a Wildman, who clears the crowds ahead of the Big Chief and makes mischief.

One aspect of New Orleans vocabulary that is heard publicly through songs but is not generally known by outsiders is the repertory of traditional Mardi Gras Indian chants. Some of these chants—most famously "Iko Iko" from a 1965 recording by the Dixie Cups—have been popularized. Mardi Gras Indian chants, songs, and prayers draw on multiple cultures and languages, including Louisiana Creole French, Isleño Spanish, English, and perhaps Native American languages (especially Choctaw, Chickasaw, and Mobilian Jargon) and African languages (possibly including Mande and Gbe). (For an ethnomusicological account of Indian chants, see Draper 1973; Sakakeeny 2002.)

Second lines are another public cultural tradition unique to New Orleans. Second lines are street parades accompanied by brass bands as part of a funeral procession or an annual parade put on by a social club or sometimes as a spectacle designed as a tourist attraction (see Regis 1999). *Buckjumping* is the term for the syncopated dancing performed by parade members and spectators at second lines.[2]

New Orleans lives to eat, and food terms are shared across the city. (For an extensive glossary, see Eble 2012.) A few common examples include *gumbo* (a

Figure 12.5. Snoball shack sign in the Eighth Ward. Photo by the author.

stew with Bantu, Choctaw, and French heritage), *po'boy* or *poorboy* (a sandwich on French bread); *dressed* (toppings on a sandwich);[3] *red gravy* (tomato sauce); *mirliton* (chayote squash); and *snoballs* (shaved ice served with flavored syrup) (figure 12.5).

French food terms include *grillades* (a meat-and-gravy dish that takes its name from the French term for *grilled meat*) and *praline* (often pronounced *plarine*; a cream, sugar, and pecan candy that takes its name from the French for *sugared almond*). Other French terms that remain in use include *lagniappe* (a little something extra; borrowed from Spanish *la ñapa* and/or from Quechua *yapay*) (Mizell-Nelson 2012). *Batture* refers to the elevated dry bed of the Mississippi River at the foot of the levee at the border of New Orleans and Jefferson *Parish* (a reflex of French *paroisse* [church parish], used instead of *county* across Louisiana). *Parraine* and *nénaine* have been widely used for *godfather* and *godmother*.

Some words are used as ambassadors for tourism, with the tourism industry using city speech as an emblem of local color. Lists of words and phrases, with a concentration on food terms and older Yat English, are staples on tourism websites, and glossaries of Mardi Gras terms are printed annually in tourist-oriented publications (e.g., Schoen 2019; Gold 2015; Taggart 2013; Ambush 2002). .For example, the tourism website Experience New Orleans (http://www.experienceneworleans.com/)features a glossary that includes,

MY-Nez
Translated: "mayonnaise"
Contributed by Sister Anne Joan: "MY-nez is a pronunciation unique to Creole New Orleanians; it reflects the French pronunciation of a visibly French word, the actual meaning of which I do not know. When I moved out of New Orleans to enter the convent, I used to avoid pronouncing it; nobody knew what I meant! Bless y'all's dawlin' hawts."

This example reinforces certain pronunciations as local (*mynez* [mayonnaise]; *r*-lessness) and presents New Orleans as providing colorful, provincial cultural content for more sophisticated visitors. While these commodified uses of vocabulary are designed to entertain tourists and often do not represent everyday speech, they amplify metalinguistic awareness of some local terms and pronunciations for both tourists and New Orleanians.

Phonological, Syntactic, and Discourse Features

More educated and non–locally oriented New Orleanians tend to speak Mainstream American English, sometimes switching between vernacular and mainstream forms or losing vernacular forms completely (White-Sustaíta 2012; Schoux Casey 2013). For example, an older New Orleans woman recalled that her mother, not wanting her to sound provincial and working class, put soap in her mouth for pronouncing *boil* (bɔɪl) as *berl* (bɚl). Another older woman recalled that she grew up saying *my-nez* ('maɪ nɛz) and later practiced saying *mayonnaise* ('mæn eɪz). Stories of this kind are common; elocution lessons were popular in the mid-twentieth century as New Orleanians, particularly women aspiring to higher social status, attempted to eradicate local features from their speech.

While the frequency of New Orleans features is now augmented by the conscious efforts of some more educated New Orleanians and newcomers to use local language, the least-educated speakers tend to use the most local features the most often. Certain grammatical features and pronunciations are used most often by less educated working-class speakers of all ethnoracial backgrounds (Schoux Casey 2013):

1. Use of idioms, including:
   Where y'at? (How are you?)
   ya mom an 'em (your mother and family)
   yeah you rite (yeah, you're right—an expression of agreeable acknowledgment)
   for true—used both to mean *Really?*" and as an asseveration (e.g., "I love the swearing, it's for true") (figure 12.6)

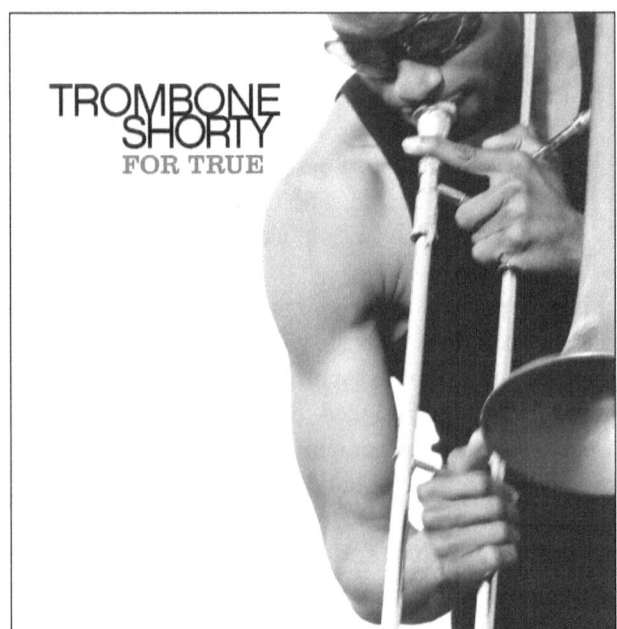

Figure 12.6. Trombone Shorty 2012 album cover. Photo by Kirk Edwards, https://www.discogs.com/Trombone-Shorty-For-True/release/4162846.

2. Use of tag elements, especially *yeah*, *no*, and personal pronouns:
   I picked up a flu bug, yeah.
   I don't like that, no.
   I need a few million, me. (Cohn 2007:30)

3. Use of the tag phrase *and (all of) that (sort of thing)* as a general extender:
   When I went to Mississippi for college and that sort of thing.
   It's hard to put two kids in the car and all that.
   Because the wood had swollen and all of that.

4. Use of triple subjects:
   And my granddaughter, her, she just crazy.
   My son, him, he better go back in January.

5. Noninversion of questions:
   What time it is? (What time is it?)
   Where he went? (Where did he go?)

6. Use of *make* in a variety of contexts (from the French *faire X* construction; e.g., *faire les courses* [do the marketing]):
   She made six [turned six] *last month.*

I'm going to make twenty-one years [complete twenty-one years] *at my job.*
We made [took] *a vacation last year.*
I don't think he'll make [be elected] *mayor again.*
I had to make the block to find a spot [go around the block looking for parking].
She's makin' groceries [grocery shopping] *right now.*

7. Use of *for* in a variety of contexts:
   I'll be there for [at] *ten.*
   Who that dog for? [Whose dog is that?]
   That term applied for [to] *the Saints.*
   Hurricane Betsy ain't got nothin' for [compared to] *Katrina.*
   It got wiped out for [during/because of] *Ivan.*
   They'll get offended for [by] *cursing.*
   No sense for [in] *stealing something you didn't have nowhere to bring it.*
   She have a lot for her mom. [She has a lot of inherited similarities to/looks like her mom.]

8. Use of *by* rather than *at*:
   Whenever something break by her house I go fix it.

9. Use of *stay by* to mean *live at*, *pass by* to mean *drop in*:
   I stayed by my sister's for six months after the storm.
   I can only pass by for a minute.

10. Use of *ride* for *drive*:
    I don't like to eat and ride.
    It's a long ride to get there.
    I would've ridden her to the hospital.

11. The *coil-curl* reversal:
    You know what kimchi is? Spurled [spɚld; spoiled] *cabbage.*
    That wasn't the pernt [pɚnt; point].
    Toin [tɔɪn]; turn] *on Royal Street.*
    The government poichased [ˈpɔɪ t͡ʃəd;] (purchased) *the home.*

The *coil-curl* reversal is nearly categorical in the speech of many less-educated African Americans and less often heard in other varieties. Impressionistic observation, however, suggests that some New Orleanians of all ethnicities and levels of educational attainment, especially older speakers, maintain the reversal in their speech.

Figure 12.7. Sign for snoball and enchilada shop, New Orleans. Photo by the author.

12. Absence or vowel-like pronunciation of *r* after vowels, so that *sugar* is pronounced *shugah* [ˈʃʊ gə] (figure 12.7)

13. Unrounding in the pronunciation of the vowel in *bomb* [ɔ] to *bum* [ʌ]: *My dad loved the trumbone* [ˈtrʌm boʊn].

14. *Th*-stopping, the pronunciation of voiced *th* as *d*, so that *these*, *that*, and *them* are pronounced *dese*, *dat*, and *dem* (figure 12.8). *Dat* is enregistered in the phrase *Who Dat*, a cheer for the team and the name for fans (the *Who Dat Nation*) of the New Orleans Saints football team.

Figure 12.8. Dr. John 2004 album cover. Photo by Cat Yellen Rebennack.

15. Metathesis (transposition of consonants) in *ask* so that it is pronounced *aks*. *Aks* is nationally associated with African American English but impressionistically is commonly used in New Orleans by many less educated speakers. (For the presence of this feature in suburban Yat English, see Carmichael 2014.)

NEW ORLEANS VARIETIES

There has been little research to date on individual varieties of New Orleans English other than Yat English. Impressionistic observation and local folk linguistic ideology suggest that other varieties do exist, and certain features have been recorded or observed. With the exception of Yat English features, these taxonomies have not been formally documented.

Yat/Chalmatian English

Carmichael (2012, 2014) and Mucciaccio (2009) document Yat, or Chalmatian English. Several features are commonly heard in New Orleans, including the *coil-curl* reversal, *r*-lessness, *th*-stopping, metathesis in *ask*, use of idioms such as *Where y'at?*, and noninversion in questions. Carmichael (2012) identifies further features of Yat speech:

1. *L*-vocalization: the pronunciation of nonsyllable initial *l* as a vowel or *w*, so that *cold* and *file* sound like *code* and *fiuw*.
2. *Price* vowel monophthongization: *I* [aɪ] sounds close to *ah* [a:].
3. Raised *bought*: the pronunciation of the vowel in *dog* and *talk* [ɔ] as a slightly higher vowel.
4. Consonant cluster reduction: the deletion of final consonants, so that *fifth* sounds like *fi'* [fɪʔ].
5. The absence of the copular verb *be* in sentences: *She gorgeous* (rather than *She is gorgeous*) and *They crazy* (rather than *They are crazy*).
6. The absence of *do* in questions: *How ya like them?*
7. The absence of subject-verb agreement: *He don't care* (instead of *He doesn't care*).

Some features documented in Yat or Chalmatian English are shared with New Orleans African American Vernacular English, particularly *price* monophthongization, consonant cluster reduction, the absence of *be* and *do*, noninversion in questions, and the absence of subject-verb agreement. White-Sustaíta (2012:51) suggests that this is because New Orleans African American

Vernacular English influenced Yat English as a result of racially integrated historical residential patterns. Settlement patterns in the city's small footprint before swamps were drained and the city expanded were unusually dense and physically integrated, which may have contributed to similarities among the city's speech varieties. At the same time, many differences are apparent between Yat and New Orleans African American Vernacular English: as White-Sustaíta (2012:51) notes, "No native or long-time resident of New Orleans would fail to perceive differences at all levels of the two dialects." For example, while Yat speakers are most often asked whether they are from New York or New Jersey, African American New Orleanians are most often asked whether they are from the Caribbean islands.

New Orleans African American Vernacular English

New Orleans African American Vernacular English is nearly totally unstudied, so these observations can be considered candidates for further research:

1. Flavored water frozen in paper or plastic cups and sold informally across the city in the summer is referred to by many names, depending on the neighborhood: *huckabuck, hucklebuck, dixie cup, iceberg, icebird, freeze cup, zip cup,* and *frozen cup* are a partial list.[4]
2. Intrusive consonants in specific words: *cawnder* for *corner, Janjuary* for *January*.
3. Use of *ya heard (me)* as frequent tag element, usually pronounced as *yurrrd me* or reduced (*yurrd*).
   I'm for [from] *the Third Ward, ya heard me.*
   I'm a catch this on video, ya heard me.
   Although it is in question form, speakers generally do not pronounce the phrase with the final rise of true questions. While *ya hear* is a stereotype of Southern American English (as in *Y'all come back now, ya hear*), *ya heard me*, where *hear* is obligatorily tensed to *heard*, is distinct from *ya hear* in form, pronunciation, and frequency of occurrence.
4. Plural marking on *French Quarter* as *French Quarters* [ˈkwɔː təz] or *the Quarters* [də ˈkwɔː təz] (Schoux Casey 2013).
5. Pronunciation of *Melpomene* Street as *Melfomeen* [ˈmɛl fə min]. Most non–African American New Orleanians pronounce the street *Melpomeen* [ˈmɛl pə min] (Dajko et al. 2012).
6. Use of *baby*, a reflex from the French *bébé*, and the shortened forms *babe* and *bé/bae*, with strangers and acquaintances as well as intimates of the speaker (see Douglas 1969:67). *Alright, baby* can be used to close a conversation between male acquaintances. *It is too, too hot, baby* can be said

to a room of strangers. Impressionistic observation supports the idea that this pronunciation of *baby*, with the first vowel extended, is distinctive. One young Ninth Ward man noted, "I'm-a tell you normally if I go out of town somewhere and I meet someone they always ask [æks] me to say one word—because you could hear that I'm from New Orleans—they always say, 'Say *baby*.' And you know, *baaaayby* [ˈbɛɪᵊː bə], it's different from everywhere else."

7. Rolling prosody is perhaps the most distinctive feature of New Orleans African American speech. Vowels are often triphthongized (extended), as in *baby*. Other examples include *paper* pronounced *paay-puh* [pɛɪᵊː pə]; *over there* pronounced *ooh-vah deh* [ˈoᵊː və dəʔ]; *crazy* pronounced *craa'-a-zy* [kɹɛɪᵊːzɪ]. Extended vowels combine with sentence stress, intonation and tag elements to produce phrases that can seem akin to Caribbean Englishes, although I know of no research corroborating or disproving a Caribbean–New Orleans English connection. (On cultural connections, see Munro and Britton 2012.)

New Orleans Creole English

The English of self-identified New Orleans Creoles has rarely been studied. One exception (Douglas 1969) studied the English of native New Orleanian speakers of Creole French and found that it was marked especially by French-influenced pronunciation of consonant and vowel sounds, including nonaspiration of initial stops (not producing a small puff of air in the pronunciation of *p*, *t*, and *k*); interdental *t* and *d* (with the tongue between the teeth rather than behind the front teeth); pronouncing "pure," longer *i*, *e*, *u*, and *o* (as they are pronounced in French); the absence of *h* at the beginning of words; the presence of tag elements at the end of a phrase (e.g., *What you doing in there, you?*); the use of French words and phrases; and the repetition of words to indicate intensity (e.g., *That cat was black, black*) (122–25). Many of these elements are also found in Cajun English, which similarly draws on a francophone history (see Carmichael, this volume).

While Douglas (1969:122) notes that "New Orleans speakers are very prone to remark "You know, Creoles always say *eeez* for *his*," the English pronunciation of New Orleans Creoles today is less French-influenced. Further, most self-identified New Orleans Creoles today consider themselves both Creole and African American, so New Orleans African American Vernacular and Creole English are closer than they have been in the past. Some features that remain particularly characteristic of Creole English include the use of many French terms, including *cher(e)* (dear) as a term of endearment; *'tit* (from *petit*) as a diminutive, so that *'tit John* refers to the son of Big or Gros John. (For folk

Figure 12.9. Sign in the historically Creole Seventh Ward. Photo by Thomas A. Klingler.

accounts of Creole terms, see D. Smith 1997; Saloy 2012.) One young Creole man suggested that a hallmark of Creole speech is frequent use of French terms: "If they don't continue to speak French on a regular basis, maybe every fifteen words you gonna hear some really native New Orleans or French expression, Creole French expression as part of the conversation."

One older Creole man substantiated this folk claim, replying to an interview question about a social club with "that Jolly Bunch is *'tit negre Americains* [little American blacks]." The use of French and the use of the diminutive *'tit* to refer to non-Creole African Americans indicates French's continuing use to demarcate Creoles as a unique group (figure 12.9). Repetition of final words and phrases is also common for Creole English speakers: "Oh, I am late, late"; "I don't know how many more will be doing that, but I like it, I like it." Carmichael (2012, 2014) found repetition to be a feature in Yat English as well, so it is possible that Yat has been influenced by French, perhaps via Creole English.

Contemporary Creoles often report an emphasis on courteous speech. One older Creole woman recalled, "When I was growing up you would see the neighbors and they would say, 'Eh, la bas! Comment ça va, cher?' ["Hey, you there! How are you, dear?"], and even to strangers you were taught to be polite." A sign on the counter of a Creole-owned store in the Gentilly neighborhood sets an explicitly courteous tone: "We Are Ladies and Gentlemen Serving Ladies and Gentlemen."

Garden District and Southern White English

New Orleans's original residents lived on a grid of streets along a bend in the Mississippi River called the Vieux Carré (Old Square) and now known as the French Quarter for its francophone colonial residents. Anglo-Americans arriving after the Louisiana Purchase settled upriver of the French portion of the city. The dividing line was Canal Street, the original demarcator of Uptown (the American, anglophone area) and Downtown (the Creole, francophone area). The most well known and wealthiest American residential neighborhood developed in the 1800s as mansions on large, verdant lots, giving rise to the name *Garden District*.

The white, American, and largely Protestant residents of this neighborhood and later other Uptown neighborhoods created a tightly knit social network and developed a distinctive way of speaking. Reinecke described the accent of "the Garden District types" as resembling "the plantation Southern dialect, with rich, full oratorical diction" (Kent 1979:C1). Other features include *r*-lessness, *price* vowel monophthongization, and the *coil-curl* reversal. This variety is that of the oldest white participants in the documentaries *Yes Ma'am* (Goldman 1981), *Yeah You Rite!* (Alvarez and Kolker 1985), and *By Invitation Only* (Snedeker 2006). While I know of no research to substantiate this claim, observation suggests that the Garden District variety is restricted to the oldest generation. Younger white members of the upper class, especially women, generally speak Mainstream American English. Upper-class white males often use some Inland Southern features, including *price* monophthongization and the *pin-pen* merger (the identical pronunciation of some front vowels before nasal consonants, so that both *ten* and *tin* are pronounced *tin*).

This general overview of features of New Orleans English varieties is neither authoritative nor exact. Much work is needed to draw a well-researched picture of New Orleans language, particularly the speech of African American, Vietnamese, and Latinx New Orleanians.[5]

INTO THE FUTURE

While there is a dearth of academic linguistic research, popular awareness of local language is robust. The city's near-drowning intensified an existing metalinguistic awareness. While Mainstream American English is spoken by non–locally oriented and more educated New Orleanians, the historical desire to sound less local has diminished. In the wake of Katrina, many New Orleanians have reevaluated local language as a unique and treasured part of the city. Further, New Orleans has experienced an influx of new residents since

2005, many of whom demonstrate their affinity for the city through linguistic means, importing local features to their talk. Some newcomers use single words such as *po'boy* or *neutral ground* or make heavy use of iconic phrases such as *yeah, you right*, and *ya heard me*. Other transplants, termed *supernatives* by the geographer Richard Campanella (2013), adopt more complex features, including rolling prosody, sentence final tags, and local uses of verbs and prepositions.

The centrality of tourism to New Orleans's economy has also heightened the performative aspect of vernacular language, as local talk is valued as a commodity for the entertainment of tourists. Because tourism is the city's most lucrative industry, local language has been promoted as a unique aspect of the city, an intangible value-added commodity for tourists and convention planners. Some parts of local language have been commodified, and nostalgia also commodifies language, as with Yat English, which is printed on T-shirts and merchandise and used in advertisements as a sign of New Orleans authenticity even though it is now suburban. Commodification and nostalgia have enregistered some parts of New Orleans English, as is also the case with French in the city (Eble 2009). Further, many New Orleanians have always been performers and celebrants of local culture and nostalgic lovers of local traditions. Language—spoken in everyday talk, sung in Mardi Gras Indian or brass band songs, or written about in popular media—is an integral part of the production and performance of localness.

New Orleans is engaged in complex sociolinguistic processes that include the interrelationship of local language and culture, gentrification, nostalgia, and commodification. The linguistic results of this interrelationship are complex: parts of New Orleans talk are commodified objects of nostalgia or entertainment, while other parts are in robust quotidian use. Some aspects of New Orleans talk are both things at once, just as New Orleans itself is both an inhabited, geographical reality and a cultural imaginary.

Both the reality and imaginary are situated within the racial binary of America. Louis Armstrong, New Orleans's most famous son and namesake of the city's airport, said "I don't care if I never see the city again. Honestly, they treat me better all over the world than they do in my hometown.... I ain't going back to New Orleans and let them white folks be whipping me on my head" (quoted in Mitchell 1999:149). Reinecke (1985:55) saw New Orleans language and culture as the synthesis of a "unique melting pot," but the famous gumbo culture of New Orleans has never been equally good for all people, as Armstrong makes clear. For New Orleans to achieve creolization in language and culture, New Orleanians of color must flourish, unthwarted by white New Orleanians, both natives and newcomers.

NOTES

1. This and all other examples are from interviews conducted by the author or direct observation unless otherwise cited.
2. The *Dictionary of American Regional English* (Cassidy and Hall 1985–2013:1:571) lists *buckjumping* as a term chiefly found in the West referring to a jumpy horse, while *buck* is listed as widely used in the Northeast in racist reference to African Americans. The origins of *buckjumping* in New Orleans to refer to a dance style have not to my knowledge been traced, although it is clearly related to buck dance, an African American folk dance associated with blues music.
3. *Po'boy* as a sandwich originated in New Orleans, while *dressed* is described in *DARE* as a New Orleans term for the act of sprinkling a substance (such as ash) on an article of clothing or other item as part of a "hoodoo" ritual. Whether *dressed* as "condiment" is a extension from that source is unknown.
4. The *Dictionary of American Regional English* (Cassidy and Hall 1985–2013) does not record any of these terms as words for frozen drink cups.
5. Audio and audiovisual resources are publicly available for people interested in New Orleans Englishes, including the Amistad Research Center, the NOLA Hiphop and Bounce Archive, and other collections in the public and university libraries; the Historic New Orleans Collection; the Hurricane Digital Memory Bank; the I-Witness Central City project at MondoBizarro.com; and the New Orleans Jazz and Heritage Foundation Archive.

WORKS CITED

Adams, Vincanne. 2013. *Markets of Sorrow, Labors of Faith: New Orleans in the Wake of Katrina.* Durham: Duke University Press.
Alvarez, Louis, and Andrew Kolker, dirs. and prods. 1985. *Yeah You Rite!* Video recording. Center for New American Media.
Ambush. 2002. *Talking that New Orleans Talk.* http://www.crescentcity.com/dictionary.htm.
Aubert-Gex, Madeleine. 1983. "A Lexical Study of the English of New Orleans Creoles Based on the Malin Questionnaire." Master's thesis, University of New Orleans.
Babbitt, E. H. 1896. "The English of the Lower Classes in New York City and Vicinity." *Dialect Notes* 1:457–64.
Baron, Robert, and Ana Cara, eds. 2011. *Creolization as Cultural Continuity and Creativity in Postdiluvian New Orleans and Beyond.* Jackson: University Press of Mississippi.
Beal, Joan. 2009. "Enregisterment, Commodification, and Historical Context: 'Geordie' vs. 'Sheffieldish.'" *American Speech* 84 (2): 138–56.
Blanton, Mackie. 1988. "New Orleans English." In *The Encyclopedia of Southern Culture,* edited by Charles Reagan Wilson and William Ferris, 780–81. Chapel Hill: University of North Carolina Press.
Brasseaux, Carl A. 2005. *French, Cajun, Creole, Houma: A Primer on Francophone Louisiana.* Baton Rouge: Louisiana State University Press.
Brasted, Chelsea. 2018. "New Orleans Sets Record with Nearly 11 Million Visitors in 2017." *New Orleans Times-Picayune,* May 1. http://www.nola.com/business/index.ssf/2018/05/new_orleans_visitors_2017_tour.html.

Brennan, Pamela. 1983. "Postvocalic /-r/ in New Orleans." Master's thesis, University of New Orleans.

Brite, Poppy Z. 2004. *Liquor*. New York: Three Rivers.

Bullard, Robert, and Beverly Wright, eds. 2009 *Race, Place, and Environmental Justice after Hurricane Katrina*. New York: Routledge.

Burnett, Katherine. 2009. "Lafcadio Hearn's Traveling Regionalism." *Global South* 32:64–82.

Campanella, Richard. 2006. *Geographies of New Orleans: Urban Fabrics before the Storm*. Lafayette: Center for Louisiana Studies, University of Louisiana at Lafayette.

Campanella, Richard. 2013. "Gentrification and Its Discontents: Notes from New Orleans." *New Geography*, March 1. http://www.newgeography.com/content/003526-gentrification-and-its-discontents-notes-new-orleans.

Campanella, Richard. 2014. "Two Centuries of Paradox: The Geography of New Orleans's African American Population, from Antebellum to Postdiluvian Times." In *Hurricane Katrina in Transatlantic Perspective*, edited by Romain Huret and Randy J. Sparks, 8–37. Baton Rouge: Louisiana State University Press.

Carmichael, Katie. 2012. "Notes from the Field: Yat English Features in Chalmette, Louisiana." *Southern Journal of Linguistics* 361:191–99.

Carmichael, Katie. 2014. "'I Never Thought I Had an Accent until the Hurricane': Sociolinguistic Variation in Post-Katrina Greater New Orleans." PhD diss., Ohio State University.

Carmichael, Katie. 2015. "'Where Y'at since the Storm?': Linguistic Effects of Hurricane Katrina." In *After the Storm: The Cultural Politics of Hurricane Katrina*, edited by Simon Dickel and Evangelia Kindinger, 149–63. Bielefeld: Transcript.

Carmichael, Katie. 2017. "Displacement and Local Linguistic Practices: R-lessness in Post-Katrina Greater New Orleans." *Journal of Sociolinguistics* 21:696–719.

Carmichael, Katie, and Kara Becker. 2016. "Raised BOUGHT in New Orleans and New York City: It's Not What You THOUGHT." Paper presented at the annual meeting of the American Dialect Society, Washington, DC, January 8.

Carmichael, Katie, and Nathalie Dajko. 2016. "Ain't Dere No More: New Orleans Language and Local Nostalgia in *Vic & Nat'ly* Comics." *Journal of Linguistic Anthropology* 26:234–58.

Cassidy, Frederic, and Joan Houston Hall. 1985–2013. *Dictionary of American Regional English*. 6 vols. Cambridge: Belknap Press of Harvard University Press.

Champagne, Christian. 2012. *The Yat Dictionary*. New Orleans: Lavender Ink.

Cohn, Nik. 2007. *Triksta: Life and Death and New Orleans Rap*. New York: Vintage.

Coles, Felice. 1997. "Solidarity Cues in New Orleans English." In *Language Variety in the South Revisited*, edited by Cynthia Bernstein, Thomas Nunnally, and Robin Sabino, 219–24. Tuscaloosa: University of Alabama.

Coles, Felice. 2003. "The Authenticity of Yat: A 'Real' New Orleans Dialect." *Southern Journal of Linguistics* 25:74–85.

Coles, Felice. 2012. "Double Identity: Isleños Are Yats, Too." *Southern Journal of Linguistics* 36 (1): 100–114.

Cooke, John, and Mackie J. V. Blanton, eds. 1981. *Perspectives on Ethnicity in New Orleans*. New Orleans: Committee on Ethnicity in New Orleans.

Dajko, Nathalie, Zach Hebert, Keith Bedney, Rebecca Beyer, Jonathan Garen, Audrey Gilmore, and Adebusola Adebesin. 2012. "Authenticity and Change in New Orleans English." *Southern Journal of Linguistics* 36 (1): 136–54.

The Data Center. 2017. "Neighborhood Change Rates: Growth Continues through 2017 in New Orleans Neighborhoods." August 17. https://www.datacenterresearch.org/reports_analysis/

neighborhood-recovery-rates-growth-continues-through-2017-in-new-orleans-neighbor hoods/.

The Data Center. 2018. "Who Lives in New Orleans and Metro Parishes Now?" January 26. https://www.datacenterresearch.org/data-resources/who-lives-in-new-orleans-now/.

DeLange, Eddie, and Louis Alter. 1947. "Do You Know What it Means to Miss New Orleans?" First performed by Louis Armstrong and Billie Holliday in *New Orleans*, directed by Arthur Lubin and produced by Jules Levey. Majestic Productions, distributed by United Artists.

DePascual, Linda, Jean Greenfield, Susan Miller, Barbara Molnar, Christye Robley, Mary Starnes, and Judith Wester. 1994. *New Orleans Neighborhood Talk: Examining the Original Dialects of the New Orleans Ninth Ward Neighborhood*. New Orleans: Loyola University of New Orleans.

Dillard, J. L. 1985. "Languages and Linguistic Research in Louisiana." In *Louisiana Folklife: A Guide to the State*, edited by Nicholas R. Spitzer, 41–42. Baton Rouge: Louisiana Folklife Program and Center for Gulf South History and Culture.

Dominguez, Virginia. 1977. "Social Classification in Creole Louisiana." *American Ethnologist* 4 (4): 589–602.

Dominguez, Virginia. 1986. *White by Definition: Social Classification in Creole Louisiana*. New Brunswick: Rutgers University Press.

Dormon, James, ed. 1996. *Creoles of Color in the Gulf South*. Knoxville: University of Tennessee Press.

Douglas, Connie. 1969. "A Linguistic Study of the English Used by New Orleans Speakers of Creole." Master's thesis, University of New Orleans.

Draper, David. 1973. "The Mardi Gras Indians: The Ethnomusicology of Black Associations in New Orleans." PhD diss., Tulane University.

Dubois, Sylvie, and Megan Melançon. 1997. "Cajun Is Dead—Long Live Cajun: Shifting from a Linguistic to a Cultural Community." *Journal of Sociolinguistics* 1 (1): 63–93.

Eble, Connie. 2003. "Englishes of Southern Louisiana." In *English in the Southern United States*, edited by Stephen Nagle and Sara L. Sanders, 173–88. New York: Cambridge University Press.

Eble, Connie. 2008. "Creole in Louisiana." *South Atlantic Review* 73 (2): 39–53.

Eble, Connie. 2009. "French in New Orleans: The Commodification of Language Heritage." *American Speech* 84 (2): 211–15.

Eble, Connie. 2012. "Food Vocabulary of New Orleans." *Southern Journal of Linguistics* 36 (1): 71–82.

Eble, Connie. 2016. "The Englishes of New York City and New Orleans: Why Are They Similar?" Paper presented at the Southeastern Conference on Linguistics, New Orleans, March 29.

Gaudin, Wendy. 2005. "Autocrats and All Saints: Migration, Memory, and Modern Creole Identities." PhD diss., New York University.

Gill, John. 1997. *Lords of Misrule: Mardi Gras and the Politics of Race in New Orleans*. Jackson: University Press of Mississippi.

Gold, Scott. 2015. *Your Guide to the Unique Vocabulary of New Orleans*. https://www.thrillist.com/lifestyle/new-orleans/your-guide-to-the-unique-vocabulary-of-new-orleans.

Goldman, Gary, dir. and prod. 1981. *Yes Ma'am: Household Domestic Workers in New Orleans*. Video recording. New York: Filmakers Library.

Hall, Abraham O. 1851. *The Manhattaner in New Orleans; or, Phases of "Crescent City" Life*. New Orleans: Morgan.

Hall, Gwendolyn Midlo. 1992. *Africans in Colonial Louisiana: The Development of Afro-Creole Culture in the Eighteenth Century*. Baton Rouge: Louisiana State University Press.

Hartman, Chester, and Gregory Squires, eds. 2006. *There Is No Such Thing as a Natural Disaster: Race, Class, and Hurricane Katrina*. New York: Routledge.
Herscher, Andrew. 2006. "American Urbicide." *Journal of Architectural Education* 60 (1): 18–20.
Higgins, Earl. 2007. *The Joy of Yat Catholicism*. Gretna, LA: Pelican.
Hirsch, Arnold. 2007. "Fade to Black: Hurricane Katrina and the Disappearance of Creole New Orleans." *Journal of American History* 94:752–61.
Hirsch, Arnold, and Joseph Logsdon. 1992. *Creole New Orleans: Race and Americanization*. Baton Rouge: Louisiana State University Press.
Johnstone, Barbara. 2009. "Pittsburghese Shirts: Commodification and the Enregisterment of an Urban Dialect." *American Speech* 842:157–75.
Kein, Sybil. 2000. *Creole: The History and Legacy of Louisiana's Free People of Color*. Baton Rouge: Louisiana State University Press.
Kent, Joan. 1979. "Talkin' New Orleans: Where Y'at?" *New Orleans Times-Picayune*, May 11, C1.
Kretzschmar, William. 2009. *The Linguistics of Speech*. Cambridge: Cambridge University Press.
Labov, William. 2006. *Principles of Linguistic Change*. Vol. 2, *Social Factors*. Malden, MA: Blackwell.
Labov, William. 2007. "Transmission and Diffusion." *Language* 83 (2): 344–87.
Labov, William, Sharon Ash, and Charles Boberg. 2006. *The Atlas of North American English*. Berlin: Mouton de Gruyter.
Lemotte, Justin. 1985. *New Orleans Talkin': A Guide to Yat, Cajun, and Some Creole*. New Orleans: Channel.
Lief, Shane. 2012. "English as a Para-Hegemonic Language in Nineteenth-Century New Orleans." *Southern Journal of Linguistics* 36 (1): 37–44.
Lind, Angus. 2005. "And Yat's a Fact." *New Orleans Times-Picayune*, May 27, Living, 1.
Lind, Angus. 2006. "Page Fences and Iceboxes: A Refresher Course in Basic Yatabonics." *New Orleans Times-Picayune*, April 17, Living, 1.
Lorando, Mark. 2007. "New Orleans from A to Z: How Do We Love Thee? Let Us Spell the Ways." *New Orleans Times-Picayune*, December 23. http://blog.nola.com/anguslind/2007/12/new_orleans_from_a_to_z_how_do.html.
Malin, Helen. 1972. "A Questionnaire of Lexical Items Used by New Orleans Speakers." Master's thesis, University of New Orleans.
Martineau, Harriet. 1838. *Retrospect of Western Travel*. New York: Harper.
Mitchell, Reid. 1999. *All on a Mardi Gras Day: Episodes in the History of New Orleans Carnival*. Cambridge: Harvard University Press.
Mizell-Nelson, Michael. 2008. "Batista-Era Havana on the Bayou." *Reviews in American History* 36 (2): 231–42.
Mizell-Nelson, Michael. 2012. "'The Curse of Lagniappe': Working Class Consumers and the Quaint Custom of Extortion." *Southern Journal of Linguistics* 36 (1): 61–70.
Mucciaccio, Francesca. 2009. "'A Gaggle a' Y'ats' and Other Stories: Tracing the Effects of Ideology on Language Change through Indexical Formation in Y'at." Honors thesis, Reed College.
Munro, Martin, and Celia Britton. 2012. *American Creoles: The Francophone Caribbean and the American South*. Liverpool: Liverpool University Press.
Olshansky, Robert, and Laurie Johnson. 2017. *Clear as Mud: Planning for the Rebuilding of New Orleans*. New York: Routledge.
Omi, Michael, and Howard Winant. 1994. *Racial Formation in the United States*. 2nd ed. New York: Routledge.

Perry, Marc. 2015. "Who Dat? Race and Its Conspicuous Consumption in Post-Katrina New Orleans." *City and Society* 71:92–114.

Pezzullo, Phaedra. 2009. "'This Is the Only Tour That Sells": Tourism, Disaster, and National Identity in New Orleans." *Journal of Tourism and Cultural Change* 7 (2): 99–114.

Picone, Michael. 2014. "Literary Dialect and the Linguistic Reconstruction of Nineteenth-Century Louisiana." *American Speech* 89 (2): 143–69.

Regis, Helen. 1999. "Second Lines, Minstrelsy, and the Contested Landscapes of Afro-Creole Festivals." *Cultural Anthropology* 14 (4): 472–504.

Regis, Helen, and Shana Walton. 2008. "Producing the Folk at the New Orleans Jazz and Heritage Festival." *Journal of American Folklore* 121 (482): 400–440.

Reinecke, George. 1951. "New Orleans Pronunciation among Children and Educated Adults." Master's thesis, Tulane University.

Reinecke, George. 1985. "The National and Cultural Groups of New Orleans." In *Louisiana Folklife: A Guide to the State*, edited by Nicholas R. Spitzer, 55–64. Baton Rouge: Louisiana Folklife Program and Center for Gulf South History and Culture.

Sakakeeny, Matthew. 2002. "Indian Rulers: Mardi Gras Indians and New Orleans Funk." *Jazz Archivist* 16:9–24.

Saloy, Mona Lisa. 2012. "Enduring Creole Terms." *Southern Journal of Linguistics* 36 (1): 169–77.

Schneider, Frank. 1996. *Gawd, I Love New Orleans*. New Orleans: FLAPS.

Schoen, Taylor. 2019. *Glossary of Mardi Gras Terms*. https://www.whereyat.com/glossary-of-mardi-gras-terms.

Schoux Casey, Christina. 2012. "Place in Sociolinguistics: New Orleans." *Southern Journal of Linguistics* 36 (1): i–viii.

Schoux Casey, Christina. 2013. "Postvocalic /r/ in New Orleans English: Language, Place, and Commodification." PhD diss., University of Pittsburgh.

Schoux Casey, Christina. 2016. "Ya Heard Me? Rhoticity in Post-Katrina New Orleans English." *American Speech* 91 (2): 166–99.

Schoux Casey, Christina. 2018. "'You Must Be Some Kind of [kɹɛɪəːzɪ], Yeah': Towards a New Orleans English Phonology." In *The Meaning of Language*, edited by Hans Götzsche, 112–26. London: Cambridge Scholars.

Seicshnaydre, Stacy, Robert A. Collins, Cashauna Hill, and Maxwell Ciardullo. 2018. *Rigging the Real Estate Market: Segregation, Inequality, and Disaster Risk*. April 5. https://www.datacenterresearch.org/reports_analysis/ rigging-the-real-estate-market-segregation-inequality-and-disaster-risk/.

Shaik, Fatima. 2015. "Remembering Hurricane Katrina: We've Come This Far by Faith." *The Root*, August 26. https://www.theroot.com/remembering-hurricane-katrina-we-ve-come-this-far-by-f-1790860929.

Smith, Darrlyn A. 1997. *The New Orleans Seventh Ward Nostalgia Dictionary, 1938–1965*. 2nd ed. Seattle: JADA.

Smith, Michael. 1994. "Behind the Lines: The Black Mardi Gras Indians and the New Orleans Second Line." *Black Music Research Journal* 14 (1): 43–73.

Smith, Michael. 2003. "Buffalo Bill and the Mardi Gras Indians." In *Mardi Gras, Gumbo, and Zydeco: Readings in Louisiana Culture*, edited by Marcia Gaudet and James C. McDonald, 16–25. Jackson: University Press of Mississippi.

Snedeker, Rebecca. 2006. *By Invitation Only*. Video recording. New Day Films.

Souther, Mark. 2006. *New Orleans on Parade: Tourism and the Transformation of the Crescent City*. Baton Rouge: Louisiana State University Press.

Spain, Daphne. 1979. "Race Relations and Residential Segregation in New Orleans: Two Centuries of Paradox." *Annals of the American Academy of Political and Social Science* 441 (1): 82–96.
Stanonis, Anthony. 2001. "'Always in Costume and Mask': Lyle Saxon and New Orleans Tourism." *Louisiana History* 42 (1), 31–57.
Stanonis, Anthony. 2006. *Creating the Big Easy: New Orleans and the Emergence of Modern Tourism, 1918–1945.* Athens: University of Georgia Press.
Hearn, Lafcadio. 2001. *Inventing New Orleans: Writings of Lafcadio Hearn.* Edited by Frederick Starr. Jackson: University Press of Mississippi.
Sublette, Ned. 2008. *The World That Made New Orleans: From Spanish Silver to Congo Square.* Chicago: Hill.
Taggart, Chuck. 2013. *A Lexicon of New Orleans Terminology and Speech.* https://gumbopages.com/yatspeak.html.
Thomas, Lynnell. 2009. "'Roots Run Deep Here': The Construction of Black New Orleans in Post-Katrina Tourism Narratives." *American Quarterly* 61 (3): 749–68.
Thomas, Lynnell. 2014. *Desire and Disaster in New Orleans: Tourism, Race, and Historical Memory.* Durham: Duke University Press.
Troutt, David, ed. 2006. *After the Storm: Black Intellectuals Explore the Meaning of Hurricane Katrina.* New York: New Press.
Troutt, David. 2015. "Disappearing Acts: Reflecting on New Orleans 10 Years after Katrina." *The Conversation*, August 28. https://theconversation.com/disappearing-acts-reflecting-on-new-orleans-10-years-after-katrina-46834.
US Census Bureau. 2018. "Quick Facts, New Orleans City, Louisiana." QuickFacts. https://www.census.gov/quickfacts/fact/table/neworleanscitylouisiana,US/PST045216.
Valdman, Albert. 1997. *French and Creole in Louisiana.* New York: Plenum.
Vaz, Kim M. 2013. *The "Baby Dolls": Breaking the Race and Gender Barriers of the New Orleans Mardi Gras Tradition.* Baton Rouge: Louisiana State University Press.
Virgets, Ronnie. 1997. *Say, Cap! The New Orleans Views of Ronnie Virgets.* Metairie, LA: Hardy.
Walton, Shana, moderator. 1996. "Language and Dialect in Louisiana, Native American Traditions." Panel at the New Orleans Jazz and Heritage Fest. Item 011.1996.002. New Orleans Jazz and Heritage Archive.
Walton, Shana, moderator. 1999. "Women of Zydeco, Cajun English." Panel at the New Orleans Jazz and Heritage Fest. Item 011.1999.015. New Orleans Jazz and Heritage Archive.
Walton, Shana, moderator. 2000. "Native American Folklore and Stories." Panel at the New Orleans Jazz and Heritage Fest. Item 011.2000.015. New Orleans Jazz and Heritage Archive.
Walton, Shana, moderator. 2001. "New Orleans and Other Louisiana Accents." Panel at the New Orleans Jazz and Heritage Fest. Item 011.2001.004. New Orleans Jazz and Heritage Archive.
White-Sustaíta, Jessica. 2012. "Sociohistorical Perspectives on Black and White Speech Relations in New Orleans." *Southern Journal of Linguistics* 36 (1): 45–60.
Wolfram, Walt, and Nathalie Schilling-Estes. 2006. *American English: Dialects and Variation.* 2nd ed. Malden, MA: Blackwell.
Woodland, James. 1987. "'In that City Foreign and Paradoxical': The Idea of New Orleans in the Southern Literary Imagination." PhD diss., University of North Carolina at Chapel Hill.

CHAPTER 13

THE LINGUISTIC SURVEY OF NORTH LOUISIANA: HISTORY AND PROGRESS

LISA ABNEY

Like much of the South, north Louisiana has generally been characterized as homogenous in terms of both culture and language. Residents who live below I-10 sometimes think of their north Louisiana counterparts as monocultural, rural, and unsophisticated—a view ably expressed by Ignatius J. Reilly, protagonist of John Kennedy Toole's novel, *A Confederacy of Dunces* (1980:19): "That was the only time that I had ever been out of New Orleans in my life. ... Speeding along in that bus was like hurtling into the abyss. By the time we had left the swamps and reached those rolling hills near Baton Rouge, I was getting afraid that some rural rednecks might toss bombs at the bus. They love to attack vehicles, which are a symbol of progress, I guess." Such depictions and those conveyed in popular media by *Duck Dynasty* and other television series provide images of north Louisiana that may contain realistic elements but reduce north Louisiana culture to a series of stereotypes that ignore the region's rich history and layers of culture. More accurate images and evidence of north Louisiana dialect and culture in printed material date to the late 1800s: Kate Chopin's first novel, *At Fault* (1890), set in Natchitoches Parish, interestingly and accurately portrays residents and the microdialects that existed and can still be found in the Parish (for a full discussion see Picone 2003, 2014). Other print sources, too, indicate bits and pieces about the dialects of north Louisiana—A. J. Leibling's *The Earl of Louisiana* (1961) includes some lexical items unique to the region, and the earlier work of Alcée Fortier (1894, 1904) similarly addresses historical and cultural/linguistic features of north Louisiana.

In the later years of the twentieth century and early twenty-first century, linguists Miguel Fuster (1997), Thomas A. Klingler (2014), Thomas A. Klingler and Nathalie Dajko (2006), Comfort Pratt (2008), and Michael D. Picone (2014) as well as anthropologists/folklorists Susan Roach (1984), Don Hatley (1991),

Maida Owens (1997), Hiram F. Gregory (2006), and Dayna Lee (2006) have worked with Anglos, African Americans, Native Americans, the Cane River French Creole Community, and the Spanish-speaking communities at Los Adaes and Spanish Lake. Beyond these few print depictions, however—most of which did not focus on English—there have been no attempts to systematically examine the speech varieties of north Louisiana.

The best previous research about the English of north Louisiana comes from the 1970s, when fieldworkers with the *Linguistic Atlas of the Gulf States* (*LAGS*) (Pederson 1986) interviewed Louisiana residents. *LAGS* researchers examined phonetic and lexical items employing nine sets of social criteria (Pederson 1986:xix). The survey grew out of linguistic atlas studies conducted by European linguists and American researchers such as Hans Kurath and Fredrick G. Cassidy in the early twentieth century. In the *LAGS* data, linguistic maps indicate phonological and lexical patterns in the region. Project director Lee Pederson's early plan for the work included interviewing two to three residents from each of the 158 units that correlated to some 590 counties and parishes from Texas to Florida:

> At least one elderly white folk informant will be interviewed from the long work sheets . . . as well as one middle-aged white informant with a high school education, to be interviewed from either the long or short work sheets. In each community where the black population in 1930 exceeded 20 percent of the local census, an elderly black folk informant will be interviewed from the long work sheets. Black informants with high school and college education, like white informants with college education, will be selected according to the judgment of the fieldworker, determined by the history and social composition of the community and the availability of such speakers for day-long interviews. (Pederson 1969:282)

LAGS fieldworkers classified Louisiana parishes employing geographic descriptors such as "Western Piney Woods" for those parishes bordering Texas from south of Shreveport to the Gulf; "Red River Basin" for parishes in central Louisiana between the Texas and Mississippi borders; and "Upper Mississippi River Basin" for the northeastern portion of the State. Southern parishes fall under the classification of "Atchafalaya River Basin" or "Lower Mississippi River Basin." *LAGS* data and methodologies present a reliable and useful corpus of information on southern speech; however, the project was never intended to delve deeply into culture, history, and language to examine how these elements have influenced dialect. Moreover, the number of people interviewed compared to the total corpus numbers and the general population do not provide a representative sample. In an effort to fill this substantial need for a systemic and longitudinal study, I have since 1997 incorporated methodologies from folklore and linguistics and have established some clear isoglosses. Not uncharacteristically, these dialect boundaries are linked to settlement patterns and historical events dating as early as 1714.

HISTORY AND SETTLEMENT PATTERNS

The story of north Louisiana settlement begins with the French, who in the early 1700s began a campaign of territorial expansion under King Louis XIV. These efforts were designed to undermine Dutch, English, and Spanish interests in the Gulf Coast Region. French settlers traveled throughout Mississippi and Louisiana, trading, exploring, and establishing outposts. In 1714, Louis Juchereau de St. Denis founded Natchitoches, the first sustained settlement of Europeans in Louisiana. From that date onward, French explorers and soldiers worked to colonize the region with the help of Catholic clergy (Pasquier 2015:1). The French brought with them an array of settlers ranging from aristocrats to indentured servants. By 1719, French colonists who had received land from the king were importing enslaved Africans to work that land. Ongoing strained relations with various Native American tribes proved problematic for the French, however, and between financial struggles, unrest in the colony, and external forces that were fragmenting governmental resources, the French abandoned the colony. In 1763, King Louis XV ceded Louisiana to the Spanish in the Treaty of Paris, which ended the Seven Years' War and diminished French control in the New World (Wall 1990:53). To say that Louisiana residents found the change difficult to embrace would be an understatement, and because the Spanish did not colonize and govern the colony actively until 1765, French residents had plenty of time to foment resentment at becoming Spanish subjects.

Antonio de Ulloa was appointed governor of the territory and in 1766 arrived with only a few men in Balize, a small settlement situated well downriver from New Orleans. Their arrival merely inflamed the locals, and Ulloa and his officials ultimately relocated to New Orleans. Because of Spain's unwillingness and inability to fiscally support the colony, Ulloa was forced to employ the services of the remaining French officials and soldiers but was ultimately overthrown and sent back to Spain. In response, the Spanish sent General Alejandro O'Reilly to New Orleans accompanied by a large military presence. O'Reilly worked to improve relations with the Native American tribes and established strong military outposts to protect the colony's fourteen thousand inhabitants from the raids of Plains' tribes and other marauders. By 1780, an array of Spanish governors—the most well-known of whom are Bernardo de

Galvez and Esteban Miro—had left their mark on Louisiana history. Under Miro's governance, the Spanish began to invite immigration. By 1784, Louisiana had grown to twenty-five thousand residents, and Miro wanted more. He offered land grants to Anglo-American settlers who swore allegiance to Spain, became Catholics, and attested that they would obey the laws of the colony (Wall 1990:70). Such efforts increased the colony's population by a factor of five by the end of the Spanish period (70). The New Louisianans were not predominantly Spanish-speaking, however, and hailed from the Canary Islands, Africa, Germany, England, Haiti, and Canada. Some of these new populations ultimately moved north from their initial points of entry into the colony.

In 1803, after Louisiana had briefly returned to French control, Napoleon Bonaparte and US president Thomas Jefferson negotiated the Louisiana Purchase, which transferred the colony to the United States and brought tremendous change in the form of rowdy and uncultured (in the eyes of the existing French population) American immigrants, often called *Kaintucks* by their French counterparts (Wall 1990:91). Many Anglo-Americans and African Americans settled in north Louisiana, where they joined the few remaining colonial French and Spanish settlers. A significant population in north Louisiana thus claims African, British, and French/Spanish heritage (Owens 1996:xxxvii). In general, north Louisiana settlers came as migrants from across the Upland South (Tennessee, the Carolinas, Georgia, Alabama, and Mississippi) and in lesser numbers from other southern states and New England. Settlers who took the lowland route often elected to establish cotton plantations along the Mississippi, Red, and Ouachita Rivers (Cash 1941; Roach-Lankford 1984), enterprises that depended heavily on enslaved people and their descendants to function.

From 1803 to 1821, the longitudinal strip of land running from south of Shreveport to the Gulf of Mexico functioned as the border between Spanish Texas and American Louisiana. This ungoverned territory became infamous as a no-man's-land, belonging neither to the Spanish nor the Americans and providing a haven for outlaws and individualists who chafed under civic constraints. The Neutral Strip, as it is known now, maintains a distinct cultural identity as a consequence of its unconventional roots (Lejeune 2015).

During the twentieth and twenty-first centuries, immigrants from Mexico, Czechoslovakia, Asia, and the Middle East have made their way to north Louisiana, continuing to enhance and expand the cultural landscape. Hispanic settlements have formed around agricultural enterprises near Natchitoches, Many, and Alexandria; however, some of these new residents have come to work in the construction industry, which has expanded quickly in the Shreveport–Bossier City region since the turn of the twenty-first century. Alexandria is home to a

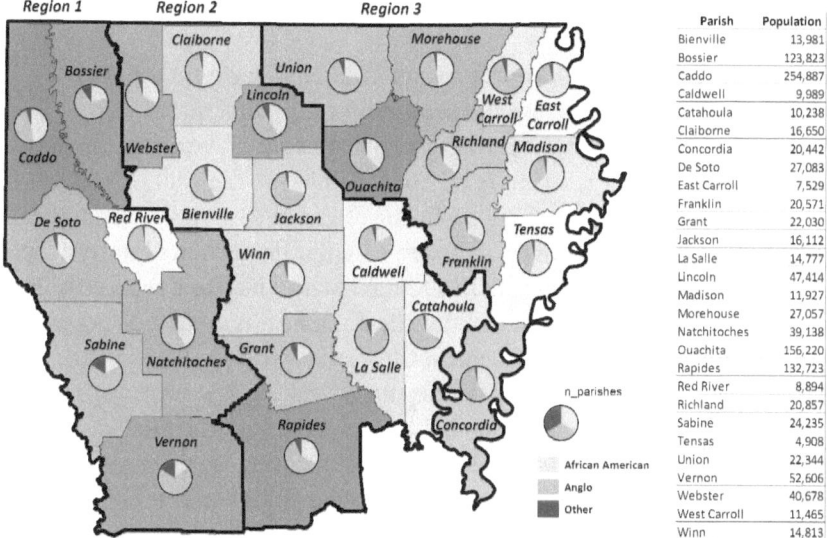

Figure 13.1. North Louisiana Linguistic Survey regions and population breakdown.
© Lisa Abney. Map by Curtis Desselles.

significant Middle Eastern community whose members are employed in the health care industry. Asian businesses abound in parts of Shreveport, Bossier City, and Alexandria.

During these in-migration periods, the Cane River Creole community, which has been vital since the 1700s, has continued its rich traditional culture, though the French language has diminished as older speakers have passed away. Similarly, the Spanish Lake and Adesaño Spanish-speaking communities have lost their native Spanish; however, cultural practices remain in isolated communities west of Natchitoches. Native American tribes remain active in the region as well, though in limited numbers.

Fully understanding the linguistic aspects of north Louisiana and appreciating the smaller regional demarcations requires some knowledge of the region's settlement patterns and geographic boundaries. Residents' cultural identities routinely affect their dialects as much as do education and social class. For instance, an interviewee in Leesville identified herself as a member of an old pioneer family, whereas respondents from Natchitoches often refer to their relatives as members of old colonial/Creole families: both of these towns are located in Region 1 (figure 13.1) of the North Louisiana Linguistic Survey. Cane River Creoles and Czechs in the Libuse and Kolin communities maintain distinctive identities that allow them to preserve their cultural practices, frequently affecting their dialects and lexical choices.

LINGUISTIC BOUNDARIES

For the purposes of this research, north Louisiana begins at a line that can be drawn horizontally across the southernmost boundaries of Vernon and Rapides Parishes, making a jog over the northern edge of Avoyelles Parish (see figure 13.1). Avoyelles is far more culturally similar to the southern parishes, with a high number of inhabitants who are of French descent and a dominant culture that remains French even though a significant portion of the residents claim Anglo-Scots-Irish descent. In addition, Marksville has a substantial Native American population (Tunica-Biloxi), another feature that distinguishes this parish from others to the north. Consequently, Avoyelles is considered part of south Louisiana as well as of Acadiana.

If I asked an Alexandria resident if he or she would consider Rapides Parish to be located in north Louisiana, the person would likely say that the city lies in central Louisiana—or CenLA, as it is most often called. Despite this insider distinction, Rapides Parish constitutes a good starting point for the survey, marking the spot where Cajun culture becomes less prominent and Anglo-Scots-Irish and African American cultural influences increase. It can be considered the gateway to the northern region (Owens 1997).

North Louisiana remains largely rural despite early twenty-first-century population surges in Bossier City and Shreveport. Monroe and Alexandria have seen only relatively modest growth since 2010. The region remains untouched by the widespread subdivision growth that has occurred in Houma, Shreveport, Bossier City, Baton Rouge, and other parts of the state (Samuels 2014; Duke 2017). The urban areas thus have remained relatively contained, while rural towns and communities have maintained their individual identities with the exception of the growth toward Minden from Bossier City.

The demographics of the twenty-eight parishes of the study have remained fairly stable since 2010. North Louisiana residents are primarily Anglo (non-Hispanic) or African American: in many cases, parish populations are almost evenly split between whites and African Americans. Some parishes function as outliers, however: Madison and East Carroll have a significantly higher numbers of African Americans than whites, while Grant, Caldwell, West Carroll, and Bossier Parishes display the reverse. Sabine Parish has the highest number of Native Americans in the region at 8.7 percent (US Census 2010, 2013).

Sabine and Natchitoches Parishes have large populations of Spanish- and French-descended residents, respectively. The Cane River Creole Community in Natchitoches Parish continues to practice its many important cultural traditions but has largely lost the French language. Spanish culture, particularly foodways, remains evident in Sabine Parish, though fewer and fewer people speak the vestigial colonial Spanish as older members of the community pass away.

THE STUDY

I initiated the Linguistic Survey of North Louisiana in 1997 after realizing that no sustained and systematized research efforts had been undertaken in the region. At that time, no work had been published about north Louisiana dialects outside of a few speakers who appear in *LAGS* data. It was clear to me, a new resident, that some north Louisiana speakers sounded different from those East Texans whose dialects I knew so well, yet I could not understand how a distance of only seventy miles could have such an impact on language. Being new to Louisiana, I hardly understood the complexities of cultures that make north Louisiana so interesting and exciting to research. However, as I began to interview residents, read Louisiana history, and learn about Louisiana's numerous ethnic, social, and economic cultural components, I came to understand just how powerfully these influences affect the development of language, especially in north Louisiana. As I listened, researched, and studied, I realized that the whole of north Louisiana had been neglected in past and contemporary linguistic studies, and I began documenting the area's dialects using methodologies similar to those in the *LAGS*.

DESIGN AND CONSTRUCTION OF SURVEY INSTRUMENT AND QUESTIONNAIRE

The data for the North Louisiana Linguistic Survey come from interviews with people who either are lifelong residents of the area or have lived the bulk of their lives in the region. The protocol employs a reading passage and questionnaire designed to elicit lexical items, phonological information in the form of minimal pairs, and other linguistic elements. The phonological data are then compared to those of an accompanying ethnographic interview that includes standard demographic survey information. Designed to elicit data about a number of subjects relating to life in Louisiana, the questionnaire asks about growing up in Louisiana, farming/gardening, superstitions, cultural practices, childhood toys and games, school/educational background, occupations, religion, community participation, and foodways. While fieldworkers and I occasionally redirect questions to clarify points or to obtain more information about certain subjects, the speakers generally direct the interview. Participants are interviewed in their homes or at public places such as community centers, churches, or senior centers. We have also conducted interviews at special events such as the Natchitoches–Northwestern State University Folk Festival and the 2003 and 2004 Ark-La-Tex Logging Extravaganza. Interviewees come from a number of cultures, educational levels, ethnicities, ages, and social classes.

Interviews initially were collected using analog tape but have been transferred to digital format as technology has advanced. Current interviews are recorded using digital recorders or iPhones/iPads or laptop computers. Once samples are collected, they are duplicated and archived at the Louisiana Folklife Center at Northwestern State University. Information regarding collection date, interviewers, interviewees, and other data are entered into a database.

Another data source for this study comes from the Louisiana Folklife Center's massive audio collection—more than five thousand hours of audio recordings, the bulk of them narrative data collected during the latter half of the twentieth and early twenty-first centuries. The collections contain an assortment of material relating to life in Louisiana, including folk culture and practices, and frequently feature extended sections of unguarded speech that provide a wealth of data for linguists.

NARRATORS AND SAMPLE SIZE

The project currently contains narratives from more than a hundred speakers. Although I have conducted and continue to conduct much of the fieldwork, I often receive assistance from graduate and undergraduate students both via course projects and through other fieldwork activities.

Because interviews can last as long as ten hours, transcription of the taped pieces can take up to four weeks per interview. Some interviews have not yet been transcribed, and work is ongoing. All transcriptions are double-checked to ensure accuracy. As we listen to the interviews, fieldworkers and I frequently hear features that warrant additional analysis. Once the data are transcribed and recordings are analyzed, data are then numerically coded to ascertain occurrence of linguistic features. This information can then be cross-referenced to region or subdialect and plotted on dialect maps.

GENERAL RESULTS

Analysis of the recordings began with impressionistic rather than instrumental transcription analysis of the reading passages, noting features of Southern English (Labov, Ash, and Boberg 2006). Although the analysis is still in its early stages, I have divided north Louisiana into three general regions (see figure 13.1). The western boundary of Region 1 is the Neutral Strip from just south of Leesville to Shreveport; the eastern boundary falls between Rapides and Natchitoches Parishes. Region 1 includes Caddo, Bossier, Red River, DeSoto, Sabine, Natchitoches, and Vernon Parishes. Region 2 begins in the west with

Bossier Parish, follows along the Red River, and is bounded by Highway 165 in the East, with a slight meander in the middle. Region 2 includes Webster, Claiborne, Lincoln, Union, Jackson, Bienville, Winn, Grant, Rapides, LaSalle, Caldwell, and Catahoula Parishes. Bordered by parts of Highway 165 on the west and by the Mississippi River on the east, Region 3 includes Concordia, Tensas, Franklin, Madison, Richland, Ouachita, Morehouse, West Carroll, and East Carroll Parishes.

In general, north Louisiana residents sound like many other American southerners. However, those from north Louisiana do not always sound like other Louisianans as a consequence of settlement patterns, education levels, social class, ethnicity, and other cultural influences.

Pin-Pen Merger

Traditional southern speakers often make no distinction between these sounds when they come before a nasal; the words are homophones. When someone asks for a *pen* or a *pin*, if context cannot make evident which item is requested, speakers will ask for clarification with "the kind you write with or the kind you wear?" Speakers in this data set, regardless of age illustrate the merger, not unlike their general southern counterparts.

Rhoticity

A commonly cited feature of Southern English is the elimination of postvocalic *r*. Some speech areas in the US South are considered *r*-less, while others are considered *r*-full, with generation, class, and race often characterizing the use of /r/ (Feagin 2014). Both older and younger speakers in Region 1 tend to use postvocalic /r/ regularly. Speakers in Regions 2 and 3, particularly older narrators, appear to be more inclined to be *r*-less. This can be seen in pronunciations such as *girl* [gʌl] and *church* [čɔjč]. Moreover, in Region 2, intrusive and linking /r/ are common as in *window* [wɪndɚ] and *Louisiana* [Luwisiˈjænɚ].

Cot-Caught Merger

A merger of the low back vowel appears to be under way in northern Louisiana. Pairs such as *caught/cot* and *hawk/hock* are homophonous for younger speakers; however, many older speakers maintain distinct phonemes.

Glide Retention

Some speakers, particularly in Region 2, retain the glide /j/ in words such as *dew* (*dyew* [dju]) and *news* (*nyews* [njuz]). This feature has generally been attributed to older speakers in the past (see Pederson 1989; Bailey 1988), and indeed, sample participants who employ it are generally over age thirty-five.

Southern Vowel Shift

Speakers in the South have been undergoing a vowel shift, particularly for the front tense vowels (Labov, Ash, and Boberg 2006). In all three regions, the southern vowel shift is frequently in evidence, as high front vowels are shifting down. For instance, /ɪ/ lowers to /æ/ before /ŋ/, so that *thing* and *sing* are rendered *thang* and *sang*. In addition, in words such as *feel* and *heel*, speakers lower and diphthongize the vowel. The low front vowel /æ/ is shifted back and sometimes diphthongized to /ɑɪ/ by speakers in Region 1 and Region 3, so that *fast* sounds more like *feist*. Simultaneously, some speakers from Regions 2 and 3 illustrate a raised /ɑ/ which sounds more like /ɑɪ/: *body* takes on a very different sound, as [ˈbɑdi] becomes [ˈbɑɪdi]. The vowel /æ/ is interesting because it shows varied movement based on environment and speaker. In Regions 2 and 3, [æ] in *wagon* raises to [ˈwɛgən] or diphthongizes to [ˈwɑɪgən], whereas in Region 1, [æ] remains [æ] or is presented as [ˈwɛgən]. Finally, in Regions 2 and 3, [æ] lengthens and raises to [e] in the word *gas*.

Further, speakers sometimes break short front vowels to elongate or glide to /j/ and go back down to /ə/, adding a syllable to a word. Hence, *gnat*, *Mary*, and *milk* are heard as [næjət], [ˈmæjəri] or [meːjəri], and [ˈmɪjəlk]. This shift occurs in many speakers, but the tendency seems most common in Region 2. Finally, some back vowels are fronted. In Region 1, I found tokens of /ʌ/ shifting to /ɪ/. So, while *cover* is generally pronounced [kʌvər], younger speakers in Region 1 sometimes rendered it closer to *kivver* [ˈkɪvər]. This appears to be less often used in Regions 2 and 3. A final example of the southern vowel shift comes with vowel lowering.

Monophthongal /ɑɪ/

The use of monophthongal /ɑɪ/—in which the diphthong /ɑɪ/ is pronounced [ɑː], thereby making *rice* and *side* sound like *rass* and *sad*—is prevalent throughout the South and is strongly in evidence in north Louisiana, which appears to belong to a core area of monophthongization, as it occurs even before voiceless consonants. While all tokens have not yet been counted, the data seem to point to rural speakers and younger speakers using the feature more often than not.

SPEECH SAMPLES

I now turn a discussion of the speech of representatives of north Louisiana to illustrate the diversity of speech varieties. Here I examine fifteen speakers of Anglo and Spanish ancestry from Regions 1 and 2 to provide an overview of the range of features present. Region 3 is not included here because the data are less robust and much of the analysis remains incomplete. In addition, I have limited the ethnicities and ages represented to offer contrasts within an ethnic group. I highlight a variety of features, including some not previously discussed, to provide examples of how social factors affect dialect. In addition, I provide longer sections of discourse from five speakers to offer a look at lexicon, sentence structure, and ideology and identity indexed by discourse topics and style. Each narrator in the sample has a unique way of sharing stories, and each individual's educational level, ethnic background, cultural background, and life experiences shape his or her narratives and speech patterns. Speakers within regions often display similarities to one another, as would be expected; however, some respondents also show idiosyncratic usages.

Region 1

Delma Perot

Perot, was seventy-one at the time of the interview and is from Black Lake, just north of Natchitoches. He was interviewed by his nephew's wife, who comes from deep East Texas. Perot has a third-grade education and worked as a farmer and fisherman on Black Lake. He is of French Creole heritage. His speech attests many of the common features discussed previously. He shows postvocalic *r*-lessness in *girls* [gʌlz], Saturday [ˈsɛtədi] (the first vowel following the pattern set by *dad*), *wart* [wɑt], and *wire* [waɪ]. Perot's vowels tend to be rounded, raised, and fronted in the cases of *r*-less words. He attests front vowel lowering, so that *sing* is pronounced *sang*. His /aɪ/ diphthong is sometimes monophthongized, producing *rat* [rat] in place of *right* [raɪt]. This is not systematic, however, as in *wire*; *inside* is also pronounced with the diphthong. The southern vowel shift is further in evidence in his pronunciation of *inside* so that the first syllable is broken into two, producing [ijənsajd]. Diphthongal /eɪ/ is lowered and laxed to /ɛ/: Labor *Day* is *Lebber Deh* [ˈlɛbrɚdɛ], *radio* is *reddio* [rɛdio], *taking* is *tekkin* [ˈtɛkin], and *railroad* is *rerrod* [ˈrɛrod]. These last examples show assimilation of /l/ to /r/ as well. He also employs the *curl-coil* reversal stereotypical of New York/New Jersey and found in New Orleans–area working-class dialects (Carmichael 2014; Carmichael and Dajko 2016): *worked* sounds similar to *woiked* [wɔɪkt], *turn* is *toin* [tɔɪn], and *furnished* is *foinished* [ˈfɔɪnɪšt]. The /æ/ in *dad* is pronounced [ɛ], so *dad* sounds like *dead* and *wagon* is *weggon* [wɛgən]. Word-final [e] becomes [i], as in *away* which is pronounced *a-whee* [ʌwi]. He rarely pronounces /r/ in a consonant cluster as [w], as in *tree* [twi]. Further, his interview contains word-final consonant deletion in *left*, which becomes *lef'* [lɛf]. He shows a neutralization of [ɪ] and [i] in many contexts: *cornmeal* sounds like *cornmill* [ˈkɔrnmɪl], *Winnie* sounds like *wienie* [wini], and *sticks* is pronounced *steeks* [stiks]. He sometimes replaces interdental fricatives with stops, so that *with* is pronounced [wɪð]. Perot's subject-verb and word form use are generally nonstandard, but this is a marker for many CenLa speakers, particularly males, who view the use of Standard English as "prissy" or inappropriate in informal situations such as storytelling. He is well known in his community and highly regarded as a storyteller.

Betty Jones

Jones, of British descent, was born and reared in Natchitoches, becoming one of the city's most ardent promoters. Even at age seventy-nine, when she was interviewed, she owned a tour service. She spearheaded the promotion of cultural and preservation efforts. Her dialect more closely resembles that of central Louisiana (Region 2) speakers than those in the Neutral Strip. She is *r*-less in most words. Like other central Louisiana speakers, she diphthongizes /æ/: *Natchitoches* is [ˈnaɪgədɪš], and *baskets* is [ˈbaɪskɪts]. Her vowels tend to be wider and farther back than those of some of the other speakers from the region, as in *all* [ɔl]. Like other CenLa speakers, she sometimes deletes the copula (the linking *be* verb) in sentences such as, *They bringing the word.*

Robert Remedies

Remedies was born and reared near Zwolle. He is a Spanish-English bilingual narrator of colonial Spanish heritage. At the time of his interview with Spanish researcher Miguel Fuster, Remedies was seventy-one years of age. His interview was conducted in both English and Spanish and shows the insularity and self-reliance of people within his community. He repeatedly self-identifies in the plural, as in "We are Spanolés." He calls the Anglo-descended members of his community "white faces." He completed the eighth grade and has worked in farming and in the timber industry. Linguistically, in some instances, he has features in common with the north-central speakers, yet his narrative contains other features that mark him as a northwestern resident. Like the north-central speakers, his speech is *r*-less, and he pronounces the [æ] as *last* [laɪst]. He replaces /r/ in a cluster with [w], so that *Shreveport* sounds like [ˈswipɔrt]. Region 1 markers in his speech include the rendering of *kids* [kɪdz] closer to *keeds* [kidz] and the diphthongization of *did* [ˈdijəd] and *chip* [ˈčijəp]. His speech shows features of African American English with the vocalization or neutralization of medial /l/ in *help* [hɛp]. He also pronounces *ask* with a final /t/: [æst].

Gil Franklin
Franklin was reared in the Leesville/Anacoco area in the Neutral Strip, and he is of Anglo-Scots-Irish and German descent. His family came to Anacoco after coming through Fort Mireau (now Monroe, Louisiana) in the 1830s from the Carolinas. He was sixty years old at the time of his interview. His mother was a teacher, and his father was a prosperous businessman. Unlike the others in his region, Franklin's dialect is *r*-full. He tends to use standard forms of English and tends not to use *-ng* fronting in words such as *working* or *riding*. His speech includes a few examples of variant pronunciations which illustrate important features listed earlier, including the classic southern neutralization and breaking of /i/ and /ɪ/, rendering *hills* as *hee-yuls* [ˈhijəlz]. He frequently monophthongizes /aɪ/—for example, in *wide* [waːd], *child* [čaːld], *find* [faːnd], *mile* [maːl], and *line* [laːn]. Another southern feature is his monophthongization of the /ɔɪ/ in *soil* to [sɔl]. Also not unusual is his raising and lengthening of the first vowel in *after*, which becomes *ayf-ter* [ˈeːftrɚ], and the raising of the [ɑ] in *on* to [on].

Don Marler
Marler, of British heritage, was reared in the Neutral Strip near the small rural towns of Hineston and Gardner. Marler is a retired social worker who lives in Texas near the Louisiana border. He does the majority of his shopping and socializing in Leesville or Many. Like Franklin, Marler raises and lengthens the /æ/ *after* to [ˈeːftrɚ] and is *r*-full. Unlike Franklin, however, Marler also retains the diphthong /aɪ/, producing *fire* [faɪr] and *pine* [paɪn]. Idiosyncratically in the sample, he renders *one* as *wan* [wɑn] rather than [wʌn]. As in much of the South, *picture* is given as [ˈpɪčrɚ], and *orange* is pronounced *are-inge* [ɑrnǰ].

Howard Blackburn
Blackburn was reared in the Neutral Strip and was ninety-one years of age at the time of his interview. Of British heritage, he worked for the railroad for many years and was actively involved transporting timber. He collects train and timber memorabilia. Blackburn, like many of the respondents in the sample, is *r*-less in some instances but not throughout his interview. This is true of other features as well: the first vowel in *passenger* is diphthongized, producing [ˈpaɪsɪnǰɚ], but he uses a standard pronunciation of *last* [læst]. The [e] of *railroad* is lowered and laxed, but he retains a distinct /l/ before /r/, producing

['rɛlrod]. Unlike others in his region, he does not raise /a/ to /o/, pronouncing *logs* [lɑgz]. He does, however pronounce *orange* as [arnj̃]. He is the only person in the samples reproduced here to pronounce *there* as [ðar].

Mary Cleveland

Cleveland is of Anglo-Scots-Irish descent and was reared in Leesville. Seventy-two at the time of the interview, she had served for many years as the curator of the Museum of West Louisiana. She graduated from college and has been actively involved in community events for many years. Cleveland's speech is often fairly standard: she presents lower levels of monophthongization of /aɪ/ than do many others in the sample. However, she does lower the /e/ and assimilates the /l/ in *railroad* [rɛrod]. *Orange* is rendered [arnj]. The rest of Cleveland's features illustrate traditional Upland South pronunciation.

G. J. "Pie" Martinez

Martinez is a logger of Spanish colonial descent whose family has lived in the Zwolle area for hundreds of years; he is a third-generation logger who has lobbied and supported safety improvements in the timber industry. Having lost an eye in an accident while loading a logging truck, he has personal reasons for his support of safety initiatives. His dialect shows less Spanish influence than that of Remedies, though they hail from the same community. Martinez, like the other Neutral Strip speakers, pronounces most words in a standard manner. He is *r*-full more often than not, for example, and he does not raise /æ/ to /ɛ/ and pronounces *daddy* as [dædi]. Martinez does, however, have a few variant pronunciations. He renders *kid* [kiːd]. He attests monophthongal /aɪ/ in *wire* [wɑːr]. He deletes the second syllable in *Saturday*, producing ['særde]; though not seen elsewhere in this sample, this is often heard in the Neutral Strip and East Texas. Following the same pattern seen in the word *orange* in other interviews, *forest* is rendered ['fɑrɪst].

Ricky Robertson

Born in Peason Ridge, Robertson has embraced history as his hobby, and he has long documented the history and culture of Louisiana's military installations. His dialect has some features common to central Louisiana in terms of subject-verb concord and verb forms, yet his phonemes are rendered more closely to those of Neutral Strip speakers. Robertson, of Anglo-Scots-Irish descent, demonstrates monophthongal /aɪ/ with *time* [tɑːm] and *tried* [trɑːd]. He attests lowering of /ɪ/ in *things* [θæŋz], making it close to *thangs*. He also demonstrates the breaking of /æ/ in *last* ['læjəst]. Unlike most Neutral Strip speakers, Robertson raises the *a* in *national* to render something closer to *nayshnul* ['neʃnəl]. *Shreveport* is rendered as ['sriport] or ['šriport].

Coiley Gewin

Gewin, seventy years old at the time of his interview, is of British heritage. He was reared on the northeastern edge of the Neutral Strip in Pleasant Hill. After graduating from high school, he entered the military; he subsequently worked in industrial plants. His speech is fairly standard. At times, he is *r*-less, but for the most part, he uses postvocalic *r*. He pronounces *night* as [naɪt] rather than [nɑːt]. The /æ/ in his interview remains [æ] as in *wagon* [wægən] rather than [ˈwɑɪgən], and the vowels in *ration* [ˈræšən] and *camps* [kæmps] are not raised as they are in other speakers' dialects. Still, with the word *gas*, Gewin has a lengthened version of the /æ/, producing [gæːs].

Scott DeBose

DeBose is twenty-eight-year-old male who was born and reared in Many and is of British heritage. His speech is standard. It is *r*-full, and he exhibits *ng*-fronting less often than do central Louisiana speakers. A rare nonstandard pronunciation includes the *cord/card* merger in the words *or* and *army*, which sound as though they are pronounced with the same vowel. In the word *Texas*, he glottalizes the /k/, making it more prominent, and stresses the first syllable more than other speakers do, producing [ˈtɛkʼsɪs]. This may be an idiosyncrasy of this particular speaker or to this particular reading; generally, his speech contains more instances of Standard American English pronunciation than does that of CenLa speakers who are closer to his age.

Region 2

Gene Chelette and John F. Lovell

These respondents grew up in Winnfield and have worked together scaling timber since 1975. They are best friends who have volumes of stories to share regarding logging and growing up in rural north-central Louisiana. Chelette is of French and British heritage, while Lovell is of British descent. Chelette and Lovell exhibit similar speech, and both are well-known and gifted storytellers. Chelette's speech is particularly notable for the deletion of consonants in medial and initial positions. For example, *handle* lacks medial /d/, becoming [ˈhænəl], and *that is* loses its initial consonant and becomes [æts]. Chelette also attests monophthongal /aɪ/, as in *hired* [hɑːrd] or *tired* [tɑːrd], and he uses *thang*: *bring* is pronounced *brang* [bræŋ]. He introduces an *r* word-finally on unstressed final syllables; *window* and *Louisiana* are pronounced *winder* [wɪndɚ] and *Louisianer* [luwisiˈjænɚ] (the final syllables having been destressed to a schwa prior to the insertion of the *r*). He retains the palatal glide in words like *knew*, which is pronounced *nyoo* [nju]. He does not raise /æ/ to /e/ but does lengthen it, producing [ˈaeːftɚ].

Bobby Horne

Horne was born and reared in the small town of Atlanta and is of British heritage. He began work in the woods at age four when he and his brother used a crosscut saw to harvest firewood for his mother. He was seventy-five years old at the time of the interview, and like the other men in the sample, he demonstrates nonstandard verb concord forms. His speech is *r*-less and exhibits high levels of /aɪ/ monophthongization in words such as *line* [lɑ:n]. He exhibits vowel breaking *limbs*, which sounds like *lee-ums* [ˈlijəmz], and he raises /æ/ to /e/ in his pronunciation of *calf*, which sounds like *cafe* [ke:f].

Narrator A

This speaker is of British Isles heritage, was reared in the town of Olla, located on Highway 165 North, and like other speakers, provides numerous examples of monophthongization of /aɪ/, including *like* [lɑ:k] and *right* [rɑt]. This speaker also uses *thang* for *thing*: *think* is pronounced *thank* [θæŋk]. Like other speakers, [i] and [ɪ] are neutralized so that *ditch* sounds like *deetch* [di:tč]. She fronts the vowel [ʊ] in *couldn't* to [ɪ], producing *kittent* [ˈkɪtn̩t]. She pronounces *there* as [thɑr]. Unlike other speakers, she backs /ʌ/ to /ɔ/, so that *big old bus* [big od bɔs] sounds a lot like *big old boss*, and *bunks* [bɔnks] sounds similar to *bonks*. She also raises the [o] in *most* to [u], producing [must].

NARRATIVE AND IDENTITY

In addition to providing phonological data, the interviews contain narratives that document cultural practices and traditions. The excerpts presented here highlight morphological and syntactic data as well as shed light on the depth of this project. Many narratives contain gems that would have been lost if we had stuck solely to the scripted question-and-answer format that some studies prescribe. Each passage has been titled to give context to the remarks, and a brief summary of narrative or discourse features follows each segment.

Employment for Women in Post–World War II Louisiana

> Let me tell you what I did to get a set of tires. Well, the government had a thing where you go out, and you take chickens, and you see if they are good layers or not. You know, and they furnished me a set of tires. Well, I read up on that thing, caught a few hens. I went and culled chickens all over the country. So what you had to do was to feel between their legs, and the bones would be far apart, they were good layers, and if it was narrow, they weren't.

I could do that, and I got a set of tires for it. That was after they closed this thing down at Esler Field. They were gettin' people lined up to have better chickens and that sort of thing.

—LOIS BATTLE, REGION 1 (BRITISH HERITAGE)

Battle's narrative focuses on life after World War II in central Louisiana and on the stories of post–World War II women in America, particularly the South. This passage displays the *you* pronoun shift as a generalizer of experience (Abney 1998). In additionally, the use of the lexical item *culled*, though not used commonly today, was popular in Battle's day. Battle commands the floor in her narrative by citing vivid and instructional examples and hooking the listener's attention with "Let me tell you what I did to get a set of tires."

Hard Times Stories in Early Twentieth-Century Louisiana

Well, I was two years old when Papa died. Carl was a month old. Papa died of pneumonia. They'd say in nine days, the crisis will pass. . . . They sent us to orphans' home. The oldest brother, he kindly caught a chip on his shoulder for his life. My half-brother and his wife sent us away. Edward [the speaker's fourteen-year-old brother who is later referenced as Dad] would have took care of us. I can just see him. I said, "Dad, didn't somebody come get me when I was in the orphans' home?" He told me "Yeah" and that they brought me back and traded me for a girl. I said "No, they didn't neither. . . . I said, "Now, Dad, who come to get us?" He said, "Well, we did"—him or Clay—but they didn't take the name of the man that they give me to. They told my brother when he came to get me, "We give him away, and we didn't take the name of the man we give him to." Back when I was in the orphans' home, if you wanted one, you just went by and got him. That was the way they done it. They couldn't remember who they give me to. It's not that a way now—the lawyers has got in on it. . . . I do have a scant memory of some of the things in the orphans' home. . . . There wadn't no books kept like they do now. But anyhow, I, uh, got a good remembrance of things from about my third birthday. I was four years old when World War I was over.

—LEE HOLLINGSWORTH, REGION 2 (BRITISH HERITAGE)

Of note in this narrative are the use of *kindly* for *kind of* and the use of nonstandard preterite verb (*done* for *did*; *they give* instead of *gave*). In addition, Hollingsworth employs a number of interjections to provide detail to the story—for instance, "It's not that way now" and "There wadn't no books." The use of the double negative, common in this excerpt, appears in many Region 2 samples.

Food and Farming Narrative

> Well, I grew up, all my life, eating wild food, because my daddy was a hunter and a fisherman. We lived on a farm. We were sharecroppers, and we didn't make very much money, so hunting and fishing were hunting and fishing for food and not for sport.... So many poor people live along the river. They rely upon the food that they can get their hands on without having to pay to make a living. The way we prepared food, we caught turtles, and you clean this turtle. You'd make a sauce piquant out of the turtle. It was enough with a vegetable to feed your family.
> —ISABEL ARCENEAUX, REGION 1 (CREOLE HERITAGE)

In this narrative, information builds regarding how the family earned a living, and the speaker uses narrative pacing to convey the story through the repetition of *we*. The last two lines illustrate the shift from *we* to *you*. *You* in this narrative may function as a generalizer, a distance marker, or a marker of inclusion (Abney 1997).

Child's Play

> We'd get some of my daddy's tobacco, me and my brothers and me and my cousins, and take off to the woods.... Then, we made us a flying jenny. You don't even know what that is, do you? We cut down a tree about this big around and split it where it would balance. Then the stub where we'd cut it off, We'd, uh, make us a peg on top of it, about this big around and then we'd take that split place with wedges—somebody'd split it and make it flare, and then one'd get on this end and one on this end, and there we went. Somebody'd push you and get you going around there, and then when you got up you couldn't stand up. We'd put pine straw in there for oiling it, make it go easier.... We made what we played with.... Made us a little log wagon. For Christmas, I'd get one little ole toy, maybe a little old car. Then I'd get a couple of apples and oranges.... Now, I've eat them blackbirds, them old crackles [*sic*], but they ain't crows. They'd just come down with a bullet, those crackles, them blackbirds.
> —COILEY GEWIN, REGION 2 (BRITISH HERITAGE)

In Gewin's narrative, the use of lexical items like *flying jenny* and *crackles* for *grackles* and the detailed narrative of the best manner in which to construct a flying jenny reflect the narrator's need for accuracy, and his focus in remembering how this is done is significant. *You* is used as an inclusion marker and generalizer of personal experience here after it appears in his early direct question to me (Abney 1996).

A Big Bird Story

Gene Chelette (GC; French and British heritage) and John F. Lovell (JL; British heritage) interviewed by Lisa Abney (LA)

> GC: I want you to tell the lady about the day we was going to south Louisiana and caught the big bird? . . . We caught a big bird; I'll let you tell that.
> JL: I'll let you go ahead; you good at it.
> JL: What was that, a ostrich?
> GC: No, it was a, uh, emu.
> JL: Well, we didn't know it . . . well, people was turnin' 'em out because they really wasn't profitable. So we was goin' to south Louisiana one morning, and uh, early, and I looked at Gene and he looked at me, and I said "Did you see that big bird run across the road?" He said "yeah." And I said "that was a **big** bird." Course, well, it stood about five foot. [gesture deixis]
> GC: Yes.
> JL: And I said, "Gene, that's one of those high-priced birds." So **we** stopped.
> GC: Now, wait a minute, before we stopped, John says, "That's one of those high-priced birds. Let's catch it." And I looked over there at the speedometer, and the bird was runnin' right down the side of the road with us, and John F. looked over there, and he was doin' about thirty miles an hour. And the bird was keepin' up with us. And I said, "There is no way we can catch this thing, you know," and he said, "Yeah, let's catch it."
> JL: Go ahead with it.
> GC: Well, anyhow, the bird could run as long as it was in the open. Well, it had got tired because it had run about four miles down the road beside us wide open. Alright, he got tired, so there was clear cut out there. We knew we couldn't catch it on foot, not in the open ground, so we thought. The bird got out in the clear cut; he stumbled and he slowed down. John F. said, "We can catch him now." So we took—we took off after the bird, and finally he jumped over a log, and the bird stumbled and fell, and John F. caught it.
> JL: **Bad** mistake. **Bad mistake.**

GC: John F. was holdin' on to that bird, hollerin', "Come here and help me." He had the beak. He said, "Get his head." And the thing had about a five-foot neck on him.

JL: And we was, we was carryin' it to the truck

GC: I told John F., "I gotta have some relief." He said, "What's the matter?" I said, "This thing is **bitin'** me."

JL: We got him to the truck.

GC: Well, we started; we put him in the back of the truck

JL: We put him in the back of the truck and tied his feet. We took off with him.

GC: Well, that bird probably weighed a hundred pounds or better. We got in the truck and took off goin' back to Winnfield with him. Tryin' to find out who he belonged to. Looked back, I looked back in the truck, and the bird was standin' up. I said, "John F., your bird's gonna jump out. We gonna have to do somethin' else with him."

JL: Aw, that was before we put him in the front.

GC: Before we put him in the front with us. I would have liked to had some of that video ... on *World's Most Funniest Videos*. John, we went in his truck that day—he's got an extended cab with two doors on the back. You know, he said, "We'll just put the bird in the back."

JL: We put the bird in the back and the sucker started hollerin' and squallin' tryin' to get out.

GC: I told John F., "We gonna have to do somethin' or he gonna kick the windows out of this thing." And uh, I said, "Let's blindfold him, maybe that'll calm him down." So I took a handkerchief out of my pocket and went back there and blindfolded him, the bird. And it was a still hollerin' and carryin' on. I told John F. "Turn on the radio, maybe he'd like some music." Turned on the radio. Got it on KWRV down there in Alexandria, and they playin' good country and western music, and he didn't like that. I said John, you better hunt somethin' else. He put on classical—he put it on public broadcasting, that's what it was.... Well, I asked John F., "Well, what are we gonna do?" He said, "Call Pam up at the sheriff's office." We called Pam, up at the sheriff's office, and she said, "Oh yeah, just bring it on in."

JL: She didn't believe us.

GC: They didn't believe us at all.

GC: We pulled up at the sheriff's department at the courthouse. I told John F., Pam was at the window on the second story up there. She hollered out, "They have got a big bird." John F. hollered up to her, "Well what do you want us to do with it?" She said, "Take him down to Sesame Street." I told John F., I said, "Tell you what let's do, let's un-blindfold this sucker, and I'll untie his legs, and open this door, and we'll let this sucker loose in downtown Winnfield." Well, about that time, animal control came up and got him.

This lengthy, humorous narrative uses repetition, detail, and well-developed narrative pacing to deliver a vivid narrative that profiles one of the pair's many adventures as longtime business partners. Of particular stylistic note in this narrative is the *ng*-fronting (*g*-dropping) in words such as *working* and *going*. The speakers share the floor, encouraging one another to "go ahead with it."

Louisiana's rich storytelling tradition lives in these narratives and provides a tremendous amount of linguistic data that can be examined for a variety of features ranging from phonological to pragmatics to discourse analysis.

CONCLUSIONS AND NEXT STEPS

Transcription and data coding for the survey are continuing, and nearly eighty samples have been coded and collated. Once the initial one hundred samples are coded, new interviews will be conducted with a focus on drawing in more African American, Native American, Hispanic, and Middle Eastern speakers who are native-born or long-term residents (thirty years or more) of Regions 1 and 2. In addition, an expansion to collection of data from participants of all backgrounds in Region 3 is underway, and once data are collected, transcribed, archived, and collated, final analysis of the samples can occur and appropriate linguistic maps will be created.

Such rich and deep interviews offer endless research possibilities, particularly because they include cultural, historical, and folklife information that might otherwise be lost to future generations.

WORKS CITED

Abney, Lisa. 1996. "Pronoun Shift in Oral Folklore, Personal Experience, and Literary Narratives, or 'What's Up with You?'" *SECOL Review* 20:203–26.
Abney, Lisa. 1998. "Textual Suppression in George Sessions Perry's *Hold Autumn in Your Hand* and Alice Walker's *The Third Life of Grange Copeland*." *Humanities in the South* 81:26–35.
Bailey, Guy. 1988. Personal interview.
Carmichael, Katie. 2014. "'I Never Thought I Had an Accent until the Hurricane': Sociolinguistics Variation in Post-Katrina Greater New Orleans." PhD diss., Ohio State University.
Carmichael, Katie, and Nathalie Dajko. 2016. "Ain't Dere No More: New Orleans Language and Local Nostalgia in *Vic & Nat'ly* Comics." *Linguistic Anthropology* 26:234–58.
Cash, W. J. 1941. *The Mind of the South*. New York: Vintage.

Chopin, Kate. 1890. *The Awakening*. Edited by Suzanne Disheroon-Green and David Caudle. Knoxville: University of Tennessee Press, 2001.
Fortier, Alcée. 1894. *Louisiana Studies: Literature, Customs and Dialects, History and Education*. New Orleans: Hansell.
Fortier, Alcée. 1904. *A History of Louisiana*. New York: Manzi, Joyant.
Fuster, Miguel. 1997. Unpublished Interviews with North Louisiana Spanish Speakers. Archived Louisiana Folklife Center.
Hatley, Donald W. 1991. "Fisher 'Bo' Snell: Kisatchie Creek Chairmaker." *Louisiana Folklife Journal* 15:1–12.
Larino, Jennifer. 2017. "These Are Louisiana's 20 Fastest-Growing Cities and Towns." *New Orleans Times-Picayune*, October 25. https://www.nola.com/business/index.ssf/2017/10/fast_growing_louisiana_cities.html.
Lee, Dayna B., and Hiram F. Gregory. 2006. *The Work of Tribal Hands: Southeastern Indian Split Cane Basketry*. Natchitoches, LA: Northwestern State University Press.
Lejeune, Keagan. 2015. *Western Louisiana's Neutral Strip: Its History, People, and Legends*. http://www.louisianafolklife.org/LT/Articles_Essays/nslejeune1.html.
Klingler, Thomas A. 2012. "Colonial Society and the Development of the Louisiana Creole." In *Language Variety in the South Revisited*, edited by Cynthia Bernstein, Thomas Nunnally, and Robin Sabino, 140–51. Tuscaloosa: University of Alabama Press.
Klingler, Thomas A. 2014. "Creole French in Louisiana/Kreyòl Andan la Louizyann." In *The Louisiana Field Guide: Understanding the Pelican State*, edited by Ryan Orgera and Wayne Parent, 89–91. Baton Rouge: Louisiana State University Press.
Klingler, Thomas A., and Nathalie Dajko. 2006. "Louisiana Creole at the Periphery." In *History, Society, and Variation*, edited by Clancy J. Clements, Thomas A. Klingler, Deborah Piston-Hatlen, and Kevin J. Rottet, 11–28. Amsterdam: Benjamins.
Labov, William, Sharon Ash, and Charles Boberg. 2006. *The Atlas of North American English: Phonetics, Phonology, and Sound Change*. Berlin: Mouton de Gruyter.
Leibling, A. J. 1961. *The Earl of Louisiana*. Baton Rouge: Louisiana State University Press.
Owens, Maida. 1997. "Louisiana's Traditional Cultures: An Overview." In *Swapping Stories*, edited by Carl Lindahl, Maida Owens, and C. Renee Harvison, xix–xlvii. Jackson: University Press of Mississippi.
Pasquier, Michael T. 2011. "French Colonial Louisiana." In *Encyclopedia of Louisiana*, edited by David Johnson. http://www.knowlouisiana.org/entry/french-colonial-louisiana.
Pederson, Lee. 1969. "The Linguistic Atlas of the Gulf States: An Interim Report." *American Speech* 44 (4): 279–86.
Pedersen Lee. 1986. *Linguistic Atlas of the Gulf States*. Vol. 1, *Handbook*. Athens: University of Georgia Press.
Pederson, Lee. 1989. *Linguistic Atlas of the Gulf States: Technical Index*. Vol. 3. Athens: University of Georgia Press.
Picone, Michael D. 2003. "Anglophone Slaves in Francophone Louisiana." *American Speech* 78:404–33.
Picone, Michael D. 2014. "Literary Dialect and the Linguistic Reconstruction of Nineteenth-Century Louisiana." *American Speech* 89:143–69.
Pratt, Comfort. 2008. "Dialect Death: The Case of Adaeseño Spanish in Northwest Louisiana." In *Recovering the U.S. Hispanic Linguistic Heritage*, edited by Alejandra Balestra, Glenn Martinez, and Irene Moyna, 191–214. Houston: Arte Público.
Roach-Lankford, Susan. 1984. *Gifts from the Hills*. Ruston: Louisiana Tech Art Gallery.

Samuels, Diana. 2014. "Baton Rouge Area's Population Growth is Suburban, While City Is Stagnant." *New Orleans Times-Picayune*, May 22. http://www.nola.com/news/baton-rouge/index.ssf/2014/05/baton_rouge_areas_population_g.html.

Toole, John Kennedy. 1980. *A Confederacy of Dunces*. New York: Grove.

US Census Bureau. 2010. *2010 Census*. http://www.census.gov/2010census/data/.

US Census Bureau. 2013. *2013 American Community Survey*. https://www.census.gov/programs-surveys/acs/data.html.

Wall, Bennett. H. 1990. *Louisiana: A History*. 3rd ed. Wheeling, IL: Harlan Davidson.

SECTION IV

New Populations

NATHALIE DAJKO

The late twentieth century saw a fairly rapid shift toward a monolingual anglophone culture in Louisiana. Still, the linguistic diversity that characterized New Orleans history continues, if perhaps on a much smaller scale. In this section we address the challenges that face three new minority populations: Spanish speakers, Vietnamese immigrants, and the speakers of less commonly spoken languages. All of these new populations face similar struggles with English-language legislation or regulations (proposed and enacted).

While never spoken by a majority of the Louisiana population, Spanish is a heritage language in the state, and its presence dates to the early years of European colonization. The dialects of Spanish that arrived with early settlers have all but disappeared, but a steady flow of new Spanish speakers is always on the horizon, and their numbers have doubled since Hurricane Katrina in 2005, although they remain very small. Here, Rafael Orozco and Dorian Dorado discuss the history of Spanish in Louisiana and describe the current Latino immigration to the state. After examining the background and linguistic features of the different dialects brought to Louisiana, they turn to the sociolinguistic context in which newly arrived Spanish speakers find themselves.

Allison Truitt then considers the challenges facing the Vietnamese community as it works to maintain its heritage language and navigate the social meaning ascribed to different dialects. Through an examination of tone and terms of address, she shows how dialectal variation may take on new meaning in an otherwise English-only context. She further documents the community's struggles with maintaining the right to use its heritage language.

Finally, Shane Lief examines the difficulties encountered by speakers of languages of lesser diffusion, including Arabic and Haitian Creole, through an in-depth examination of the causes and effects of language regulations passed by New Orleans's Taxicab and For Hire Vehicles Bureau. An encounter with a taxi driver who does not speak the local dominant language may cause fear among members of the public, while the drivers struggle to deal with the changing linguistic reality of a city that is both reliant on tourism for its livelihood and striving to maintain its identity in the face of change.

CHAPTER 14

SPANISH IN LOUISIANA: A STORY OF UNPLANNED LANGUAGE REVIVAL

RAFAEL OROZCO AND DORIAN DORADO

The Spanish language was brought to the Americas during the fifteenth and sixteenth centuries mainly via soldiers, colonists, settlers, priests, and colonial administrators (Penny 2002). The United States has approximately fifty million Spanish speakers—the second-largest concentration in the world, surpassed only by Mexico ("Spanish" 2019). Spanish is thus an important language in the United States. The South has hosted communities of Hispanic origin dating back to the arrival of the conquistadors in the sixteenth century. However, different political and historical events, particularly during the nineteenth century, marked a separation between former Spanish colonies (Texas, New Mexico, and California) in the Southwest and the Southeast, the territory that the United States acquired either by transfer from Great Britain or by direct purchase, as in the case of Louisiana.

The sociolinguistic situation of Spanish in the United States has been studied from different perspectives. The *Enciclopedia del Español en los Estados Unidos* (López Morales 2009) constitutes the most extensive and comprehensive compilation. Most existing studies have explored the Isleño, Brule, and Adaeseño patrimonial Spanish varieties. However, Spanish has undergone a resurgence in Louisiana since the latter part of the twentieth century, and this revival has not yet received adequate study. This chapter fills a void in our collective knowledge of Spanish in the United States. We begin by discussing the early Spanish presence in Louisiana and the patrimonial varieties of Louisiana Spanish. Subsequently, we turn our attention to the revival of Spanish in Louisiana, and we address its current situation in the Pelican State.

FIRST SPANISH PRESENCE IN LOUISIANA

The presence of Spanish-speaking speech communities in Louisiana dates back to the sixteenth century, when Spaniards first came to the area. The first European to explore the territory, Spain's Hernando de Soto, died in 1542 on the banks of the Mississippi River near what is today the town of Ferriday, Louisiana. In the late seventeenth century, migrants from France began to settle on the Gulf Coast, and in 1718 New Orleans was established; it became the administrative seat of the colonial Louisiana territory in 1723 (Din 2014:2). Several decades later, according to the terms of the 1762 Treaty of Fontainebleau, France ceded all of New France to Spain (Armistead 1991). Until then, however, the Spanish presence in Louisiana was rather insignificant, with very few inhabitants in Upper Louisiana (also called Spanish Illinois) (Din 2014:4). In 1778, one year after Bernardo de Gálvez became governor, new Spanish-speaking communities began to emerge, largely fueled by almost three thousand settlers, mainly from the Canary Islands, who arrived between 1783 and 1788 (Din 2014:15). These settlers and their descendants eventually became known as Isleños (Islanders).

The Canary Islanders dispersed and established settlements along the bayous around New Orleans and on both sides of the Mississippi River as well as throughout the Delta (Coles 2007:3). Settlers from other regions of Spain subsequently arrived, bringing their language and culture to a region that already possessed heavy French linguistic and cultural influences. During their first century in Louisiana, the Isleños' relative isolation from English speakers was key to maintaining the Spanish language. However, the English-only educational practices in effect in the early 1900s appear to have prompted a decline in the number of those who remained fluent in Spanish (Kammer 1941:64; Coles 2007:3). Samper and Hernandez (2009:79) indicate that Spaniards continued to arrive in Louisiana regularly until well into the twentieth century.

While most of the Canary Islanders settled southeast of New Orleans in what later became St. Bernard Parish, where their few remaining descendants live today, a smaller group settled in what is now Ascension Parish and became known as the Brule. Holloway (1997:ix) notes that despite remarkable similarities, the Brules' Spanish was clearly distinguishable from that of the Isleños. Another Spanish-speaking community that developed in Louisiana was that of the Adaeseños, who settled in the northwestern part of the state, near the Texas border.

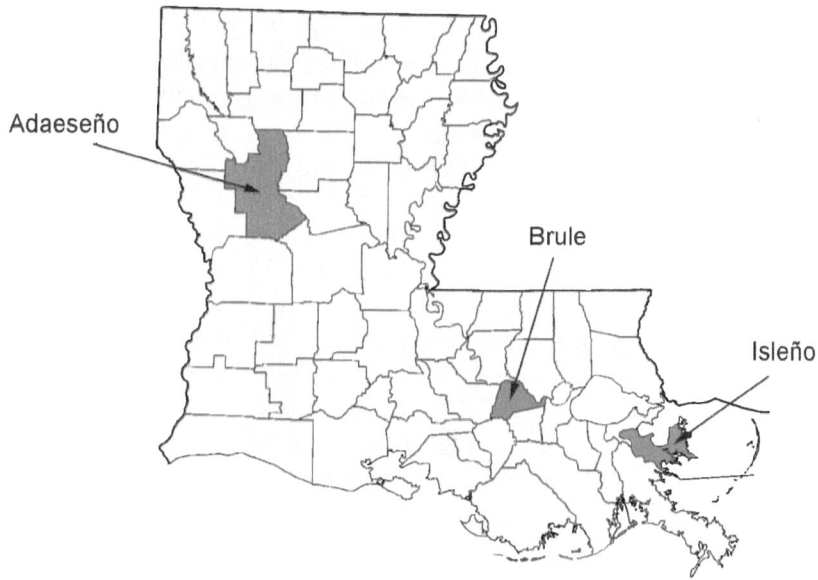

Figure 14.1. Ancestral varieties of Louisiana Spanish. Map by authors based on map available at https://legacy.lib.utexas.edu/maps/states/louisiana.gif.

PATRIMONIAL VARIETIES OF LOUISIANA SPANISH

Louisiana's main Spanish patrimonial varieties—Adaeseño, Isleño, and Brule (Armistead 1991; Lipski 1996, 2008; Moreno Fernández 2009)—together with those spoken in New Mexico, constitute some of the oldest Spanish varieties found in the United States (fig. 14.1). These patrimonial Spanish varieties were preserved partly through their isolation from other Spanish-speaking communities (Lipski 1990b:1), which contributed to the preservation of archaic elements that reflect the linguistic usage of earlier centuries (Lipski 2008:209). These varieties of Spanish have gradually declined to the point of extinction, largely as a consequence of inevitable sociolinguistic events within each speech community.

Adaeseño, also known as Sabine River Spanish, constitutes one of the least-known ancestral Spanish varieties documented in the United States (Lipski 1985, 1987). It developed on both sides of the Sabine River in present-day Natchitoches and Sabine Parishes in northwestern Louisiana and Nacogdoches County in eastern Texas. This region was explored as part of the colonization of Mexico, and two Spanish priests founded the mission of San Miguel de Cuéllar de los Adaes in 1717 (Pratt 2004:20–22). The communities that subsequently developed consisted mainly of mixed-race individuals, as the original settlers included Spaniards and Native Americans, with subsequent migrants arriving from Mexico (Lipski 1990b:2, 2008:216). These Spanish-speaking pockets were completely unknown outside of their immediate surroundings for many decades. Consequently, their linguistic situation remained unstudied until the late 1970s (Lipski 1985:5, 1987:112). Although the members of this speech community have not called themselves Adaeseños, the scholars who have studied the group have used this name (Lipski 1987:114; Pratt 2004:31).

The original settlers, as well as others who joined them throughout the eighteenth century, came mostly from the northern Mexican state of Coahuila (Lipski 1987:121). Thus, Adaeseño Spanish essentially derives from northern Mexican Spanish and shares very few similarities with Isleño and Brule. Phonologically conservative, Adaeseño features the general retention of coda consonants and the absence of complete neutralizations found in other dialects. Syllable- and word-final /s/ is normally retained as [s], with a low proportion of cases of aspiration (Lipski 1990b:4). As it occurs in Isleño and other isolated or vestigial Spanish varieties, Adaeseño features frequent cases of (1) phonological misidentification, (2) total relexification, and (3) both unstable and sporadic variation. Some common examples include *rabilán* < *gavilán* (hawk), *bujero* < *agujero* (hole), *buja* < *aguja* (needle), *jalote* < *guajalote* (turkey), *amaricano* < *americano* (American) (Lipski 2008:217–218). Adaeseño morphosyntax is complex, as it combines Mexican, archaic, popular, and vestigial tendencies with other external influences. Its most salient features include the almost complete absence of the subjunctive mood and the exclusive use of the periphrastic future. In addition, in expressing nominal possession, possessive adjectives are commonly replaced by possessive periphrases as in *la casa de ella* instead of *su casa* (her house) (Pratt 2004:94–95). The lexicon constitutes a combination of archaic, rural/popular, and Mexican Spanish items mixed with indigenous elements and French loanwords. Some Mexicanisms include *cacahuate* (peanut), *petate* (mat), and *tejón* (raccoon). Archaisms include *calzón/calzones* (pants), *lumbre* (fire), and *peje* (fish) (Lipski 2008:219; Pratt 2004:149–51). The remaining members of this community still live in Nacogdoches County, Texas, and in the communities of Ebarb, Noble, Spanish Lake, and Zwolle in Louisiana.

Isleño is the best-known Louisiana patrimonial Spanish variety. It was brought to this region toward the end of the eighteenth century—during the Spanish colonial period—by settlers from the Canary Islands. After the French and Indian War (1754–63), France sought to prevent Louisiana from becoming a British territory by offering it to Spain, setting the stage for the arrival of the Isleños (Din 1988). The first group of Isleños, mainly soldiers and their families, arrived in 1778 (Samper and Hernández 2009). As they settled in their new land, they often became fishermen and trappers to provide for themselves and their families (Samper and Hernández 2009). Although the first wave of Isleño migration to Louisiana involved the military, subsequent waves of Canary Islanders were sent to Louisiana to populate the colony with Spanish speakers and to act as a barrier between the French colonists and American military expansion (Coles 1993:124). The Isleño enclave developed in what is today St. Bernard Parish, about thirty-five miles southeast of New Orleans, in the innermost Louisiana marshlands. The original community constituted "a close-knit social network structure and included mostly lower-class individuals" (Coles 1993:124). As with the Adaeseño community, Isleños remained virtually unknown to the outside world for many decades. Until the second half of the twentieth century, the Isleño territory still lacked functioning roads, leaving residents completely isolated from other communities. Moreover, the absence of electricity (until the 1940s), phone lines (until the 1950s), and running water (until the 1960s) enhanced the remoteness of the Isleño community.

Historians, folklorists, linguists, and other social scientists who study the origins and evolution of this Spanish enclave have addressed various elements of the Isleño community and their language (Coles 2007:7). There are no recorded mentions of the Isleño community during its first century of existence, and the first known scholarly discussion of Isleño Spanish appeared in Alcée Fortier's *Louisiana Studies* (1894). Another half century passed before Claudel (1945) published some Isleño folktales. According to Lipski (1990a:viii), MacCurdy (1950), the seminal monograph that broke the ground for serious linguistic investigation of Isleño Spanish, constitutes one of the most complete studies of the variety, providing a background sketch of this dialect and exploring its lexicon, with an extensive glossary of items (Coles 2007:7). Craddock (1981) and Varela (1986) describe the dialect's main linguistic characteristics. Several works produced in the 1990s explore the gradual erosion of Isleño (see Coles 1991b; Holloway 1997; Lestrade 1999; Lipski 1990a). Coles (1991a, 1993) further addresses its obsolescence and discusses maintenance efforts made by the Isleño speech community.

The Isleño community's isolation has meant that its Spanish did not evolve concurrently with the rest of the language (Lipski 2008:210). The dialect developed from "a popular, uneducated variety representative of the rural speech of southern Spain and the Canary Islands" (Lipski 1990a:14). Phonetically and phonologically, Isleño is quite similar to Andalusian and Canary Island Spanish, exhibiting radical cases of consonantal reduction and neutralization. For instance, word- and syllable-final /s/ is normally aspirated to [h] or completely elided, so that *los isleños* is realized as [loh.ih.le.ɲo] (Lipski 2008:212). Its most salient morphosyntactic characteristics include the frequent use of the clitic pronoun *los* for first-person plural reference as in the case of *nos vamos > los vamos* (let's go). Archaic and analogical forms are also quite frequent, including the use of feminine forms for nouns that are grammatically masculine in modern Spanish, as in *la mar* (the sea), *la calor* (the heat), *la color* (the color) (Lipski 2008:213). Also, as with Adaeseño, in expressing nominal possession, possessive adjectives are commonly replaced by possessive periphrases, as in *la casa de él* instead of *su casa* (his house). The Isleño lexicon contains numerous cases of ancestral lexical preservation, including such archaic lexical items as *asina* (thus), *entuavía* (still), and *naide* (nobody) (Lipski 2008:212–14). Further, as the members of this community became English dominant throughout the twentieth century, numerous English loanwords and calques entered the lexicon (Lipski 1990a:68), among them *farmero* (farmer), *fuhnó* (furnace), *grocería* (grocery store), *guachimán* (watchman), *lonchá* (to eat lunch), *marqueta* (market), *suiche* (switch), *troleá* (to trawl) (Lipski 1990a:73–80). MacCurdy (1950), Lipski (1990a) and Coles (2007) provide detailed descriptions of the Isleño structural characteristics, with separate sections that cover phonetics and phonology, morphology, syntax, and the lexicon.

Present-day Isleños live throughout southeastern Louisiana, though their traditional cluster remains in Delacroix Island, St. Bernard Parish, approximately twenty-five miles southeast of New Orleans. The incursion of English meant that by 1990, the ancestral dialect had already reached an agonic state and became a dying variety (Coles 1993). There have been eleven to twelve generations of Isleños since their arrival in Louisiana to the present. Up to about the seventh generation—that is, until approximately the 1930s—Isleño was spoken in the home. After about the middle of the twentieth century, English gradually became the preferred home language. Furthermore, some members of the ninth generation claim that they can still understand Isleño Spanish but choose not to speak it because there is no need for it in their current environment. It is presumed that members of the tenth and eleventh generations neither understand nor speak Isleño and have detached themselves completely from the Isleño culture (Los Isleños Heritage and Cultural Society 2015). At the turn of the twenty-first century, no speaker was monolingual in Isleño (Coles 2007:3). Today Isleño has fewer than ten speakers, all of them over the age of seventy-five. For all practical purposes, this variety of Spanish is virtually defunct, as it is no longer the community's main vehicle of communication (Coles 2015). In other words, Isleño Spanish will be declared officially dead with the passing of its last remaining native speakers. Although the Isleños' full assimilation into American life has caused the loss of their language variety, their culture remains alive, and they take pride in their heritage (Los Isleños Heritage and Cultural Society 2015).

Brule, a sister variety of Isleño, also developed in southern Louisiana in the late eighteenth century. The Brule speech community formed on the west bank of the Mississippi, approximately fifty miles west of New Orleans, in what later became Ascension Parish, predominantly in the Donaldsonville area (Lipski 2008; Samper and Hernandez 2009). Since the Brules are also of Canary origin, their variety of Spanish has essentially the same linguistic characteristics found in Isleño (Lipski 2008). Nevertheless, those who are familiar with both varieties report that Brule is clearly distinguishable from Isleño (Holloway 1997:ix). Similar to Isleño, Brule Spanish also preserves many archaic linguistic characteristics (Samper and Hernández 2009). Like the Adaeseños and Isleños but unlike most other US Hispanic communities, the Brule community was never revived by immigration. Brule remained almost completely isolated, so the language with the most influence on the Brules was Cajun French rather than Spanish or English (Samper and Hernández 2009). No speaker of Brule was known to be alive at the turn of the twenty-first century, and the language is thus extinct (Samper and Hernández 2009).

Thanks to their unique circumstances, all three Louisiana patrimonial Spanish varieties remained strong for well over a century. They constitute remarkable examples of linguistic preservation, as immigrant speech communities in the United States usually shift to English by the third generation (Escobar and Potowski 2015:20; Lipski 2008:55). Nevertheless, all three varieties of Spanish gradually declined during the twentieth century, largely as a result of sequences of unfavorable sociolinguistic events that occurred as their communities opened to the outside world. The language shift into English ensued primarily as members of the three groups assimilated into American life, facilitated by government policies such as English-only public education (Lipski 2008:211). In the Adaes region, public education was virtually nonexistent until well into the twentieth century (Smith and Hitt 1952:107; Lipski 1985:10). The same is true for the Isleño community, where the use of Spanish was prohibited in the public schools (Coles 2007:3). Only those whose occupations involved strong intragroup contacts and did not need to learn English to earn a living preserved their proficiency in Spanish longer (Coles 1993). Consequently, in all three of these speech communities, Spanish became the subordinate language, with its use restricted to the home environment; by 1950, only a few individuals retained proficiency (Coles 2007:5; Holloway 1997:28; Pratt 2004:187). As the twentieth century progressed, maintaining the linguistic heritage became even more difficult as many members of these communities out-married. By the mid-1980s, the patrimonial Spanish varieties no longer served as the main vehicle for oral communication (see Armistead 1983:1; Coles 2015). At the turn of the twenty-first century, the remaining speakers of the ancestral Louisiana Spanish varieties were mostly over the age of seventy, and no fluent speakers were younger than fifty (see Pratt 2004:193–95). Today, Brule has ceased to exist, while Adaeseño and Isleño are moribund.

MODERN-DAY HISPANIC PRESENCE IN LOUISIANA

After Louisiana's admission to the United States in 1812, New Orleans became the major American port on the Gulf of Mexico and established itself as the US gateway to the Americas (Hoffman 1992). Although the flow of Hispanics into Louisiana has never stopped, their origin shifted, as most of those who arrived after the Louisiana Purchase were technically Latinos—that is, born in Latin America. Cuba had served as a stopover between the Canary Islands and Louisiana, and many Isleños were born in Cuba. Regular maritime traffic between New Orleans, Cuba, and Mexico subsequently facilitated the formation of Cuban and Mexican communities in Louisiana. Concurrently, New Orleans served as port of entry for thousands of Latin Americans of various origins. However, most of them moved on to other parts of the United States (Sluyter et al. 2015).

Despite remaining relatively small, Louisiana's Hispanic and Latino population slowly diversified during the twentieth century, with its stronghold remaining in metropolitan New Orleans. The 1930 Census found 1,083 New Orleans residents of Mexican birth, 299 born in Cuba, and fewer than 100 born in Honduras. The relocation of the United Fruit Company headquarters to New Orleans in 1933 brought large numbers of Hondurans, since United Fruit owned large banana plantations there (Sluyter et al. 2015:69), and a vibrant Honduran community developed. By 1950, Hispanics represented about 2 percent of the state population. Yet, Hispanics constituted the fastest-growing portion of the American population during the latter part of the twentieth century, reaching 22.4 million (9 percent of the total) in 1990 (US Census Bureau 1993). Growth accelerated even more over the next decade, with Hispanics accounting for 12.5 percent of the population nationwide. However, Louisiana's numbers remained low, with just 107,738 Latinos in the state (2.4 percent of the population) according to the 2000 Census (US Census Bureau 2007). In 2005, Hurricanes Rita and Katrina devastated southern Louisiana, and in the aftermath of those natural disasters, Louisiana received a large influx of Hispanics, many of whom arrived to work in the rebuilding efforts. By 2010, Louisiana's Hispanic population totaled 192,560 (4.2 percent) (US Census Bureau 2011). Although that number is much lower than the national average (17.1 percent), it had grown by 1 percent since 2000. In Texas, by contrast, Latinos constitute 35.5 percent of the population; however, the percentage of Latinos in Louisiana is higher than the 1.8 percent found in Mississippi, its neighbor to the east.

As in New Mexico, the influx of Latin American (primarily Central American) Spanish-speaking immigrants facilitated the revival of Spanish in Louisiana (see Lipski 2008:211–12). A considerable number of Louisiana's Hispanic and Latino residents have relocated from other states rather than arrived directly from their countries of origin (Campos Molina 2009:38). As occurs nationally, most are of Mexican origin, though southern Louisiana has so many Hondurans that New Orleans has been considered to have "the second-largest urban concentration of Hondurans in the world" (Gruesz 2008:140). Louisiana's Hispanic population also includes Puerto Ricans, Cubans, other Central Americans (mainly Guatemalans and Salvadorans), South Americans (primarily Colombians and Ecuadorians), and Spaniards (US Census Bureau 2010). The largest Hispanic concentration is found in the New Orleans metropolitan area (5.2 percent) and specifically in Kenner, where Hispanics constitute 22.4 percent of the population. Concurrently, the Hispanic presence in the state's second- and third-largest cities, Baton Rouge (3.3 percent) and Shreveport (2.5 percent), respectively, falls below the overall rate for the state (US Census Bureau 2010).

The significant growth of the Louisiana Hispanic population has affected businesses and the media. Grocery stores carry food, beverages, and other products from Latin American countries. In the Baton Rouge and New Orleans metropolitan areas in particular, athletic and sports apparel shops feature goods with logos from all over the Hispanic world. Restaurants and food trucks across the state specialize in Honduran, Salvadoran, and Mexican cuisine. Spanish-language media outlets have sprung up to serve the Hispanic population, including New Orleans radio stations WFNO La Caliente 830 AM, KGLA Tropical Caliente 105.7 FM and 1540 AM, and the online station Vocero Radio (http://www.voceroradio.com/). Spanish radio programming is broadcast in Baton Rouge by KDDK La Nueva 105.5 FM, in Lafayette by KFXZ Juan 1520 AM, and in Shreveport by KSYR La Invasora 92.1 FM. Bilingual Spanish-English newspapers and magazines have also appeared. The New Orleans monthly *El Tiempo New Orleans* (http://www.eltiemponeworleans.com) focuses on local and international news on various topics such as immigration, the economy, and social functions, while a bilingual print and online newspaper, *Jambalaya News: El Periódico Bilingüe de la Comunidad* (http://www.jambalayanews.com), primarily targets the state's Central American–descended population. Telemundo New Orleans Channel 42 broadcasts Spanish-language television programming, including the popular *telenovelas* (soap operas) that are an important part of Hispanic culture (http://libguides.tulane.edu/latinos_NOLA). Moreover, all cable and satellite providers carry Spanish-language programming from around the world.

The presence of the Spanish language and Hispanic culture appears to be more prevalent in Louisiana than ever before. However, these recently established Latino communities have not been sufficiently studied, perhaps because Louisiana does not constitute one of the main sites of massive Hispanic immigration and is better known for its French culture than for its Hispanic influence.

CHARACTERISTICS OF MODERN-DAY LOUISIANA SPANISH

Recent investigations have focused on the communities in southeastern Louisiana that are currently home to the largest concentrations of Spanish speakers. This emerging body of research consists mainly of studies that explore sociolinguistic patterns as they manifest regarding phenomena such as calques, variable subject personal pronoun expression, the expression of futurity, forms of address, and perceptual attitudes toward Spanish in Louisiana.

Calques

Lexical borrowings and calques inevitably occur in situations of linguistic contact such as those in Louisiana (see Weinreich 1953:36–38). Calques result from the transfer of a word's meaning into an existing lexical item in the recipient language (Silva-Corvalán 1994:170–75). A typical example of an English word calqued into Spanish is that of *aplicación*, which takes the meaning of English *application*, in place of its standard Spanish equivalent, *solicitud*. In the speech of Honduran and Salvadoran southern Louisiana Spanish-English bilinguals, calques are most strongly conditioned by collocations, by the preceding word's lexical category, by age, by education, and by socioeconomic status (Bivin 2013). Collocations exert the strongest conditioning effect, with relative pronouns and conjunctions most favoring the production of calques. The preceding word's lexical category has the second-strongest effect, with calques most frequently occurring around relative pronouns as well as immediately after conjunctions, adjectives, and verbs. Concurrently, the social predictors reveal that calquing is strongly promoted by younger and less educated individuals with lower income levels. Conversely, calques are disfavored by older and more educated speakers with higher incomes (Bivin 2013). The author found that calquing among southern Louisiana Hondurans and Salvadorans is as noteworthy as it is among Mexican Americans in Los Angeles (Silva-Corvalán 1994) and Cubans, Puerto Ricans, and Mexicans in Gainesville, Florida (Dorado 2006).

Subject Personal Pronoun Expression

Variable subject personal pronoun expression (e.g., *nosotros vamos* alternating with *vamos* to mean "we go") constitutes a morphosyntactic characteristic that Spanish inherited from Latin. Vidal-Covas (2013) explores this linguistic variable in the speech of Puerto Rican Spanish speakers in Puerto Rico and Baton Rouge, Louisiana, to determine the overt pronominal rate and the predictors that probabilistically condition the usage of overt pronominal subjects. Louisiana Puerto Ricans' pronominal rate (37 percent), although representative of Caribbean Spanish, is not significantly higher than the pronominal rate in Puerto Rico. This finding suggests that, as with Colombians in New York City (Orozco 2018) and Hondurans in Louisiana (Estrada Andino 2016), the influence of dialectal leveling and convergence coming from other Spanish speakers strongly competes with the influence of language contact with English. Vidal-Covas (2013) finds that variable subject pronoun expression among Louisiana Puerto Ricans is strongly conditioned by linguistic predictors. Moreover, these predictors, as well as the effects of their individual factors, are consonant with what occurs throughout the Hispanic world in both bilingual and monolingual speech communities. Thus, contact with English has not yet prompted significant differences in subject pronoun expression.

The Expression of Futurity

Futurity is expressed in Spanish by means of a linguistic variable that consists of three variants: the morphological future, the simple present, and the periphrastic future. In a comparative study of the expression of futurity in the Spanish of Mexicans in Louisiana and the sociolinguistically understudied city of Xalapa, Mexico, Kyzar (2014) explores the distribution of futurity variants and the predictors conditioning their occurrence. The effects of five social and nine linguistic predictors were tested by means of statistical regression analyses. Results indicate that as in New York City (Orozco 2018), the periphrastic future registers the highest rate of occurrence (67.6 percent), whereas the morphological future is disappearing. A comparison of Kyzar's findings with those of other studies (Orozco 2007a; Lastra and Martín Butragueño 2010; Claes and Ortíz-López 2011; Gutiérrez 1995; Blas Arroyo 2008) suggests that Mexicans in Louisiana are at a more advanced stage in the evolution of the expression of futurity than most other Hispanic speech communities. As reported in other studies (see Orozco 2007a, 2018), type of verb is the linguistic predictor that most strongly influences the expression of futurity. Both age and educational level condition the use of the future. Gender, however, shows no significant effect, which differs from what occurs in Colombia and New York City (Orozco 2007b, 2015), Mexico City (Lastra and Martín Butragueño 2010), and Puerto Rico (Claes and Ortíz López 2011). In general, the effects of linguistic factors are consistent with those in other speech communities and reflect the universality of the process of grammaticalization. The lack of statistical significance for gender suggests that women and men have similar sociolinguistic behaviors. Kyzar's (2014) findings open the possibility of exploring other linguistic variables in these and other communities to determine whether the social trends found are limited to the expression of futurity or to the communities under study.

Forms of Address

The use of multiple second-person forms of address constitutes one of the most intriguing cases of variation in contemporary Spanish. The heavy Central American presence in Louisiana results in a large proportion of users of *vos* as the preferred second-person-singular form of address (*you*), whereas most Spanish speakers use *tú*. Estrada Andino (2016) studies the use of second-person address forms among southeastern Louisiana Hondurans, finding that in Louisiana as well as in their native country, Hondurans perceive the use of *vos* as characteristic of their Spanish. Nevertheless, in Louisiana, the use of *tú* has increased at the expense of both *vos* and *usted*. This decrease in the use of *voseo* (i.e., the preferential use of *vos*) as the second-person singular form of address is driven mainly by speakers who have been in the United States for more than ten years. It is also similar to what occurs in Central American communities elsewhere in the United States and may reflect dialectal convergence. Moreover, those with lower educational attainment are less accepting of *voseo* and appear to hold negative attitudes toward this practice. In general, Estrada Andino's findings, as well as those of Campos Molina (2009) and Sullivan (2010), suggest that dialect convergence plays an important role in Louisiana Spanish, just as it does in New York City (see Orozco 2015, 2018).

PERCEPTIONS TOWARD SPANISH

The study of perceptions toward Spanish in Louisiana employs folk linguistics methodology (Niedzielski and Preston 2000:63) to explore two different perspectives. One seeks to determine whether Louisiana Hispanics and Latinos perceive that their Spanish has changed as a result of living in the United States; the other explores the attitudes of native English-speaking Louisiana residents toward different varieties of Spanish.

Campos Molina (2009) explores Latino Louisianans' perceptions of how their Spanish has changed. Her informants maintain frequent communication with friends and relatives in their countries of origin but perceived changes in their Spanish and attributed those changes mainly to contact with Spanish speakers of other nationalities. Louisiana Hispanics also feel that learning

English has affected their Spanish, particularly in their use of code-switching and lexical borrowings. Nevertheless, they do not feel that the effect of English is as strong as that of their regular interactions with speakers of other varieties of Spanish.

Sullivan (2010) investigates attitudes toward the word *Spanglish* and toward Spanish-English code-switching using data obtained through a survey completed by 183 participants including Spanish-English bilinguals and monolingual English speakers. Multivariate analyses uncovered that five predictors condition opinions toward code mixing. The respondents' native language influences their attitudes toward code-switching, with native Spanish speakers less apt to have positive opinions. Moreover, the attitudes and perceptions of both monolinguals and bilinguals merit further study. Gender also seems to influence language attitudes, as is evidenced by the divergent tendencies observed in the opinions of the men and women surveyed as well as by the respondents' maternal language repertoire. In general, the participants demonstrate an understanding of language contact and bilingualism and seem to recognize that in language contact situations, the combination of two or more languages is something expected rather than a deviant sociolinguistic behavior. Likewise, the term *Spanglish* is deemed appropriate for describing the combination of Spanish and English linguistic elements. However, most respondents do not feel that Spanglish constitutes a language in itself. Overall, this investigation presents an innovation to the field of sociolinguistics, as the attitudes under study had never been examined quantitatively or at this level.

Orozco and Dorado (2016) surveyed 559 people (335 women and 224 men) from various backgrounds born between 1937 and 2000, with 77.3 percent born between 1991 and 1997 and 1995 the most frequent year of birth. Most of the respondents resided in the Baton Rouge metropolitan area. They completed a one-page questionnaire with multiple-choice and fill-in-the-blank items intended to elicit their attitudinal perceptions as well as demographic information. Nearly three-quarters (73 percent) of those surveyed felt that it is important to speak other languages besides English in the United States. However, given Louisiana's cultural heritage, we expected this percentage to be higher. When asked what language they would like to learn, 39 percent selected Spanish, while 20.6 percent chose French. Among our sample, 89 percent were aware of regional variations in Spanish, and 61 percent felt that Spanish is spoken more properly or more correctly in certain places or regions, with such perceptions slightly more common among women (63 percent) than men (59 percent). Almost half (47 percent) of respondents selected Spain as the ideal location to study Spanish, with Mexico placing second and Argentina third. Furthermore, 23.3 percent found Peninsular Spanish the most pleasant variety and stated that if they were to become fluent, they would prefer to sound like

Spaniards. Positive perceptions toward Peninsular Spanish were more prevalent among women than men. Respondents also perceived Mexican, Peruvian, Colombian, and Cuban Spanish as pleasant.

Although survey participants evaluated Mexican and Argentine Spanish positively, Caribbean and Central American varieties were rated unfavorably. The positive evaluations of Peninsular and Argentine Spanish are congruent with those of Miami Cubans (Alfaraz 2002) and residents of the Mexican state of Veracruz (Orozco and Nemogá 2012). Likewise, the respondents echoed the negative perceptions of Central American and Caribbean Spanish prevalent in Mexico (Orozco and Nemogá 2012). These findings suggest that in addition to holding attitudes on language at all levels (Garnett 2010:2), people are aware of language variation in languages they do not speak fluently. In particular, Louisianans exhibit awareness of the differences between various varieties of Spanish, suggesting that widespread perceptions of varieties of Spanish transcend language boundaries.

The long-standing consequences of linguistic contact are well known. However, despite a recent surge in research, linguistics as a discipline still lacks definite answers to what happens in the incipient stages of simultaneous language and dialect contact situations. The sociolinguistic situation of the emerging twenty-first-century Louisiana Hispanic community has barely been explored. Thus, only further research can shed light on what exactly happens during the initial stages of a language contact situation and help answer emerging or, as yet, unanswered questions while providing a foundation for future research. As Thomason and Kaufman (1988:213) assert, research on current contact situations is needed to obtain a more thorough understanding of the role played by the sociolinguistic context in contact-based linguistic change. The contact between Spanish and English in Louisiana provides a unique opportunity for short-term diachronic exploration. Studies of this sort, as Weinreich (1953:104) proposes, "make it possible to clarify basic problems involving longer time spans as well." The contact between different varieties of Spanish is no less intriguing. And research on Louisiana's smaller Spanish-speaking communities offers an important counterpoint to research on such cities as Los Angeles, New York, and Miami that have large Hispanic populations.

WORKS CITED

Alfaraz, Gabriela G. 2002. "Miami Cuban Perceptions of Varieties of Spanish." In *Handbook of Perceptual Dialectology*, edited by Dennis R. Preston, 1–11. Amsterdam: Benjamins.

Armistead, Samuel G. 1983. "Spanish Riddles from St. Bernard Parish." *Louisiana Folklore Miscellany* 5 (3): 1–8.

Armistead, Samuel G. 1991. "Tres Dialectos Españoles de Luisiana." *Lingüística Española Actual* 13:279–301.

Bivin, Alexandria. 2013. "'Mi Mamá Es Cinco Cuatro': A Study of the Use of Calques in Hondurans and Salvadorans in Southern Louisiana." Master's thesis, Louisiana State University.

Blas Arroyo, José Luis. 2008. "The Variable Expression of Future Tense in Peninsular Spanish: The Present (and Future) of Inflectional Forms in the Spanish Spoken in a Bilingual Region." *Language Variation and Change* 20 (1): 85–126.

Campos Molina, Dally. 2009. "Sociolinguistic Characteristics of the Latino Population in the Baton Rouge Metro Area." Master's thesis, Louisiana State University.

Claes, Jeroen, and Luis Ortíz-López. 2011. "Restricciones Pragmáticas y Sociales en la Expresión de Futuridad en el Español de Puerto Rico." *Spanish in Context* 8 (1): 50–72.

Claudel, Calvin. 1945. "Spanish Folktales from Delacroix, Louisiana." *Journal of American Folklore* 58:208–24.

Coles, Felice. 1991a. "The *Isleño* Dialect of Spanish: Language Maintenance Strategies." In *Sociolinguistics of the Spanish-Speaking World: Iberia, Latin America, United States*, edited by Carol Klee and Luis Ramos-García, 312–28. Tempe: Bilingual Press/Editorial Bilingüe.

Coles, Felice. 1991b. "Social and Linguistic Correlates to Language Death: Research from the Isleño Dialect of Spanish." PhD diss., University of Texas at Austin.

Coles, Felice. 1993. "Language Maintenance Institutions of the Isleño Dialect of Spanish." In *Spanish in the United States: Linguistic Contact and Diversity*, edited by John M. Lipski and Ana Roca, 121–33. Berlin: Mouton de Gruyter.

Coles, Felice. 2007. *Isleño Spanish*. Munich: Lincom Europa.

Coles, Felice. 2015. "Commodifying the Preservation of Isleño Spanish." Paper presented at the 82nd Southeastern Conference on Linguistics (SECOL), Raleigh NC, April 10.

Craddock, Jerry. 1981. "New World Spanish." In *Language in the USA*, edited by Charles A. Ferguson and Shirley Brice Heath, 196–211. Cambridge: Cambridge University Press.

Din, Gilbert. 1988. *The Canary Islanders of Louisiana*. Baton Rouge: Louisiana State University Press.

Din, Gilbert. 2014. *Populating the Barrera: Spanish Immigration Efforts in Colonial Louisiana*. Lafayette: University of Louisiana at Lafayette Press.

Dorado, Dorian. 2006. "Spanish-English Bilinguals in Gainesville, Florida: A Cross-Generational Study of the Use of Calques." Master's thesis, University of Florida.

Escobar, Anna María, and Kim Potowski. 2015. *El Español de los Estados Unidos*. Cambridge: Cambridge University Press.

Estrada Andino, Monika. 2016. "El Tú No Es de Nosotros, Es de Otros Países: Usos del Voseo y Actitudes Hacia Él en el Castellano Hondureño." Master's thesis, Louisiana State University.

Fortier, Alcée. 1894. *Louisiana Studies*. New Orleans: Hansell.

Garnett, Peter. 2010. *Attitudes to Language: Part of Key Topics to Sociolinguistics*. New York: Cambridge University Press.

Gruesz, Kirsten Silva. 2008. "The Mercurial Space of 'Central' America: New Orleans, Honduras, and the Writing of the Banana Republic." In *Hemispheric American Studies*, edited by Caroline F. Levander and Robert S. Levine, 140–65. New Brunswick: Rutgers University Press.

Gutiérrez, Manuel J. 1995. "On the Future of the Future Tense in the Spanish of the Southwest." In *Spanish in Four Continents: Studies in Language Contact and Bilingualism*, edited by Carmen Silva-Corvalán, 214–23. Washington, DC: Georgetown University Press.

Hoffman, Paul E. 1992. *Luisiana*. Madrid: Mapfre.
Holloway, Charles E. 1997. *Dialect Death: The Case of Brule Spanish*. Amsterdam: Benjamins.
Kammer, Edward. 1941. *A Socio-Economic Survey of the Marshdwellers of Four Southeastern Louisiana Parishes*. Washington DC: Catholic University of America Press.
Kyzar, Kendall. 2014. "El Futuro es Perifrástico: Un Análisis Sociolingüístico de la Expresión de Futuridad en dos Comunidades Mexicanas." Master's thesis, Louisiana State University.
Lastra, Yolanda, and Pedro Martín Butragueño. 2010. "Futuro Perifrástico y Futuro Morfológico en el Corpus Sociolingüístico de la Ciudad de México." *Oralia* 13:145–71.
Lestrade, Patricia. 1999. "Trajectories in Isleño Spanish with Special Emphasis on the Lexicon." PhD diss., University of Alabama.
Lipski, John M. 1985. "Sabine River Spanish: Vestigial 18th Century Mexican Spanish in Texas and Louisiana." *Southwest Journal of Linguistics* 8:5–24.
Lipski, John M. 1987. "El Español del Río Sabinas: Vestigios del Español Mexicano en Luisiana y Texas." *Nueva Revista de Filología Hispánica* 35:111–28.
Lipski, John M. 1990a. *The Language of the Isleños: Vestigial Spanish in Louisiana*. Baton Rouge: Louisiana State University Press.
Lipski, John M. 1990b. "Sabine River Spanish: A Neglected Chapter in Mexican-American Dialectology." In *Spanish in the United States: Sociolinguistic Issues*, edited by John J. Bergen, 2–13. Washington DC: Georgetown University Press.
Lipski, John. 1996. "Los Dialectos Vestigiales del Español en los Estados Unidos: Estado de la Cuestión." *Signo y Seña* 6:459–89.
Lipski, John. 2008. *Varieties of Spanish in the United States*. Washington DC: Georgetown University Press.
López Morales, Humberto, ed. 2009. *Enciclopedia del Español en los Estados Unidos*. Madrid: Instituto Cervantes, Santillana.
Los Isleños Heritage and Cultural Society. 2015. Telephone interview with spokesperson. 22 February.
MacCurdy, Raymond. 1950. "The Spanish Dialect of St. Bernard Parish, Louisiana." Master's thesis, University of New Mexico.
Moreno Fernández, Francisco. 2009. "Caracterización del Español Patrimonial." In *Enciclopedia del Español en los Estados Unidos*, edited by Humberto López Morales, 179–99. Madrid: Instituto Cervantes, Santillana.
Niedzielski, Nancy, and Dennis R. Preston. 2000. *Folk Linguistics*. New York: Mouton de Gruyter.
Orozco, Rafael. 2007a. "The Impact of Linguistic Constraints on the Expression of Futurity in the Spanish of New York Colombians." In *Spanish in Contact: Policy, Social, and Linguistic Inquiries*, edited by Kim Potowski and Richard Cameron, 311–28. Amsterdam: Benjamins.
Orozco, Rafael. 2007b. "Social Constraints on the Expression of Futurity in Spanish-Speaking Urban Communities." In *Selected Proceedings of the Third Workshop on Spanish Sociolinguistics*, edited by Jonathan Holmquist, Augusto Lorenzino, and Lotfi Sayahi, 103–12. Somerville, MA: Cascadilla.
Orozco, Rafael. 2015. "Castilian in New York City: What Can We Learn from the Future?" In *New Perspectives on Hispanic Contact Linguistics in the Americas*, edited by Sandro Sessarego and Melvin González-Rivera, 347–72. Madrid: Iberoamericana/Vervuert.
Orozco, Rafael. 2018. *Spanish in Colombia and New York City: Language Contact Meets Dialectal Convergence*. Amsterdam: Benjamins.
Orozco, Rafael, and Dorian Dorado. 2016. "Perceptual Attitudes towards Spanish in the United States." Paper presented at Sociolinguistics Symposium 21, Murcia, Spain, June 17.

Orozco, Rafael, and Maritza Nemogá. 2012. "Veracruz Speech Perceptions: The Best Spanish is Spoken Here?" Paper presented at the International Workshop on Spanish Sociolinguistics, Tucson, AZ, April 12.

Penny, Ralph. 2002. *A History of the Spanish Language.* 2nd ed. New York: Cambridge University Press.

Pratt, Confort. 2004. *El Español del Noroeste de Luisiana: Pervivencia de un Dialecto Amenazado.* Madrid: Verbum.

Samper, José Antonio, and Clara Eugenia Hernández. 2009. "La Luisiana." In *Enciclopedia del Español en los Estados Unidos*, edited by Humberto López Morales, 75–79. Madrid: Instituto Cervantes, Santillana.

Silva-Corvalán, Carmen. 1994. *Language Contact and Change: Spanish in Los Angeles.* Oxford: Oxford University Press.

Sluyter, Andrew, Case Watkins, James P. Chaney, and Annie M. Gibson. 2015. *Hispanic and Latino New Orleans: Immigration and Identity since the Eighteenth Century.* Baton Rouge: Louisiana State University Press.

Smith, T. Lynn, and Homer Hitt. 1952. *The People of Louisiana.* Baton Rouge: Louisiana State University Press.

"Spanish." 2019. In *Ethnologue: Languages of the World*, edited by David M. Eberhard, Gary F. Simons, and Charles D. Fennig. 22nd ed. Dallas: SIL International. http://www.ethnologue.com/language/spa.

Sullivan, Sarah. 2010. "Popular Attitudes and Beliefs toward the Mixing of Spanish and English." Master's thesis, Louisiana State University.

Thomason, Sarah G., and Terrence Kaufman. 1988. *Language Contact, Creolization, and Genetic Linguistics.* Berkeley: University of California Press.

US Census Bureau. 1993. *1990 Census of Population, Social and Economic Characteristics: Louisiana.* Washington, DC.

US Census Bureau. 2007. *2000 Census of Population and Housing.* Washington, DC.

US Census Bureau. 2011. *The Hispanic Population: 2010.* Washington, DC.

Varela, Beatriz. 1986. "El Español de Luisiana." In *Actas del II Congreso Internacional sobre el Español de América*, edited by José G. Moreno de Alba, 273–77. Mexico City: Universidad Autonoma Nacional de Mexico.

Vidal-Covas, Lee-Ann. 2013. "El Uso Variable de los Pronombres Sujetos en el Castellano Puertorriqueño Hablado en Luisiana y Puerto Rico." Master's thesis, Louisiana State University.

Weinreich, Uriel. 1953. *Languages in Contact: Findings and Problems.* London: Mouton, 1967.

CHAPTER 15

VIETNAMESE IN LOUISIANA

ALLISON TRUITT

In 2008, the Terrebonne Parish School Board reportedly considered a proposal to require all commencement speeches to be delivered in English only (Pleasant 2008). The proposal came in response to a speech delivered by cousins Hue and Cindy Vo, co-valedictorians of Ellender High School and the daughters of Vietnamese immigrants. Cindy Vo reportedly addressed her parents with the Vietnamese expression, "Nhìn lên mình không bằng ai, nhìn xuống không ai bằng mình," which she translated as "Being one's own person."[1] As the controversy brewed, Cindy remarked, "Out of the whole speech, it's one sentence dedicated to [my parents] to give them thanks." Her cousin added, "It's very important to my parents that I keep my culture. I felt that if I expressed myself in Vietnamese, it would be more heartfelt." The school board's proposal to enforce English only during commencement stirred questions about whether a ban on other languages would infringe on the rights of students, especially in a region that proudly marketed its diverse linguistic heritage. Warren Perrin, then president of the Council for the Development of French in Louisiana, noted, "It would seem the French, who have been subjects of prejudice, would be more sensitive to the issue. I find that extremely ironic." While Perrin discounted the lingering discrimination against French speakers, he did draw attention to the region's long history of linguistic inequality.

Terrebonne Parish is located in Acadiana, a twentieth-century term given to the twenty-two-parish area in south Louisiana in which large numbers of francophones, including three thousand Acadians, settled in the eighteenth and nineteenth centuries and in which French is still spoken by a large number of (primarily elderly) residents. In the early twentieth century, French speakers faced restrictions on their use of their native language in public schools. By the 1960s, *Cajun* (a shortened form of *Acadian*) was marketed as part of Louisiana's rich linguistic and cultural landscape (Trépanier 1991). In 1974, the revised Louisiana state constitution enshrined ethnic diversity by recognizing "the right of the people to preserve and promote their respective historic, linguistic, and cultural origins." Yet the Terrebonne School Board's proposal to require English during commencements exposed just how tenuous those rights to preserve linguistic and cultural origins still are, whether by new populations like Vietnamese or by ethnic French speakers.

The presence of both French and Vietnamese speakers testifies to how histories of displacement and migration have shaped the linguistic landscape of south Louisiana. But while the promotion of French in Louisiana has received some financial support from the French government, Vietnamese diasporic communities have a far more strained relationship with present-day Vietnam, a fact that has implications for the linguistic landscape. The first Vietnamese who arrived in Louisiana were refugees who fled after the collapse of South Vietnam in 1975. They were more urbanized and educated than those refugees in the second wave (1978–90s), known as the Boat People, who were from rural areas or of ethnic Chinese descent. The third wave consisted of veterans and their immediate families who were resettled through the Humanitarian Operation Program and the Orderly Departure Program. Today, new pathways of migration have opened through sponsorship by families, religious organizations, and schools, ensuring that the majority of Vietnamese in the United States are still classified as foreign-born or first-generation immigrants. The high value placed on maintaining cultural heritage and language reflects how the Vietnamese American experience has been framed by war, loss, and displacement. In the 1990s, Carl Bankston and Min Zhou (1998) demonstrated how students in New Orleans who identified strongly as Vietnamese tended to succeed academically, a seeming paradox given how many adult Vietnamese migrants in the study perceived Americanization as the major threat. Consequently, even though Vietnamese remains the primary language spoken in many households, community leaders express concern over the gap between different generations' cultural values and linguistic practices. While the Terrebonne Parish School Board viewed Cindy Vo's use of Vietnamese as an affront, many Vietnamese Americans in the audience viewed her speech as a testimony to her parents having raised their daughter well.

In this chapter, I provide an overview of the demographics of the Vietnamese in Louisiana, drawing attention to how the social histories of resettlement have given the population linguistic characteristics that are different from those of the US Vietnamese population as a whole. I then examine two salient features of language, dialectal variation and terms of address. Dialectal variation is significant insofar as it indexes place-based identities in Vietnam that are, in turn, perceived as reinscribing the Cold War division of Vietnam into two hostile regimes. By contrast, terms of address are important pragmatic practices that conform to what anthropologist Hy Van Luong (1987) calls a native model of and for reality that emphasizes hierarchy and solidarity. Because Vietnamese is a minority language, the settings in which it is used are restricted, thereby affecting how and when such a model is actually realized. As the example of Cindy and Hue Vo's high school commencement speech makes clear, the prominence of Vietnamese on Louisiana's linguistic landscape remains powerful and even threatening in certain settings. I conclude by turning to the problem of language rights and how Vietnamese community-based organizations in Louisiana have led efforts to ensure that those constitutional rights are recognized and protected.

VIETNAMESE RESETTLEMENT PATTERNS IN SOUTHEASTERN LOUISIANA

Vietnamese constitute the largest immigrant group in Louisiana (Migration Policy Institute 2016). In the 1970s, the New Orleans metropolitan area was one of the initial gateway cities for refugee resettlement. Since the late 1990s, however, population growth in the region has slowed considerably compared to other coastal states, especially Texas, Georgia, and Florida. Moreover, while Louisiana still has the country's tenth-largest Vietnamese population, it differs from the Vietnamese population in the United States as a whole in several prominent ways. Local community leaders estimate that more than half of the Vietnamese in Louisiana identify as Catholic, even though a plurality of Vietnamese in the United States identity as Buddhist (40 percent) rather than Christian (36 percent) (Pew Research Center n.d.:12). This phenomenon has been attributed to the role of Associated Catholic Charities of New Orleans in resettling refugees in the late 1970s. In contrast to federal policies that led to the dispersal of Vietnamese families around the country to encourage assimilation, Catholic Charities recruited Vietnamese priests and their congregants, a model of resettlement that emphasized communal and cultural ties as a means of integration. Today, the three neighborhoods where Vietnamese refugees were initially resettled—Village de l'Est (or Versailles) in eastern New Orleans, Woodlawn, and Marrero—are still home to prominent Vietnamese churches and central to Vietnamese cultural life in southeastern Louisiana.

The most well-known Vietnamese community in Louisiana is located on the eastern edge of New Orleans. Taking its name from the Versailles Armes apartment complex, where refugees were initially resettled, the neighborhood has attracted both scholarly and media attention for both its distinctiveness and its recovery efforts in the wake of Hurricane Katrina (Nguyen 2015;

VanLandingham 2017). Along with an active commercial area with several small grocery stores, a video store, a pharmacy, restaurants, cafés, and other services, the neighborhood also boasts a Saturday morning "crouching market"—so named because the vendors squat on the pavement to sell their wares. The institutional focal point of the neighborhood is unquestionably Mary Queen of Vietnam Church, which offers a bilingual Vietnamese-language nursery and preschool, although English is the predominant language, as well as Sunday language classes for children of the Catholic congregation.

Southeastern Louisiana appealed to refugees and migrants not only because of the institutional connections with the Catholic Church but also because the subtropical climate and the opportunities to work in the commercial fishing and seafood industry shaped secondary migration patterns in the 1980s. By 1990, Vietnamese migrants made up 5 percent of those employed in Louisiana's fishing industry, and by 2010, local residents estimated that as many as one-third of Louisiana's 12,400 licensed commercial fishermen were Vietnamese (Bankston and Zhou 1996). However, dependence on the fishing industry rendered communities and households economically vulnerable, especially following Hurricane Katrina and the 2010 BP oil spill. Vietnamese had difficulties accessing government assistance, thereby highlighting how constitutionally protected rights to preserve and promote linguistic origins must also be accompanied by mechanisms to ensure language access for residents. Yet even a seemingly obvious solution such as hiring translators can become contentious when the diverse ways of speaking Vietnamese incite lingering resentment against the Socialist Republic of Vietnam.

THE POLITICS OF LINGUISTIC VARIATION

Vietnamese is a Mon-Khmer language within the Austroasiatic family spoken throughout mainland Southeast Asia. Today, Vietnamese can rightfully be considered a global language as more than 3.7 million speakers now reside in more than one hundred countries, including more than 1.3 million in the United States alone (A. T. Pham 2010:5). Vietnamese is often classified into two major dialects, Northern Vietnamese and Southern Vietnamese, although some scholars include Central Vietnamese as a third major dialect. While the differences in dialect do not impair mutual intelligibility, they do index place-based identities, which in turn map onto the political division of Vietnam into the US-allied Republic of Vietnam (1956–75) and the communist Democratic Republic of Vietnam (1945–76). After the South Vietnamese regime fell to northern troops in 1975, the two governments were integrated into the Socialist Republic of Vietnam in 1976. Consequently, dialectal variation often

Table 15.1. Vietnamese Tones and Their Orthographic Representation

Tone	Orthography	Example
Level (Vietnamese, dấu ngang)	a	la (to scold)
Rising (Vietnamese, dấu sắc)	á	lá (leaf)
Falling (Vietnamese, dấu huyền)	à	là (to be)
Low falling-rising (Vietnamese, dấu hỏi)	ả	lả (weak)
High falling-rising broken by a glottal stop (Vietnamese, dấu ngã)	ã	lã (flow downward)
Low falling (Vietnamese, dấu nặng)	ạ	lạ (strange)

marks not only place but the political orientation to the Cold War division of Vietnam (A. H. Pham 2008:35).

Much of the dialectal variation can be traced to tone. In Vietnamese, tone is lexical, which means that every syllable must carry a tone. Standard Vietnamese orthography uses six diacritics to denote tone, thereby reinforcing the language's lexical quality: "One symbol represents one sound and one sound is represented by one symbol" (A. H. Pham 2008:22). The orthographic representations are represented as shown in table 15.1.

The Northern Vietnamese dialect has long been considered the standard dialect, in part because of how closely its sounds map onto orthography. The Red River Delta in northern Vietnam is popularly depicted as the birthplace of Vietnamese culture, so as Vietnamese rulers extended their domains to the southern regions, the Viet people mingled with other groups, thus transforming how Vietnamese was spoken in the central and southern regions. For example, the Southern dialect has only five of the six tones attested in the Northern Vietnamese dialect. Linguists, however, offer alternative explanations for the difference in tonal inventories. Some argue the contour tones in the Southern dialect have merged into a single tone (Kirby 2010), whereas others propose that the widespread claim of an underlying unity in Vietnamese tonal inventory may reflect social perceptions rather than the strategies listeners actually use to identify tones (Brunelle 2009:94). Speakers thus ascribe meanings to the Northern and Southern dialects that extend far beyond the tonal variations and differences in voice quality measured by linguists. Today in Vietnam, speakers are exposed to a national education system and the mass media, thereby narrowing the gaps among different dialects. However, among Vietnamese who fled the country after 1975, these dialectal and lexical variations are not simply markers of regional difference but signals of political preference.

Speakers of the Northern Vietnamese dialect are often presumed to be sympathetic with the present-day Socialist Republic of Vietnam, even though dialect variation has never neatly mapped onto political preferences even among

Vietnamese speakers in the United States. In Louisiana, the Northern dialect characterizes the phonetic patterning of older Vietnamese, many of whom lived in Catholic parishes in northern Vietnam and then fled south to the Republic of Vietnam in 1954 before evacuating the country in 1975. The vast majority of these early migrants were Catholic and retained their regional dialect, a pattern expressed in speakers using the Northern Vietnamese dialect in the Versailles neighborhood.

Tonal differences are not the only linguistic features presumed to signal political preferences. The lexicon of Vietnamese spoken today in the Socialist Republic of Vietnam has diverged from the Vietnamese spoken in the 1970s, above all in the southern region, as new words are added and old words die out. However, Vietnamese who left in 1975 tend to associate unfamiliar words used in current Vietnamese spoken in Vietnam as "communist" (A. H. Pham 2008:34–35). The political stakes of lexical variation became evident during community meetings with Vietnamese fisherfolk after the 2010 Deepwater Horizon oil spill. White fisherfolk initially accused Vietnamese refugees of overfishing (Starr 1981), but they have since been credited with revitalizing the industry. Nevertheless, differences in cultural meanings and linguistic access resurfaced during efforts to compensate fisherfolk after the oil spill. Many Vietnamese lacked the linguistic skills and documents needed to attest to their losses, especially as many people circulated their catches within the community in lieu of formal payment. Claims for compensation were eventually categorized as "subsistence use," a concept formulated in Alaska in the 1990s to ensure that native fishing communities received adequate compensation following the Exxon-Valdez oil spill (Esclamado 2011:32). Many Vietnamese fisherfolk regarded the BP-sponsored interpreters with suspicion because they used "communist terminology," as community activist Daniel Nguyen explained: "BP had people coming in from Vietnam who were using the wrong dialect, offensive dialects. There's post and pre-1975 language. With post-1975 language, you have a split, you have American-based Vietnamese and you have Vietnamese-based Vietnamese—and that's considered Communist Vietnamese, so they were using Communist terminology, which was really offensive to people here, who fled from the Communist regime" (Sullivan 2012).

The strained relationship between "American-based Vietnamese and Vietnamese-based Vietnamese" underscores how Vietnamese in Louisiana have forged a collective identity not only in the context of a host society in which the dominant language is English but also in their continued opposition to the contemporary Socialist Republic of Vietnam. Community members scrutinize materials for teaching Vietnamese, even children's books, for images and symbols deemed unacceptable, such as the flag of the Socialist Republic of Vietnam rather than the "Freedom and Heritage" flag (the yellow flag with three horizontal red stripes adopted by the Republic of Vietnam) preferred by many community leaders. Efforts to patrol language materials reflect more than just a "nostalgic melancholy for the unrealized, idealized pre-war educational and intellectual potential" (Lam 2006:10); such efforts also reflect the complicated linguistic landscape that interpreters and teachers must navigate. Even within the intimate spaces of the family, language variation can be contentious, as the elaborate system of terms of address makes evident.

TERMS OF ADDRESS AND COMPETING MODELS OF PERSONHOOD

The dilemmas facing immigrant communities like the Vietnamese include not only the acquisition of English by the immigrant or first generation but also the maintenance of the heritage language by the second and later generations. Dialect and lexical differences conjure up Cold War political divisions that animate Vietnamese communities in Louisiana, but shifts in the pragmatic dimensions of person reference in Vietnamese reveal how linguistic practices within diasporic communities collide with dominant language ideologies in the United States. Consequently, linguistic practices that encode solidarity and hierarchy take on heightened meaning in the face of American notions of personhood that valorize individualism and self-reliance.

Like other Southeast Asian languages, Vietnamese has a far more structurally elaborate system of reference than Indo-European languages. In English, speakers use *I*, a pronoun that designates but does not define the subject. Linguist Emile Benveniste developed a theory of personal pronouns called shifters in recognition of the fact that interlocutors may shift *I* and *you* depending on who is speaking. In French and German, speakers may index social relationships by selecting one of two words that correspond to the English second-person singular pronoun *you*, a distinction characterized as a binary opposition between a *T*-form (French *tu*, German *du*) and a *V*-form (French *vous*, German *sie*). The *T*-form indexes solidarity between the speaker and addressee as well as informality, while the *V*-form indexes distance, formality, or respect. As in English, however, the use of the pronouns is reciprocal: the speaker is always *I, je,* or *Ich*, and the addressee *you, tu/vous,* or *du/sie*.

In contrast, the Vietnamese model of address draws on family membership as the dominant model for determining person reference. For example, a mother calls herself *mẹ* (mother) and addresses her child as *con* (child), and her child responds by calling himself *con* and his mother *mẹ*. Unlike in English, these terms do not shift but rather designate the role and rank of the speaker and addressee. Anthropologist Hy Van Luong (1987:63) has called the importance of kinship terms an "organic unity model" because of how the terms structure social interactions that emphasize solidarity. However, the organic unity model is not the only available one. Other models allow speakers to convey parity or even challenge rank, but doing so requires speakers to "step outside the system" through their selection of address and self-reference forms (Sidnell and Shohet 2013). For example, historian David Marr (2000) has argued that *tôi* (I) became popularized during the colonial period as a way of translating *je*, the first-personal singular in French. Yet in American English, speakers who use the first-person singular *I* are not stepping outside the system but rather assenting to a system in which personhood emphasizes individualism and autonomy.

In contrast to dialectal and lexical variations that signal political preferences, terms of address convey moral orientations to the group or collective. When Vietnamese speakers address one another in English, they sometimes include nominal forms such as *chị* (older sister) or *anh* (older brother) or even terms such as *em* (young one) and *con* (child) when speaking to children, a pragmatic dimension that indexes recognition of the moral universe conveyed by the Vietnamese system even when the primary language of communication is English. Such strategies depend on mutual recognition of the speaker and addressee to accept this system and the premises of intersubjectivity that it conveys. Yet not every speaker accepts those premises, which chafe against models of personhood in broader society. Vietnamese speakers may avoid using terms of address, relying instead on proper names or even reverting to English pronouns such as *I* and *you*.

In this respect, personhood is also marked by naming practices. Vietnamese raised or born in the United States often take on Anglicized names, a strategy of accommodating the dominant role of English. This practice has antecedents in baptismal rituals in the Catholic Church where individuals are formally recognized as members who now require a name that is not "foreign to Christian sensibility," according to Canon 855 of the 1983 Code of Canon Law (Beal, Coriden, and Green 2000:1044–45). People commonly switch between names, using an American name deemed appropriate for public or civic engagement and a Vietnamese name that conveys belonging within the family. This practice is not limited to Catholics. Buddhists also undergo an initiation rite, "going for refuge," in which they vow to follow the five precepts and are then given a Buddhist or dharma name by the monastic presiding over the ceremony. People use their dharma name within the Buddhist community and their given name in other contexts, demonstrating a flexibility with naming practices.

Both terms of address and naming practices raise the question of how children enter into language and negotiate the diverse linguistic resources available to them. Linguistic variation is framed in part by Cold War politics in which Northern Vietnamese is not viewed as the standard but rather as a signal of political preference and, in the case of eastern New Orleans, the transplantation of Catholic communities not once but twice. Linguistic strategies of pronoun use and naming make evident how Vietnamese models of personhood differ substantially from mainstream American ones. Children tend to use English at school and when speaking not only to their peers but even their siblings, thus widening the gap between the language spoken at home with parents and grandparents and the language spoken in public spaces and with their peers. Consequently, the conditions for maintaining Vietnamese across generations are unstable. Religious organizations are important institutions that emphasize the role of heritage language. Vietnamese churches as well as Buddhist temples offer language classes for youth on Sunday. However, these classes cannot compete with a widely held view held among some Vietnamese families that English offers the surest route toward academic success and future economic stability. After Hurricane Katrina, the head pastor of Mary Queen of Vietnam spearheaded a charter school that offered Vietnamese-language instruction as a world language and was initially located on church grounds. Yet people hesitated to enroll their children over concerns about the school's academic quality and rigor. After four years, the charter school was taken over by a higher-performing charter school with a significant population of Vietnamese students but no dedicated language instruction or translation services.

VIETNAMESE ON LOUISIANA'S LINGUISTIC LANDSCAPE AND SOUNDSCAPE

Vietnamese and other minority languages draw attention to how language is an "ideological object invested with social and cultural interests" (Blommaert, Collins, and Slembrouck 2005: 199), not just a vehicle for meaning. While for Vietnamese in Louisiana, dialect and lexical variation as well as pragmatic features such as naming and terms of address make visible the fault lines within community formation, Vietnamese is made visible even to non-Vietnamese-speaking residents. Visual depictions of Vietnamese construct commercial zones as "ethnic" and make government services appear more accessible than they actually are.

Linguists have proposed that the presence of signage in the form of billboards, street names, and even brochures creates a linguistic landscape that heightens the visibility of minority languages (Landry and Bourhis 1997). Billboards along the Crescent City Connection, the bridge spanning the Mississippi River, advertise local casinos in Vietnamese language, especially leading up to the lunar new year (Tết), reminding drivers of Vietnamese economic power. Candidates running for political office and social welfare groups pass out brochures translated into Vietnamese at festivals held at Buddhist temples and Catholic churches. Even New Orleans parking meters list Vietnamese as a language choice. The inclusion of Vietnamese-language resources demonstrates awareness of Louisiana's linguistically diverse communities.

Not all these resources are intended for non-Vietnamese audiences. Vietnamese residents also produce their own materials, including a New Orleans-based Vietnamese-language radio show; two newspapers highlight Vietnamese-language services, obituaries, community-based announcements, and translations of stories of general interest. Since 1999, Radio Free Vietnam Louisiana has broadcast programs around the world and provided a vital resource by translating important public announcements regarding social services and recovery initiatives after Hurricane Katrina. *Sức Khỏe* (Health) is a magazine that focuses specifically on issues related to health care, targeting older Vietnamese with limited ability to access material in English. In Versailles, the signage on commercial buildings advertise services available in Vietnamese, such as insurance, banking, title companies, and auto showrooms where one or more employees speak Vietnamese. Across the Mississippi River lies the Hong Kong Market, a former Walmart building now housing a large Asian grocery store that offers an array of vegetables and fruit whose names are provided in Vietnamese and Chinese, underscoring how signs function "primarily as an index of ethnicity and for its purely aesthetic qualities rather than for its semantic content" (Berry and Henderson 2002:192). However, if the visibility of Vietnamese indexes purely "aesthetic qualities," or difference in a multicultural landscape, the use of speech is still contested, as the case of the Terrebonne commencement speech makes clear.

Commercial signage, radio programs, newspapers, and even collective spaces of worship are thus part of the linguistic resources of Vietnamese in Louisiana. Nevertheless, Vietnamese speakers living in Louisiana continue to struggle for their language access rights. Community-based organizations, often staffed by young Vietnamese Americans, provide vital resources for ensuring that the rights of Vietnamese speakers are recognized.

LANGUAGE RIGHTS

Since Hurricane Katrina, several community-based organizations, including the Mary Queen of Vietnam Community Development Corporation, the Vietnamese American Young Leaders Association, and Vietnamese Initiatives in Economic Training, have begun to raise awareness of the interests of Vietnamese-speaking residents. As the neighborhood and surrounding communities have undergone demographic shifts, these organizations have also adapted to address the needs of linguistically diverse constituents, including migrants from Central America. Language rights and language access have guided programming efforts and have not been limited to Vietnamese.

Federal laws recognize the rights of "limited English proficiency" residents, and in Southeastern Louisiana, the languages most spoken in addition to English are Vietnamese and Spanish. Nationwide, households identified as Vietnamese tend to have very high rates of a language other than English spoken at home. According to the 2007–9 American Community Survey, 87.5 percent of Vietnamese households speak a language other than English at home, a level surpassed only by Hmong households, although these data do not capture how many of the households are bilingual, with adults primarily speaking Vietnamese and children speaking English. In New Orleans, the Vietnamese American Young Leaders Association and the Asian American Legal Defense and Education Fund have addressed the problems facing bilingual households by filing a complaint based on Title VI of the Civil Rights Act, which bars discrimination by schools that receive federal money. The complaint alleged that the New Orleans public schools had failed to serve nonnative English-speaking families (Dreilinger 2013). In support of its complaint, the Young Leaders Association conducted a survey that showed a majority of Asian American and Latino respondents said that no adult at their school spoke their parents' native language and that three-quarters of parents were not offered interpreters for important school meetings.

The question of access and language rights goes beyond schooling to include citizens' basic right to participate in elections. In 1975, Congress amended the Voting Rights Act to require certain jurisdictions to provide bilingual materials and translation support. Because the laws vary from state to state, confusion arose in the 2012 General Election when a poll worker did not allow limited-English-proficient Vietnamese voters ballots in Vietnamese because that language was not a covered Section 203 language in the parish or state. Mary Queen of the Vietnam Community Development Corporation has been active in ensuring that Vietnamese residents receive such assistance, translating materials after both Hurricane Katrina and the Deepwater Horizon oil spill. In the spring of 2015, the US Centers for Disease Control formally opened a community-based clinic where clients could receive translation services as well as counseling in Vietnamese. How such activities will continue to shape the Vietnamese presence in southeastern Louisiana remains to be seen, but the struggle has spurred these organizations to fight for language access for minority-language speakers, even those who speak languages different from the ones on which the organizations focus. In addressing the audience in Vietnamese, Hue and Cindy Vo were not excluding members of the audience but rather fulfilling one of the promises enshrined in the Louisiana constitution.

NOTES

1. Another possible translation would be, "Looking up, I'm not equal to anyone; looking down, no one is equal to me." The expression conveys a sense of social hierarchy in its reminder to strive toward success as well as to be respectful and considerate of others.

WORKS CITED

Bankston, Carl L., III, and Min Zhou. 1996. "Go Fish: The Louisiana Vietnamese and Ethnic Entrepreneurship in an Extractive Industry." *National Journal of Sociology* 10 (1): 37–55.
Berry, Kate A., and Martha L. Henderson. 2002. *Geographical Identities of Ethnic America: Race, Space, and Place.* Reno: University of Nevada Press.
Beal, John P., James A. Coriden, and Thomas J. Green. 2000. *New Commentary on the Code of Canon Law.* New York: Paulist Press.
Blommaert, Jan, James Collins, and Stef Slembrouck. 2005. "Spaces of Multilingualism." *Language and Communication* 25 (3): 197–216.
Brunelle, Marc. 2009. "Tone Perception in Northern and Southern Vietnamese." *Journal of Phonetics* 37 (1): 79–96.
Dreilinger, Danielle. 2013. "New Orleans Public Schools Inadequate for Non-English Speakers, Critics Say." *New Orleans Times-Picayune*, August 1. https://www.nola.com/education/index .ssf/2013/08/groups_to_file_complaint_alleg.html.
Esclamado, Leo. 2011. "Ensuring Justice: Claiming Livelihood for Communities in the U.S. Gulf Coast after the BP Oil Spill Disaster." *Michigan Journal of Social Work and Social Welfare* 2(1): 24–38.
Kirby, James. 2010. "Dialect Experience in Vietnamese Tone Perception." *Journal of the Acoustical Society of America* 127 (6): 3749–57.
Lam, Mariam Becvi. 2006. "The Cultural Politics of Vietnamese Language Pedagogy." *Journal of Southeast Asian Language Teaching* 12 (2): 1–19.
Landry, Rodrigue, and Richard Bourhis. 1997. "Linguistic Landscape and Ethnolinguistic Vitality: An Empirical Study." *Journal of Language and Social Psychology* 16 (1): 23–49.
Luong, Hy V. 1987. "Plural Markers and Personal Pronouns in Vietnamese Person Reference: An Analysis of Pragmatic Ambiguity and Native Models." *Anthropological Linguistics* 29 (1): 49–70.
Marr, David G. 2000. "Concepts of 'Individual' and 'Self' in Twentieth-Century Vietnam." *Modern Asian Studies* 34 (4): 769–96.
Migration Policy Institute. 2016. *State Immigration Data Profiles.* https://www.migrationpolicy .org/data/state-profiles/state/demographics/LA.
Nguyen, Marguerite. 2015. "Vietnamese American New Orleans." *Minnesota Review* 84 (1): 114–28.
Pew Research Center. N.d. *Asian Americans: A Mosaic of Faiths.* http://www.pewforum.org/ 2012/07/19/asian-americans-a-mosaic-of-faiths-overview.
Pham, Andrea Hoa. 2004. *Vietnamese Tone: A New Analysis.* New York: Routledge.
Pham, Andrea Hoa. 2008. "The Non-Issue of Dialect in Teaching Vietnamese." *Journal of Southeast Asian Language Teaching* 14:22–39.

Pham, Andrew T. 2010. *The Returning Diaspora: Analyzing Overseas Vietnamese (Viet Kieu) Contributions toward Vietnam's Economic Growth.* https://ideas.repec.org/p/dpc/wpaper/2011.html.

Pleasant, Matthew. 2008. "Officials Consider English-Only Graduation Speeches." *Houma Today*, June 29. http://www.houmatoday.com/article/20080629/ARTICLES/80629032.

Starr, Paul D. 1981. "Troubled Waters: Vietnamese Fisherfolk on America's Gulf Coast." *International Migration Review* 15 (1–2): 226–38.

Sullivan, Zoe. 2012. "Law in Translation." http://www.lifeofthelaw.org/2012/10/podcast-culture-of-litigation/.

Trépanier, Cécyle. 1991. "The Cajunization of French Louisiana: Forging a Regional Identity." *Geographical Journal* 157 (2): 161–71.

VanLandingham, Mark. 2017. *Weathering Katrina: Culture and Recovery among Vietnamese Americans.* New York: Sage.

Zhou, Min, and Carl Bankston. 1998. *Growing Up American: How Vietnamese Children Adapt to Life in the United States.* New York: Sage.

CHAPTER 16

DIVERSE LINGUISTIC COMMUNITIES AND ENGLISH "FLUENCY" IN NEW ORLEANS

SHANE LIEF

Throughout the United States, people who speak languages of lesser diffusion, such as Arabic, Haitian Creole, or Yorùbá, must contend with xenophobic reactions to their speech varieties. In the city of New Orleans, such challenges have varied from relatively innocuous instances of misrecognition to cases of systematic discrimination. Between June and August 2015, I surveyed fifty anonymous people belonging to smaller linguistic communities, revealing a general pattern of interaction: the vast majority speak their home language on a daily basis, but most often only with their family and friends, sometimes with their neighbors, and almost never with the general surrounding population. This is hardly surprising, since many New Orleanians who are native English speakers—like other anglophones throughout the United States—are generally monolingual, and the chances that they might know, for example, more than a couple of phrases in Arabic, are minuscule. Many interactions with nonspeakers seem to be positive: even if lesser-known languages are not shared or recognized by monolingual English speakers, their usage is often greeted with friendly curiosity in personal encounters between individuals. By and large, these English-speaking New Orleanians are described as reacting "positively" to different languages, finding the newly encountered speech to be intriguingly "authentic." At the same time, however, some curious New Orleanians were reported to have a habit of looking at people speaking other languages as if they were "not normal."

Throughout New Orleans history, these linguistic communities have been documented only sporadically. Efforts have included surveys of libraries in Louisiana (Riquelmy 1994) and discussions of immigrant communities throughout the state (Owens and Green 2012), without offering much specific data on individual languages. However, recent Census data on smaller language groups offer a more precise picture of the current situation in New Orleans. Moreover, members of these communities are defined not only by the languages they speak but also by the degrees of English fluency they are perceived as possessing. They must navigate an unpredictable territory of language ideology (Haviland 2003) in a city with a rich and varied cultural history that, ironically, has been mostly celebrated in English, even if spiced up every now and then with a French or Spanish phrase.

LANGUAGE DATA

The results of the American Community Survey conducted by the US Census Bureau provide a snapshot of these linguistic communities in the New Orleans greater metropolitan area. This information is based on data collected from 2009 to 2013 and represents the "most comprehensive data ever released from the Census Bureau on languages spoken less widely in the United States" (US Census Bureau 2015a). According to the Detailed Language Tables for Core-Based Statistical Areas, out of the combined population of 1,130,973 in New Orleans and suburban Metairie, 1,005,347 people speak only English at home, while 125,626 speak a language other than English (US Census Bureau 2015b). Table 16.1 shows the number of speakers for many less widely spoken languages.

The Census data leave some important questions unanswered. For example, although more than 125,000 people have a home language that is not English, the data do not indicate how many are bilingual in English (or another language) and how many are monolingual in their reported language. Also, some languages are unspecified or underspecified ("Other Native North American languages"), and others are sometimes grouped according to geographical or political criteria rather than strictly linguistic criteria ("Kru, Ibo, Yoruba"; "African"). Most egregiously, wherever the term *Indian* is used, "it cannot be determined if the respondent spoke a Native American language or spoke a language from India" (US Census Bureau 2015b). Nonetheless, the Census information provides an overview of New Orleans's diverse linguistic communities.

Just over one-tenth of the population (11.1 percent) speaks languages other than English at home, a lower number than is found in any of the fifteen largest US metro areas. The three major US cities with the highest such percentages are Los Angeles (54 percent), Miami (51 percent), and San Francisco (40 percent) (US Census Bureau 2015a). Fewer than a hundred languages are spoken in New Orleans, whereas many other US cities have much greater linguistic diversity: the New York metro area, for example, has almost two hundred languages (table 16.2).

Table 16.1. Languages Spoken at Home and Ability to Speak English, Population Five Years and Over, New Orleans and Metairie, Louisiana, 2009–2013

Language	Number of Speakers	Margin of Error	Self-Reported Population Speaking English Less Than "Very Well"	Margin of Error
All languages	1,130,973	194	52,888	1,930
Speak only English at home	1,005,347	2,367	—	—
Speak a language other than English at home	125,626	2,379	52,888	1,930
Spanish	72,350	1,541	33,650	1,379
Vietnamese	15,640	832	8,354	724
French (including Patois, Cajun)	10,563	797	1,933	320
French	9,850	730	1,845	327
Chinese (including Cantonese, Mandarin, other Chinese languages)	3,826	608	1,915	451
Chinese	3,355	569	1,735	452
Arabic	3,280	955	710	307
Portuguese	1,910	548	915	408
Tagalog	1,600	357	446	164
German	1,500	214	200	79
Urdu	1,217	487	578	250
Italian	1,021	203	227	108
Korean	962	343	586	248
Russian	768	262	259	161
Japanese	763	225	360	153
Hindi	679	245	55	46
Croatian	560	367	180	139
Persian	509	258	102	77
Gujarati	503	235	132	87
Bengali	490	279	170	181
Kru, Ibo, Yoruba	340	127	35	34
Greek	339	137	74	48
Telugu	315	160	a	a
Amharic	295	179	115	99
Indonesian	280	198	155	170

Language	Number of Speakers	Margin of Error	Self-Reported Population Speaking English Less Than "Very Well"	Margin of Error
Polish	257	112	56	49
Mandarin	240	106	85	55
Turkish	235	149	130	132
Dutch	220	128	b	—
Thai	209	123	63	60
Hebrew	209	102	56	66
Laotian	198	178	168	154
Mon-Khmer, Cambodian	196	122	128	79
Norwegian	175	111	40	36
Marathi	175	171	b	—
Swahili	160	80	a	a
Hungarian	137	121	38	35
Formosan	130	110	75	65
Other and unspecified languages	125	64	34	33
Czech	120	95	a	a
Panjabi	115	107	a	a
Tamil	115	64	a	a
Cushite	110	126	65	66
Cantonese	105	63	a	a
Serbo-Croatian	95	73	35	39
Bulgarian	90	67	a	a
Danish	80	63	a	a
Romanian	75	46	a	a
Hmong	67	87	9	14
Lithuanian	65	89	a	a
Bantu	65	39	30	31
African	60	48	a	a
Jamaican Creole	55	39	a	a
Kannada	55	48	b	—
Malay	55	58	a	a
Sebuano	55	58	a	a
Chamorro	50	61	b	—

Yiddish	43	48	2	5
Malayalam	40	41	a	a
Armenian	37	62	10	18
Other Native North American languages	37	44	b	—
Berber	35	44	a	a
Serbian	30	38	a	a
Ukrainian	30	40	b	—
Nepali	30	28	b	—
Sinhalese	30	33	20	28
Navajo	28	48	b	—
Swedish	25	31	b	—

a Data withheld to avoid disclosure.
b Either too few or no sample observations were available to compute an estimate.
The margin of error can be interpreted roughly as providing a 90 percent probability that the interval defined by the estimate minus the margin of error and the estimate plus the margin of error (the lower and upper confidence bounds) contains the true value.
The category *Indian* as well as several aggregate estimates and other less useful entries have been omitted.
Source: US Census Bureau 2015b

Table 16.2. Number of Languages Spoken in Fifteen Largest US Metro Areas, 2009–2013

Metropolitan Area	Number of Languages Spoken at Home
New York	192
Los Angeles	185
Washington, DC	168
Seattle	166
San Francisco	163
Phoenix	163
Dallas	156
Chicago	153
Philadelphia	146
Atlanta	146
Houston	145
Riverside, California	145
Boston	138
Miami	128
Detroit	126
Source: US Census Bureau 2015a	

The pattern of European language groups in New Orleans resembles a miniature sketch of the city's conventional historical narrative. The continuing presence of substantial francophone and hispanophone communities can be seen as emblematic of the earlier colonial regimes of France and Spain, but the current populations are mostly descended from people who came to Louisiana after it became a part of the United States in the early nineteenth century. The substantial Portuguese-speaking community shows recent trends in the city's shifting demographics as an increasing number of Brazilians have made New Orleans their home throughout the past century. The next two highest populations of speakers of European languages, German and Italian, echo the historical presence of these linguistic communities in New Orleans: a substantial wave of immigrants from German-speaking Europe fled political turbulence in 1848, while many Italian speakers came to New Orleans during the last two decades of the nineteenth century and the first decade of the twentieth century (Merrill 2005; Gauthreaux 2014). The institutional remnants of these historic communities, such as the Deutsches Haus on the outskirts of New Orleans (which represents the "German Presence in the Gulf South" [http://deutscheshaus.org/]) and the American Italian Cultural Center downtown, serve as important cultural symbols for speakers of these languages, whether they are visitors or permanent residents of the city. The relatively high percentage of these groups in New Orleans goes against the grain national trends: both German and Italian were spoken by fewer US individuals in 2011 than in 1980, with Italian having a "net decline of about 900,000" during that period (Ryan 2013:5).

New Orleans currently has relatively high proportions of Vietnamese and Arabic speakers. Both languages were among the ten fastest-growing languages nationwide between 2000 and 2011 (Ryan 2013:8), yet Chinese remains the country's third-largest language group, trailing English and Spanish. In New Orleans, however, Vietnamese ranks third. As the fifth-largest language group in New Orleans, the Arabic-speaking community comprises at least 2.6 percent of the population that speaks another language besides English at home. The vast majority (more than 75 percent) of the smaller language communities have fewer than a thousand speakers.

It is a perennial challenge to get accurate information about smaller linguistic communities, especially when these groups face economic and political difficulties and are understandably wary of official attempts to track and tabulate their existence.

MUNICIPAL INSTITUTIONS

When it comes to key institutions and social organizations in the city of New Orleans, the language gap can involve substantial hardship for people who speak languages of lesser diffusion. As might be expected for any major metropolitan area, translation and interpretation services have been incorporated into the city's hospital infrastructure. Most local medical institutions, such as Ochsner Medical Center, have an "international department" or an equivalent service that helps patients and their families communicate their needs to health care providers. At the other end of the spectrum, only in the decade since Katrina has the local prison system engaged the services of much-needed interpreters, mostly through the public defender's office, which has a very small staff: as of 2015, the office had only one or two Spanish interpreters available on any given day to serve the entire Orleans Parish prison population. Members of smaller linguistic communities have even less hope of communicating with authorities. In 2013, one monolingual Polish speaker languished behind bars for several days before someone could be found to interpret for him. As of 2015, the ballooning incarceration industry had not yet availed itself of services such as the Language Access Network, which provides video remote interpretation to health care facilities in the area. Caught in the city's jails, people who speak languages of lesser diffusion find their voices are imprisoned along with their bodies.

Somewhere in the middle of the range of such city institutions and their structural responses to multilingualism stands New Orleans's Taxicab and For Hire Vehicles Bureau. The city's taxicabs represent a challenging context for people who speak languages of lesser diffusion. In particular, taxicab drivers from different countries must navigate a dynamic social landscape including both local residents and a continuous flow of international visitors who flood New Orleans for the city's many festivals. The issue of English-language proficiency among taxicab drivers erupted into a legal controversy in 2011, as the question of English fluency became conflated with general concerns about a transportation system seen as dirty and dangerous. A moral panic over this particular form of transportation turned a very familiar occurrence—hailing a taxi with a driver whose native language was not English—into an experience perceived as fraught with peril, offering a useful path for exploring the widespread anglophone fear of other languages and the difficulties awaiting those who speak languages of lesser diffusion in New Orleans.

In English-speaking communities throughout the United States, language is often seen as a "neutral" vehicle for communication, a mere "instrument of denotation" (Silverstein 1996:287). It is likewise commonly assumed that language policies can be generated according to "objective" criteria, with the idea that all people who come within the purview of these laws can simply comply with the proposed boundaries of linguistic behavior as long as they have the ability to tailor their speech habits accordingly and possess the correct civic spirit. In this view, languages are merely "linguistic tools, like hammers or pliers, [and] can be picked up, without undue effort, by all responsible citizens" (Haviland 2003:766). Language use is thus treated as a matter of conscious will and legal responsibility. A set of language standards can then serve a political function, acting as a raw means of exerting cultural hegemony hidden behind a legal jargon that denies historical and cultural contexts.

CASE STUDY: THE LINGUISTIC IDEOLOGY OF TAXICAB SERVICES

During the summer of 2011, after a series of reported corruption and bribery scandals at the New Orleans Ground Transportation Bureau (previously known as the Taxicab Bureau), reformers made a renewed push to clean up the industry. Emulating other cities that had already enshrined certain protections for taxicab customers into legal codes, the New Orleans City Council began to draft a Passengers' Bill of Rights, including certain linguistic stipulations. By late September, the language policy component had become more specific: taxicab drivers would be required to speak fluent English. Over the next three months, the legislative process took various twists and turns as a consequence of several factors, including the economic motivations of the Convention and Visitors Bureau, which oversees New Orleans's vast tourist industry and has much invested in the city's marketing image; a municipal government that constantly focuses on maintaining a positive image in the eyes of its citizens; various linguistic communities that expressed solidarity against a nationwide tide of anti-immigrant sentiments encoded in laws that discriminate against those who speak languages other than English; the taxi drivers themselves; and the ill-defined but powerful undercurrent of xenophobia felt by some native New Orleanians, whose pride in hosting visitors from other countries is often contradicted by fear of "strange" people and cultures.

As the architects of the taxicab language policy and their allied linguistic engineers wrangled over how to implement the English requirement, few official documents described the proposed law. In fact, the absence of official language during the law's embryonic stages provided a space for public prejudice to run riot. Instead of representing an objective framework for social interaction, language policy functioned as a projection screen for a broad range of unarticulated anxieties: fear of the physical proximity of strangers, fear of cultural loss, and general fears of uncertainty. The debate revolving around the "cleanup" of the taxicab industry in New Orleans also revealed the close connection between languages of lesser diffusion and perceptions of English fluency.

In early June 2011, the *New Orleans Times-Picayune* had reported a number of problems regarding taxicab services in New Orleans (Simerman 2011a). Not only had an inspector for the Ground Transportation Bureau been indicted for bribery and filing false records, but a major federal investigation was also underway involving a taxi driver who had been accused of rape. The driver had retained his taxi license even "after several arrests, including a highway shooting in 2007 that resulted in four attempted-manslaughter charges in St. Charles Parish, for allegedly shooting through his cab window at an SUV with two adults and two children inside" (Simerman 2011a). In response to this and other reported problems, Mayor Mitch Landrieu hired Malachi Hull to serve as deputy director of the Department of Safety and Permits for Ground Transportation and charged him with "overhaul[ing] the agency's operations and its oversight of taxis, pedicabs, for-hire vehicles and carriages" (Carr 2011).

During the course of the summer, City Hall felt pressure to revamp "an agency with a long reputation for corruption" (Simerman 2011b). By late August, it was clear that large-scale changes were being considered: new rules initiated by city council member Kristin Gisleson Palmer would ensure that "taxi passengers for the first time would be protected by a 'bill of rights' guaranteeing them a clean and 'noise-free' vehicle, as well as a driver who knows the street grid, speaks good English and doesn't use a cellphone while driving" (Krupa 2011). In mid-July, an amended ordinance (Gisleson Palmer, Clarkson, and Guidry 2011) stated that taxicab passengers should be provided with a "passengers' rights notice which specifies the rights of passengers in for-hire vehicles," including a "driver who speaks and understands English." By the beginning of September, this text had been modified to declare that "applicants for certificates of public necessity and convenience and for-hire vehicle driver's permits are required to fluently speak English" (Gisleson Palmer and Guidry 2011).

On September 24, 2011, the *Times-Picayune* described the "continuing push by the Landrieu administration and the council to clean up the city's oft-derided taxi industry," drawing a parallel between language use, cleanliness, and criminality (Eggler 2011a). Noting that a "sizeable proportion of New Orleans' cab drivers now come from Middle Eastern countries, with others coming from Latin America or other nations where English is not the principal language," the article reported that Gisleson Palmer had "heard stories of drivers whose English is so limited that they cannot understand passengers' instructions about where they want to go": "drivers hand passengers cellphones so they can give their destination to an English speaker, who then translates the information into the driver's native language," reinforcing the notion that speech simply constituted an "instrument of denotation" (Eggler 2011a). However, given that the new law did not specify criteria for determining fluency, there were no safeguards to prevent the language policy from serving as an ad hoc device for denying applications based on other reasons.

Gisleson Palmer's legislative director told me in a December 2011 interview that the Taxicab Passengers' Bill of Rights was part of a series of legislative reforms pushed by the hospitality industry, several of whose members had complained that taxicabs did not have a good reputation and that problems were "systemic." Two members of the Taxicab and For Hire Vehicles Bureau had been fired the previous year as a consequence of "lots of corruption"—several ongoing investigations, including one by the FBI. Since taxicabs are an "important component of New Orleans' multibillion-dollar tourist industry" (Eggler 2011b), the New Orleans Convention and Visitors Bureau was asking for higher standards. In response, Gisleson Palmer's office began working on new standards based on the needs of New Orleans and "best practices of other cities," taking the legislation's text was "from other cities who have Passenger Rights such as New York City, Los Angeles, Miami–Dade County, Palm Springs, and Indianapolis." However, finding the original wording, which stated that "applicants for [Certificates of Public Necessity and Convenience] or driver's permits must be 18 years of age and must be able to read and write English," to be "very vague" and seeking to put some kind of "threshold in place," Gisleson Palmer's office added *fluently speak*.

The Hispanic Chamber of Commerce and the Vietnamese American Young Leaders Association of New Orleans later contacted Gisleson Palmer's office seeking to have those two words removed. Representatives of these groups had attended an October 14 public hearing on the legislation, and such language raised a "red flag" for them. The wording was reminiscent of contemporaneous laws being passed in other parts of the country, such as English-language initiatives targeting immigrants in Alabama (see Picone 2018) and Arizona. Given that the text of New Orleans's proposed law had been drawn from other municipal laws, this fear of succumbing to a national pattern of linguistic xenophobia was well founded.

According to Cyndi Nguyen (2011), executive director of the Vietnamese Initiatives in Economic Training, the proposed legislation sent shock waves throughout the minority communities of New Orleans. Nguyen had immediately viewed the measure as an attack not just on the "Vietnamese-speaking community" but also on all people who did not speak English as their first language—"Arabic individuals, Mexican individuals: "This is about limited-English-fluency communities." Gisleson Palmer and her staff were "very upset" to learn that the legislation was perceived as threatening, and they removed *fluently speak* was removed from the text. The ordinance currently includes a "Passengers' Rights Notice" stating merely that passengers are entitled to a "driver who speaks and understands English and is knowledgeable of the metropolitan area" ("Passengers' Rights" 2018).

But while language-minority communities had one fear, native speakers of English had another. In December 2011, I interviewed "Kelley," owner and operator of a taxi repair shop founded by his family decades earlier. The shop still bore evidence of the three feet of floodwaters that had inundated the shop in the wake of Hurricane Katrina.

Kelley launched into a seamless personal account of forty years of New Orleans taxicab history that incorporated both myths regarding a "golden age" (i.e., things were better in the good old days) and evidence of upward progress (i.e., the last vestiges of corruption are being eliminated). He equated English fluency with plans to "clean up the industry"—non-English-speaking drivers had been a "downside" and the past two municipal administrations had "dropped standards." Kelley also argued that a great divide existed between responsible, "more Americanized" cab companies, which are "bred on locals" and have drivers who know street names and take their passengers to "clubs and neighborhoods," and "nonradio" companies that shuttle passengers back and forth between hotels and the airport and that have drivers who do not know the city at all and cannot speak English. According to Kelley, one woman caught a cab at the airport but soon discovered that the driver could not understand anything she was saying. He handed her a cell phone so she could talk to one of his family members, and then she handed the phone back to the driver, so that the directions could be explained to him in his own language. (This anecdote also appeared in the *Times-Picayune* on September 24, 2011 [Eggler 2011a].)

Kelley also told a story about the "Haitian mafia": when a Haitian cab driver friend who speaks with a "thick French accent" hailed a cab on Canal Street and asked for a ride to Kelley's shop, the driver refused. When the friend insisted on his right to be driven to his destination, the driver got out of the car, baseball bat in hand, and yanked the man out of the back. The driver of the next vehicle in line at the taxi stand, also a Haitian, then issued a veiled threat: "You know they call this the Big Easy—sometimes people just disappear." The circulation of many such stories among both anglophone and francophone New Orleanians reinforces a menacing stereotype that has developed during the two centuries since the Haitian Revolution.

On the one hand, Kelley talked about progress in the form of improved standards and technological innovations such as the "digital dispatch," which eliminates the need for a human dispatcher who might play favorites among drivers. In this area, Kelley's narrative emphasized the idea that the old system was bad and the new one was good. On the other, however, Kelley's discussion of immigrant taxi drivers reverted to invoking the "golden age." For many years, the business had just been "black and white," and "everyone was very nice." But when foreigners entered the business, they brought "arrogancy" and were always "bartering the prices." Kelley, in contrast, had always had "straight prices."

Kelley directly addressed the issue of language, implying that language use was simply a matter of choice—"They think that's cool, speaking different languages."—before turning to fears of physical danger, which he termed "the safety thing." He sketched a scenario where cabs were hurtling down I-10 at around seventy miles per hour, with the drivers "gibberishing in a different language" and the passengers afraid for their lives. He told the story in the past tense, as though it had already happened, yet made it plural, generalizing the pseudo-anecdote, with *they* clearly referring to foreign-born cab drivers and the English-speaking passengers positioned as terrified captives who must survive the experience of another language.

While all potential passengers share the desire to communicate effectively with the driver and municipal authorities are bound legally and ethically to oversee services that impact the public, language policy can also be driven by fears that have little direct relation to the taxicab service. Taxicab drivers as well as passengers would be most affected by the new legislation, and the drivers seemed to have little confidence that the process would be fair. Like many other drivers I interviewed, a native Nigerian whose original language was Kalabari invoked physical safety in discussing the issue: he understood that the "service industry" needed to be "organized," but "we must remember those who need a job—humanity—cabbies who put their life on the line" in dealing with the public. Moreover, having strict language policies in place doesn't "fit the New Orleans tradition," which is characterized by "gumbonism" [sic]—a welcome blend of cultures.

This vaunted New Orleans quality is rife with paradox. While most residents like to believe that their city is entertaining and "exotic" for outsiders, many locals also fear "outsiders." Such anxieties surface within a context of sanitized interaction—that is, people are increasingly accustomed to associating with others only by choice. As many services have become automated and depersonalized (e.g., online shopping), face-to-face personal interaction has diminished. Public space keeps contracting, and with social media acting as an accelerant, fewer physical encounters between strangers occur. Given these conditions, many people might experience a heightened phobia of unplanned interactions with individuals from different cultures. The cab ride can be seen as a blast from the interactive past, where a person must negotiate geography with a stranger and spend at least several minutes in physical proximity. An encounter with a stranger causes a spike in the awareness of linguistic traits, which are immediately associated with the experience. Fear of the unknown thus quickly becomes attached to a strange accent. Responding to questions about language fluency, Kelley quickly focused on the passengers' possible physical danger. According to his view, if language is indeed "the road map of experience" (Silverstein 1996:292), a foreign language threatens to drive us over the guardrails, while English will keep us from plunging off the I-10 overpass.

This attitude toward other languages can be called "linguistic paranoia," a state of mind in which "speaking a language other than English is taken as inherently insulting or threatening" (Haviland 2003:764). This linguistic paranoia collects in the catch basin of urban legends as expressed by the taxicab meter specialist or Gisleson Palmer, who tell the same anecdote about cell phone interpreters. In turn, this anxiety dovetails with the fearmongering that reached a fever pitch in another *Times-Picayune* article about the experience of riding in taxicabs in New Orleans (Krupa 2011):

> Whenever she climbs into a taxi, Catherine Hunter imagines what it would be like if she weren't from New Orleans. Usually, she's horrified. From broken seat belts and busted air-conditioning units to drivers who don't know their way around town, Hunter, a recruiter for Tulane University's Freeman School of Business, can't help but fear that the for-hire rides her prospective students get around town reflect poorly on the city—and the institution— she's trying to sell.
>
> "It's an embarrassment," Hunter said. "It's not clean and it's not cute and it's not old-world patina or charm. I just don't understand why these blighted cabs, which at the very least create a bad impression and at the very worst endanger our visitors, are allowed to continue."

There is a power in accumulated anecdotes, the litany of proverbial taxicab horror stories, sometimes experienced directly by the storyteller, other times passed through many minds, and in most cases embellished for dramatic effect. In this context, "fluency" often bears no relation to taxicab service but instead combines fear of other cultures and fear of physical danger.

To their credit, Gisleson Palmer and her staff removed the term *fluently* from the law and were responsive to community needs. However, according to Nguyen, official institutions are often slow to perceive such needs. Speaking to power—specifically, power as embodied in people who act as official representatives of city services and institutions—takes energy and time. Doing so can be challenging for native speakers of English, let alone anyone speaking a nonstandard variety of English. As Nguyen (2011) indicated, people also find themselves defined by exclusion and belong to "limited-English-fluency communities."

In the summer of 2014, several years after hiring Hull to "clean up" the taxicab industry, Mayor Landrieu fired him after a number of scandals: one taxicab inspector had pepper-sprayed and handcuffed a cab driver, while another inspector had physically assaulted a French Quarter tour guide (Eggler 2014). In addition, the taxicab industry has faced new competitive pressures from transportation alternatives such as Uber Black, a "premium luxury car service" that began operating in New Orleans in 2014. In April 2015, the mayor signed an ordinance "setting out regulations for Uber and other ride-hailing services" (Adelson 2015). Taxi drivers joined the taxi companies in fighting the ordinance, "arguing that they are being held to higher—and costlier—standards than the new services looking to enter the market" (Adelson 2015). Now that private corporations have entered the fray, the battle over passengers' right to English fluency has almost become moot. Uber has opened the floodgates to the taxi labor pool, bringing in many native English speakers using their own cars as cabs and crowding out dozens of taxicab drivers who do not speak English as their first language.

Ironically, while the city council and the Convention and Visitors Bureau worried about public perceptions of New Orleans, the taxi driver from Nigeria who stood at the receiving end of the shifting language policy pointed out that cultural diversity—the "gumbonism" of New Orleans—constitutes the substance behind the image they seek to create. This business-based fear of risk parallels the fear of chance encounters with a foreign language and culture. In an atmosphere of linguistic paranoia where New Orleanians fearfully perceive people who speak other languages as dangerous xenophones—sources of strange sounds—English fluency is invoked as an objective metric of reliability and protection for law-abiding citizens and businesses, even though language is not simply a denotational instrument and the definition of *fluency* is notoriously fluid.

Because New Orleans is not quite as multilingual as other US cities, people belonging to smaller linguistic communities must grapple with a "standard language ideology" that presupposes not only the use of English in public contexts but also the widespread preference for a neutral, idealized version of that language. To the extent that people deviate from this abstract ideal of communication, they might find themselves "cut off from the everyday privileges and rights of citizenship" (Lippi-Green 2012:71). As the debate over taxicab drivers' fluency in English shows, this ideology plays a decisive role in shaping public discourse and hence public policy.

More insidiously, language ideology shapes our collective understanding of the city itself: for almost three centuries, the story of New Orleans has mainly been told in French, Spanish, and English. Just as colonial historians (Usner 2006) have realized the need to pay attention to smaller indigenous groups who lived in the vicinity of early New Orleans and who played such a key role in sustaining the settlement through its first fragile decades, we must put extra effort into acknowledging the smaller linguistic communities that contribute to the life of the city today. By remembering this multilingual reality, we can recover a sense of the Choctaw name for New Orleans, Balbancha—the place where different languages are spoken. Doing so would not only lead to a more accurate idea of what New Orleans sounds like but also instantiate the image of the welcoming spirit cultivated by many New Orleanians.

WORKS CITED

Adelson, Jeff. 2015. "Mayor Signs Ride-Hailing Law, and Uber Says It Will Soon Enter New Orleans Market." *New Orleans Advocate*, April 15. http://www.theadvocate.com/new_orleans/news/politics/article_559d4a15-36d3-5c9b-8db2-55f813e12a01.html.

Carr, Martha. 2011. "New Orleans Taxicab Bureau's New Leader Was Taxi Director for Atlanta Police." *New Orleans Times-Picayune*, June 7. http://www.nola.com/politics/index.ssf/2011/06/mitch_landrieu_names_new_taxic.html.

Eggler, Bruce. 2011a. "Cab Drivers Now Required to Fluently Speak English." *New Orleans Times-Picayune*, September 24. http://www.nola.com/politics/index.ssf/2011/09/new_orleans_taxicab_drivers_no.html.

Eggler, Bruce. 2011b. "Taxi Access for People with Disabilities Addressed by New Orleans City Council." *New Orleans Times-Picayune*, November 5. http://www.nola.com/politics/index.ssf/2011/11/taxi_access_for_people_with_di.html.

Eggler, Bruce. 2014. "Malachi Hull Dismissed as Taxicab Bureau Director." *New Orleans Advocate*, July 4. http://www.theadvocate.com/new_orleans/news/politics/article_3307297a-c4a8-5382-bd73-7e7e83f2e2dc.html.

Gauthreaux, Alan G. *Italian Louisiana: History, Heritage, and Tradition*. Charleston, SC: History Press.

Gisleson Palmer, Kristin, Jackie Clarkson, and Susan Guidry. 2011. "An Ordinance to Amend and Re-Ordain Article V of Chapter 162 of the Code of the City of New Orleans." Calendar no. 58,590, no. 24563, Mayor Council Series, July 21. https://library.municode.com/la/new_orleans/munidocs/ordinance_documents?nodeId=0102420110RDINANCESPDF.

Gisleson Palmer, Kristin, and Susan Guidry. 2011. "An Ordinance to Amend and Re-Ordain Section 162-182 of the Code of the City of New Orleans." Calendar no. 28,651, no. 24596, Mayor Council Series, September 1. https://library.municode.com/la/new_orleans/munidocs/ordinance_documents?nodeId=0102420110RDINANCESPDF.

Haviland, John B. 2003. "Ideologies of Language: Some Reflections on Language and U.S. Law." *American Anthropologist* 205 (4): 764–74.

Krupa, Michelle. 2011. "Taxi Service in New Orleans May Get Major Overhaul." *New Orleans Times-Picayune*, August 28. http://www.nola.com/politics/index.ssf/2011/08/taxi_service_in_new_orleans_ma.html.

Lippi-Green, Rosina. 2012. *English with an Accent: Language, Ideology, and Discrimination in the United States*. 2nd ed. New York: Routledge.

Merrill, Ellen C. 2005. *Germans of Louisiana*. Gretna, LA: Pelican.

Nguyen, Cyndi. 2011. Telephone interview by author, December 14. Owens, Maida, and Laura Marcus Green. 2012. "The Many Faces of the Bayou State: New Populations in Louisiana." http://www.louisianafolklife.org/LT/Articles_Essays/newpops.html.

"Passengers' Rights Notice." 2018. *Code of Ordinances, City of New Orleans, Louisiana*. Codified through Ordinance No. 27704, adopted March 8 (Supp. No. 84, Update 1). https://library.municode.com/la/new_orleans/codes/code_of_ordinances?nodeId=PTIICO_CH162VEHI_ARTVDRRE_S162-455PARINO.

Picone, Michael D. 2018. "Multilingual Alabama." In *Language in Alabama: History, Diversity, Function, and Change*, edited by Thomas E. Nunnally, 18–49. Tuscaloosa: University of Alabama Press.

Riquelmy, Christina. 1994. "Louisiana Libraries and Ethnic-Group Documentation." *LLA Bulletin* 57 (1): 52–61.

Ryan, Camile. 2013. "Language Use in the United States: 2011." https://www.census.gov/prod/2013pubs/acs-22.pdf.

Silverstein, Michael. 1996. "Monoglot 'Standard' in America: Standardization and Metaphors of Linguistic Hegemony." In *The Matrix of Language: Contemporary Linguistic Anthropology*, edited by Donald Brenneis and Ronald K. S. Macaulay, 284–306. Boulder, CO: Westview.

Simerman, John. 2011a. "Federal Investigators Are Looking at New Orleans Taxicab Bureau." *New Orleans Times-Picayune*, June 2. http://www.nola.com/crime/index.ssf/2011/06/federal_investigators_are_look.html.

Simerman, John. 2011b. "New Orleans Taxicab Bureau Investigator Suspended." *New Orleans Times-Picayune*, June 16. http://www.nola.com/politics/index.ssf/2011/06/new_orleans_taxicab_bureau_inv.html.

US Census Bureau. 2015a. "Census Bureau Reports at Least 350 Languages Spoken in U.S. Homes." ReleaseCB15-185. November 3. https://www.census.gov/newsroom/press-releases/2015/cb15-185.html.

US Census Bureau. 2015b. "Detailed Languages Spoken at Home and Ability to Speak English for the Population 5 Years and Over: 2009–2013." October. https://www.census.gov/data/tables/2013/demo/2009-2013-lang-tables.html.

Usner, Daniel H., Jr. 2006. "American Indians in Colonial New Orleans." In *Powhatan's Mantle: Indians in the Colonial Southeast*, rev. ed., edited by Gregory A. Waselkov, Peter H. Wood, and Tom Hatley, 163–86. Lincoln: University of Nebraska Press.

ABOUT THE CONTRIBUTORS

LISA ABNEY serves as a professor of English at Northwestern State University in Natchitoches, Louisiana. She is the principal investigator for the Linguistic Survey of North Louisiana and conducts research in the ways that language, folk culture, and literature of the American South intersect and interact. She has coedited two collections of essays about Louisiana writers; coedited a volume of the *Dictionary of Literary Biography*, *Twenty-First Century American Novelists* (Farmington Hills, MI: Thomson/Gale, 2004); and served as an editor of *Voices of the American South* (New York: Pearson/Longman, 2004).

PATRICIA ANDERSON holds a doctorate in anthropology from Tulane University. She has been a member of the Kuhpani Yoyani Luhchi Yoroni (Tunica Language Working Group) since 2011. She is the creator of the Tunica Dictionary app and online dictionary and has co-produced Tunica materials such as the Tunica Language Textbook and a Tunica children's book.

ALBERT CAMP is the coordinator of English as a Second Language studies and an instructor in the Interdepartmental Program in Linguistics at Louisiana State University. His dissertation, "L'Essentiel ou Lagniappe: The Ideology of French Revitalization in Louisiana," focuses on efforts to revitalize French through the state's public school systems.

KATIE CARMICHAEL is an assistant professor of English linguistics at Virginia Tech. Her research focuses on sociolinguistic variation in dialects of French and English found in Louisiana.

CHRISTINA SCHOUX CASEY is an assistant professor of English linguistics in the Department of Culture and Global Studies at Aalborg University. Her research weaves together linguistic and discourse analysis with work in anthropology and humanistic geography and theories of reproduction from critical sociology and philosophy. She edited a special edition of the *Southern Journal of Linguistics* focusing on New Orleans (2012), and her work has appeared in *American Speech*, the *Journal of Language and Sexuality*, and *Gender and Language*.

NATHALIE DAJKO is an assistant professor of anthropology at Tulane University. She has published in the *Journal of Linguistic Anthropology*, *Language in Society*, and several edited volumes, in both French and English.

JEFFERY U. DARENSBOURG is a tribal council member and head of the Alligator Band, Atakapa-Ishak Nation of Southwest Louisiana and Southeast Texas. He holds a doctorate in cognitive science from the University of Louisiana at Lafayette.

DORIAN DORADO is assistant professor of Spanish linguistics and language program supervisor and coordinator for the basic Spanish program at the Louisiana State University. Her scholarly interests are second-language acquisition and pedagogy, language variation and change, bilingualism, and language contact.

CONNIE EBLE is a retired professor of English at the University of North Carolina at Chapel Hill. She is a New Orleans native whose research focuses on English slang and on variation in American English with a special focus on Louisiana. She has served as editor of *American Speech* and as president of the Southeastern Conference on Linguistics, the Linguistic Association of Canada and the United States, the South Atlantic Modern Language Association, and the American Dialect Society. She is the author of *Slang and Sociability: In-Group Language among College Students* (Chapel Hill: University of North Carolina Press 1996).

DANIEL W. HIEBER is a doctoral candidate in linguistics at the University of California at Santa Barbara. He focuses on the documentation, description, and revitalization of languages in the US Southeast and East Africa. He works primarily with Chitimacha and Gusii, an underdocumented and endangered language of southeastern Kenya, where he does fieldwork. He was previously a linguist with the software company Rosetta Stone, where he worked in the Endangered Languages Program to create language-learning software with a variety of Native North American communities.

DAVID KAUFMAN is a linguistic anthropologist and independent scholar who holds a doctorate in Anthropology from the University of Kansas. He is the author of *Clues to Lower Mississippi Valley Histories: Language, Archaeology, and Ethnography* (Lincoln: University of Nebraska Press, 2019), based on his dissertation.

GEOFFREY KIMBALL holds a doctorate from Tulane University and is an independent scholar who has worked with the Koasati language for more than thirty years. He is the author of *Koasati Grammar* (Lincoln: University of Nebraska Press, 1991) and *Koasati Dictionary* (Lincoln: University of Nebraska Press, 1994) and the translator of *Koasati Traditional Narratives* (Lincoln: University of Nebraska Press, 2010).

THOMAS A. KLINGLER is Richard V. and Seola Arnaud Edwards Associate Professor of French at Tulane University. His research focuses on the French and Creole languages in Louisiana. He is the author of *If I Could Turn My Tongue Like That: The Creole Language of Pointe Coupee Parish, Louisiana* (Baton Rouge: Louisiana State University Press, 2003) and coeditor of the *Dictionary of Louisiana Creole* (Bloomington: Indiana University Press, 1998) and the *Dictionary of Louisiana French as Spoken in Cajun, Creole, and American Indian Communities* (Jackson: University Press of Mississippi, 2010).

BERTNEY LANGLEY formerly served as secretary-treasurer for the Coushatta Tribal Council and currently holds the position of cultural adviser to the Coushatta Tribe of Louisiana.

LINDA LANGLEY is a retired professor of anthropology at McNeese State University. She currently serves as the tribal historic preservation officer for the Coushatta Tribe of Louisiana.

SHANE LIEF is a doctoral candidate in linguistics at Tulane University, from which he also holds a master's degree in Musicology. Born and raised in New Orleans, he has researched the development of musical traditions and languages in the Lower Mississippi River Valley, focusing on how multilingual environments generate competing visions of social order.

TAMARA LINDNER is an associate professor and the coordinator of the French language program in the Department of Modern Languages at the University of Louisiana at Lafayette. She is coeditor of *The Dictionary of Louisiana French: As Spoken in Cajun, Creole and American Indian Communities* (Jackson: University Press of Mississippi, 2010) and the *Anthologie de la Littérature Louisianaise d'Expression Française, de 1682 à Nos Jours* (Sudbury: Prise de Parole/Lafayette: University of Louisiana at Lafayette Press, 2017).

JUDITH M. MAXWELL is Louise Rebecca Schawe and Williedell Schawe Professor of Linguistics and Anthropology at Tulane University. She has served as the director of Oxlajuj Aj, Tijonïk Kaqchikel since 1987 and as the director of Kuhpani Yoyani Luhchi Yoroni working group, the Tulane collaboration with the Tunica-Biloxi Tribe of Louisiana, since 2010. Her research interests include indigenous languages of Central and North America, discourse analysis, language and culture revitalization, and bilingual education.

RAFAEL OROZCO is an associate professor of Spanish linguistics at Louisiana State University. He is the author of *Spanish in Colombia and New York City: Language Contact Meets Dialectal Convergence* (Amsterdam: Benjamins, 2018) and coeditor of *Subject Pronoun Expression in Spanish: A Cross-Dialectal Perspective* (Washington, DC: Georgetown University Press, 2015). His scholarly interests include sociolinguistics, Caribbean Spanish, and Spanish in the United States.

ALLISON TRUITT is an associate professor of anthropology at Tulane University. Her research focuses on economics and globalization in Southeast Asia, particularly Vietnam. She is the author of *Dreaming of Money in Ho Chi Minh City* (Seattle: University of Washington Press, 2013).

SHANA WALTON is an associate professor of English at Nicholls State University. She is coeditor of *Ethnic Heritage in Mississippi: The Twentieth Century*, published by University Press of Mississippi.

ROBIN WHITE is an associate professor of languages and literature at Nicholls State University, where she teaches French, English, and comparative literature. A Pittsburgh native who has lived and studied in Ireland, Mali, Benin, and France, she holds a doctorate in Francophone studies from Louisiana State University.

INDEX

Acadia/Acadians, xvii–xviii, 70, 76–78, 82–84, 86–87, 108–12, 126, 141–47, 155–56, 159–60, 163–66, 168, 208, 246
Acolapissa, 5
Africa/Africans, vii, 69–70, 76, 86, 92, 101, 103, 142–43, 153, 155–56, 161, 166, 169, 172, 176, 178–85, 191, 195, 197, 200–201, 206, 208, 215, 223, 260
African Americans/blacks, 84, 90–91, 94, 102–3, 109, 133, 154, 158, 160, 162, 166, 169, 176–85, 194, 204, 206, 208, 213, 223, 270, 272. *See also* Creole/creolization
Agglutination, 95, 101
Akensas, 26
Akokisa, 65
Alabama language (Alabamu), 37–39
Allemands, 85. *See also* Germanic/German
Alphabet, xiv, 6, 9, 19, 30–31, 153
Americans/Americanization/America, 22, 88, 105, 109, 124, 127, 139, 141, 172, 194, 200, 232, 245, 247, 269
Ancestors, xvii, 5, 15–16, 84, 86–87, 104, 109, 111, 161, 178, 213, 231, 234–35
Anglo-Americans/anglophones/whites, xvii, 69–70, 84, 90–91, 94, 102–3, 110, 127, 133, 140, 142–43, 145–46, 148, 150, 154–56, 160–63, 171–72, 174–79, 181, 187, 191, 195–96, 202, 204, 206, 208, 213–16, 227, 251, 253, 259, 265, 270
Antebellum period, 127, 142, 174
Apalachee, 43
Appalachian English, 166
Arabic, 227, 259, 261, 264, 268
Archaic period/forms, 3, 12, 232–35
Ascension Parish, 230, 235

Assumption Parish, 143
Atakapa/Attakapa, xvi, 4, 6, 12, 18, 22, 38, 61, 64–68
Atchafalaya Basin/Atchafalaya River, 5, 82, 160, 204
Austroasiatic language family, 249
Authenticity, 165, 174, 181, 196, 259
Avoyelles, 48
Avoyelles Parish, xv, 38, 48, 80, 82, 208
Awakened language/reawakening language, 6, 45–46, 59, 61, 67

Balbancha, 273
Balize, 205
Bantu, 186, 262
Bayougoula, 5
Belize, 176
Bengali, 261
Berber, 263
Bidialectal speakers, 91
Bienville Parish, 211
Bilingual/bilingualism, xv, xx, 41, 72, 92, 109, 111, 117–19, 134, 142, 144, 146–50, 152, 164–65, 237–39, 241, 249, 256, 260
Biloxi, Mississippi, 69
Biloxi language, 38, 48, 50
Bogalusa, 5
Borders/boundaries, xviii, 5, 93, 178, 183, 186, 204–8, 210, 215, 230, 242, 266
Bossier City, Louisiana/Bossier Parish, 206–8, 210–11
Boundary. *See* Borders/boundaries
BP Deepwater Horizon oil spill, 67, 249, 251, 256–57
Brasseaux, Carl, 76–78, 83, 88, 91, 105, 108, 124, 126–27, 138, 142, 153, 161, 170, 178, 197

279

Brasseur, Patrice, 88, 105, 139
Breaux Bridge, Louisiana, 70, 92–93, 96, 98–99, 106
Bulgarian, 262

Caddo language/Caddoan, 5, 66
Caddo Parish, 210
Cadien/Cadjin, 139. *See also* Cajun/Cajunization
Cajun/Cajunization, xvii–xviii, 38–39, 41, 65, 71, 75–76, 78, 80, 93, 102–3, 108–24, 128–29, 132–33, 150–51, 156–72, 193, 208, 235, 246, 261. *See also* Acadia/Acadians; Cadien/Cadjin
Calcasieu Parish, 38, 43, 66
Caldwell Parish, 208, 211
California, 51, 112, 229, 263
Calque, 59, 165, 234, 238
Cambodian, 262
Campos Molina, Dally, 237, 240
Canada/Canadians, xvi–xvii, 9, 35, 47, 69, 76, 79, 88, 112, 125–26, 130, 206
Canary Islands, 126, 206, 230, 232–33, 235–36
Cantonese, 261–62
Caribbean, xvi, 192–93, 239, 242
Carolinas, 206, 215
Castellano/Castilian, 243, 244, 245
Catahoula, 90–91, 211
CenLA, 208, 214, 217
Chalmette, Louisiana, 181, 191
Charenton, Louisiana, 9–10, 17, 19–20
Chawasha, 5, 10, 17
Cherokee, 29
Chickasaw, 4, 6, 47, 185
Chitimacha/Chetimachas/ChitimaCha, xvi, 4–6, 9–27, 38–39, 43, 48, 51, 63, 276
Choctaw, 3–6, 12, 29, 38, 43, 48, 50, 59, 64, 66, 79, 185–86, 273
Coahuila, 232
CODOFIL (Council for the Development of French in Louisiana), xvii, 69, 72, 102, 104, 123, 128–38, 147, 150–51, 161
Colonial/colonialism, xvi–xvii, xix, 5, 9, 15–17, 48, 63–64, 67, 69–70, 72, 75–76, 91, 101, 103, 105, 107–8, 125–27, 141–44, 153, 176–78, 195, 200, 205–8, 213–14, 216, 224, 227, 229–33, 243, 253, 264, 272, 274

Colombians, 237, 239, 242
Columbia University, 20
Commodity/commodification, xviii, xx, 102, 159, 168–69, 174, 180, 187, 196
Concordia Parish, 211
Coushatta, 6, 28–36, 42, 48. *See also* Koasati
Creole/creolization, xvi–xvii, 19, 65, 70–73, 75–77, 82, 84–86, 88–109, 111, 124, 132–33, 139, 142–44, 150–51, 153–54, 156–58, 160–63, 169–72, 174–78, 181, 183–85, 187, 193–97, 199–202, 204, 207–8, 220, 224, 227, 245, 259, 262, 277
Croatian, 176, 261–62
Curriculum, 22–23, 32, 147, 150
Czech, 206–7, 262

Daigle, Jules, 71–72, 150
Deepwater Horizon. *See* BP Deepwater Horizon oil spill
Delacroix Island, Louisiana, 234
DeSoto Parish, 210
Deutsches Haus, 264. *See also* Allemands; Germanic/German
Dialect/dialectology, xvii–xx, 4, 37, 71, 75–79, 83–84, 87, 91–92, 101, 104–9, 114, 123, 150, 155–57, 160, 162–66, 168, 175, 180–81, 192, 195, 203–5, 207, 209–10, 213–17, 227, 232–34, 239–40, 242, 247, 249–54
Diaspora, 247, 252
Diffusion, 15, 227, 259, 265, 267
Diglossia, 92
Discourse, 11, 21, 59, 146, 164, 187, 213, 218, 223, 272, 275
Displacement, xvii, 247
Domengeaux, James, 129, 137
Douglas, John, 34, 39, 43, 156, 175, 192–93

Ebarb, Louisiana, 232
Eble, Connie, 146, 156, 162–63, 169, 175, 178, 185, 196
Eckert, Penelope, 169, 171
Ecuadorians, 237
El Salvador/Salvadorans, 237–38, 243
Ellis, Elizabeth, 4, 6–7
Elton, Louisiana, 29, 35–36, 38, 41
Enslaved/enslavement, xvii–xviii, 9, 69–70, 77, 91, 103, 106, 126, 142, 144, 154, 161, 176, 178, 205–6

Ethnicity, xvii, 67, 71, 78, 94, 105, 111, 122, 128, 176, 189, 209, 211, 213, 255
Evangeline Parish, 80–82, 84

Ferriday, Louisiana, 230
Festivals, 175, 209, 254, 265
Florida, 5, 9, 28, 162–63, 204, 238, 248
Fluency, xv, xix, 10, 21, 29, 33, 38, 45, 50, 59, 65–66, 70–72, 116, 120–21, 133, 136–38, 147, 152, 159, 161, 163, 165, 230, 235, 241–42, 259–61, 263, 265–69, 271–73
Fogelson, Raymond, 15–16, 20, 24–27, 43, 68
French/francophone, 76, 78, 85, 104, 109–10, 125, 129, 140, 142–43, 145–53, 169, 193, 195, 246, 264

Gaelic, 155
Gauthier, Louisiana, 83, 88
Gender, 53–54, 61, 63, 94–96, 158, 179, 239, 241
Gentilly, 194
Georgia, xviii, 28, 206, 248
Germanic/German, 81, 176, 273. *See also* Allemands
Gisleson Palmer, Kristin, 267–68, 271, 273
Globalization, 278
Goddard, Ives, 11, 17, 24
Guidry, Richard, 150, 167
Gujarati, 261

Haas, Mary, xv, 4, 6, 12, 22, 30, 41, 46, 49–51, 53, 56–59, 61
Haiti/Haitians, 70, 77, 82, 90–92, 126, 142, 156, 176, 206, 227, 259, 269
Hall, Gwendolyn Midlo, 141
Hebrew, 262
Henderson, Louisiana, 90–91
Henry, Jacques, 102, 109, 124, 129, 159, 165, 168
Hernandez, Clara, 230, 235
Hindi, 261
Hispanics, 46, 112, 156, 179, 206, 208, 223–24, 229, 235–37, 239–40, 242, 264, 268
Hmong, 256, 262
Holloway, Charles, 230, 233, 235, 244
Hondurans/Honduras, 176, 179, 236–40, 243
Horvath, Barbara, 156, 162–63, 166–69
Houma language/United Houma Nation, 4–5, 85, 87, 160

Houma, Louisiana, 208
Houston, Texas, 48, 263
Hungarian, ix, 262

Iberia Parish/New Iberia, Louisiana, 38, 103
Iberville Parish, 10
Ibo, 260–61
Identity, xvi–xvii, xx, 6, 71, 84–86, 93–94, 104, 110, 123–24, 139, 146, 156, 160, 167, 206–8, 213, 218, 228, 245, 247–49, 251
Ideology, 21, 116, 127–28, 130–34, 137–38, 160, 191, 213, 252, 254, 260, 266, 272
"Iko Iko," 185
Immersion, xvii, 32–33, 43, 72, 130–41, 146–52
Immigrants/immigration, xvi, xviii–xix, 38, 70, 75–77, 83, 108, 126–27, 141–42, 146, 155, 177, 206, 227, 235–37, 246–48, 252, 257, 259, 264, 266, 268–69
Inalienable/inalienability, 51, 56–57, 62
Indigenous languages/indigenous people, xv–xvii, 3–5, 23–25, 28, 32–34, 37, 45–49, 79, 85–87, 91, 178, 272
Indonesian, 261
Integration, language, 15, 142, 192, 248–49
Intonation, xviii, 51, 169, 193
Ireland, xviii, 77
Ishak, xvi, 5–6, 51, 61, 64–68. *See also* Atakapa/Attakapa
Isleño, 185, 199, 229–36
Isolation, 38–39, 57, 75, 109, 125, 230–31, 233
Italy/Italians, 34, 141, 144, 151, 155, 176, 261, 264

Jackson, Jason, 15–16, 20, 24–26
Jackson, Mississippi, 48
Jackson Parish, 211
Jamaican Creole, 262
Jesuits, 3, 9, 17, 46, 50, 144
Johnson, William Ely, 50, 58
Johnstone, Barbara, 175, 200
Juchereau de St. Denis, Louis, 9, 205

Kalabari, 270
Kinshasa, Democratic Republic of the Congo, 150
Klingler, Thomas, xvii, 71, 73, 76–79, 81, 84, 86, 94, 96–102, 124, 160–61, 194, 203
Kniffen, Fred, 5, 7, 16, 25, 64, 67

Koasati, xv–xvi, 5–6, 28–44. *See also* Coushatta
Korea, 112, 261

Lacombe, Louisiana, 43, 76
Lafayette, Louisiana, xvii, 35, 71, 83, 103–5, 110, 112, 123, 133, 144, 150–51, 157–58, 160, 198, 237
Lafourche Parish/Bayou Lafourche, 5, 70, 72, 79–85, 87–88, 104, 146, 150, 155, 160
Lake Pontchartrain, 90, 162, 179, 183
Landrieu, Mitch, 267, 271
Landry, Christophe, 103–4, 112, 143, 254
Langley, Bertney, 6, 34, 42
Language reconstruction, 22, 43
Laotian, 262
LaSalle Parish, 43, 211
Latinos/as/x, 148, 195, 227, 236–37, 240, 256
Lincoln Parish, 211
Linguistic Atlas of the Gulf States (*LAGS*), 204, 209
Lipski, John, 231–36
Lithuanian, 141, 262
Logsdon, John, 142, 144, 176, 178
López Morales, Humberto, 229, 244–45

MacCurdy, Raymond, 233–34
Malay, 262–63
Mandarin, 147, 261–62
Mande, 185
Marksville, Louisiana, xv–xvi, 3, 38, 43, 48, 61, 63, 86, 208
Mesoamerica, 11, 16
Mexico/Mexicans, 229, 231–32, 241–42, 244
Minority people/minority languages, 41, 132, 181, 227, 248, 254, 256, 269
Mississippi Delta, 17, 230, 250
Missouri, 45, 143
Mizell-Nelson, Michael, 174, 186
Mobile, Alabama, 9, 69, 90
Mobilian Jargon, 4, 38–39, 185
Multilingualism, xix, 15, 146, 265, 272–73
Muskogean, 4–5, 12–15, 28, 37, 45, 51, 64

Nacogdoches, Texas, 231–32
Natchez, 3–5, 46–47, 51
Natchez, Mississippi, 69

Natchitoches, Louisiana, xviii, 5, 69, 76, 83, 88, 90, 93, 103, 203, 205–10, 213–14, 224, 231
Neologisms, 58–59, 62
Nepali, 263
Neumann(-Holzschuh), Ingrid, 76, 88, 91–94, 96, 98–100, 106–7
New Orleans, Louisiana, xviii–xix, 63, 69–70, 72, 77, 90, 95, 103, 123, 128, 139–58, 162–63, 166, 170–71, 173–87, 189–203, 205, 213, 223–25, 227, 230, 233–34, 236–37, 243, 245, 247–48, 253, 255–57, 259–61, 263–77
Nigeria, 112, 270, 272

Ofo, 5, 43–44, 48
Orthography, 18–19, 30, 34, 42, 61, 82, 93, 250
Ouachita language, 5
Ouachita Parish, 3, 206, 211

Panjabi, 262
Pedagogy, 6, 30, 32, 49, 59–60, 94, 148, 151–52, 257, 276
Peruvian, 242
Phonetic/s, 19, 26, 35, 105–7, 166, 168–69, 171, 204, 224, 233–34, 251, 257
Phonology, 22, 25–26, 52, 56, 88, 105, 158, 171–72, 187, 198, 204, 209, 218, 223–24, 232–34
Picone, Michael, 71, 75, 78–79, 82, 87–89, 101, 106, 124, 159, 161, 167, 172–73, 201, 203, 224
Pointe au Chien Indian Tribe (PACIT), 86
Pointe Coupee Parish, 90–91, 93, 96, 98–99, 102–7, 171
Positionality, 12, 15, 51, 55, 57–58
Prehistory, 11, 15, 25
Pronominal/pronouns, 54, 79–80, 82, 84, 87, 96–98, 165, 172, 188, 219, 223, 233, 238–39, 252–54, 257, 278
Prosody, 169, 193, 196
Puerto Rico, 237–39, 243, 245

Quebec, 50, 61, 82, 84, 129, 153
Quechua, 186
Quinapisa, 5
Quizquiz, 46

Racial discrimination/racism, 102–3, 176–77, 181, 184, 196

INDEX 283

Racial identity, 90–91, 102–3, 161, 176–79, 184, 192, 196–97, 201
Rapides Parish, 43, 208, 210–11
Regional/regionalism, xvii–xx, 60–61, 70–71, 75–76, 78–79, 81–82, 84–88, 101, 106, 108–9, 112, 150, 157, 160, 162, 164, 166, 169–70, 172–73, 182, 197–98, 207, 241, 250–51, 258
Reinecke, George, 155–56, 158, 175–76, 180–81, 195–96, 201
Rhetoric, 145, 158, 171
Rhoticity, 88, 170, 198, 211
Richland Parish, 211
Romanian, 262
Rosetta Stone, 10–11, 22–26, 276

Sabine Parish, 208, 210, 231
Sabine River Spanish, 231, 244
Scots, 208, 215–16
Seattle, Washington, 263
Segregation, xv, 201–2
Semifluent speakers/semispeakers, 33, 43, 70, 132, 137
Serbian, 263
Shreveport, Louisiana, xviii, 135–36, 151, 204, 206–8, 210, 214, 216, 237
Sinhalese, 263
Siouan, xv, 5, 24–25, 43, 61, 63
Slavery. *See* Enslaved/enslavement
Sociolinguistic situations/behaviors/patterns, xx, 88, 92–93, 106, 124, 139, 157, 169–71, 196, 198–99, 223, 227, 229, 231, 235, 238–45, 275, 278
Southeastern US languages, 12, 15–16, 19, 24, 26–27, 36, 51, 61, 63, 88–89, 157–58, 199, 224, 234, 238, 240, 243–44, 248–49, 256, 276
Southwest, xvi, 6, 28, 37, 65–68, 89–90, 94, 105–6, 138, 153–54, 157–58, 160, 170–72, 229, 243–44, 276
Spain, xvi, 35, 48, 161, 177, 179, 202, 205–6, 230, 232–33, 241, 244, 264
Spanglish, 241
Spanish, vi–viii, xvi–xvii, xix, 9, 18, 28–29, 46, 48, 59, 63, 69–70, 78–79, 81, 91, 95, 101, 126, 130, 141–42, 144, 146–47, 161, 167, 176, 185–86, 202, 204–8, 213–14, 216, 224, 227, 229–45, 256, 260–61, 264–65, 272, 276
Spanish Illinois (Upper Louisiana), 230

St. Martin Parish, 11, 14, 34, 92, 112
Standardization, 18, 127, 132, 274
Stigmatization, 91, 102, 109, 113, 122
Storytelling, 58, 86, 149, 167, 214, 217, 223, 271
Stylistics, 78, 156, 170, 223
Swadesh, Morris, 10–11, 13–14, 16, 18–23, 25–27
Swahili, 262
Swanton, John, xvi, 4, 9–12, 15, 17–21, 23, 27, 30, 34, 36, 43, 46, 49–51, 58–59, 61, 63–68
Swedish, 263
Syntax/syntactic, 107, 158, 165, 172, 187, 218, 234

Tagalog, 261
Tallapoosa, 37
Tamil, 262
Tangipahoa Parish, 5
Tchoupitoulas Street, New Orleans, 182
Telugu, 261
Tensas Parish, 211
Terrebonne Parish, 4, 9, 70, 79–83, 85, 87, 104, 149, 155, 158, 160, 172, 246–47, 255
Texas/Texans, xvi, 6, 28, 36–38, 48, 62, 65–68, 94, 106, 112, 160, 204, 206, 209, 213, 215–17, 229–32, 236, 243–44, 248, 276
Thai, 262
Thibodaux, Louisiana, xviii, 80, 83, 157, 168, 170
Tourism/tourists, xviii, 62, 69, 105, 123, 128, 131, 147, 168–69, 174, 180, 182–83, 185–87, 196–97, 201–2, 228, 266, 268
Tradition, 21, 35, 37, 40, 44, 114, 150, 162, 164–65, 170, 173, 182, 185, 196, 202, 208, 218, 223, 270, 273, 277
Tunica/Tunican, xv–xvi, 4–6, 12, 38, 41, 45–63, 160
Turkish, 262

Ukrainian, 263
Urdu, 261

Valdman, Albert, 70–71, 73, 78–79, 87–89, 92–94, 101, 105–9, 124, 132, 139, 146, 154, 159, 161, 169–70, 172, 178, 202
Variation, xviii, 20, 61, 71–72, 75–85, 87–89, 94, 99, 105–6, 108, 114, 139, 153, 156–58, 166–67, 169–72, 175, 198, 202, 215, 223–24, 227, 232, 239–43, 247, 249–54, 275–76
Venezuela, 112

Venice, Louisiana, 69
Veracruz, Mexico, 242
Vermilion Parish, 66, 112, 150
Vernacular, 108–9, 123–24, 132, 157–58, 162, 170–72, 175, 180, 187, 191–93, 196
Vietnam/Vietnamese, xix, 176, 179, 195, 227, 246–58, 261, 264, 268, 278
Vocabulary, xviii, 14, 17–19, 24–27, 35, 39, 50, 62, 66, 79, 106, 108, 182, 185, 187, 199–200

Washa (Ouacha), 4–5, 10, 16–17
Winn Parish, 211, 217, 222–23

Xalapa, Mexico, 239

Yagenecito (Yagnechito), 5, 16–17
Yat, xviii, 156–57, 163, 175, 177, 180–81, 186, 191–92, 194, 196, 198–200, 202
Yiddish, 141, 263
Yoruba, 259–61
Yugoslavia, 176

Zwolle, Louisiana, 214, 216, 232

www.ingramcontent.com/pod-product-compliance
Lightning Source LLC
Chambersburg PA
CBHW021804220426
43662CB00006B/175